➢ 2ND EDITION ◄

A COMPLETE GUIDE TO GUN LAW IN VIRGINIA

VIRGINIA GUN LAW
Armed And Educated

Copyright © 2021 Stanley Marie, LLC
All rights reserved.
No part of this book may be reproduced in any form or by any means without permission in writing from the publisher.

Written by Gilbert Ambler and published in the United States of America.

U.S. Law Shield, LLC
ISBN 978-0-578-30437-3

To order additional books by phone or
for wholesale orders call (877) 448-6839.

TABLE OF CONTENTS

PREFACE v

CHAPTER ONE 1
**Brief Legal History Of The Right To Bear Arms
And The Laws Regulating Firearms**
    I. Introduction And Overview 1
    II. Do I Have A Constitutional Right As An Individual To Keep And Bear Arms? 2
    III. Major Firearms Statutes Every Gun Owner Needs to Know 12

CHAPTER TWO 19
**Know Your Rights: Part I
The Fourth Amendment: Understanding Police Power
Some Basic Legal Concepts**
    I. Introduction And Overview 19
    II. What Is The Fourth Amendment? 20
    III. Legal Levels Of Proof 21
    IV. What Is A Search? 24
    V. What Is A Seizure? 25
    VI. Police Power 25
    VII. Encounters With The Police 27
    VIII. The Fifth Amendment 31
    IX. What Happens If The Police Violate My Rights? 32

CHAPTER THREE 37
**Know Your Rights: Part II
The Fourth Amendment: Understanding
The Warrant Requirement in Virginia**
    I. Introduction And Overview 37
    II. What Is The Warrant Requirement? 38

CHAPTER FOUR 45
**Know Your Rights: Part III
The Fourth Amendment: Exceptions To The Warrant Requirement**
    I. Introduction And Overview 45
    II. When Can The Police Search Or Arrest Me Without A Warrant? .. 46
    III. When Can The Police Search My Home Without A Warrant? 51
    IV. When Can The Police Search My Vehicle Without A Warrant? 54
    V. Other Search Issues 58

CHAPTER FIVE **63**
Legal Definitions And Classifications Of Firearms:
What Is Legal?
    I. Definition Of Firearm 64
   II. Ammunition 74

CHAPTER SIX..................................... **87**
Purchasing, Transferring, And Possessing Firearms
    I. Laws Of Purchasing And Possessing: The Basics 87
   II. Minimum Age To Possess Vs. Minimum Age To Purchase 88
  III. The Federal Firearm License System 89
  IV. Background Check Systems in Virginia 95
   V. Federal And Virginia Law On Disqualifications For Purchasing
      And Possessing Firearms 98
  VI. Understanding "Private Sales" Laws 125
 VII. Buying, Selling, And Transferring Through An FFL 129
VIII. What If I'm Denied The Right To Purchase A Firearm?......... 134
  IX. Additional Considerations In Firearms Purchasing And
      Possession Laws 136
   X. Ammunition: The Law Of Purchasing And Possession 140

CHAPTER SEVEN................................. **145**
When Can I Legally Use My Gun: Part I
Understanding The Law Of Justification
Some Basic Legal Concepts
    I. Introduction And Overview 145
   II. Ignorance Of The Law Is No Excuse! 145
  III. Force Vs. Deadly Force................................. 146
  IV. Self-Defense Must Be Either "Justified" Or "Excused"......... 150
   V. Warning Shots....................................... 166
  VI. Brandishing... 167
 VII. Mutual Combat 168
VIII. Right To Resist Unlawful Arrest.......................... 169
  IX. The Virginia Criminal Trial.............................. 169

CHAPTER EIGHT **173**
When Can I Legally Use My Gun: Part II
Defense of Others
Understanding When Force and Deadly Force Can Be Legally
Used To Defend Another Person
    I. Introduction And Overview 173
   II. Defense Of Others In Virginia 174

CHAPTER NINE ... 179
When Can I Legally Use My Gun: Part III Defense Against Animals
  I. Defense Against Animals ... 179

CHAPTER TEN ... 189
When Can I Legally Use My Gun: Part IV Understanding When Deadly Force Can Be Used To Protect Property
  I. Can I Use Deadly Force To Protect My Property? ... 189

CHAPTER ELEVEN ... 195
What Crimes Can I Be Charged With When My Use Of Deadly Force Is Not Justified?
  I. Introduction And Overview ... 195
  II. Crimes Against Persons ... 195
  III. Crimes Against Society ... 198
  IV. The Aftermath ... 200

CHAPTER TWELVE ... 203
Law Of Handgun Carry: Part I The Concealed Handgun Permit Qualifications, Requirements, Appeals, And Regulations
  I. Application For Resident CHP Process ... 204
  II. Application For Non-Resident CHP Process ... 211
  III. Disqualified Individuals Ineligible To Obtain A CHP ... 213
  IV. CHP Reciprocity ... 217

CHAPTER THIRTEEN ... 219
Law Of Handgun Carry Part II: What, How, And Where You Can Legally Carry With A Concealed Handgun Permit
  I. Introduction ... 219
  II. Virginia Is An Open Carry State ... 220
  III. Law Of Concealed Carry Of A Firearm ... 222
  IV. Firearm Prohibitions By Premises ... 224
  V. Traveling Across State Lines With Firearms ... 243
  VI. Air Travel With A Firearm ... 246
  VII. Frequently Asked Questions ... 252

CHAPTER FOURTEEN ... 257
Restoration Of Firearms Rights: The Law Of Pardons And Expungements
  I. Is It Possible To Restore A Person's Right To Bear Arms? ... 257
  II. Federal Law ... 259
  III. Virginia Law ... 264

CHAPTER FIFTEEN **271**
I'm Being Sued For What?
Civil Liability If You Have Used Your Gun
    I. What Does It Mean To Be Sued? 271
    II. What Might You Be Sued For? Gun-Related Claims In Civil Courts 280
    III. The Virginia Civil Trial: An Overview 292
    IV. Insurance 295

CHAPTER SIXTEEN **299**
Beyond Firearms: Knives, Blackjacks, Nunchucks, Throwing Stars, And Tasers
    I. Introduction 299
    II. Weapons Regulated By Va. Code § 18.2-308 300
    III. Stun Weapons 304
    IV. Other Weapons 305
    V. Prohibited Premises For Regulated Weapons 308

CHAPTER SEVENTEEN **323**
The National Firearms Act & The Virginia Uniform Machine Gun Act: Silencers, Short-Barreled Weapons, and Machine Guns
    I. Virginia Uniform Machine Gun Act 324
    II. What Is The National Firearms Act? 325
    III. What Firearms Does The NFA Regulate? 326
    IV. Process and Procedure For Obtaining NFA Firearms 341

APPENDICES **349**
    Appendix A: Selected Virginia Statutes 349
    Appendix B: Selected Federal Forms 599

ABOUT THE ATTORNEY AUTHOR **613**

PREFACE

U.S. LawShield would like to thank its members and others who made the previous edition of *Virginia Gun Law: Armed And Educated* an overwhelming success. As many Virginians know, the Virginia Legislature created, amended, and repealed several laws that impact the Second Amendment rights of gun owners. In order to keep Virginians up to date on the law, U.S. LawShield has prepared this revised 2nd Edition of *Virginia Gun Law: Armed And Educated.*

As lawyers with years of representing law-abiding gun owners in cases all over the United States, we have seen how well-intended people exercising their Second Amendment rights get mixed up in the legal system through just plain not understanding the law. Through this edition, we are continuing with our commitment to produce the best one-volume resource that provides any gun owner with a base level of knowledge about laws that gun owners need to know.

The law can be complicated, overlapping, hard to understand, and in some cases, completely arbitrary to the point of confusion. Laws are often written by lawyers for lawyers or are the result of political compromises generating confusing laws that the courts are left to interpret. After years of legal work in the arena of firearms law, we found there did not exist a resource that explained gun law in a manner that was easy for everyone to understand—because understanding the law goes far beyond just reading statutes or regulations. If you do not know either the process by which the law is being administered or how the courts are interpreting the meaning of the law, then you don't understand the full legal story.

That is why we wrote and will continue to revise the Armed And Educated series. It is a one-volume guide to the minimum law every gun owner needs to know to stay legal. Whenever appropriate, we tried to present useful analysis and real-world applications. Our goal was to explain the "law" so gun owners could inform and educate themselves. Thousands of attorney hours have gone into producing this resource, always with the goal in mind of education. Our collective legal experience has taught us well that anyone can become ensnared in the legal system. Many people firmly believe that "it" can't happen to them. Even people who have never been in trouble before can find themselves in the world of law, lawyers, and law enforcement through ignorance of the law.

We are committed to helping protect Second Amendment rights for all legal gun owners. It is our passion and our mission. We want people to know the law, because only through eternal vigilance will we protect our cherished right to bear arms. If you own a gun, the laws concerning firearms and their use apply to you. Ignorance of the law is not a valid legal excuse. Therefore, if you want to stay legal, know the law. We hope you enjoy reading it as much as we enjoyed writing it!

> CHAPTER ONE ◄

BRIEF LEGAL HISTORY OF
THE RIGHT TO BEAR ARMS
And The Laws Regulating Firearms

I. INTRODUCTION AND OVERVIEW

The right to own and carry a firearm in Virginia is guaranteed by both the United States Constitution and the Constitution of the Commonwealth of Virginia, but that was not always the case. In May of 1776, the Colony of Virginia, which was the first permanently settled English colony in North America, declared its independence from the British Empire largely over taxation and representation matters to become the independent Commonwealth of Virginia. In June of 1776, the Virginia Declaration of Rights and Constitution of the Commonwealth of Virginia were created. George Mason and James Madison are credited with drafting most of both documents. The Virginia Declaration of Rights proclaimed the inherent rights of man, was the first constitutional protection of individual rights, and was the precursor to the United States Bill of Rights.

The Virginia Constitution was the first written constitution adopted by the people's representatives in the history of the world. The original Virginia Constitution of 1776 was enacted in conjunction with the Declaration of Independence. The Virginia Constitution defines and limits the powers of government and the basic rights of its citizens. The Declaration of Rights was later incorporated within the Constitution of Virginia.

In June of 1788, the United States Constitution became the supreme law of the United States of America when it was ratified by thirteen American sovereign and independent states. The original version of the U.S. Constitution did not include any specific enumerated guaranteed individual rights; however, the first Congress of the United States adopted amendments to the U.S. Constitution, ten of which were ratified by the states and are known as the Bill of Rights. Virginian James Madison is hailed as the "Father of the Constitution" for his pivotal role in drafting and promoting the U.S. Constitution and the Bill of Rights. The Second Amendment specifically addresses firearms because it protects the right of the people to keep and bear arms.

II. DO I HAVE A CONSTITUTIONAL RIGHT AS AN INDIVIDUAL TO KEEP AND BEAR ARMS?

Yes. The United States Supreme Court has decided that an individual has a constitutional right to keep and bear arms. This flows from the Second Amendment, which states simply:

> A well-regulated Militia, being necessary to the security of a free State, the right of the people to keep and bear Arms, shall not be infringed.

Additionally, the Constitution of the Commonwealth of Virginia in Article I, Section 13 states in relevant part:

> "That a well-regulated militia, composed of the body of the people, trained to arms, is the proper, natural, and safe defense of a free state; therefore, the right of the people to keep and bear arms shall not be infringed."

However, this right is not absolute and it is permissible for there to be regulations that place reasonable restrictions on the use, purchase, possession, and carrying of firearms that we will discuss in detail.

From a plain reading, there are two important parts to this amendment: first, that a well-regulated militia is necessary to the security of a free state, and second, that there is a right of the people to keep and bear arms.

Notably, the Virginia constitution contains the critical word "therefore" between the prefatory clause which addresses the importance of the militia, and the operative clause which grants the right.

For years, because of the absence of the word "therefore" in the Second Amendment of the United States Constitution, and before the issue was decided, anti-gun activists have tried to argue that the Second Amendment only applied to "militias" and not to individuals. Luckily, this argument is not the law. Nevertheless, despite the U.S. Supreme Court rulings stating otherwise, this myth seems to persist. What do these parts of the Second Amendment of the U.S. Constitution mean? Are they the same, or are they different?

A. What is a "well-regulated militia"?

As we discussed earlier, the first part of the Second Amendment references a "well-regulated militia." What is a well-regulated militia? The U.S. Supreme Court has held what this phrase does and does not mean. In 1939, in the case of *United States v. Miller*, 307 U.S. 174 (1939) (ironically, a ruling that upheld federal firearms regulations), the Court defined a "militia" as comprising "all males physically capable of acting in concert for the common defense." Based on how the amendment was drafted, the Court stated, it was clear that the militia predated Article I of the Constitution, because unlike armies and navies, it did not have to be created by Congress. What then is "well-regulated" per the Court? It is exactly what it sounds like: the imposition of discipline and training. So, is this just the National Guard?

No. In the case of *D.C. v. Heller*, 554 U.S. 570 (2008), the U.S. Supreme Court stated that the well-regulated militia is not the state's military forces, but a separate entity altogether. The Supreme Court stated that the word "militia" referred to the body of the people, and they—the people—were required to keep a centralized government in check. The Court considered and rejected the position that the National Guard is the current militia under the Second Amendment.

Va. Code § 44-1 also addresses who is in the militia at the state level. The law says that the militia is made up of "all able-bodied residents of the Commonwealth who are citizens of the United States and all other able-bodied persons resident in the Commonwealth who have declared their intention to become citizens of the United States, who are at least 16 years of age and, except as hereinafter provided, not more than 55 years of age." While not a prerequisite to enjoying the right to keep and bear arms, if you are an able-bodied citizen of Virginia between the ages of 16-55, you automatically are a member of the unorganized militia!

B. How has the phrase "right to keep and bear arms" been interpreted by the courts?

One of the first cases to directly deal with the Second Amendment was *United States v. Miller*. In *Miller*, the U.S. Supreme Court found that the National Firearms Act ("NFA"), which imposed registration requirements on machine guns, short-barreled weapons, destructive devices, and other similarly unique firearms, did not violate the Second Amendment. The Court used the reasoning that possession of weapons regulated by the NFA did not reasonably relate to the preservation or efficiency of a well-regulated militia; therefore, the NFA was upheld as constitutional.

UNITED STATES v. MILLER, 307 U.S. 174 (1939)

THE FACTS
The defendants, Miller and Layton, transported a double-barrel 12-gauge shotgun with a barrel length of less than 18 inches from Oklahoma to Arkansas, and were being prosecuted under the National Firearms Act (which required certain types of firearms to be registered and a tax to be paid). Defendants challenged the NFA as an unconstitutional violation of the Second Amendment.

THE LEGAL HOLDING
Upheld the National Firearms Act as constitutional and not a violation of the Second Amendment.

An interesting quirk of history in the *Miller* case (and not a shining moment for the legal system) is that Miller's attorney never appeared at the arguments before the U.S. Supreme Court because he was court-appointed and had not been paid. There was no written brief and no legal representation at oral arguments by the party arguing that the law was unconstitutional. The Court only heard the government's side. To make matters worse, Miller was shot to death before the decision was rendered.

C. 69 years later, the U.S. Supreme Court interprets the Second Amendment again: *D.C. v. Heller*

It would be 69 years after *Miller* until the U.S. Supreme Court addressed the Second Amendment directly again. Except this time the Court would hear both the Government's and the Defendant's arguments. Fortunately, freedom and Second Amendment rights prevailed in court that day. The Court held that individuals have a right to keep and bear arms.

DISTRICT OF COLUMBIA v. HELLER, 554 U.S. 570 (2008)

THE FACTS

Heller applied for a handgun ownership permit and was denied; without such a permit, D.C. required that all firearms (including rifles and shotguns) be kept unloaded and disassembled, or bound by a trigger lock, even in a person's own home.

THE LEGAL HOLDING

1. The Supreme Court found that the Second Amendment protects an individual right of firearms ownership for the purpose of self-defense and is not connected with any militia or military purposes; it further elaborated that individual self-defense is "the central component" of the Second Amendment. Further, handguns are the primary defensive weapon of choice and are protected by the Second Amendment.

2. A well-regulated militia is not the state's military forces.
3. The Court also discussed what the phrase "bear arms" meant: "wear, bear, or carry… upon the person or in clothing or in a pocket, for the purpose… of being armed and ready for offensive or defensive action in a case of conflict with another person."
4. The District of Columbia regulation was held to be unconstitutional.
5. The Court concluded that the right to bear arms is not completely absolute. Reasonable provisions and restrictions have been upheld.

Keep in mind *D.C. v. Heller* was a split 5-4 decision; only one Justice away from a completely different outcome, where the Second Amendment (according to the dissent) had "outlived its usefulness and should be ignored."

D. Can states ignore the Second Amendment? *McDonald v. City of Chicago*

D.C. v. Heller was fantastic, but there was a slight quirk: the District of Columbia is under the exclusive jurisdiction of Congress and is not part of any state. Therefore, the case shed no light on the question of what states can do when it comes to regulating or banning firearms. How do state constitutions interact with the Second Amendment? Can states ban guns outright? Two years after *Heller*, *McDonald v. City of Chicago* sought to answer these questions.

McDONALD v. CITY OF CHICAGO, 561 U.S. 742 (2010).

THE FACTS:

A Chicago city ordinance banned handgun possession (among other gun regulations). McDonald was a 76-year-old retired maintenance engineer who wanted a handgun for self-defense.

Chicago required that all handguns had to be registered, but refused all handgun registration after a 1982 citywide handgun ban.

THE LEGAL HOLDING:
The Supreme Court held that the Second Amendment is fully applicable to the states and that individual self-defense is "the central component" of the Second Amendment. Therefore, the Second Amendment prohibits states from enacting bans on handguns for self-protection in the home.

E. Legal limitations of the right to keep and bear arms

The U.S. Supreme Court has stated: "Of course the right [to keep and bear arms] was not unlimited, just as the First Amendment's right of free speech was not." Courts may have struggled over the years with what the Second Amendment means, but they have been resolute that there is an element of self-defense. The *Heller* Court stated that, "The Second Amendment does not protect the right to carry arms for any sort of confrontation," focusing their decision on self-defense.

Further, the *Miller* Court stated that the weapons protected were those "in common use at the time" of the decision. This is supported by historical traditions of prohibiting the carry of "dangerous and unusual weapons" that are commonly used by criminals offensively, as opposed to by law-abiding citizens for defensive purposes.

The Second Amendment does not protect against legislative prohibitions on firearm possession by felons and the mentally ill. *Heller* made this point in its decision, and many circuit court cases such as *U.S. v. Everist* had previously used the same reasoning prior to Heller. The Fifth Circuit Court of Appeals in *U.S. v. Everist* stated that the Second Amendment is subject to, "limited narrowly tailored specific exceptions or restrictions for particular cases that are reasonable; it is clear that felons, infants and those of unsound mind may be prohibited from possessing firearms." *U.S. v. Everist*, 368 F.3d 517, 519 (5th Cir. 2004). Along this same train of thought, the U.S. Supreme Court did not want to eliminate laws that imposed conditions and qualifications on the commercial sales of firearms.

It also does not mean that the Second Amendment includes the right to carry anywhere a person wants. The *Heller* Court stated that their opinion was not meant to allow the carrying of firearms in sensitive places, such as schools and certain government buildings.

F. The future of the Second Amendment

How will the Second Amendment be treated going forward? With the passing of Supreme Court Justice Antonin Scalia, one of the key supporters and author of the 5–4 decision that was Heller, the split-down-the-middle Supreme Court truly seemed poised to either continue protecting firearms rights, or backslide to the position that the Second Amendment only applies to militia activity. When the dust settled, Justice Scalia's empty seat ended up going to Neil Gorsuch. How Justice Gorsuch has treated the Second Amendment in the past will be a central component of its future. Brett Kavanaugh is a tried-and-true supporter of the right to bear arms. Additionally, President Trump was able to appoint Amy Coney Barrett to the seat left vacant by the passing of Ruth Bader Ginsburg. Justice Barrett is known as a strong Second Amendment advocate, and her appointment may be one of the lasting and very positive effects of the Trump legacy. Her appointment and confirmation bodes well for the future of the Second Amendment.

Although Justice Scalia's opinion in *Heller* established the right for individuals to bear arms, it includes the famous caveat: "Like most rights, the right secured by the Second Amendment is not unlimited." *D.C. v. Heller*, 554 U.S. at 595. That sentence left open the possibility that some gun regulations could pass muster, without spelling out the criteria for constitutionality. Overall, these regulations can be generalized into three major archetypes: those that impose registration requirements on firearms or their owners; those that ban certain types of firearms or firearm accessories; and those that prohibit the carrying of firearms in public (be it through impossible-to-obtain licensing schemes, or piecemeal prohibition).

The sheer volume of such cases allowing the erosion of the Second Amendment is alarming, but not as alarming as how many are denied certiorari.

In the years since *McDonald*, there have been more than 70 U.S. circuit court opinions upholding state restrictions on the Second Amendment that the U.S. Supreme Court has refused to review. These restrictions include requiring the registration of firearms, prohibiting "large capacity" magazines, banning certain firearms as "assault weapons," and creating classes of individuals who are restricted from owning firearms.

A Ninth Circuit case that many observers thought the U.S. Supreme Court would review is *Peruta v. County of San Diego*, 742 F.3d 1144 (9th Cir. 2014). On June 26, 2017, the Supreme Court again denied certiorari. However, Justice Thomas along with newly appointed Justice Gorsuch issued an opinion decrying the Court's decision and stated therein:

> The Court's decision to deny certiorari in this case reflects a distressing trend: the treatment of the Second Amendment as a disfavored right. ... The Constitution does not rank certain rights above others, and I do not think this Court should impose such a hierarchy by selectively enforcing its preferred rights. ... For those of us who work in marbled halls, guarded constantly by a vigilant and dedicated police force, the guarantees of the Second Amendment might seem antiquated and superfluous. But the Framers made a clear choice: They reserved to all Americans the right to bear arms for self-defense. I do not think we should stand by idly while a State denies its citizens that right, particularly when their very lives may depend on it. *Peruta v. California*, 198 L.Ed.2d 746 (Mem) (2017) (THOMAS, J., dissenting from denial of certiorari).

It appears that Justice Gorsuch and Thomas's pleas were heard. With Justice Kavanaugh, and now Justice Barrett appointed to the bench, the belief is that there is now a firm majority on the Court who would give the Second Amendment the reverence it is due.

In 2019, the Supreme Court heard a Second Amendment case called *New York State Rifle and Pistol Association v. New York*. In early 2020, the Court ruled the case moot, holding that there was no active controversy for them to resolve due to New York City and New York State voluntarily changing the laws that were challenged. Nonetheless, the concurring and dissenting opinions expressed a strong desire that the Supreme Court address Second Amendment issues in the near future. Fortuitously, these desires may be answered with another New York Case. In the fall of 2021 the Supreme Court will hear *New York State Rifle and Pistol Association v. Corlett*. The case revolves around New York's "may issue" licensing scheme, that recognizes no broad right to possess a firearm outside of the home. This case will be more difficult for the State of New York to moot, and therefore, we may be set for a landmark decision on the Second Amendment in early 2022.

PRACTICAL LEGAL TIP

Currently, the two most important court decisions fortifying our gun rights are *Heller* and *McDonald*. But those cases could have gone either way! The makeup of the Court is a little bit different today, but this serves as an important reminder on why the appointment of Justices is so important, and so often hotly contested! –Gilbert

III. MAJOR FIREARMS STATUTES EVERY GUN OWNER NEEDS TO KNOW

At the federal level, there are plenty of laws and regulations that concern firearms, but this section will focus on some of the more major legislative actions that all gun owners need to know.

A. Gun Control Act of 1968

The Gun Control Act of 1968 ("GCA") was enacted by Congress to "provide for better control of the interstate traffic of firearms." This law is primarily focused on regulating interstate commerce in firearms by generally prohibiting interstate firearms transfers except among licensed manufacturers, dealers, and importers; however, interstate commerce has been held by the courts to include nearly everything. It also contains classes of individuals to whom firearms should not be sold. For the specifics of who can and can't purchase a firearm, please refer to Chapter 6. Among other things, the GCA created the Federal Firearms License ("FFL") system, imposed importation restrictions on military surplus rifles (adding a "sporting purpose test" and a "points system" for handguns), and marking implemented requirements.

B. The Brady Handgun Violence Prevention Act

The Brady Handgun Violence Prevention Act, commonly referred to as the Brady Law, instituted federal background checks (the National Instant Criminal Background Check System, or "NICS") for firearm purchasers in the United States. It also prohibited certain persons from purchasing firearms. (*See* Chapter 6 for more information on who can or can't purchase a firearm).

C. The Firearm Owners' Protection Act

The Firearm Owners' Protection Act ("FOPA") revised many provisions of the original Gun Control Act, including "reforms" on the inspection of FFLs. This same Act updated the list of individuals prohibited from purchasing firearms that was introduced by the GCA. The FOPA also banned the ownership by civilians of any machine gun that was not registered under the National Firearm Act ("NFA") as of May 19, 1986. FOPA created what is called a "safe passage" provision of the law, which allows for traveling across states with a firearm. Finally, FOPA prohibited a registry for non-NFA items that directly linked firearms to their owners.

D. The Public Safety and Recreational Firearms Use Protection Act

The Public Safety and Recreational Firearms Use Protection Act, commonly referred to as the Federal Assault Weapons Ban, was a subsection of the Violent Crime Control and Law

Enforcement Act of 1994. It banned outright the manufacture and transfer of certain semi-automatic firearms and magazines. This ban grandfathered in previously legally owned weapons, but no prohibited firearm could be acquired or manufactured after September 13, 1994. With great foresight, the drafters of this law included a so-called "sunset provision," which stated that the ban would expire 10 years later unless renewed. The ban expired in 2004, and all attempts to renew it have been unsuccessful.

E. The Gun-Free School Zones Act of 1995

The Gun-Free School Zones Act of 1995 modified the prior Gun-Free School Zones Act of 1990, which the Supreme Court found unconstitutional. Most notably, the rewritten law makes it a crime to possess a firearm within 1,000 feet of a school zone. A school zone includes any public, private, or religious K-12 school. There are some notable exceptions in the law, which allow firearms in a school zone. The law does not apply to the possession of a firearm:

> (i) on private property not part of school grounds;
> (ii) if the individual possessing the firearm is licensed to do so by the State in which the school zone is located or a political subdivision of the State, and the law of the State or political subdivision requires that, before an individual obtains such a license, the law enforcement authorities of the State or political subdivision verify that the individual is qualified under law to receive the license;
> (iii) which is—
>   (I) not loaded; and
>   (II) in a locked container, or a locked firearms rack which is on a motor vehicle;

> (iv) by an individual for use in a program approved by a school in the school zone;
> (v) by an individual in accordance with a contract entered into between a school in the school zone and the individual or an employer of the individual;
> (vi) by a law enforcement officer acting in his or her official capacity; or
> (vii) that is unloaded and is possessed by an individual while traversing school premises for the purpose of gaining access to public or private lands open to hunting, if the entry on school premises is authorized by school authorities.

Unfortunately, this law failed to consider a major issue when carving out exceptions, which was reciprocal licenses. There is an exception to allow you to carry a loaded firearm in a school zone if you are licensed by the state, or a political subdivision of the state you are in and had a background check conducted as part of the licensing process. This means that a license or permit holder could generally carry within 1,000 feet of a school zone in the issuing state. However, the exception does not protect those traveling in a state with an out-of-state license or permit even if it is recognized by that state.

F. The National Firearms Act

The National Firearms Act ("NFA") regulates and imposes a statutory excise tax on the manufacture and transfer of certain types of firearms and weapons: machine guns, short-barreled weapons, suppressors, explosive devices, and "any other weapons" ("AOWS") (AOWs can range from everyday objects that are actually firearms, such as an umbrella that can fire a round, to other weapons the ATF decides to place in this category). The tax is $200 if you make or transfer an item other than the transfer of AOWs; the tax for transferring AOWs is $5. The NFA is also referred to as Title II of the federal firearms laws. (*See* Chapter 17 for more information on how to navigate the NFA while remaining legal).

G. Can local governments in Virginia be prohibited from making certain gun laws?

Yes, in some areas. The Virginia courts have acknowledged that the Constitution of Virginia allows the legislature to create laws to prohibit certain types of carrying weapons, and have upheld "unlawful carrying" laws and license requirements. Along those lines, the Virginia legislature can and does prohibit local governments from adopting or enforcing some gun laws. A Virginia locality may not adopt any gun law inconsistent with existing Virginia statutory law.

Va. Code § 15.2-915 states that generally a locality cannot regulate: the purchase, possession, transfer, ownership, carrying, storage, or transporting of firearms, ammunition, or combinations of firearms and ammunition other than those expressly authorized by the Code of Virginia. Unfortunately, beginning July 1st, 2020, the Code of Virginia will allow localities to regulate the possession, carrying, and transportation of firearms and ammunition in a variety of locations.

These locations include any buildings, public parks, and public recreation or community centers owned or operated by the locality or by any authority created by the locality. This ability for local control also extends to buildings not owned or controlled by a locality, during the time that the locality is using them (and only in the portion of the building that the locality is using).

Localities can now also regulate the possession of firearms or ammunition in public streets or sidewalks that are in a permitted event area (or at an event that would otherwise require a permit) and in parking lots, sidewalks, and other locations adjacent to the permitted event area. Whether such restrictions will be allowed to stand remains to be seen. These laws have been challenged by multiple lawsuits, including a suit against the City of Winchester, Virginia, who implemented such laws, brought on behalf of U.S. LawShield, Gun Owners of America, Virginia Citizens Defense League, and other organizations and individuals.

PRACTICAL LEGAL TIP

Unfortunately, allowing localities to regulate firearms in locations where a permit is required will greatly change the legality of carrying a firearm at many protest and lobbying events. This may have been a direct response to the historic turnout at the Virginia Citizens Defense League's January 2020 lobby day. –Gilbert

Fortunately, unless and until such laws are struck down by the courts, localities are not permitted to create gun-free zones or enact regulations without providing notice. If a locality wishes to regulate firearms or ammunition in one of the above specifically enumerated areas over which they may exert control, they must first provide notice of the restrictions at every entrance, and at every appropriate area of ingress and egress.

This does not mean that there are not other regulations that apply to only specific areas of the state. This simply means that any such regulations that apply to only particular localities come from the state level, not the local level.

> CHAPTER TWO ◄

KNOW YOUR RIGHTS: PART I
THE FOURTH AMENDMENT:
Understanding Police Power
Some Basic Legal Concepts

I. INTRODUCTION AND OVERVIEW

It's 3 a.m. and the police barge into your home with a search warrant. They're at the wrong address and your family is terrorized; what are your rights? An officer approaches you on the street and asks to pat you down for weapons; what are your rights? The government listens to your private telephone calls or looks through your private documents; what are your rights? An officer wants to search your vehicle during a traffic stop; what are your rights? The answers to all these questions are found in the jurisprudence of the Fourth Amendment to the U.S. Constitution. The court cases and legislation coming out of this area are some of the fastest changing and most hotly contested in the country right now. Everything from when the police can take your DNA, to what parts of your house the police can look in, the use of "no-knock warrants," to searching a smartphone are disputed topics. Commonly known as the law of "search and seizure," this is the most crucial protection we have from the government prying into our private lives and property. Let's take a closer look at Fourth Amendment rights.

II. WHAT IS THE FOURTH AMENDMENT?

The constitutional restriction on governmental searches and seizures is one of the first attempts by any society to protect the people from the government itself. Simply put, the Fourth Amendment stops government agents (often the police, but applicable to any person acting under government authority) from interfering with, searching, or seizing a person without first establishing "probable cause" and securing a warrant. The actual text of the Fourth Amendment reads:

> The right of the people to be secure in their persons, houses, papers, and effects, against unreasonable searches and seizures, shall not be violated, and no Warrants shall issue, but upon probable cause, supported by Oath or affirmation, and particularly describing the place to be searched, and the persons or things to be seized.

A. Why was this protection included in the Bill of Rights?

The men who drafted the U.S. Constitution and its first 10 amendments, the Bill of Rights, wanted to keep the government from gaining overarching power to abuse its citizens. The Fourth Amendment, specifically, is a result of these founding fathers' disgust and concern with the British "writ of assistance." These writs were widely used by Great Britain in the American colonies, and functioned as general search and seizure warrants with no requirement they state what locations to search or what items to seize. To make matters even worse, they never expired and could be transferred from person to person. The result was a blanket authorization by the British government to interfere with the private affairs of the colonists, with no real restrictions, checks, or balances. The goal of the Fourth Amendment was to restrict the police and provide "security" to Americans against a snooping, abusive government.

B. How is the government limited today?

Today's driving force in Fourth Amendment law is called the "reasonable expectation of privacy." This concept recognizes that private affairs follow the person, and are not necessarily confined to a particular location (such as a home or car). When an individual is guaranteed a reasonable expectation of privacy, the government must obtain a warrant from a neutral magistrate (or satisfy an exception as discussed in Chapter 4) before conducting a lawful search or seizure. This reasonable expectation of privacy is what we think of as our "right to privacy." While it is not a right specifically guaranteed in the Bill of Rights, it is a principle that comes from courts interpreting the Fourth Amendment over the decades.

III. LEGAL LEVELS OF PROOF

Officers must meet certain standards of proof before engaging in many police encounters with citizens. In order to lawfully detain, search, or arrest, the police must obtain certain levels of proof to believe that a person is connected to some criminal activity. What are these levels of proof and how are they defined in Virginia?

A. Reasonable suspicion

Reasonable suspicion is the legal standard that a police officer must have in order to legally stop and detain a person or "pat down" a person for weapons or contraband (a Terry Stop, discussed below). What does this murky concept mean? It is a very low standard of proof, and requires a minimal level of objective evidence. Reasonable suspicion occurs when a police officer has "suspicion that is reasonable. It is not something more than suspicion. And it can hardly be called proof." *Mason v. Commonwealth*, 64 Va. App. 292 (2015). Reasonable suspicion cannot be based on a mere hunch or guess. Unfortunately, the facts and reasons can be subject to interpretation, and the U.S. Supreme Court and the Virginia Supreme Court have found reasonable suspicion from conduct that is as consistent with innocent activity as it is with criminal activity. For example, reasonable suspicion can come from your car being too clean, being too dirty, driving under the speed limit, or driving the exact speed limit, depending on the situational factors.

TERRY v. OHIO, 392 U.S. 1 (1968)

THE FACTS

John Terry was stopped and frisked by a veteran police officer when the officer spotted Terry and another man repeatedly walking up and down a street and peering into store windows. During the search, the officer found a concealed handgun in Terry's possession, which was a violation of Ohio law. The officer testified that he conducted the frisk because he suspected the men were "casing" a store for a potential robbery.

THE LEGAL HOLDING

The Supreme Court held that an officer may stop a suspect and perform a brief search for weapons when he has a reasonable belief that the person may be engaging in criminal activity and is potentially armed. This ruling made history by providing the government an avenue to search on a standard less than probable cause.

As you can see, Mr. Terry did nothing more than lawfully walk up and down the street and look in some store windows—an activity that is done by millions on a daily basis.

B. Probable cause

Probable cause is the minimum legal standard of proof required by law before a police officer may lawfully arrest someone or search a vehicle without a warrant, or, for a judge or magistrate to issue a search warrant or arrest warrant. This relatively low level of proof is defined by the U.S. Supreme Court as available trustworthy facts that would lead a reasonable person to believe that the person under investigation had committed or is committing an offense. *See Beck v. Ohio,* 379 U.S. 89 (1964). Probable cause is evaluated on a case by case basis and has no precise formula. Sometimes, a person is eligible for certain defenses or exceptions to shield him from criminal responsibility. Unfortunately, an officer does not need to investigate and rule out all possible defenses and exceptions before developing probable cause that an offense is being committed.

C. Preponderance of the evidence/clear and convincing evidence

Preponderance of the evidence and clear and convincing evidence are standards of proof that predominantly apply to civil causes of action. (*See* Chapter 15 for more information on these terms and civil liability generally).

D. Beyond a reasonable doubt

This is the highest level of legal proof, and is the standard of proof that must be established in trial before a person can be convicted of a criminal act. How is it defined? Virginia courts often use model jury instructions that say proof beyond a reasonable doubt "does not require proof beyond all possible doubt, nor is the Commonwealth required to disprove every conceivable circumstance of innocence. However, suspicion or probability of guilt is not enough for a conviction. There is no burden on the defendant to produce any evidence. A reasonable doubt is a doubt based on your sound judgment after a full and impartial consideration of all the evidence in the case." Virginia Model Jury Instructions, Inst. No. 2.100 (2019).

In general, it has been described as the level of certainty that a reasonable person should have before unplugging the life support system for a loved one, or the certainty that a person would need in packing their parachute before jumping out of a perfectly good aircraft. The government must provide this level of evidence before a conviction may occur. In short, the State needs reasonable suspicion to detain a person, probable cause to arrest a person, and proof beyond a reasonable doubt to convict a person.

IV. WHAT IS A SEARCH?

What definition do courts give to the term "search" under the Fourth Amendment? A search must be: 1) an intrusion into an individual's reasonable expectation of privacy; and 2) made by a government agent. If the examination or investigation of a person, place, or property does not violate someone's reasonable expectation of privacy, or was not done by a government agent, it is not subject to the restrictions of the Fourth Amendment.

The most common searches are of the home, vehicle, and person. However, the Fourth Amendment is not limited to these areas. As stated above, a search can occur anywhere a person has a reasonable expectation of privacy. For example, searches often include private documents, bank records, electronic communications, DNA samples, and countless other intrusions into private affairs.

V. WHAT IS A SEIZURE?

If the government demonstrates the appropriate level of proof, it may make a seizure of either a person or property.

A. What is a seizure of a person?

Someone is "seized" when a reasonable person would understand from the conduct of a police officer and the circumstances surrounding the encounter that he or she was not free to terminate the encounter and leave the interaction. Two elements must be satisfied for an act to constitute a seizure of a person: 1) there is a show of authority by the officer; and 2) the citizen submits to that authority. This kind of seizure occurs during investigatory stops, detentions, and arrests (*See* Section VII, "ENCOUNTERS WITH THE POLICE").

B. What is a seizure of property?

The government has "seized" property under the Fourth Amendment anytime a government agent creates a meaningful interference with a person's possessory right in the property. To seize, the government must show probable cause that the property was: 1) illegal; 2) evidence of a crime; or 3) "fruit" or property acquired as a result of a crime.

VI. POLICE POWER

The power of police is bestowed through legislation, and affects the rights of individuals when the balance of interests favors the health, safety, and maintenance of the general public over the individual's rights to act as he or she pleases free from government interruption, intrusion, or prohibition.

A. What is the role of police?

There are many different police organizations. Most often, we encounter police employed by the State of Virginia, individual counties, municipalities, school districts, *etc.* There is no general federal police power. However, there are law enforcement bodies controlled by the U.S. government that enforce laws in arenas specifically under federal control. Federal law enforcement bodies (often referred to as "bureaus") include the Federal Bureau of Investigation; the Bureau of Alcohol, Tobacco, Firearms and Explosives; United States Immigration and Customs Enforcement; United States Park Police, and many others.

Though it's hard to generalize the day to day routines of these vastly different agencies, law enforcement functions performed by police can be broken down into three broad areas: 1) maintaining order through general patrols and surveillance, particularly with high visibility policing; 2) enforcing the laws against violators and apprehending and arresting those suspected of breaking the law; and 3) providing services unrelated to criminal activity, such as rendering first aid, helping distressed citizens, *etc.* For example, a patrol officer on a usual day can patrol streets, investigate a burglary, and help get a cat out of a tree—all before lunchtime.

It's the "law enforcement" function that we are most concerned about in this chapter. This is where the police commit the most intrusion and are most likely to run up against (or through!) the rights of individuals.

B. Limits on police power

The U.S. and state constitutions serve as the greatest restraint on police power. Specifically, the Fourth, Fifth, and Sixth Amendments to the U.S. Constitution, and the case law that has flowed from these amendments, function to keep the government in check with strict consequences for violations. (*See* Section IX just ahead for a detailed explanation of what happens when the police violate your rights).

VII. ENCOUNTERS WITH THE POLICE
A. When do my Fourth Amendment rights matter?

The Fourth Amendment is designed to protect citizens during encounters with the police and other government agents. These encounters take several different forms. The Fourth Amendment does not cover a private citizen interacting with other private citizens.

B. Voluntary encounter

A police officer can approach any person who is located in a "public place" and engage them in ordinary conversation, just as any other person could do. This can be very casual: "Lovely weather," or "Nice boots." A person who finds themselves in a voluntary encounter with a police officer is fully within their rights to not engage in conversation or to walk away.

Courts have decided that the act of walking away from a police officer during a voluntary encounter does not create a reasonable suspicion that they are involved in criminal activity. However, any statements given or observations made during a voluntary encounter may establish reasonable suspicion to detain or probable cause to search and/or arrest a person. Any evidence found during the voluntary encounter may be used in court based on the person's consent in talking with the police officer. (*See* Chapter 4 for more issues on consent).

> **EXAMPLE:**
> Jim is walking to a bus stop when the police approach and ask where he is going. Jim ignores them just as the bus pulls up. Jim has a legal right to get on the bus without being detained by the police.

C. Temporary detention

A temporary detention occurs when a police officer stops and holds a person, restricting their right to walk away. A police officer is legally justified in conducting a temporary detention when the officer has "reasonable suspicion" based on specific articulable facts that a person has broken, is breaking, or will break the law. While lawfully detained, a police officer may check arrest warrants, frisk the outside of clothing, remove weapons, or handcuff and place a person in the back of a squad car.

There is no requirement for a police officer to read a person their Miranda Rights warning (*see* discussion of *Miranda v. Arizona*, just ahead) during a temporary detention. What a person says to the police and the surrounding circumstances of the detention may give rise to probable cause to arrest even if the detention was based on completely different suspicion. Any evidence obtained during the temporary detention may be used against that person in court.

> **EXAMPLE:**
> Police receive a call about a man wearing a red shirt who is causing a commotion at the park. Upon arrival, the police observe a man matching the description who appears intoxicated. The police have reasonable suspicion to detain this man for criminal investigation.

D. Arrest

Police may arrest a person if they have probable cause to believe a crime has been or is being committed. A formal arrest occurs when someone is placed into custody in a manner such that a reasonable person would believe they have been deprived of their freedom. At the point of arrest, most of the person's legal rights and protections are triggered, including the right to remain silent, the right to counsel, *etc.*

Remember: Don't waive your rights without talking to your lawyer!

> **EXAMPLE:**
> Police are called to the scene of a convenience store robbery. While the police are talking to the clerk, the clerk says "There he is!" and points to Sam walking down the street. The police lawfully detain Sam, pat him down, and find a pistol and a wad of cash in Sam's jacket. Sam can now be lawfully arrested based on probable cause.

E. "Community caretaking"

This encounter doesn't fit nicely into the categories of police interactions. An officer may approach a citizen if he "reasonably believes" the citizen is in need of assistance. It was expressly allowed in Virginia by the Court of Appeals in the case of *Commonwealth v. Waters*, 20 Va. App. 285 (1995) relying on the

U.S. Supreme Court case of *Cady v. Dombrowski*, 413 U.S. 433 (1973). Courts will determine whether the officer was reasonable by looking to the level and nature of distress exhibited, the location of the individual, the ability to receive assistance from others, and the extent to which the individual posed a danger to himself or others. A community caretaking encounter does not provide the right to search absent independent reasonable suspicion or probable cause, and generally only applies to public property. However, the incriminating information an officer gets from this encounter can give him reasonable suspicion for an investigation or probable cause for an additional detention or arrest. In 2021, a unanimous Supreme Court, in *Caniglia v. Strom* 141 S. Ct. 1511 (2021) decided that this community caretaking exception does not extend broadly enough to allow the warrant-less search of a home.

EXAMPLE:

A police officer observes Emily vomiting out of the passenger window of a moving vehicle. The officer can lawfully conduct a traffic stop of the automobile to determine whether Emily needs medical attention. While the officer is conducting the stop, he determines that both Emily and the driver are intoxicated and arrests Emily for public intoxication and the driver for driving while intoxicated.

F. Traffic stops

The most common encounter with the police are traffic stops. The police have the ability to make a traffic stop for any violation that they witness. It is commonly said that the police officer can follow a car for ten minutes and observe some traffic violation that would allow him to stop a car. In 2014, the U.S. Supreme Court in the case of *Navarette v. California*, 134 S.Ct.1683, 572 U.S. 393 (2014), held that the police can make a traffic stop or other temporary detention based upon information provided by an anonymous person. This ruling could profoundly impact Fourth Amendment law in the future.

VIII. THE FIFTH AMENDMENT

A. What are my rights against self-incrimination?

The Fifth Amendment to the U.S. Constitution protects an individual from being compelled to be a "witness against himself," among other rights. This means the state cannot force a person to make statements or testify in court, especially when they are against their own self-interest or are incriminating.

B. Do the police have to read the Miranda Rights warning after every arrest?

No! The Miranda Rights warning is not required simply because a person is placed into handcuffs and charged with a crime. This warning is only required when the police: 1) place a person in custody; and 2) wish to interrogate that person.

Whether or not someone is in "custody" for the purposes of Miranda Rights is determined by analyzing the facts and circumstances to determine if his or her freedom of action has been deprived in a significant way. Generally, an arrest will equate to "custody." However, there are some circumstances in which a person has not been arrested but is in "custody" for the purposes of the Miranda Rights warning. If the police do not wish to interrogate the person in custody, there is no need for a Miranda Rights warning. However, if the police wish to ask questions of the individual in custody to further their own investigation or to obtain a confession, they must administer this warning.

MIRANDA v. ARIZONA, 384 U.S. 436 (1966)

THE FACTS

The decision of Miranda v. Arizona actually addressed four different cases. In each case, the criminal suspect was questioned by law enforcement for many hours, isolated in an interrogation room with no outside communication, and ultimately each suspect gave a confession to law enforcement. None of the four defendants were advised of their Fifth Amendment rights during the interrogation process.

THE LEGAL HOLDING

The Court held that "there can be no doubt that the Fifth Amendment privilege is available outside of criminal court proceedings and serves to protect persons in all settings in which their freedom of action is curtailed in any significant way from being compelled to incriminate themselves." The Court concluded that, "the prosecution may not use statements, whether exculpatory or inculpatory, stemming from custodial interrogation of the defendant unless it demonstrates the use of procedural safeguards effective to secure the privilege against self-incrimination. By custodial interrogation, we mean questioning initiated by law enforcement officers after a person has been taken into custody or otherwise deprived of his freedom of action in any significant way." The result of this holding is the "Miranda Warning" we are familiar with today. When a suspect is subjected to a custodial interrogation by law enforcement officers, the resulting statements are not admissible unless the suspect first knowingly waived his or her rights.

IX. WHAT HAPPENS IF THE POLICE VIOLATE MY RIGHTS?
A. Exclusionary rule

What can you do when the government has overstepped its limits and violated your Fourth or Fifth Amendment rights? If a person is found to be in possession of criminal evidence or contraband, and they are successful in persuading the judge that the police officer's search, seizure, or interrogation was unconstitutional, their recourse is found in a legal principle called the exclusionary rule. The exclusionary rule states that illegally obtained evidence is "fruit of the poisonous tree" and cannot be used as evidence in the criminal trial of the person, even if this results in a guilty person going free. The exclusionary rule exists at both the federal level and the state level.

1. The federal exclusionary rule

There are a few judicially recognized exceptions to the exclusionary rule where the "illegally obtained" evidence may still be admissible against the accused. This includes evidence found in "good faith" reliance on a search warrant later determined to be legally defective, or a statute later declared to be unconstitutional. Evidence may also be admitted if it has become sufficiently disassociated with the illegal police action, it was legally obtained from an independent source, or it would have been inevitably discovered through other legal means. The U.S. Supreme Court has also ruled that the government may use illegally obtained evidence if the police officer made a "reasonable" mistake of fact or of law. Further, any evidence excluded during the prosecution phase of a criminal trial can later be admissible if the defendant or defendant's attorney "opens the door" to the issue by referring to it in the testimony at trial.

In order to take advantage of the exclusionary rule, the person charged with the crime has to have "standing" to make the evidentiary challenge. What does this mean? Simply that the person making the challenge had an expectation of privacy, was wronged by the police action, and their personal Fourth or Fifth Amendment rights were violated.

2. The exclusionary rule in Virginia
While Virginia recognizes the exclusionary rule, Virginia courts are also willing to examine whether any exceptions to the exclusionary rule exist. One of the biggest loopholes is termed the "good-faith exception," which Virginia courts discussed in the case of *Collins v. Commonwealth* Va. App. LEXIS 289 (2018).

In *Collins* the Virginia Court of Appeals recognized that "the United States Supreme Court established a good-faith exception to the exclusionary rule, applicable when a search is conducted pursuant to a warrant subsequently determined to be defective for Fourth Amendment purposes." *Ward v. Commonwealth*, 273 Va. 211, 222, 639 S.E.2d 269, 274 (2008). "Under the good-faith exception, '[w]here a police officer has an objectively reasonable belief that the issuing magistrate had probable cause to issue the search warrant, the officer may rely upon the magistrate's probable cause determination and the evidence [obtained pursuant to the defective warrant] will not be excluded.'" *Sowers v. Commonwealth*, 643 S.E.2d 506 (Va. App. 2007). This decision stands for the proposition that so long as the officer conducting a search had a good reason to believe that the warrant giving him authority to search was valid, evidence will not be excluded solely because of a later determination that the warrant was unlawful.

B. Section 1983 Claim
When a person's civil rights, including their rights against illegal searches are violated by a police officer, a person may file a civil lawsuit under Title 42 United States Code § 1983, which

is commonly referred to as a "Section 1983 Claim." The United States Supreme Court has ruled that a police officer and his or her department may be liable for monetary damages if a person's civil rights are violated. However, there is a huge exception to this rule. If the court finds a reasonable police officer could have believed a search, seizure, or other action was lawful, a police officer will be cloaked with qualified immunity that legally excuses the officer from civil liability. This means a person whose rights have been violated will have to show that a police officer knew his or her conduct was objectively unreasonable under a clearly established rule of law. This is a very high burden and will make a Section 1983 Claim an uphill battle for any aggrieved person. To bring a successful Section 1983 Claim, a person must show:

1) a person acting under the color of law (for example, a police officer acting within the scope of their employment as a police officer);
2) deprived the individual of their rights guaranteed by the U.S. Constitution or laws of the United States; and
3) is not protected by qualified immunity.

➢ CHAPTER THREE ◂

KNOW YOUR RIGHTS: PART II
THE FOURTH AMENDMENT:
Understanding The Warrant Requirement in Virginia

I. INTRODUCTION AND OVERVIEW

The text of the Fourth Amendment requires that the government have a warrant based on probable cause when they want to invade our privacy or place us under arrest. Unfortunately, the words of the Fourth Amendment are not the end of the story. Over the years, the courts and the legislature have chipped away at the warrant requirement and created an incredible number of exceptions. So many, in fact, that today there are far more searches and seizures conducted without a warrant than with one. Despite this sad reality, warrants remain the general rule, and it is important to understand how they are obtained and executed.

II. WHAT IS THE WARRANT REQUIREMENT?

Let's start with the most basic question—what is a warrant? A warrant is a document issued by a government official, typically a magistrate judge, authorizing a police officer to arrest a person, or search and/or seize property. A search warrant gives the government authority to conduct a search of a specified place and seize evidence of criminal acts or to install monitoring equipment in or on certain property. A magistrate can also issue a warrant that authorizes the "seizure" of a human being. This is called an arrest warrant, and it directs a law enforcement officer to arrest and bring "the body of the person" accused of criminal wrongdoing in front of the court.

A. How is a warrant issued?

First, police learn of activity leading them to believe a search or seizure of property will reveal evidence of a crime or that a person has committed a criminal act. Police might gather this information through their own investigation and first-hand knowledge or through information gathered by a confidential informant ("CI"). Next, the police officer drafts a sworn statement supporting the request to arrest or search. Police will include all relevant facts they have gathered in their investigation or from their CI. Officers will often include photos, maps, or other visual evidence with the officer's sworn statement. After the warrant is drafted, a neutral magistrate judge reviews the sworn statement and determines whether or not the officer has articulated probable cause for the arrest or search. (*See* Chapter 2 for the definition of probable cause). If probable cause has been established, the judge signs the warrant, and police may then execute the warrant. This means the police now have full authority to search and/or seize property or persons described in the warrant.

EXAMPLE:

Justin is arrested for possession of crack cocaine. Justin tells police where he bought the crack. Police write an affidavit describing details given by Justin about the crack house on Maple Street. The requested search warrant and attached affidavit are given to a judge who signs both, thus authorizing police to raid the crack house.

THE GENERAL WARRANT PROCESS:

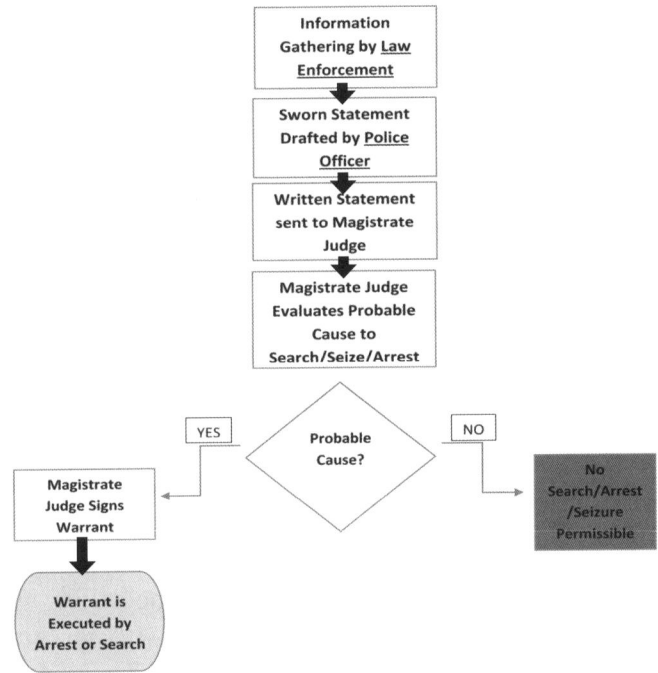

B. The "particularity requirement"

The text of the Fourth Amendment dictates that warrants must "particularly describe" the person or place at issue. How does this "particularity requirement" look in practical application? The warrant must specifically identify the person to be arrested, or describe the property to be searched and seized. It must be done in such a manner that the average person could find the location or identify the persons and places named in the warrant. In an arrest warrant, particularity is generally satisfied by including the name and date of birth of the person to be arrested, the crime alleged, and the name of the victim, if any. A search warrant's requirements are a little more complicated. To cover all bases, a search warrant generally includes three separate descriptions of the location—the street address, visual characteristics of the land or building, and descriptors from the county property records. More often than not, police officers will attach a photo of the location to the search warrant. The warrant must also describe the items the police want to seize and what they believe will be found in the location. Once probable cause is established and the warrant is signed, it may be executed by a police officer.

C. How is a warrant executed?
1. General rule-police must "knock and announce"
It is generally required that the government "knock and announce" their presence before entering a premises to execute a warrant. However, in most of the country there is an exception to this requirement, and this exception swallows the rule. If the police can state reasonable suspicion to believe that if they knocked or announced before entering it would be "dangerous, futile, or would frustrate the search's purpose," then they may disregard the knock and announce requirement. The police can ask in advance that the warrant dispense with the knock and announce requirement, or they may claim the circumstances surrounding the actual search justified dispensing with the knock and announce requirement at

the time the warrant was executed. In practice, the potential for destruction of evidence and issues of officer safety will almost always supersede the knock and announce requirement. What does this mean? The police may possibly break down your door without any warning to execute their warrant. This general exception has been greatly limited by Virginia. Beginning March 1st, 2021, Virginia Code § 19.2-56 has been amended to prevent police from executing no-knock warrants. If the police do execute a no-knock warrant, any evidence that they obtain may be excluded from court pursuant to the statute.

2. Is there a limit on destruction of your property?
It is a violation of the Fourth Amendment to cause unnecessary and excessive destruction of property when executing a search warrant. However, as the U.S. Supreme Court clarified in *U.S. v. Ramirez*, 523 U.S. 65 (1998), this violation does not mean that the evidence against you should be thrown out (see the previous chapter's discussion of the exclusionary rule). Practically speaking, the police can justify highly destructive acts in the course of their search. If it is "necessary" in the execution of the search warrant, the police may go as far as ripping up your carpets or tearing open your furniture to find what they are looking for.

3. How long do the police have to execute a warrant?
Va. Code § 19.2-56 states that a search warrant must be executed within fifteen days. The code requires that "any search warrant not executed within 15 days after issuance thereof shall be returned to, and voided by, the officer who issued such search warrant."

4. What if you are in the wrong place at the wrong time?
You are at a friend's home when the police knock on the door with

a search warrant for that address; what happens to you, the innocent bystander? In the event that the police do not have probable cause to arrest or search other individuals present at the scene, they may be temporarily detained during the course of the search for purposes of controlling the scene, officer safety, the preservation of evidence, or checks for outstanding arrest warrants. If there exists no probable cause that a detained person who is not named in the warrant is involved in criminal activity, they must be released. However, you may find yourself detained for several hours before the police decide to release you.

D. Do the police always need a warrant to perform a search and seizure?

No! The following chapter describes the many ways in which the warrant requirement has been eroded.

E. In Virginia, what can be searched and/or seized?

The Code of Virginia lays out in detail what may be searched and/or seized. Section 19.2-53 reads:
- A. Search warrants may be issued for the search of or for specified places, things or persons, and seizure therefrom of the following things as specified in the warrant:
  1. Weapons or other objects used in the commission of crime;
  2. Articles or things the sale or possession of which is unlawful;
  3. Stolen property or the fruits of any crime;
  4. Any object, thing, or person, including without limitation, documents, books, papers, records or body fluids, constituting evidence of the commission of crime; or
  5. Any person to be arrested for whom a warrant or process for arrest has been issued.

Notwithstanding any other provision in this chapter to the contrary, no search warrant may be issued as a substitute for a witness subpoena.

B. Any search warrant issued for the search and seizure of a computer, computer network, or other device containing electronic or digital information shall be deemed to include the search and seizure of the physical components and the electronic or digital information contained in any such computer, computer network, or other device.

C. Any search, including the search of the contents of any computer, computer network, or other device conducted pursuant to subsection B, may be conducted in any location and is not limited to the location where the evidence was seized.

As you can see, almost anything is subject to a search and/or seizure with a warrant. What about when the police don't have a warrant? In the next chapter, we will discuss in detail the many, many exceptions to the warrant requirement.

> CHAPTER FOUR ◄

KNOW YOUR RIGHTS: PART III
THE FOURTH AMENDMENT:
Exceptions To The Warrant Requirement

I. INTRODUCTION AND OVERVIEW

You are driving late at night when you look into your rearview mirror and see flashing blue and red lights. When the officer approaches your window, he tells you he is going to search your car because he saw you making "furtive movements." What are your rights? You are walking around your neighborhood when an officer approaches and tells you that you match the description of a burglary suspect. He frisks you for weapons. Can he do this without a warrant? When does the law allow police to avoid the warrant process to make an arrest or conduct a search of your private property?

Courts have eroded the strong protection of the warrant requirement over the years—there are so many present day exceptions to obtaining a warrant that the exceptions now swallow the rule. This chapter will discuss the many ways police can conduct warrantless arrests and warrantless searches of your body, vehicle, and home.

II. WHEN CAN THE POLICE SEARCH OR ARREST ME WITHOUT A WARRANT?

A. Stop and frisk

If a police officer has developed reasonable suspicion a person has committed a crime, he can detain and pat down that person to search for weapons. This "stop and frisk" is commonly referred to as a Terry Stop. *Terry v. Ohio*, 392 U.S. 1 (1968), confines this type of search to "…guns, knives, clubs, or other hidden instrumentalities for the assault of the police officer." Recall from Chapter 2 that reasonable suspicion is an extremely low standard. An officer has to have just a little more than a hunch that you might be involved in criminal activity. A Terry Stop is limited to an over-the-clothes search for weapons; however, if an officer can determine through touch alone that a person is in possession of contraband (the "plain feel" doctrine), he can confiscate the contraband and charge the person with a criminal violation. How far does plain feel go? While the officer cannot squeeze, move, or manipulate the things in your pockets to see if the items feel like contraband, it is not uncommon for police officers to claim they could tell by plain feel that someone was in possession of a crack rock or a marijuana joint. If an officer feels contraband in your pockets, he can arrest you, and the evidence found on your body will be admissible in court.

Just how easy is it for an officer to decide he has reasonable suspicion to search you? A quick-thinking officer can justify a Terry

Stop and frisk of virtually anyone he decides is suspicious. Most states have laws on the books that criminalize loitering, sometimes called "obstructing a right of way." If an officer sees you walking down the sidewalk and decides to search you, all the officer has to do is wait for you to stop and look at your phone, bend over to tie your shoe, or stop to look into a storefront. He now has reasonable suspicion that you are committing the crime. *Terry v. Ohio* gives the officer permission to detain and search you for weapons and other contraband.

In 2017, the United States Fourth Circuit Court of Appeals issued an opinion in the case *U.S. v. Robinson*, 846 F.3d 694 (4th Cir. 2017), which addressed a stop and frisk search situation that is relevant to all legal firearm owners. The Court reasoned that an anonymous tip about the presence of a firearm triggered a police officer's right to engage in a Terry Stop, even if the act of carrying a firearm is not illegal under state law. Under the reasoning of the Fourth Circuit's opinion, anyone exercising their Second Amendment rights effectively surrenders their Fourth Amendment rights against warrantless detentions and searches.

B. On-site arrest

In Virginia, the police have been given broad powers of arrest. Va. Code § 19.2-81 says that police can arrest someone for the following reasons:

    Such officers may arrest without a warrant any person who commits any crime in the presence of the officer and any person whom he has reasonable grounds or probable cause to suspect of having committed a felony not in his presence.

    Such officers may arrest without a warrant any person whom the officer has probable cause to suspect of operating any watercraft or motorboat while:

(i) intoxicated in violation of subsection B of § 29.1-738 or a substantially similar ordinance of any county, city, or town in the Commonwealth; or

(ii) in violation of an order issued pursuant to § 29.1-738.4 and may thereafter transfer custody of the person arrested to another officer, who may obtain a warrant based upon statements made to him by the arresting officer.

Any such officer may, at the scene of any accident involving a motor vehicle, watercraft as defined in § 29.1-733.2 or motorboat, or at any hospital or medical facility to which any person involved in such accident has been transported, or in the apprehension of any person charged with the theft of any motor vehicle, on any of the highways or waters of the Commonwealth, upon reasonable grounds to believe, based upon personal investigation, including information obtained from eyewitnesses, that a crime has been committed by any person then and there present, apprehend such person without a warrant of arrest. For purposes of this section, "the scene of any accident" shall include a reasonable location where a vehicle or person involved in an accident has been moved at the direction of a law-enforcement officer to facilitate the clearing of the highway or to ensure the safety of the motoring public.

Such officers may, within three hours of the alleged offense, arrest without a warrant at any location any person whom the officer has probable cause to suspect of driving or operating a motor vehicle, watercraft or motorboat while intoxicated in violation of §§ 18.2-266, 18.2-266.1, 46.2-341.24, or subsection B of § 29.1-738; or a substantially similar ordinance of any county, city, or town in the Commonwealth, whether or not the offense was committed in such officer's presence.

Such officers may arrest, without a warrant or a capias, persons duly charged with a crime in another jurisdiction upon receipt of a photocopy of a warrant or a capias, telegram, computer printout, facsimile printout, a radio, telephone or teletype message, in which photocopy of a warrant, telegram, computer printout, facsimile printout, radio, telephone or teletype message shall be given the name or a reasonably accurate description of such person wanted and the crime alleged.

Such officers may arrest, without a warrant or a capias, for an alleged misdemeanor not committed in his presence when the officer receives a radio message from his department or other law-enforcement agency within the Commonwealth that a warrant or capias for such offense is on file.

Such officers may also arrest without a warrant for an alleged misdemeanor not committed in their presence involving (i) shoplifting in violation of § 18.2-96 or 18.2-103 or a similar local ordinance, (ii) carrying a weapon on school property in violation of § 18.2-308.1, (iii) assault and battery, (iv) brandishing a firearm in violation of § 18.2-282, or (v) destruction of property in violation of § 18.2-137, when such property is located on premises used for business or commercial purposes, or a similar local ordinance, when any such arrest is based on probable cause upon reasonable complaint of the person who observed the alleged offense. The arresting officer may issue a summons to any person arrested under this section for a misdemeanor violation involving shoplifting.

Because the police in Virginia may arrest when they have probable cause that almost any infraction has occurred or is occurring, there are literally thousands of criminal offenses for which a person may be arrested. Almost everyone who drives a car or walks around in public violates some minor law on a daily basis and is subject to arrest if a police officer so desires. For example, if you are driving an automobile, you can be arrested for having a burnt-out light around your license plate, an expired registration sticker, crossing a solid line on the roadway, failing to signal a lane change, failing to signal prior to turning, or hundreds of other infractions. This can be equally true if you are on a bicycle or even in a wheelchair or riding a horse because the Virginia Motor Vehicle Code regulates bicycle riders, personal mobility vehicles, and animals in public. Va. Code § 46.2-800.

C. Warrantless apprehension of suspected dangerous persons with mental illness, "red flag laws"

In recent years, there has been a nationwide push for "extreme risk protective orders" or "red flag laws" specifically designed to remove firearms from individuals who are accused of engaging in conduct or making statements that others may deem "dangerous." Beginning July 1, 2020, and pursuant to Va. Code § 19.2-152.13, upon petition of a Law Enforcement Officer or Commonwealth Attorney and after an independent investigation, an emergency substantial risk order may be issued to seize firearms for up to 14 days or until a hearing occurs. This law is discussed in further detail in Chapter 6. However, many gun rights advocates believe that red flag laws exist only to harass gun owners. For the last several decades, Virginia has had a process which allows a magistrate to sign a temporary detention order which allows someone to be detained and evaluated for purposes of ensuring that they are not a danger to themselves or others. Va. Code § 37.2-809.

III. WHEN CAN THE POLICE SEARCH MY HOME WITHOUT A WARRANT?

Your home is about as private as any place can get. The government should always be required to get a warrant to search this ultra-private space, right? Wrong! There are several scenarios where the police can legally search your home or its surrounding areas without a warrant. The following is a discussion of the most important exceptions.

A. Exigent circumstances

The police may enter and search a home in response to "exigent circumstances." Police officers typically claim exigency in order to protect life, protect property, prevent the destruction of evidence, or pursue a fleeing felon.

Once the crisis is contained, a further search of the home is not permitted. However, officers may seize any evidence or contraband that is in plain view inside the home. Further, what they see while in the home may be used to support probable cause for a search warrant.

EXAMPLE:

The police are chasing Curtis, a robbery suspect, through a neighborhood. Unfortunately, Curtis decides to evade the cops by running into Eric's home! Because the police are in hot pursuit of an alleged felon, they have every right to enter Eric's home without a warrant, and may search any place in his house that Curtis could possibly be hiding. To make matters worse, they see on Eric's kitchen counter what they believe is drug paraphernalia. They can now seize these items to investigate and use them to arrest Eric or to develop probable cause for a search warrant.

B. Open fields

The police don't need a warrant to march around and search the open fields outside your home. What is an open field? It's any area "out of doors in fields, except in the area immediately surrounding the home." *Oliver v. United States*, 466 U.S. 170, 178 (1984). The area immediately surrounding your home is the "curtilage," and the police have to get a warrant to search this area. Why are the open fields different from the spaces immediately adjacent to your home? Courts have said that people do not have a reasonable expectation of privacy in the open fields outside because open fields aren't private enough to invoke the protections of the Fourth Amendment.

C. Abandoned property

Courts have consistently held that persons cannot object to the seizure and evidentiary admission of abandoned property. An officer only has to have a reasonable belief that a person has abandoned the property. Because of that, any reasonable expectation of privacy in the property is lost. The most notable example of abandoned property is your garbage on the street awaiting collection.

What does it take to abandon an object? In the case of *Hawley v. Commonwealth*, a man asked permission to leave a car at a motel for three or four days. After the car sat at the hotel for eight to ten days, the manager of the hotel called the police and had the vehicle towed. When the police towed the vehicle, they searched it. In doing so they found stolen contraband that they traced to the defendant Hawley. Hawley argued that the search of the vehicle was a violation of his Fourth Amendment rights. Unfortunately for him, the Virginia Supreme Court ruled that he could not challenge the admissibility of the contraband in his trial, because he had abandoned the car! *Hawley v. Commonwealth*, 144 S.E.2d 314 (1965).

D. Plain view

An officer may, without a warrant, seize contraband and evidence of criminal activity that is in plain view. The plain view doctrine, as courts have analyzed, has three requirements:
1) the officer must lawfully make an initial intrusion or be in a lawful position to see the items;
2) the officer must make the discovery inadvertently and may not use plain view as pretext; and
3) it must be immediately apparent that the items are contraband or evidence of a crime.

What does it mean to be in a "lawful position" to see the items? An officer walks up to your front door, and through your living room window, he sees your elaborate methamphetamine operation. He may enter and seize the items because they are in plain view. By contrast, if an officer suspects you have a meth lab somewhere in your home and decides to jump your fence to look into your back window, anything he sees from that vantage does not fall under the "plain view" doctrine.

1. Can the police use sense-enhancing devices?

It depends. Law enforcement's use of binoculars to peer into your home or your property is lawful and can constitute plain view. Similarly, aerial views of your property by airplane or helicopter are plain view and do not require a warrant. Infrared imaging and dog sniffs of your home, however, require warrants based on probable cause and do not constitute plain view (or smell). New technology poses questions that the legislature and the court have to decide. For example, under current Virginia law, police must obtain a warrant before using a drone to search your property. Va. Code § 19.2-60.1.

2. Can the police claim "plain view" if you have "No Trespassing" signs?

Yes. A "No Trespassing" sign does not stop law enforcement officials from seizing items in plain view on your property. A "No Trespassing" sign might stop an officer from searching through your abandoned property or from physically setting foot on your property (unless one of the exceptions applies), but courts often allow officers to skirt this requirement by claiming they did not see any posted "No Trespassing" sign before entering the property.

IV. WHEN CAN THE POLICE SEARCH MY VEHICLE WITHOUT A WARRANT?

Many Americans would be shocked to learn that the Fourth Amendment provides very little protection for their personal vehicles. The Supreme Court justified this lessened expectation of privacy in the 1925 case of *Carroll v. United States*. In *Carroll*, the Court reasoned that a car's mobility makes it more difficult for the police to secure a search warrant, and because automobiles are already subject to increased government regulation, people should not expect the same security against warrantless searches that they have in their homes. As a result, there are very few circumstances in which the police have to seek a warrant to search a vehicle.

A. The probable cause search

This is the farthest reaching exception to searching without a warrant. In order to legally search a vehicle, a police officer only has to articulate probable cause that a crime has been, will be, or is being committed. (*See* detailed discussion of probable cause, Chapter 2). Once this occurs, an officer can search anywhere in the vehicle that could contain evidence of that crime without the requirement of obtaining a warrant.

It is a common misconception that a police officer cannot search containers, bags, or other self-contained personal items present in a vehicle. Unfortunately, this is most often not the case. A police officer may search any part of the vehicle, including the glove box or trunk, which could contain evidence of the crime for which they developed probable cause.

For example, if an officer smells the odor of phencyclidine ("PCP") in a vehicle, he may search anywhere in the vehicle that could contain PCP. Since PCP could be stored in a very small space, there will be virtually no restrictions on where the officer may look. By contrast, if the officer has probable cause to believe you are a felon in possession of an AR-15, he will not be able to look in your glove box, center console, or small locked briefcase, as an AR-15 could not reasonably be stored in any of these locations.

What about the wheel well and body panel of the vehicle? An officer must have probable cause that contraband or evidence of a crime is specifically contained within these areas of your vehicle to justify a warrantless search. This makes some sense, because searching these areas is more intrusive and damaging to your personal property than searching the passenger compartment.

How does the law treat other modes of transportation? Boats and planes are treated like motor vehicles, and warrantless searches are lawful based on probable cause. RVs and houseboats, however, are a different story—if the RV or houseboat is stationary and being used as a home at the time law enforcement wishes to conduct a search, they must seek a warrant. If the RV or houseboat is traveling, it is likely subject to a warrantless search.

B. Plain view in a motor vehicle

Just like an officer may seize contraband and evidence of a crime in plain view from your home and/or person (described in detail above), he may seize these items if they are in plain view in your vehicle. So, if a person left contraband lying out in plain view on your dashboard, an officer can seize it as evidence and arrest the person—no warrants required.

C. Search incident to arrest

Regardless of what the arrest was for, there is an exception to the warrant requirement that permits an officer to perform a warrantless search during or immediately after a lawful arrest. The exception is limited to the person arrested and the area immediately surrounding the person in which the person may gain possession of a weapon, in some way effect an escape, or destroy or hide evidence.

If a person is arrested in the very near vicinity of their vehicle, this power to search will often extend to the passenger compartment of the vehicle. In 2009, the U.S. Supreme Court addressed this authority to search in the case of *Arizona v. Gant*, 556 U.S. 332 (2009). In *Gant*, the Court held that a search of the passenger compartment of the vehicle was lawful only if it was reasonable to believe the arrestee might access the vehicle at the time of search, or that the vehicle contained evidence of the crime for which the person had been arrested. Assume that an officer slaps the cuffs on you right outside your open car door for the aforementioned crime of unlawful carry. Now, the police can search your entire passenger compartment incident to your arrest! However, if you are arrested several yards away from your parked car, *Gant* does not allow the search of your car as being "incident" to the arrest.

D. Inventory search

The inventory search is the all-encompassing catch-all that will allow a thorough search of your vehicle anytime it comes into police custody. Anytime you are arrested with your vehicle, the police are authorized to remove the car and impound it for safe keeping. The contents of the car must be "inventoried" to protect the property of the person arrested as well as to protect the police from any false allegations of stealing or losing the property. For the search to provide admissible evidence, courts require that the police department must have procedures in place for performing inventories of automobiles. In practice, virtually every police agency has a valid inventory search policy. Many times, the police will use this opportunity to perform a thorough search of the car, its trunk, and all of its contents. The courts have determined that this "inventory" can be done without a warrant and any contraband or other evidence of criminal activity that is lawfully obtained constitutes admissible evidence. *South Dakota v. Opperman*, 428 U.S. 364 (1976).

E. Consent

In practice, this is the most common way police officers gain access to your home or vehicle to conduct a search. Most people are conditioned to respect the authority of a police officer, and so many people have a hard time saying no when an officer demands permission to search. An officer can ask permission to search for any reason or no reason at all. There is no evidentiary standard required to ask a person for consent to conduct a search. The officer must simply obtain consent "voluntarily."

What is "voluntariness"? Virginia courts have said that consent "loses its validity only if it is involuntary or the product of a manipulative 'exploitation' by the police of an earlier unconstitutional search or seizure." *Kyer v. Commonwealth*, 45 Va. App. 473 (2005). Virginia courts have further said that "whether consent was in fact voluntary or was the product of duress or coercion, express or implied, is a question of fact to be determined from the totality of all the circumstances." *Walls v. Commonwealth*, 2 Va. App. 639 (1986).

Do people have the right to refuse consent? Yes! However, an officer does not need to inform you of your right to refuse consent. Your knowledge of your ability to refuse a search is only one element that will be considered when the courts examine whether you voluntarily gave consent. *Walls v. Commonwealth*, 2 Va. App. 639 (1986). In fact, it is very possible that in Virginia an officer may gain consent to search your vehicle by saying something to the effect of "I'm going to search your vehicle now, okay?" If you agree, you have given voluntary consent! How far does consent go? A person may limit the scope of their consent, and anything found outside that scope will not be admissible evidence. For example, if you grant an officer consent to look in your glove compartment, he may not use that same consent to conduct a search of your trunk.

V. OTHER SEARCH ISSUES
A. Inventory once in custody

No warrant is required to search an individual once they are in custody and booked into jail. Personal possessions are accounted for and logged into police custody. Depending on the officers and the offense you are suspected of committing, this search can be very invasive. Unfortunately, once you are in custody, there is no more permission needed for an officer to bring out the rubber gloves.

B. GPS tracking

The U.S. Supreme Court decision of *U.S. v. Jones*, 565 U.S. 400 (2012), determined that the installation and tracking of a GPS device on a vehicle is a Fourth Amendment search requiring a warrant. However, the Court has not yet issued any guidelines as to what conditions are required for the issuance of a warrant for GPS tracking.

C. Smart phones

In today's day and age, you might be hard-pressed to find someone who does not carry a smart phone on their person at all times. Most of these tiny, portable computers are overflowing with personal information such as texts, personal contacts, schedules, emails, and photos. What happens when police find a smart phone, say in an inventory search like the one above? How has Fourth Amendment jurisprudence kept up with this technological development? In 2014, the U.S. Supreme Court handed down *Riley v. California*, 134 S.Ct. 2473 (2014), which directly addresses this issue. In *Riley*, the Court distinguished cell phones from other objects found on an individual by stating:

> Cell phones differ in both a quantitative and a qualitative sense from other objects that might be kept on an arrestee's person. The term "cell phone" is itself misleading shorthand; many of these devices are in fact minicomputers that also happen to have the capacity to be used as a telephone. They could just as easily be called cameras, video players, rolodexes, calendars, tape recorders, libraries, diaries, albums, televisions, maps, or newspapers. One of the most notable distinguishing features of modern cell phones is their immense storage capacity. Before cell phones, a search of a person was limited by physical realities and

tended as a general matter to constitute only a narrow intrusion on privacy. *Riley v. California*, 134 S.Ct. 2473, 2478-79 (2014).

Due to these distinguishing features, the Court ultimately concluded that police must obtain a warrant based on probable cause to search the contents of a cell phone. However, the Court left open the question of whether or not a smart phone can be searched without a warrant if there are exigent circumstances or if the phone itself is the instrumentality of the crime.

D. Highly regulated businesses

Warrantless searches have been permitted by the courts if carried out by the state's administrative agents in any business or activity that is highly regulated by the government. For example, agents from the Bureau of Alcohol, Tobacco, Firearms and Explosives may conduct an audit of a gun store, or the Virginia Alcoholic Beverage Authority may send their agents to inspect liquor stores or bars.

E. Airports/international borders

Warrantless searches are permitted at borders and airports under the legal theory that individuals have implicitly consented to be searched while traversing an international border or getting on an airplane. Further, warrantless searches are justified by public interest and the great risk to public safety in these areas.

F. Probationers/parolees

Persons on probation and parole have a lessened expectation of privacy due to their highly monitored status. As a result, they may be searched on reasonable suspicion alone. This standard even applies to the person's cell phone! Persons subject to government supervision lose nearly all of their Fourth Amendment rights.

G. Dog sniffs

As it applies to vehicles, a dog sniff is not considered a search under the Fourth Amendment. An officer may detain you for a reasonable amount of time to await a canine to conduct a sniff. If the dog alerts on your vehicle, the officer then has probable cause to conduct a search of the vehicle for narcotics without a warrant. However, a dog sniff of the front porch of a home is a search under the Fourth Amendment, and cannot be done in the absence of a warrant. This is because the dog sniff takes place on the curtilage of the home, which is a place where the occupant of the home has an expectation of privacy.

What is a "reasonable" amount of time? Courts examine this under the totality of the circumstances on a case by case basis. For example, in a large city with many canine officers, it is probably unreasonable to detain someone for over an hour to await the dog. In a small county with only one canine officer, this long wait may not be unreasonable if the dog is out on another crime scene. Ultimately, the lengths to which an officer is allowed to go to detain and search a particular person will be fought after the fact in the courtroom on this kind of "totality of the circumstances" analysis.

The U.S. Supreme Court in *Rodriguez v. United States*, 135 S.Ct. 1609 (2015), added some clarity to the legality of dog sniff detentions at the conclusion of a traffic stop. The Court ruled that once the officer has concluded his investigation into the traffic stop, he may not detain a citizen to wait for a drug dog without independent reasonable suspicion that the person is in possession of illegal narcotics. Expect to see many lengthy traffic stops in the future as police officers attempt to stay on the right side of this decision.

H. Drones

The use of drones has become more and more prevalent. This includes aerial surveillance by both private individuals and law enforcement. While many states allow police to fly drones anywhere a civilian can, Virginia takes the minority approach in generally requiring police to obtain a warrant before using a drone to search a particular area. Some exceptions exist, such as after an Amber Alert is issued, or to survey the scene of a crash to aid in reconstruction photos. Va. Code § 19.2-60.1.

> CHAPTER FIVE ◄

LEGAL DEFINITIONS AND CLASSIFICATIONS OF FIREARMS:
WHAT IS LEGAL?

Before discussing the law of firearms and all its different facets, it is important first to understand what the law defines as a "firearm." Firearms laws are governed on both the federal and state levels; therefore, throughout this chapter we will explore the interactions that federal and Virginia law have on the purchase and possession of firearms.

I. DEFINITION OF FIREARM
A. What is a firearm under federal law?

FEDERAL DEFINITION

> Under federal law, a firearm is defined as "any weapon (including a starter gun) which will or is designed to or may readily be converted to expel a projectile by the action of an explosive." 18 U.S.C. § 921(a)(3). The federal definition of a firearm also includes the frame or receiver of any such weapon, any firearm muffler or silencer, or any "destructive device."

Why might it be important to know the different ways the term "firearm" is defined under federal and state law? It is because if a person finds themselves charged with a crime by federal authorities, the federal definition of a firearm will apply. Likewise, if the charge is under a violation of state law, then the state definition will apply. Thus, the primary difference in the definitions and their impact on a defendant charged with a crime involving a firearm lies with how a person may be in trouble with the law. As we see in the next sections, the definitions of what does and does not constitute a firearm, although similar in many aspects, contain an array of differences that make violating the law unwittingly easy.

B. What is a firearm under Virginia law?

VIRGINIA DEFINITION

> Under Virginia law, a firearm is defined as, "any weapon that will or is designed to or may readily be converted to expel single or multiple projectiles by the action of an explosion of a combustible material; or the frame or receiver of any such weapon."

C. Unfinished "80 percent" frames and receivers

During the firearm manufacturing process, raw materials such as metals and polymers eventually emerge from their unmanufactured form into something readily identifiable and usable as a firearm. Legislatures have had to grapple with at what point a block of raw material becomes a firearm as it is machined and processed. The federal government (through the ATF) has drawn a distinction between unfinished firearm frame or receiver blanks, which are unregulated, and finished firearm frames or receivers, which are subject to federal regulation under the Gun Control Act. The unfinished frame or receiver blanks are commonly sold as 80 percent lowers. This distinction has been followed by most states. This position is relied upon for the proposition that only after a frame or receiver is machined or manufactured beyond 80 percent does it become a firearm, and subject to federal and state regulation. It retains the same classification as the raw material before it has been manufactured or machined beyond 80 percent completion. Keep in mind, the ATF does not use the term "80 percent" but simply classifies items as "finished" or "unfinished." Therefore, an unfinished frame or receiver can be sold and shipped through the mail without regulation. It is not considered a firearm in its unfinished format but merely a metal or plastic block, akin to a paperweight. Once the item is finished, it becomes classified as a firearm and governed by all applicable laws, including possession and transfer. Of course, gun owners must remain vigilant to watch for changing definitions and requirements. Homemade firearms (called Privately Made Firearms—PMF—by the Biden administration), have been the target of many recent proposed legislative and interpretive changes. The rules surrounding these weapons could change at any point.

D. Handguns, rifles, and shotguns

Federal law and Virginia law both classify and define firearms into categories of handguns and long guns (rifles and shotguns). This section will provide an overview of how both federal and Virginia laws classify firearms as well as the physical requirements for a firearm to be legal.

1. What is a handgun?

The term "handgun" is defined as any firearm that is designed to be fired by using only one hand. While it is true that most individuals will use two hands when firing a handgun for safety and accuracy purposes, the emphasis in the legal definition of a handgun rests purely in its design to be held or fired with a single hand. For this reason, many "braced" pistols seem to be under scrutiny by the ATF. Essentially, the ATF is questioning whether such items are truly designed with the intent to be fired from one hand. Gun owners need to remain watchful, because which weapons are classified as "handguns" may change in the future

> **FEDERAL DEFINITION**
>
> The United States Code of Federal Regulations defines a handgun as "(a) any firearm which has a short stock and is designed to be held and fired by the use of a single hand; and (b) any combination of parts from which a firearm described in paragraph (a) can be assembled."

> **VIRGINIA DEFINITION**
>
> Va. Code § 18.2-307.1 defines a handgun as "any pistol or revolver or other firearm, except a machine gun, originally designed, made, and intended to fire a projectile by means of an explosion of a combustible material from one or more barrels when held in one hand."

2. What is a rifle?

FEDERAL DEFINITION

Federal law defines a rifle as "a weapon designed or redesigned, made or remade, and intended to be fired from the shoulder, and designed or redesigned and made or remade to use the energy of the explosive in a fixed metallic cartridge to fire only a single projectile through a rifled bore for each single pull of the trigger." 27 CFR § 478.11. In addition, a legal rifle must have a barrel length of 16 inches or greater, and includes any weapon made from a rifle which is at least 26 inches overall in length.

VIRGINIA DEFINITION

Va. Code § 29.1-100 defines a rifle as "a weapon designed or redesigned, made or remade, and intended to be fired from the shoulder, and designed or redesigned and made or remade to use the energy of the explosive in a fixed metallic cartridge to fire only a single projectile through a rifled bore for each single pull of the trigger."

Minimum lengths

In order for a rifle to not be subject to the National Firearms Act, it must have a barrel of at least 16 inches in length. The ATF procedure for measuring barrel length is accomplished by measuring from the closed bolt (or breech-face) to the furthermost end of the barrel or permanently attached muzzle device.

Below is an example of a rifle that does not meet the minimum barrel length requirement after measurement.

The barrel is measured by inserting a dowel rod into the barrel until the rod stops against the bolt or breech-face. The rod is then marked at the furthermost end of the barrel or permanently attached muzzle device, withdrawn from the barrel, and then measured. Any measurement of less than 16 inches will classify the rifle as being short-barreled under federal law and would subject the firearm to the NFA.

Short-barreled rifles and regulation by the NFA is further discussed in Chapter 17. Note: for overall length, rifles with collapsible/folding-stocks are measured from the "extreme ends," unless the stock is "easily detachable," in which case it is measured without the stock.

3. What is a shotgun?

A shotgun is a firearm that is usually designed to be fired from the shoulder. It is generally a smooth-bore firearm, which means that the inside of the barrel is not rifled. A shotgun uses the energy of a fixed shell to fire a number of small spherical pellets called shot or a solid projectile called a slug. The shot pellets from a shotgun spread upon leaving the barrel, and the power of the burning charge is divided among the pellets, which means that the energy of any one ball of shot is fairly low.

Federal and Virginia definition of a shotgun

The federal and Virginia legal definitions of a shotgun are the same. It is "a weapon designed or redesigned, made or remade, and intended to be fired from the shoulder, and designed or redesigned and made or remade to use the energy of the explosive in a fixed shotgun shell to fire through a smooth bore either a number of ball shot or a single projectile for each single pull of the trigger." 27 CFR § 478.11. Like rifles, legal shotguns have requirements for minimum barrel and overall lengths. Shotgun barrels must be at least 18 inches long and must also comply with the same 26 inch overall length requirement.

Minimum lengths

In order for a shotgun to not be subject to the National Firearms Act or classified as a short-barreled firearm, it must have a barrel of at least 18 inches in length. The ATF procedure for measuring the barrel length of a shotgun is the same as it is for a rifle. Below is an example of a shotgun that does not meet the minimum barrel length requirement after measurement.

Any measurement of less than 18 inches will classify the shotgun as a short-barreled weapon and illegal under federal law unless the requirements of the NFA are satisfied. (*See* Chapter 17 for short-barreled shotguns and other non-compliant firearms). Note: The collapsible/folding-stock rule that applies to rifles applies to shotguns as well.

Numerous questions have surrounded the release of the Mossberg 590 Shockwave. The firearm has a pistol grip, shoots shotgun shell ammunition, has a barrel length of 14 inches and an overall length of around 26½ inches. On March 2, 2017, the ATF issued a letter that states the Shockwave is not a firearm regulated by the NFA. Instead, it is a GCA firearm that is regulated as any other common firearm that is available to the public. Consequently, Mossberg has marketed the 590 Shockwave as a non-NFA weapon that does not require a tax stamp for possession. The ATF determination relies on the fact that it is made without a shoulder stock and instead has a "bird's head" grip.

E. The federal standards for antique or replica firearms

When is a firearm not legally a "firearm"? It is when the law defines it as not being one, such as with "antique" firearms.

1. Federal definition of "antique firearm"

1898 or prior

The federal definition of firearm under Title 18, Section 921 of the United States Code excludes "antique firearms." Even though an antique firearm still functions ballistically similar to a "modern" firearm, under federal law, antique firearms are regulated differently. An antique firearm under federal law includes any firearm with a matchlock, flintlock, percussion cap, or similar type of ignition system manufactured in or before 1898 or any replica of a firearm just described so long as the replica "is not designed or redesigned for using rimfire or conventional centerfire fixed ammunition, or uses rimfire or centerfire ammunition that is no longer manufactured in the United States and is not readily available in ordinary channels of commerce." 18 U.S.C. §§ 921(16)(A) and (B). So, an "antique firearm" is not a "firearm" for purposes of federal regulation; it is an "antique firearm."

Muzzle loading

In addition, federal law does not consider "any muzzle loading rifle, muzzle loading shotgun, or muzzle loading pistol, which is designed to use black powder, or a black powder substitute, and which cannot use fixed ammunition" as a firearm. Be aware, however, that the term "antique firearm" does not include: any weapon which incorporates a firearm frame or receiver; any firearm which is converted into a muzzle loading weapon; or any muzzle loading weapon which can be readily converted to fire fixed ammunition by replacing the barrel, bolt, breechblock, or any combination of these parts. *See* 18 U.S.C. § 921(a)(16)(C).

F. Highly regulated firearms under federal law

Under federal law, several types of firearms are regulated by the National Firearms Act. These firearms include:
- Short-barreled shotguns;
- Short-barreled rifles;
- Machine guns;
- Firearm silencers or suppressors;
- Weapons or devices capable of being concealed on the person from which a shot can be fired;
- Pistols or revolvers having a smooth bore (as opposed to rifled bore) barrel designed to fire a fixed shotgun shell;
- Pistols or revolvers with a vertical handgrip;

- Destructive devices; and
- Weapons classified as "Any Other Weapon," or AOWs.

See 26 U.S.C. § 5845. (*See* Chapter 18 discussing the National Firearms Act for more information on these weapons).

Keep in mind, however, many of these weapons may be legally possessed with proper compliance under the National Firearms Act. (*See* Chapter 17 for more information on these prohibited weapons and the NFA).

G. What firearms are illegal under Virginia law?

Under the Virginia Code, several firearms are illegal to possess. Also, the National Firearms Act regulates and restricts certain firearms. (*See* Chapter 17 for more information on the NFA).

1. Plastic firearms

Va. Code § 18.2-308.5 defines a "plastic firearm" as any firearm, including machine guns and sawed-off shotguns, as containing less than 3.7 ounces of electromagnetically detectable metal in the barrel, slide, cylinder, frame, or receiver which does not generate an image that accurately depicts its shape when subjected to X-ray machine inspection. It is unlawful for any person to manufacture, import, sell, transfer, or possess any plastic firearm. A violation is a felony punishable by up to 10 years in prison! The recent trend of firearm files being downloaded from the internet and 3D printed causes concern for the possibility that this law may be violated. Often, 3D printed designs force the maker to use metal parts as inserts to avoid running afoul of this law.

2. Striker 12

Va. Code § 18.2-308.8 specifies the Striker 12, also known as a "streetsweeper," or any semi-automatic folding stock shotgun of like kind with a spring tension drum magazine capable of holding twelve shotgun shells, is prohibited. The Striker 12 is a 12-gauge shotgun with a revolving cylinder that was designed for riot control and combat. It is unlawful to import, sell, possess, or transfer the Striker 12 or any firearm of like kind. A violation is a felony punishable by up to five years in prison.

3. Assault firearms

Virginia does not outlaw "assault firearms" but does define them. Va. Code § 18.2-308.2:01 defines an "assault firearm" as any semi-automatic center-fire rifle or pistol which expels single or multiple projectiles by action of an explosion of a combustible material and is equipped at the time of the offense with a magazine which will hold more than 20 rounds of ammunition or designed by the manufacturer to accommodate a silencer or equipped with a folding stock.

4. Machine guns

The Uniform Machine Gun Act of the Code of Virginia regulates machine guns in Virginia. Va. Code § 18.2-288 defines any weapon which shoots or is designed to shoot automatically more than one shot, without manual reloading, by a single function of the trigger, as a machine gun. While it is legal to possess a machine gun in Virginia, so long as the provisions of the National Firearms Act (*see* Chapter 17) are met, Virginia has recently outlawed the possession of "trigger activators" which are commonly known as "bump stocks." Virginia law defines a trigger activator as a "device designed to allow a semi-automatic firearm to shoot more than one shot with a single pull of the trigger by harnessing the recoil energy of any semi-automatic firearm to which it is affixed so that the trigger resets and continues firing without additional physical manipulation of the trigger by the shooter."

H. How big of a gun can a person possess?

Federal law dictates that any firearm which has any barrel with a bore of more than one-half inch in diameter is a "destructive device" and is subject to the National Firearms Act. Possession of any such firearm without the proper paperwork associated with NFA firearms is illegal. Note, however, that some shotguns are regulated differently. (*See* Chapter 17 for more information on destructive devices and the NFA).

II. AMMUNITION

No discussion concerning firearm law would be complete without examining laws concerning the ammunition that goes into a firearm. Just like firearms, the law regulates the possession, sale, and even composition of "legal" ammunition. This section addresses the essential aspects of the law concerning ammunition and what gun owners need to know, both under federal and state law.

PRACTICAL LEGAL TIP

Even with firearms, having the right tool for the job is important. Practically speaking, you should choose the firearm and ammo that you feel most comfortable using. Recent advancements in ammunition technology have made smaller rounds that many in the past had dismissed as inadequate into formidable defensive choices. –Gilbert

A. Ammunition types

Ammunition is categorized by its type and assembly; not by use.

1. Fixed ammunition

Fixed ammunition is characteristically used in most small arms such as handguns and rifles. Fixed ammunition is also called a cartridge. This type of ammunition consists of a container for the propellant charge (cartridge case) and a projectile that flies downrange at the target. The propellant charge, priming, and ignition system are assembled inside the cartridge case and are not alterable. The cartridge case is firmly attached to the projectile by crimping or cement. The cartridge case remains in the weapon after firing and is ejected near it or is consumed during firing.

Centerfire ammunition

A centerfire cartridge is a cartridge with a primer located in the center of the cartridge case head. The primer is a separate and replaceable component. Centerfire cartridges are the most popular variety of ammunition in almost all cartridge sizes.

Rimfire ammunition

Rimfire is a method of ignition for metallic firearm cartridges as well as the cartridges themselves. It is called rimfire because the firing pin of a gun strikes and crushes the base of the cartridge's rim to ignite the primer. This is in contrast to the more common centerfire method, where the firing pin strikes the primer cap at the center of the base of the cartridge. The rim of the rimfire cartridge is essentially an extended and widened percussion cap which contains the priming compound, while the cartridge case itself contains the propellant powder and the projectile (bullet). Once the rim of the cartridge has been struck and the bullet discharged, the cartridge cannot be reloaded, because the head has been deformed by the firing pin impact.

2. Separable ammunition

Separable ammunition also consists of the cartridge case and projectile, but the case is not attached firmly to the projectile and can be removed in the field and altered. The projectile may either consist of "shot" or a "slug." This type of ammunition is used in shotguns.

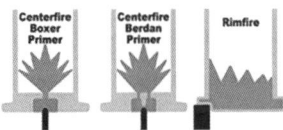

B. Ammunition size

Ammunition is generally expressed in a measurement. Most of the world uses a metric rating, while the commercial market in the United States uses a U.S. standard measurement. Handgun and rifle ammunition is measured by the caliber, which is simply a measurement of the internal diameter of the barrel measured in millimeters or inches and is approximately equal to the diameter of the projectile that is fired. The larger the caliber, the bigger in diameter the ammunition.

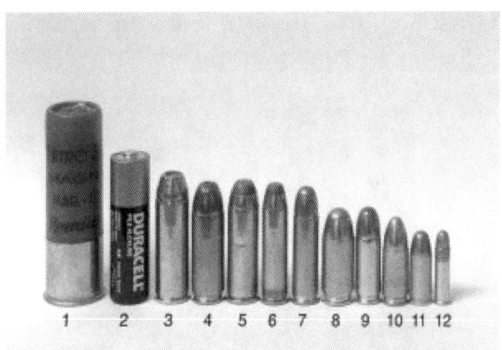

Different calibers of handgun ammunition

Pictured above: Shotgun shell; (2) AA Battery; (3) .454 Casull; (4) .45 Winchester Magnum; (5) .44 Remington Magnum; (6) .357 Magnum; (7) .38 Special; (8) .45 ACP; (9) .38 Super; (10) 9mm Luger; (11) .32 ACP; and (12) .22 LR

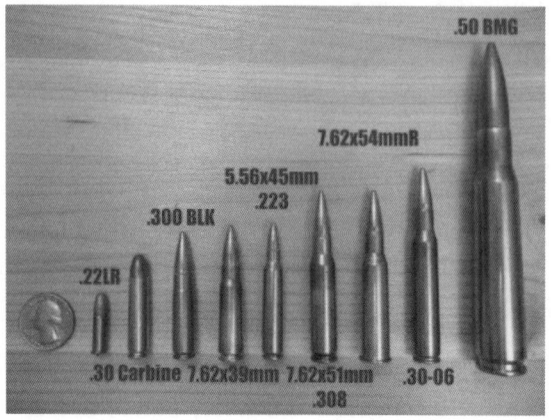

Shotgun ammunition, on the other hand, comes in self-contained cartridges loaded with some form of shot or slug which is designed to be fired from a shotgun. Shotgun shells are generally measured by "gauge." The gauge of a firearm is a unit of measurement used to express the diameter of the barrel.

Left-to-right: .410, 28ga, 20ga, 12ga

C. Bullet type

There are numerous styles of bullets that can be put into a cartridge of any caliber of ammunition. Different types of bullets have different effects when they strike a target. For example, the hollow-point round design causes the bullet to expand (or mushroom) rapidly when it hits soft tissue and therefore, to stop in soft-tissue targets. More of the energy of the bullet is deposited in the intended target because of the mushrooming, and the bullet is more likely to stop a perpetrator from doing what he is doing. Some manufacturers have further developed the hollow-point rounds to make them more lethal such as the R.I.P. ammunition, Black Talons, *etc.*, which star outward upon impact in order to do more internal damage.

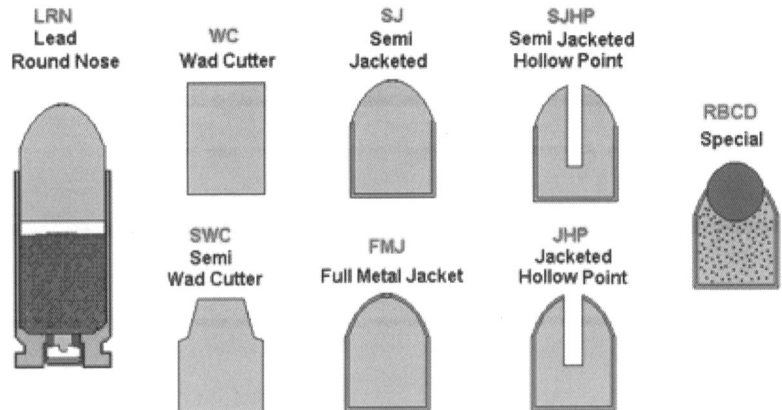

D. How does the law define ammunition?

1. Federal definition of ammunition

Under federal law, the term "ammunition" is defined under 18 U.S.C. § 921(a)(17)(A) and means "ammunition or cartridge cases, primers, bullets, or propellant powder designed for use in any firearm." Thus, the federal definition of ammunition includes the finished product and all of the components in making a round of ammunition. However, the federal definition of ammunition does not include:

   1) any shotgun shot or pellet not designed for use as the single, complete projectile load for one shotgun hull or casing; or
   2) any unloaded, non-metallic shotgun hull or casing not having a primer. *See* 27 CFR § 478.11.

In other words, individual ammunition components are legally defined as ammunition themselves, even if they are simply parts, except that shotgun ammunition components, if not completely assembled, are not ammunition.

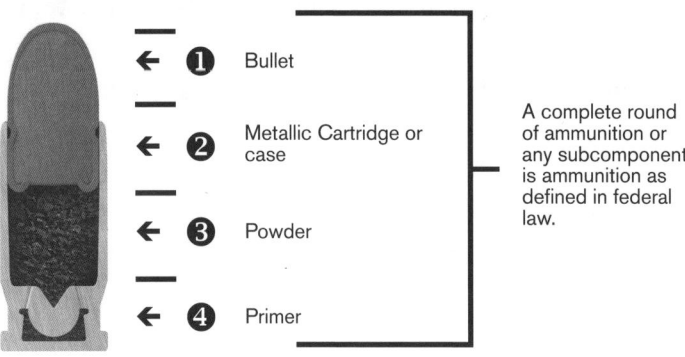

2. Virginia definition of legal ammunition

Va. Code § 18.2-308.2 defines "ammunition for a firearm" as: "the combination of a cartridge, projectile, primer, or propellant designed for use in a firearm other than an antique firearm."

Va. Code § 18.2-308.2 also defines explosive material: Explosive material means any chemical compound mixture, or device, the primary or common purpose of which is to function by explosion; the term includes, but is not limited to, dynamite and other high explosives, black powder, pellet powder, smokeless gun powder, detonators, blasting caps and detonating cord but shall not include fireworks or permissible fireworks.

E. What ammunition is illegal?

1. Federal law

Armor-piercing handgun ammunition is prohibited under federal law. The federal definition of armor-piercing ammunition is found in 18 U.S.C. § 921(a)(17)(B) and means "[1] a projectile or projectile core which may be used in a handgun and which is constructed entirely (excluding the presence of traces of other substances) from one or a combination of tungsten alloys, steel, iron, brass, bronze, beryllium copper, or depleted uranium; or [2] a full jacketed projectile larger than .22 caliber designed and intended for use in a handgun and whose jacket has a weight of more than 25 percent of the total weight of the projectile." The production, sale, importation, delivery, and possession of armor-piercing ammunition is discussed in Chapter 6. Over the past several years the proliferation of weapons classified as "handguns," which shoot ammunition typically reserved for rifles, has caused concern that certain rifle ammunition may run afoul of this law.

Under federal law, while there is no blanket prohibition on the mere possession of armor-piercing ammunition, it is prohibited under four conditions:

Prohibition one: it is illegal to make or import armor-piercing ammunition.
Under 18 U.S.C. § 922(a)(7) it is unlawful for any person to manufacture or import armor-piercing ammunition unless:
1) the manufacture of such ammunition is for the use of the United States, any department or agency of the United States, any state, or any department, agency, or political subdivision of a state;
2) the manufacture of such ammunition is for the purpose of exportation; or

3) the manufacture or importation of such ammunition is for the purpose of testing or experimentation and has been authorized by the United States Attorney General.

Prohibition two: it is illegal for manufacturers and importers to sell or deliver armor-piercing ammunition.

Federal law states that it is unlawful for any manufacturer or importer to sell or deliver armor-piercing ammunition unless such sale or delivery is:
1) for the use of the United States, any department or agency of the United States, any state, or any department, agency, or political subdivision of a state;
2) for the purpose of exportation; or
3) for the purpose of testing or experimentation and has been authorized by the United States Attorney General.

See 18 U.S.C. § 922(a)(8).

Prohibition three: an FFL or other license-holder cannot sell or deliver armor-piercing ammunition without the proper documentation.

Under 18 U.S.C. § 922(b)(5), it is unlawful for any licensed importer, licensed manufacturer, licensed dealer, or licensed collector to sell or deliver armor-piercing ammunition to any person unless the licensee notes in his records, as required under 18 U.S.C. § 923, the name, age, and place of residence of such person if the person is an individual, or the identity and principal and local places of business of such person if the person is a corporation or other business entity.

Prohibition four: it is illegal to possess armor-piercing ammunition if a person is involved in a crime of violence or drug-trafficking.

Pursuant to 18 U.S.C. § 924(c)(5), it is unlawful for "any person who, during and in relation to any crime of violence or drug trafficking crime (including a crime of violence or drug trafficking crime that provides for an enhanced punishment if committed by the use of a deadly or dangerous weapon or device) for which the person may be prosecuted in a court of the United States, uses or carries armor piercing ammunition." Individuals who use or carry armor-piercing ammunition in the commission of a crime of violence or during a drug-trafficking crime are subject to heightened sentencing standards should they be found guilty.

As you can see, while possession of armor-piercing ammunition itself is not illegal, obtaining armor-piercing ammunition without violating one of the foregoing prohibitions is almost impossible.

However, it should be noted that not all ammunition that can pierce armor is actually armor-piercing. The federal definition contains specific requirements for a particular round of ammunition's composition in order to make it armor-piercing (*i.e.,* composed of certain alloys). As a practical example, 5.7 millimeter ammunition for an FN Five-seveN handgun or a PS90 rifle, while capable of piercing armor based on its size and velocity, is not ammunition that is armor-piercing as defined under the law because such ammunition, sold commercially, is primarily for sporting purposes according to the ATF.

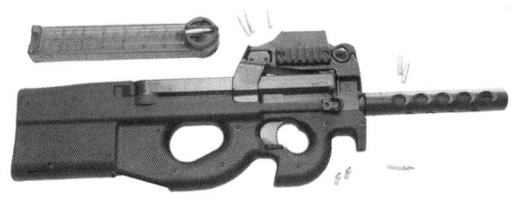

PS90

2. Virginia restricted firearm ammunition definition

Va. Code § 18.2-308.3 defines "restricted firearm ammunition" as bullets, projectiles or other types of ammunition that are: (i) coated with or contain, in whole or in part, polytetrafluorethylene or a similar product; (ii) commonly known as "KTW" bullets or "French Arcanes": or (iii) any cartridges containing bullets coated with a plastic substance with other than lead or lead alloy cores, jacketed bullets with other than lead or lead alloy cores, or cartridges of which the bullet itself is wholly comprised of a metal or metal alloy other than lead. However, this definition does not include shotgun shells or solid plastic bullets.

F. Does modifying traditional ammunition make it illegal?
1. Federal law

No. Outside of armor-piercing ammunition, there is no handgun or long gun ammunition that is prohibited under federal law. In fact, there are many examples of hollow-point rounds which are modified in a way to become more lethal such as the R.I.P. ammunition, Black Talons, *etc.*, which star outward upon impact in order to do more internal damage. Such ammunition, though it looks different from traditional ammunition, is perfectly legal.

2. Virginia law

No. Virginia law contains no provisions specifically related to modifying ammunition. While it is unlawful to possess "restricted ammunition" (as described in section 5 (II)(E)(2) of this chapter) during the commission of a crime, there is no specific Virginia law preventing the modification of ammunition.

G. Is it legal to use ammunition that works in both handguns and rifles?

Generally yes, except for armor-piercing ammunition that is used principally in handguns. This is because the federal definition of armor-piercing ammunition contemplates handguns only. Beyond armor-piercing ammunition, it is legal to use ammunition that is available in common calibers and that functions in both handguns and rifles.

> CHAPTER SIX ◄

PURCHASING, TRANSFERRING, AND POSSESSING FIREARMS

I. LAWS OF PURCHASING AND POSSESSING: THE BASICS

The laws of purchasing, selling, gifting, or otherwise transferring a firearm are distinct and different from the laws of possessing a firearm. It may be legal for someone to possess a firearm, and it still be illegal for them to "purchase" the firearm. Further, each of these sets of laws for "purchasing" or "possessing" has a federal and a state component, both of which must be satisfied in order to stay on the right side of the law.

On the federal level, the Bureau of Alcohol, Tobacco, Firearms and Explosives ("ATF") is charged with regulating firearms including sales, purchases, and transfers through Federal Firearms Licensees ("FFLs" or "dealers"); however, a multitude of federal agencies can be involved in any given firearms law investigation or police function, most currently falling under a branch of the U.S. Department of Justice.

There is no direct state-level equivalent to the ATF in Virginia, but the Department of State Police ("VSP") plays a significant role with respect to criminal background record checks, investigations, and enforcement of firearm sales and transfers by firearm dealers. Local law enforcement agencies typically have little to no role regarding the sale or transfer of firearms, but will routinely investigate and enforce firearm possession offenses.

II. MINIMUM AGE TO POSSESS VS. MINIMUM AGE TO PURCHASE

Federal law controls all FFL firearms transactions and requires that a person be 21 years of age or older before they may purchase a handgun or 18 for the purchase of a long gun. With some notable exceptions, under federal law, a person must generally be at least 18 years of age in order to possess a handgun or ammunition for a handgun. *See* 18 U.S.C. § 922(x)(2). But unlike the law on purchasing a long gun, there is no federal age requirement for the possession of a rifle or shotgun. Va. Code § 18.2-308.7 makes it unlawful for anyone under the age of 18 (also defined as a minor/child/juvenile) to knowingly or intentionally possess or transport any handgun or assault firearm. A violation of this section is a misdemeanor punishable by up to 12 months in jail. Note: There are exceptions to this minimum age to possess requirement, which we will discuss later. There is no Virginia age requirement for the possession of long guns such as a rifle or a shotgun unless the shotgun comes with a magazine that will hold more than seven rounds. Virginia law does not have a minimum age for the possession of ammunition.

Traditionally, according to federal law, a person must be 21 years of age or older before they may purchase a handgun or ammunition for a handgun from a firearm dealer. A 2021 panel of the Fourth Circuit found that the prohibition on sales of handguns by firearm dealers to those between the ages of 18 and 21 was unconstitutional. If this decision stands, in the future even 18 year olds may be able to enjoy their constitutional right to buy firearms from a firearm dealer. Additionally, a person must be 18 years of age or older before they may purchase a long gun or ammunition for a long gun from a firearm dealer. While under federal law, a handgun or long gun could be purchased in a private sale by a person who is 18 years of age, Virginia law has now eliminated private sales within the state. Firearm dealer transactions, private sales, and ammunition are discussed later in this chapter.

MINIMUM AGE TO PURCHASE FIREARMS	FEDERAL LAW: FROM DEALER	VIRGINIA LAW: PRIVATE SALE
Handgun	21	18
Long gun	18	18

III. THE FEDERAL FIREARM LICENSE SYSTEM

An FFL or Federal Firearms License is a license required by federal law for those persons or entities that are engaged in the business of buying and selling firearms. A federal firearms licensee is often called an "FFL" or "dealer."

When an individual purchases, sells, or transfers a firearm through a firearm dealer, the dealer and the individual must both comply with specific legal requirements, paperwork, and procedures concerning the buying, selling, or transferring of those firearms.

A. Who must obtain an FFL?

Federal law requires a federal firearms license if a person is engaged in business as a firearms dealer, manufacturer, or importer. For the purposes of our discussion in this chapter, a person is engaged in the business when the person "devotes time, attention, and labor to dealing in firearms as a regular course of trade or business with the principal objective of livelihood and profit through the repetitive purchase and resale of firearms, but such term shall not include a person who makes occasional sales, exchanges, or purchases of firearms for the enhancement of a personal collection or for a hobby, or who sells all or part of his personal collection of firearms." 18 U.S.C. § 921(A)(21)(C).

There is no exact number of sales or transfers that constitutes "occasional sales, exchanges, or purchases of firearms." In 2016, the Obama administration prompted the ATF to clarify that 1) "A person can be engaged in the business of dealing in firearms regardless of the location in which firearm transactions are conducted" (internet sales and gun show sales may still require a license); 2) "[E]ven a few transactions, when combined with other evidence, can be sufficient to establish that a person is 'engaged in the business.'" For example, courts have upheld convictions for dealing without a license when as few as two firearms were sold or when only one or two transactions took place, when other factors also were present. The administration also made sure to remind people that violations are punishable by up to five years in prison and a fine of up to $250,000.

ATF also released a pamphlet called *Do I Need A License To Buy And Sell Firearms? Guidance to help you understand when a Federal Firearms License is required under federal law*. Similar to the administration's directive, the pamphlet notes that:

> Courts have identified several factors relevant to determining on which side of that line your activities may fall, including: whether you represent yourself as a dealer in firearms; whether you are repetitively buying and selling firearms; the circumstances under which you are selling firearms; and whether you are looking to make a profit. Note that while quantity and frequency of sales are relevant indicators, courts have upheld convictions for dealing without a license when as few as two firearms were sold, or when only one or two transactions took place, when other factors were also present.

The pamphlet can be found at this link: www.atf.gov/file/100871.

B. FFL firearm transaction overview

Any attempted purchase or transfer of a firearm from an FFL dealer will trigger legal requirements imposed by both the federal and Virginia law. Such an event will require a firearm transaction record. These requirements will include processing federal and Virginia forms to ensure that the purchaser is neither prohibited from making the purchase nor from possessing a firearm under federal and Virginia law.

The first thing that a prospective purchaser will typically do is select a firearm to purchase from the firearm dealer. After a selection has been made, the prospective purchaser is required to show proper identification and complete ATF Form 4473 and Virginia

Department of State Police Form SP-65. These forms require the applicant purchaser, under penalty of law, to provide accurate identifying information, as well as answer certain questions in order to establish whether the applicant purchaser may legally purchase and possess a firearm.

In Virginia, the FFL submits the executed forms along with a criminal background check request to the Virginia Department of State Police's Firearms Transaction Program ("VFTP"). The VFTP was created by the Virginia Department of State Police to provide a timely point-of-sale approval or disapproval decision regarding the sale or transfer of all firearms (except antiques) based upon the results of a criminal history record information check and purchaser answers to potentially disqualifying questions. The criminal background check requirement is further explained in section IV of this chapter.

VSP Form SP-65 is the Virginia equivalent form that is required by Va. Code § 18.2-308.2:2.

Additionally, the dealer must also sign ATF Form 4473 and retain it for at least 20 years. The ATF is permitted to inspect as well as receive a copy of Form 4473 from the dealer both during audits and during the course of a criminal investigation. An FFL dealer's ATF Form 4473 records must be surrendered to the ATF in the event the FFL dealer retires or ceases business.

C. Sale of multiple handguns must be reported to the ATF

Under federal law, firearm dealers are required to report to the ATF any sale or transfer of two or more pistols, revolvers, or any combination of pistols and revolvers to an unlicensed (non-FFL) individual that takes place at one time or during any five consecutive business days. *See* 18 U.S.C. § 923(g)(3). This report is made to the ATF on Form 3310.4 and is completed in triplicate with the original copy sent to the ATF, one sent to the VSP, and one retained by the dealer and held for no less than five years. In addition Virginia law found at Va. Code § 18.2-308.2:2 makes it a crime to purchase more than one handgun during a 30-day period.

There are multiple exceptions to this law. Some of the more common exceptions are for those with a valid Concealed Handgun Permit, those who purchase a new handgun from a dealer on the same day they trade an old handgun in, and for those who have had an old handgun stolen or irretrievably lost (after such loss or theft has been reported to police) and for collectors of firearms who submit to an "enhanced background check." Other exceptions for this law exist for those purchasing handguns on behalf of law enforcement agencies or security companies licensed within the state.

D. Special duty of firearms dealers involving minors

Federal law requires that FFLs who deliver handguns to non-licensees display at their licensed premises (including temporary business locations at gun shows) signs that customers can readily see. These signs are provided by the ATF and contain the following language:

(1) The misuse of handguns is a leading contributor to juvenile violence and fatalities.

(2) Safely storing and securing firearms away from children will help prevent the unlawful possession of handguns by juveniles, stop accidents, and save lives.

(3) Federal law prohibits, except in certain limited circumstances, anyone under 18 years of age from knowingly possessing

a handgun, or any person from transferring a handgun to a person under 18.

(4) A knowing violation of the prohibition against selling, delivering, or otherwise transferring a handgun to a person under the age of 18 is, under certain circumstances, punishable by up to 10 years in prison.

In addition to the displayed sign, federal law requires FFLs to provide non-licensee customers with a written notification containing the same four points as listed above as well as Sections 922(x) and 924(a)(6) of Title 18, Chapter 44 of the United States Code. This written notification is available as a pamphlet published by the ATF entitled "Youth Handgun Safety Act Notice" and is sometimes referred to as ATF Information 5300.2. Alternatively, this written notification may be delivered to customers on another type of written notification, such as a manufacturer's brochure accompanying the handgun or a sales receipt or invoice applied to the handgun package. Any written notification delivered to a customer other than the one provided by the ATF must include the language described here, and must be "legible, clear, and conspicuous, and the required language shall appear in type size no smaller than 10-point type." 27 CFR § 478.103(c).

E. What is a private sale?

A private sale of a firearm is a sale of a firearm by individual private parties that are not licensed firearm dealers, and for which no ATF Form 4473 or VSP Form SP-65 is completed. Private sales in Virginia have been outlawed pursuant to Va. Code § 18.2-308.2:5. Private transfers of firearms, which are permissible in some limited situations will be discussed later in the chapter.

Note: While private sales are generally outlawed in Virginia, an ongoing legal challenge to the law exists, and for the time being an injunction has been issued to allow the private sale of a handgun to a minor between the ages of 18 and 21 who is otherwise not prohibited from firearm ownership.

IV. BACKGROUND CHECK SYSTEMS IN VIRGINIA

The National Instant Criminal Background Check System ("NICS")is the system for determining if a prospective firearm purchaser is eligible to purchase a firearm. Virginia also uses a state-based background check system. In Virginia, after a prospective purchaser completes ATF Form 4473 and VSP Form SP-65, the firearms dealer initiates the NICS background check process with the VSP Firearms Transaction Center. The VSP is the point of contact between the FFL and the NICS.

The NICS and Virginia background check systems will check the applicant purchaser against multiple different databases containing various types of records. The NICS searches the National Crime Information Center ("NCIC") consisting of the Wanted Persons File, Protection Order File, Interstate Identification Index ("III"), Deported Felons File, US Secret Service Protective File, Foreign Fugitive File, the ATF, Violent Felon File, and NICS indexes: Illegal/Unlawful Aliens File, Mental Defectives/Commitments File, Dishonorable Discharges, Citizenship Renunciants, Controlled Substance Abuse File and Denied Persons File. The Virginia search is accessed through the Virginia Criminal Information Network ("VCIN"), which include Virginia's wanted and missing persons files and protective orders, Virginia's criminal history record files, and Virginia's database of adjudications of legal incompetence and incapacity, as well as involuntary commitments to mental institutions for inpatient or outpatient treatment.

NICS is also tasked with ensuring that a prospective purchaser is not listed on the Virginia voluntary "do not sell list." The "do not sell list" is created by statute, and allows anyone over the age of 18 to apply in writing to the Department of State Police to be added to the list. When applying for placement on the voluntary "do not sell list" the applicant must provide photo identification with the application. When an individual is added to the list, they are notified of their status on the list by mail by the Virginia Department of State Police.

Once on the list, a person may be removed only by submitting a removal request and waiting 21 days.

The response to background check requests from the NICS system come in three basic forms: approved, delayed, or denied. According to the Federal Bureau of Investigation ("FBI"), NICS checks are usually determined within minutes of initiation. The Brady Handgun Violence Prevention Act of 1993 states that the FBI has three business days to make its decision to approve or deny the transfer; however, according to Va. Code § 18.2-308.2:2, and beginning July 1st, 2021, the VSP has until the end of the firearm dealer's fifth business day to advise the firearm dealer of the decision to either approve or deny the transfer.

If an identification is not made in one or more of the background check files, the computer responds "APPROVED" and a unique computer-generated approval number is provided to the firearm dealer for the transaction. The firearm may be transferred upon the dealer's receipt of the approval number. The "DENIED" response means that the transfer may not take place. The "DELAYED" response means that the purchase or transfer may not legally proceed. If a possible identification is made during the background checks, then the computer responds "DELAYED" and a review of the information/record is conducted to determine probable identification and lawful eligibility of the prospective firearms purchaser. The firearm dealer is notified immediately upon a final determination of eligibility. In the case of electronic failure or other circumstances beyond the control of the VSP, the firearm dealer shall be advised immediately of the reason for such delay and be given an estimate of the length of such delay. After such notification, the VSP shall, as soon as possible but in no event later than the end of the firearm dealer's next business day, inform the requesting firearm dealer if the purchaser is disqualified. Exception: The VSP has up to 10 days to inform the firearm dealer of a background check response in instances involving non-resident background checks for the purchase or transfer of a rifle or shotgun.

A. What transactions require background checks?
A background check is required before any sale, rental, trade, or transfer between any person and a FFL-licensed firearm dealer can be complete unless an exception is provided under the law.

B. What transactions do not require a background check?
The VSP is not required to conduct a NICS background check under the following circumstances:
  i. Transactions between persons who are licensed as firearms importers or collectors, manufacturers or dealers pursuant to 18 U.S.C. § 921 *et seq;*
  ii. Purchases by or sales to any law enforcement officer or agent of the United States, the Commonwealth or any local government, or any campus police officer; or
  iii. Transactions of antique firearms, curios or relics.

V. FEDERAL AND VIRGINIA LAW ON DISQUALIFICATIONS FOR PURCHASING AND POSSESSING FIREARMS

Federal law lists categories of persons disqualified from legally purchasing and possessing a firearm. This list comprises disqualifications that come from several different pieces of federal legislation including the Gun Control Act of 1968, the Brady Handgun Violence Prevention Act, and the Violence Against Women Act. If a person buys or attempts to buy a firearm from an FFL, they must not be disqualified under any of the laws. Before an FFL may sell or otherwise transfer a firearm, the purchaser must fill out an ATF Form 4473 and a VSP Form SP-65. This form has questions concerning each of the criteria that disqualify a person to purchase a firearm under federal law. These disqualifications include:

1) if the person is not the actual purchaser of the firearm—also known as a "straw man purchaser";
2) if the person is under indictment or information in any court for a felony or any other crime for which the judge could imprison the person for more than one year;
3) if the person has ever been convicted in any court for a felony or other crime for which the judge could imprison the person for more than one year or found guilty or adjudicated delinquent as a juvenile 14 years of age or older at the time of the offense of a delinquent act that would be a felony if committed by an adult;
4) if the person is a fugitive from justice;
5) if the person is an unlawful user of, or addicted to, marijuana, or any depressant, stimulant, narcotic drug, or controlled substance; (The Federal Gun Control Act defines an addicted person, or unlawful user, as a person who has a conviction for

use or possession of a controlled substance within the past year or persons found through a drug test to use a controlled substance unlawfully, provided that the test was administered within the past year.);

6) it is illegal for any person to purchase or transport a handgun who, within a 36-consecutive-month period, has been convicted of two misdemeanor drug offenses;

7) if the person has ever been adjudicated as mentally defective or has been committed to a mental institution; has ever been acquitted by reason of insanity and prohibited from purchasing, possessing or transporting a firearm pursuant to Va. Code § 18.2-308.1:1 or any substantially similar law of any other jurisdiction, been adjudicated legally incompetent, mentally incapacitated or adjudicated an incapacitated person and prohibited from purchasing a firearm pursuant to Va. Code § 18.2-308.1:2 or any substantially similar law of any other jurisdiction, or been involuntarily admitted to an inpatient facility or involuntarily ordered to outpatient mental health treatment and prohibited from purchasing a firearm pursuant to Va. Code § 18.2-308.1:3 or any substantially similar law of any other jurisdiction;

8) if the person has been dishonorably discharged from the Armed Forces;

9) if the person is subject to an active final protective order or a protective order restraining the person from harassing, stalking, or threatening the person's child, or an intimate partner or child of such partner;

10) if the person is currently subject to an emergency substantial risk order or substantial risk order (both often called a red flag order);

11) if the person has been convicted in any court for a misdemeanor crime of domestic violence;
12) if the person has ever renounced their United States citizenship;
13) if the person is an alien illegally in the United States;
14) if the person is admitted under a non-immigrant visa and does not qualify for an exception; and
15) if the applicant is on the Virginia voluntary do not sell list.

The purchaser must legally affirm that they are not subject to any of the criteria listed above before they may purchase a firearm. If a prospective purchaser answers any question on the form in a manner that indicates they are legally disqualified, it is illegal for the FFL to sell that person the firearm, and it is illegal for the purchaser to complete the transaction or possess the firearm. It is also illegal and a felony to make any false oral or written statement with respect to ATF Form 4473 and/or VSP Form SP-65 and to exhibit any false or misrepresented identification with respect to the transaction. Certain violations of the Gun Control Act pursuant to 18 U.S.C. § 921 are punishable by up to 10 years in prison and/or up to a $250,000 fine. Va. Code § 18.2-308.2:2(K) makes any willful and intentional materially false statement on the consent form or on such firearm transaction records as may be required by federal law a felony punishable by up to 10 years in prison.

A. Understanding who is disqualified
1. Can I buy a firearm for another person?
No. This would be a "straw man" purchase. Purchases for third persons are often called "straw man" purchases and are illegal. If you are not the actual purchaser, beware! In order to legally purchase a firearm from a dealer, you must be the "actual purchaser or transferee." If you are not the actual purchaser or transferee, then

it is illegal for you to complete the transfer or sale under federal and Virginia law. If you are not the actual purchaser, beware!

In fact, the ATF has a campaign called "Don't Lie for the Other Guy" that is targeted at (as they term it on their website) detection and deterrence of "straw man" purchases. The ATF website lists numerous examples of prosecutions for "straw man" purchases, and a United States Supreme Court case examined and upheld federal law on this matter. *Abramski v. United States*, 134 S.Ct. 2259 (2014).

So who is the "actual" buyer or transferee so as not to be a "straw man"? The ATF states that you are the actual "transferee/buyer if you are purchasing the firearm for yourself or otherwise acquiring the firearm for yourself (*e.g.*, redeeming the firearm from pawn/retrieving it from consignment, or a firearm raffle winner)." The ATF goes on to state "you are also the actual transferee/buyer if you are legitimately purchasing the firearm as a gift for a third party."

EXAMPLE:
Bobby asks John to purchase a firearm for Bobby because he will be out of town during the gun sale. Bobby gives John the money for the firearm. John then buys the firearm with Bobby's money and gives Bobby the firearm.

John is not the "actual buyer" (he is legally a "straw man") of the firearm and if John indicates that he is the "actual buyer" of the firearm on ATF Form 4473, then he has committed a federal crime. However, it should be noted that the Supreme Court ruling in *Abramski* reaffirmed that "gifts" of firearms are not illegal straw man purchases. The important element in this crime is who provided the money for the purchase.

When completing ATF Form 4473, if a person checks "yes" to the box asking if the person is the "actual purchaser," then that person cannot have engaged in a separate transaction to sell or transfer the firearm privately. Please note: The U.S. Supreme Court's ruling held that a person cannot legally purchase a firearm on behalf of another even if the person receiving the firearm would not otherwise be prohibited from making the purchase themselves. So don't buy a firearm for another person no matter how good a friend, relative, or person they are—it is a crime!

PRACTICAL LEGAL TIP

Thinking about buying a gun on behalf of your buddy? Not a good idea! This is true even if your friend is legally able to purchase the weapon himself. –Gilbert

Va. Code § 18.2-308.2:2(L1) states that any person who attempts to solicit, persuade, encourage, or entice any dealer to transfer or otherwise convey a firearm other than to the actual buyer, as well as any other person who willfully and intentionally aids or abets such person, is guilty of a felony punishable by up to five years in prison.

Va. Code § 18.2-308.2:2(M) states that any person who purchases a firearm with the intent to (i) resell or otherwise provide such firearm to any person who he knows or has reason to believe is ineligible to purchase or otherwise receive from a dealer a firearm for whatever reason or (ii) transport such firearm out of the Commonwealth to be resold or otherwise provided to another person who the transferor knows is ineligible to purchase or otherwise receive a firearm, shall be guilty of a felony punishable by up to 10 years in prison with fines of up to $100,000. A mandatory minimum term of imprisonment of five years applies if more than one firearm is transferred. Note: This section shall not apply to the purchase of a firearm by a person for the lawful use and possession for his child, grandchild, or individual for whom he is the legal guardian if such child, grandchild, or individual is ineligible to purchase a firearm solely because of his age pursuant to Va. Code § 18.2-308.7.

Va. Code § 18.2-308.2:2(N) also makes it illegal for any person who is ineligible to purchase or otherwise receive or possess a firearm in Virginia to solicit, employ, or assist any person in violating Va. Code § 18.2-308.2:2(M). A violation of this section is a felony punishable by up to 10 years in prison with fines of up to $100,000, and with five years of the prison sentence being a mandatory minimum term of imprisonment.

Va. Code § 18.2-308.2:1 makes it illegal for any person to sell, barter, give or furnish, or have in his possession or under his control with the intent to sell, barter, give or furnish, any firearm to any person he knows is prohibited from possessing or transporting a firearm pursuant to Va. Code §§ 18.2-308.1:1, 18.2-308.1:2, 18.2-308.1:3, 18.2-308.2, subsection B of Va. Code § 18.2-308.2:01, or Va. Code § 18.2-308.7 and says that such a person shall be guilty of a felony punishable by up to 10 years in prison with a fine of up to $100,000. However, this prohibition shall not be applicable when the person convicted of the felony, adjudicated delinquent or acquitted by reason of insanity has (i) been issued a permit pursuant to subsection C of Va. Code § 18.2-308.2 or been granted relief pursuant to subsection B of Va. Code §§ 18.2-308.1:1, 18.2-308.1:2, or 18.2-308.1:3 (ii) been pardoned or had his political disabilities removed in accordance with subsection B of Va. Code § 18.2-308.2, or (iii) obtained a permit to ship, transport, possess, or receive firearms pursuant to the laws of the United States.

FREQUENTLY ASKED QUESTIONS FROM ATF WEBSITE

Q: TO WHOM MAY AN UNLICENSED PERSON TRANSFER FIREARMS UNDER THE GCA?

A: A person may sell a firearm to an unlicensed resident of his state, if he does not know or have reasonable cause to believe the person is prohibited from receiving or possessing firearms under federal law. A person may loan or rent a firearm to a resident of any state for temporary use for lawful sporting purposes, if he does not know or have reasonable cause to believe the person is prohibited from receiving or possessing firearms under federal law. A person may sell or transfer a firearm to a licensee in any state. However, a firearm other than a curio or relic may not be transferred interstate to a licensed collector. [18 U.S.C. 922(a)(3) and (5), 922(d), 27 CFR 478.29 and 478.30]

> **Q: MAY A PARENT OR GUARDIAN PURCHASE FIREARMS OR AMMUNITION AS A GIFT FOR A JUVENILE (LESS THAN 18 YEARS OF AGE)?**
>
> A: Yes. However, possession of handguns by juveniles (less than 18 years of age) is generally unlawful. Juveniles generally may only receive and possess handguns with the written permission of a parent or guardian for limited purposes, *e.g.*, employment, ranching, farming, target practice or hunting.
> [18 U.S.C. 922(x)]

Bureau of Alcohol, Tobacco, Firearms and Explosives. (2021). Firearms - Frequently Asked Questions - Unlicensed Persons [online] Available at: https://www.atf.gov/firearms/firearms-frequently-asked-questions-unlicensed-persons [Accessed 2 February 2021].

Instead of the previous example where Bobby gave John money to purchase a firearm for him, if John decides to buy a firearm with his own money and then give the firearm to Bobby as a present, John is the actual buyer/transferee of the firearm. Since John is the actual buyer, there exists no sham or "straw man," and the purchase is legal.

2. A person cannot purchase a firearm if they have been convicted or are under "indictment or information" for a felony or certain misdemeanors

If a person has been convicted of a felony or other crime for which a judge may sentence, or could have sentenced the person to more than one year imprisonment, that person may not legally purchase a firearm (unless the crime was a state misdemeanor punishable by imprisonment of two years or less). *See* 18 U.S.C. § 921(a)(20)(B). Likewise, if a person is under "indictment" or "information" for a felony, or any other crime for which a judge may sentence the person to more than one year imprisonment, that person is disqualified from purchasing a firearm. An "indictment" or "information" is a formal accusation of a crime punishable by imprisonment for a term exceeding one year. It is important to point out that the actual sentence received is not the determining factor for disqualification; rather, it is the possible maximum sentence. A person may have only been sentenced to 30 days imprisonment, but if the crime for which they were charged allowed a maximum penalty of five years, then that person is disqualified. *See Schrader v. Holder*, 831 F.Supp.2d 304 (D.D.C. 2011, aff'd, 704 F.3d 980 (D.C. Cir. 2013)).

Va. Code § 18.2-308.2 states that it is unlawful for any person to knowingly and intentionally possess or transport any firearm or ammunition for a firearm:

(i) who has been convicted of a felony;

(ii) who was adjudicated delinquent as a juvenile 14 years of age or older at the time of the offense of murder in violation of Va. Code § 18.2-31 or Va. Code § 18.2-32, kidnapping in violation of Va. Code § 18.2-47, robbery by the threat or presentation of firearms in violation of Va. Code § 18.2-58, or rape in violation of Va. Code § 18.2-61; or

(iii) who is under the age of 29 and who was adjudicated delinquent as a juvenile 14 years of age or older at the time of the offense of a delinquent act which would be a felony if committed by an adult, other than those felonies set forth in clause (ii), whether such conviction or adjudication occurred under the laws of the Commonwealth, or any other state, the District of Columbia, the United States or any territory.

Note: Any of the above persons may possess in his residence or the curtilage thereof a stun weapon as defined by Va. Code § 18.2-308.1.

Any person who violates Va. Code § 18.2-308.2 shall be guilty of a felony punishable by up to five years in prison. However, this section shall not apply to:

(i) any person who possesses a firearm or ammunition for a firearm while carrying out his duties as a member of the Armed Forces of the United States or of the National Guard of Virginia or of any other state,

(ii) any law-enforcement officer in the performance of his duties,

(iii) any person who has been pardoned,

(iv) any person whose right to possess firearms or ammunition has been restored under the law of another state,

(v) any person adjudicated delinquent as a juvenile who has completed a term of service of no less than two years in the Armed Forces of the United States or if such person received an honorable discharge from the Armed Forces of the United States after such term of service.

3. What does it mean to be a "fugitive from justice" so as to be disqualified from purchasing a firearm?

A "fugitive from justice" is a person who, after having committed a crime, flees from the jurisdiction of the court where the crime was committed. A fugitive from justice may also be a person who goes into hiding to avoid facing charges for the crime of which he or she is accused. Such individuals are not eligible to purchase or possess firearms.

4. Unlawful users of or persons addicted to drugs are disqualified from purchasing firearms

Federal law is very broad in that it disqualifies persons from the purchase of firearms if they are either users of or addicted to marijuana or any depressant, stimulant, narcotic drug, or any controlled substance. Under federal law, an "addict" is defined as a person that "habitually uses any narcotic so as to endanger the public morals, health, safety, or welfare, or who is so far addicted to the use of narcotic drugs as to have lost the power of self-control with reference to his addiction." 21 U.S.C. § 802(1). However, in using the terms "users of," no such frequency or dependence seems contemplated in the words, nor did Congress give further guidance. Illegal users and addicts are prohibited from purchasing firearms from any person under federal law, and are likewise prohibited from possessing firearms. *See* 18 U.S.C. §§ 922(d) and (g).

In late 2016, the ATF felt compelled to revise its Form 4473 to include the following statement in bold lettering:
WARNING: THE USE OR POSSESSION OF MARIJUANA REMAINS UNLAWFUL UNDER FEDERAL LAW REGARDLESS OF WHETHER IT HAS BEEN LEGALIZED OR DECRIMINALIZED FOR MEDICAL OR RECREATIONAL PURPOSES IN THE STATE WHERE YOU RESIDE.

This has caused a great amount of concern as to whether or not a person who holds a prescription or license to buy marijuana is automatically prohibited from purchasing or possessing firearms. As more and more states decriminalize marijuana, this is an issue that must ultimately be resolved.

Adding to the confusion of what prohibits someone as an unlawful user is conflicting case law between various federal court circuits. In the Ninth Circuit case of *Wilson v. Lynch* the court held that a prohibition on firearms ownership by someone who held a medical marijuana card from the state was lawful, even without evidence that the individual had ever used marijuana. On the other end of the spectrum, where Virginia lies inside the Fourth Circuit, case law seems to stand for the proposition that to be convicted under federal law as an unlawful user of a controlled substance in possession of a firearm, the state has to prove a "pattern and recency" of drug use to sustain a conviction. To accomplish this the state must be able to show that the defendant's "drug use was sufficiently consistent, 'prolonged' and close in time to his gun possession." *United States v. Williams*, 216 F. Supp. 2d 568 (E.D. Va. 2002).

Keep in mind that Virginia also criminalizes possession of a firearm while simultaneously possessing a controlled substance at the state level.

Furthermore, Va. Code § 18.2-308.1:5 makes it illegal for any person to purchase or transport a handgun who, within a 36-consecutive-month period, has been convicted of two misdemeanor drug offenses under former Va. Code §§ 18.2-248.1:1, 18.2-250, or 18.2-250.1. However, the ineligibility shall be removed upon expiration of a period of five years from the date of the second conviction, provided the person has not been convicted of any such offense within that period.

5. A person can't legally buy or possess firearms if they are "mentally defective"

What does "mentally defective" mean? A person is considered to have been adjudicated as "mentally defective" if there has been a "determination by a court, board, commission, or other lawful authority that a person, as a result of marked subnormal intelligence, or mental illness, incompetency, condition, or disease: is a danger to himself or others, or lacks the mental capacity to contract or manage his own affairs." The term "mentally defective" includes a finding of insanity by a court in a criminal case, and those persons found incompetent to stand trial or found not guilty by reason of lack of mental responsibility. 27 CFR § 478.11.

"Mentally defective" also includes a person who has been committed to a mental institution by a court, board, commission, or other lawful authority, or a commitment to a mental institution involuntarily. The term includes commitment for mental defectiveness or mental illness, and also includes commitment for other reasons, such as drug use. However, it does not include a person in a mental institution for observation or a voluntary admission to a mental institution. Individuals who have been adjudicated as mentally defective are also prohibited from possessing firearms under federal law.

Va. Code § 18.2-308.1:1 makes it unlawful for any person to knowingly and intentionally purchase, possess, or transport any firearm after having been acquitted by reason of insanity and committed to the custody of the Commissioner of Behavioral Health and Developmental Services for any felony or select misdemeanors pursuant to statute. A violation of this section is a misdemeanor offense punishable by imprisonment for up to 12 months.

Va. Code § 18.2-308.1:2 makes it unlawful for any person who has been adjudicated legally incompetent, mentally incapacitated, or incapacitated to purchase, possess, or transport any firearm. A violation of this section is a misdemeanor offense punishable by imprisonment for up to 12 months.

Va. Code § 18.2-308.1:3 makes it unlawful for any person to purchase, possess, or transport a firearm who has been involuntarily admitted to a facility or ordered to mandatory outpatient treatment pursuant to Va. Code § 19.2-169.2, involuntarily admitted to a facility or ordered to mandatory outpatient treatment as the result of a commitment hearing pursuant to Va. Code § 37.2-814, or who was the subject of a temporary detention order pursuant to Va. Code § 37.2-809 and subsequently agreed to voluntary admission pursuant to Va. Code § 37.2-805. A violation of this section is a misdemeanor offense punishable by imprisonment for up to 12 months.

6. A person subject to a protective or restraining order may not purchase or possess a firearm

Under 18 U.S.C. § 922(g)(8), firearms may not be sold to or received by a person subject to a court order that: (a) was issued after a hearing which the person received actual notice of and had an opportunity to participate in; (b) restrains the person from harassing, stalking, or threatening an intimate partner or child of such intimate partner or person, or engaging in other conduct that would place an intimate partner in reasonable fear of bodily injury to the partner or child; and (c) includes a finding that such person represents a credible threat to the physical safety of such intimate partner or child; or by its terms explicitly prohibits the use, attempted use, or threatened use of physical force against such intimate partner or child that a person would reasonably be expected to cause bodily injury. An "intimate partner" of a person is the spouse or former spouse of the person, the parent of a child of the person, or an individual who cohabitates with the person.

Va. Code § 18.2-308.1:4(A) makes is unlawful for any person to purchase or transport any firearm while a protective order is in effect that was entered subject to: (i) Va. Codes §§ 16.1-253.1, 16.1-253.4, 16.1-278.2, 16.1-279.1, 19.2-152.8, 19.2-152.9, or 19.2-152.10; (ii) an order issued pursuant to subsection B of Va. Code § 20-103; (iii) an order entered pursuant to subsection E of Va. Code § 18.2-60.3; (iv) a preliminary protective order entered pursuant to subsection F of Va. Code § 16.1-253 where a petition alleging abuse or neglect has been filed; or (v) an order issued by a tribunal of another state, the United States or any of its territories, possessions, or commonwealths, or the District of Columbia pursuant to a statute that is substantially similar to those cited in clauses (i), (ii), (iii), or (iv). Any person with a concealed handgun permit shall be prohibited from carrying any concealed firearm, and shall surrender his permit to the court entering the order, for the duration of any protective order referred to herein. A violation of this section is a misdemeanor offense punishable by imprisonment for up to 12 months.

However, pursuant to subsection C of Va. Code § 18.2-308.1:4 and after having been served with a protective order under Va. Code § 16.1-279.1 or Va. Code § 19.2-152.10, such person may continue to possess and transport any firearm possessed at the time of service for a period of 24 hours for the purposes of surrendering the firearms to law enforcement, or selling or transferring any such firearm to any person who is not otherwise prohibited by law from possessing such firearm. A violation of this section is a felony punishable by up to five years in prison.

Within 48 hours of service of a protective order pursuant to Va. Code § 16.1-279.1 or Va. Code § 19.2-152.10, an individual who is subject to the order shall certify in writing that such person does not possess any firearms or that all firearms possessed by such person have been surrendered, sold, or transferred and file such certification with the clerk of the court that entered the protective order. Willful failure to provide such certification in writing constitutes contempt of court.

Because an individual may again become eligible to possess firearms after expiration of the protective order, they may choose to surrender weapons to law enforcement during the course of their prohibition rather than sell them. However, in this situation where weapons are surrendered to law enforcement, be aware that law enforcement is not liable for loss, deterioration, theft, or damage to firearms. Furthermore, law enforcement may destroy firearms in their possession if a written request for return of the weapons is not submitted within 120 days of expiration of the related protective order.

Additionally, any protective order will disqualify an individual from obtaining a concealed handgun permit and shall also prohibit one from carrying any concealed firearm with a previously issued permit. (Va. Code § 18.2-308.09.) A previously issued concealed handgun permit shall be surrendered to the court entering the order for the duration of any protective order.

7. Domestic violence issues and disqualifications

Both Virginia and federal laws prevent those who have been convicted of crimes of domestic violence from possessing firearms and ammunition. The Virginia prohibition is recent and goes into effect July 1, 2021. It is found at Va. Code § 18.2-308.1:8 which states:

A. Any person who knowingly and intentionally purchases, possesses, or transports any firearm following a misdemeanor conviction for an offense that occurred on or after July 1, 2021, for (i) the offense of assault and battery of a family or household member or (ii) an offense substantially similar to clause (i) under the laws of any other state or of the United States is guilty of a Class 1 misdemeanor.

B. For the purposes of this section, "family or household member" means (i) the person's spouse, whether or not he resides in the same home with the person; (ii) the person's former spouse, whether or not he resides in the same home with the person; or (iii) any individual who has a child in common with the person, whether or not the person and that individual have been married or have resided together at any time.

C. Any person prohibited from purchasing, possessing, or transporting a firearm pursuant to subsection A shall be prohibited from purchasing, possessing, or transporting a firearm for three years following the date of the conviction at which point the person convicted of such offense shall no longer be prohibited from purchasing, possessing, or transporting a firearm pursuant to subsection A. Such person shall have his firearms rights restored, unless such person receives another disqualifying conviction, is subject to a protective order that would restrict his rights to carry a firearm, or is otherwise prohibited by law from purchasing, possessing, or transporting a firearm.

Although the Virginia law purports to restore firearm rights for those convicted of a misdemeanor crime of domestic violence after three years from the date of conviction, it is unsettled whether such restoration would serve to also restore firearm rights at the federal level. The federal prohibitions come from what is known as the Violence Against Women Act in 1994 and amended in 1996. This is an often misunderstood law, and, in fact, the ATF has numerous "Frequently Asked Questions" concerning this disqualification on its website: www.atf.gov. The ATF does a good job of explaining the scope of this subject in its FAQs. Due to the complexity of this issue, the ATF examples are included here:

FREQUENTLY ASKED QUESTIONS FROM ATF WEBSITE

Q: WHAT IS A "MISDEMEANOR CRIME OF DOMESTIC VIOLENCE"?

A: "misdemeanor crime of domestic violence" is an offense that:
(1) is a misdemeanor under federal, state, or tribal law;
(2) has, as an element, the use or attempted use of physical force, or the threatened use of a deadly weapon; and
(3) was committed by a current or former spouse, parent, or guardian of the victim, by a person with whom the victim shares a child in common, by a person who is cohabiting with or has cohabited with the victim as a spouse, parent, or guardian, or by a person similarly situated to a spouse, parent, or guardian of the victim.

However, a person is not considered to have been convicted of a misdemeanor crime of domestic violence unless:
(1) the person was represented by counsel in the case, or knowingly and intelligently waived the right of counsel in the case; and
(2) in the case of a prosecution for which a person was entitled to a jury trial was tried, either –
  (a) the case was tried by a jury, or
  (b) the person knowingly and intelligently waived the right to have the case tried by a jury, by guilty plea or otherwise.

In addition, a conviction would not be disabling if it has been expunged or set aside, or is an offense for which the person has been pardoned or has had civil rights restored (if the law of the jurisdiction in which the proceedings were held provides

for the loss of civil rights upon conviction for such an offense) unless the pardon, expunction, or restoration of civil rights expressly provides that the person may not ship, transport, possess, or receive firearms, and the person is not otherwise prohibited by the law of the jurisdiction in which the proceedings were held from receiving or possessing firearms.
[18 U.S.C. 921(a)(33); 27 CFR 478.11]

Editor's note: A significant number of people make the mistake of overlooking or forgetting about a court issue or family law judicial proceeding. However, if you meet the above criteria, you are federally disqualified from possessing a firearm. The fact that it may have happened a long time ago, or that you did not understand the ramifications, is legally irrelevant.

Q: MUST A MISDEMEANOR CRIME OF DOMESTIC VIOLENCE (MCDV) BE DESIGNATED AS A "DOMESTIC VIOLENCE" OFFENSE?

A: No. A qualifying offense need not be designated as a domestic violence offense. For example, a conviction for assault may qualify as an MCDV even if the offense is not designated as a domestic violence assault.
[18 U.S.C. 921(a)(33) and 922(g)(9); 27 CFR 478.11 and 478.32(a)(9)]

Q: DOES THE PROHIBITION ON RECEIPT OR POSSESSION OF FIREARMS AND AMMUNITION APPLY IF THE PERSON WAS CONVICTED OF AN MCDV PRIOR TO THE ENACTMENT OF 18 U.S.C. 922(G)(9) ON SEPTEMBER 30, 1996?

A: Yes.

> Editor's note: For those wondering why this is not an unconstitutional ex post facto, law, multiple federal appeals courts have ruled against that argument and the Supreme Court has consistently declined to review any of those cases, effectively accepting the ruling of the courts of appeals and upholding the law.

Q: IS AN INDIVIDUAL WHO HAS BEEN PARDONED, OR WHOSE CONVICTION WAS EXPUNGED OR SET ASIDE, OR WHOSE CIVIL RIGHTS HAVE BEEN RESTORED, CONSIDERED CONVICTED OF A MISDEMEANOR CRIME OF DOMESTIC VIOLENCE?

A: No, as long as the pardon, expungement, or restoration does not expressly provide that the person may not ship, transport, possess, or receive firearms. A restoration of civil rights, however, is only effective to remove the federal firearms disability if the law of the jurisdiction provides for the loss of civil rights for a conviction of such a misdemeanor.
[18 U.S.C. 921(a)(33); 27 CFR 478.11]

Q: IS THE RELATIONSHIP BETWEEN THE PARTIES AN ELEMENT OF AN MCDV?

A: No. The "as an element" language in the definition of "misdemeanor crime of domestic violence" only applies to the use of force provision of the statute and not the relationship provision. However, to be disabling, the offense must have been committed by someone whose relationship to the victim meets the definition in the Gun Control Act (GCA).
[18 U.S.C. 921(a)(33); 27 CFR 478.11]

Editor's note: This basically means that if illegal force was used against another person, regardless of the language in the underlying statute, if the illegal force was used against a member of the protected class under the statute, federal law will deem this as satisfying the requirements and disqualify the individual from purchasing and possessing firearms.

Q: IN DETERMINING WHETHER A CONVICTION IN A STATE COURT IS A "CONVICTION" OF A MISDEMEANOR CRIME OF DOMESTIC VIOLENCE, DOES FEDERAL, STATE OR TRIBAL LAW APPLY?

A: The law of the jurisdiction determines whether a conviction has occurred. Therefore, if the law of the jurisdiction does not consider the person to be convicted, the person would not have the federal disability.
[18 U.S.C. 921(a)(33); 27 CFR 478.11]

Q: DOES THE DISABILITY APPLY TO LAW ENFORCEMENT OFFICERS?

A: Yes. The Gun Control Act was amended so that employees of government agencies convicted of misdemeanor crimes of domestic violence would not be exempt from disabilities with respect to their receipt or possession of firearms or ammunition. Thus, law enforcement officers and other government officials who have been convicted of a disqualifying misdemeanor may not lawfully possess or receive firearms or ammunition for any purpose, including performance of their official duties. The disability applies to firearms and ammunition issued by government agencies, purchased by government employees for use in performing their official duties, and personal firearms and ammunition possessed by such employees.
[18 U.S.C. 922(g)(9) and 925(a)(1); 27 CFR 478.32(a)(9) and 478.141]

Q: ARE LOCAL CRIMINAL ORDINANCES "MISDEMEANORS UNDER STATE LAW" FOR PURPOSES OF 18 U.S.C. 922(D)(9) AND (G)(9)?

A: Yes, assuming a violation of the ordinance meets the definition of "misdemeanor crime of domestic violence" in all other respects.

Q: WHAT STATE AND LOCAL OFFENSES ARE "MISDEMEANORS" FOR PURPOSES OF 18 U.S.C. 922(D)(9) AND (G)(9)?

A: The definition of misdemeanor crime of domestic violence in the Gun Control Act (GCA) includes any offense classified as a "misdemeanor" under federal, state or tribal law. In States that do not classify offenses as misdemeanors, the definition includes any State or local offense punishable by imprisonment for a term of 1 year or less or punishable by a fine.
[18 U.S.C. 921(a)(33); 27 CFR 478.11]

Q: WHAT SHOULD AN INDIVIDUAL DO IF HE OR SHE HAS BEEN CONVICTED OF A MISDEMEANOR CRIME OF DOMESTIC VIOLENCE?

A: Individuals subject to this disability should immediately dispose of their firearms and ammunition, such as by abandonment to a law enforcement agency.
[18 U.S.C. 922(g)(9); 27 CFR 478.32]

Bureau of Alcohol, Tobacco, Firearms and Explosives. (2021). Misdemeanor Crime of Domestic Violence. [online] Available at: https://www.atf.gov/qa-category/misdemeanor-crime-domestic-violence [Accessed 2 February 2021].

PRACTICAL LEGAL TIP

If you or a loved one are going through court proceedings involving family issues and a restraining or protective order is entered in your case, it can suspend your ability to purchase or possess firearms. Language in the court order prohibiting any acts of family violence, whether or not family violence actually occurred, make it so the person whom the order impacts is legally barred from the purchase or possession of any firearm. Believe it or not, the Juvenile & Domestic Relations and Domestic Relations Courts have the ability to suspend your Second Amendment rights. –Gilbert

8. Illegal aliens or aliens admitted under a non-immigrant visa

Persons who are illegally in the United States may not legally purchase, possess, or transport firearms. Generally, non-immigrant aliens are also prohibited from legally purchasing, possessing, or transporting firearms.

Exceptions for non-immigrant aliens

However, a non-immigrant alien who has been admitted under a non-immigrant visa is not prohibited from purchasing, receiving, or possessing a firearm if the person falls within one of the following exceptions:

1) if the person was admitted to the United States for lawful hunting or sporting purposes or is in possession of a hunting license or permit lawfully issued in the United States;

2) if the person is an official representative of a foreign government who is accredited to the United States Government or the Government's mission to an international organization having its headquarters in the United States;
3) if the person is an official representative of a foreign government who is en route to or from another country to which that alien is accredited;
4) if the person is an official of a foreign government or a distinguished foreign visitor who has been so designated by the Department of State;
5) if the person is a foreign law enforcement officer of a friendly foreign government entering the United States on official law enforcement business; or
6) if the person has received a waiver from the prohibition from the Attorney General of the United States.

See 18 U.S.C. § 922(y).

Va. Code § 18.2-308.2:2(B) states that no firearm dealer shall sell, rent, trade, or transfer from his inventory any assault firearm to any person who is not a citizen of the United States or who is not a person lawfully admitted for permanent residence.

Va. Code § 18.2-308.2:01 makes it unlawful for any person who is not a citizen of the United States or who is not a person lawfully admitted for permanent residence to knowingly and intentionally possess or transport any firearm or assault firearm or to knowingly and intentionally carry about his person, hidden from common observation, an assault firearm. A violation of this section is a felony punishable by up to five years in prison with a $2,500 fine.

B. Criminal liability for allowing a minor access to firearms

Va. Code § 18.2-309 states that it is illegal for any person to sell, barter, give or furnish a handgun to any minor. A violation of this section is a felony punishable by up to five years in prison; however, this law does not apply to any transfer made between family members or for the purpose of engaging in a sporting event or activity. The federal law also makes it illegal to sell, transfer, or deliver a handgun and handgun ammunition to a minor, but there are some exceptions, which we will discuss momentarily. A violation of the federal version of this law is punishable by up to 10 years in prison.

Va. Code § 18.2-56.2 states that it is unlawful for any person to recklessly leave a loaded, unsecured firearm in such a manner as to endanger the life or limb of any child under the age of 14. A violation of this section shall be a Class 1 misdemeanor punishable by up to a year imprisonment and a fine of up to $2,500. Additionally, it is unlawful to knowingly authorize a child under the age of 12 to use a firearm except when the child is under the supervision of an adult. A violation of this section is also a Class 1 misdemeanor punishable by up to 12 months in jail.

C. When may a minor legally possess a handgun?

As we discussed, Va. Code § 18.2-308.7 states that "it is unlawful for anyone under the age of 18 to knowingly or intentionally possess or transport any handgun or assault firearm." A violation of this statute is a misdemeanor and is punishable by up to 12 months in jail. However, this law does not apply to the following:
1) any minor (i) while in his home or on his property; (ii) while in the home or on the property of his parent, grandparent,

or legal guardian; or (iii) while on the property of another who has provided prior permission, and with the prior permission of his parent or legal guardian if the minor has the landowner's written permission on his person while on such property;

2) any minor who, while accompanied by an adult, is at, or going to and from, a lawful shooting range or firearms educational class, provided that the weapons are unloaded while being transported;

3) any minor actually engaged in lawful hunting or going to and from a hunting area or preserve, provided that the weapons are unloaded while being transported; and

4) any minor while carrying out his duties in the Armed Forces of the United States or the National Guard of this Commonwealth or any other state.

Additionally, the federal law similarly states that it is unlawful for a minor to knowingly possess a handgun or handgun ammunition. A violation of this statute is punishable by no more than one year of imprisonment. However, this law does not apply to the following according to 18 U.S.C. § 922(x)(3):

1) in the course of employment;

2) in the course of ranching or farming, target practice, hunting, or a course of instruction in the safe and lawful use of a handgun;

3) with the prior written consent of the minor's parent with exceptions;

4) members of the Armed Forces of the United States or the National Guard who possess or are armed with a handgun in the line of duty;

5) a transfer by inheritance of title (but not possession); and
6) possession taken in self-defense or defense of others against a residential intruder.

VI. UNDERSTANDING "PRIVATE SALES" LAWS

The firearms transaction forms and background checks we previously discussed that are required for firearm dealer transactions do not apply to private transfers conducted in Virginia among Virginia residents where the firearm is given as a gift. However, private transfers are only permissible in very specific instances. It is important to recognize that the private sale of firearms without a background check being conducted on the purchaser is outlawed in Virginia by Va. Code § 18.2-308.2:5. This code section says that a criminal history background check must be obtained by a firearms dealer with a determination from the State Police that the purchaser is not prohibited by state or federal law before any transfer of a firearm occurs where "money, goods, services, or anything of value" has been obtained for the firearm. By statute, a dealer may not charge more than $15 for performing this service. There are a couple of exceptions. One exception provided in Va. Code § 18.2-308.2:5(B)(1) allows the sale of a firearm to an authorized representative of the Commonwealth as part of an authorized gun buy-back or give-back program.

Another exception found in Va. Code § 18.2-308.2:5(B)(2) allows a private sale to occur when the sale occurs at a firearms show, as defined in Va. Code § 54.1-4200, and the seller has received a determination from the Department of State Police (who are present at every gun show to perform background checks) that the purchaser is not prohibited under state or federal law from possessing a firearm in accordance with Va. Code § 54.1-4201.2.

Selling or purchasing a firearm in Virginia in violation of Va. Code § 18.2-308.2:5 is a Class 1 misdemeanor, punishable by up to 12 months imprisonment and a fine of up to $2,500.

Because only the transfer of a firearm for something of value is prohibited in Virginia, the bona fide gift of a firearm, or loan of a firearm in Virginia is permissible so long as it is to another Virginia resident, who is not otherwise prohibited from possessing the weapon. *See* previous note under section III, subsection E of this chapter on the private sale exemption for minors between the ages of 18 and 21.

A. Residency requirements

In order for the private gift of a firearm to be legal in Virginia, both parties must be Virginia residents. This means that a Virginia resident is prohibited from selling or transferring a firearm to a resident of another state. It is a violation of the federal law if the seller or transferor knows or has reasonable cause to believe that the purchaser does not reside in the same state as the seller/transferor. One exception to this prohibition on gifts of firearms to a resident of a different state is the gift of a firearm in a will or in another testamentary (by bequest) or intestate succession (without a will) upon death, provided that the firearm is legal in the other state. Note: A private individual may complete a firearm transfer or sale to a resident of another state, but the seller must follow a procedure that requires the use of a federal firearm dealer.

The federal law also makes it illegal for a non-firearm dealer individual to transport into or receive in his state of residence a firearm purchased or otherwise obtained from a resident of another state, other than a firearm received upon death through intestate succession (without a will) or by bequest (through a will). *See* 18 U.S.C. § 922(a)(3).

How does the law determine a person's residence when buying or selling a firearm?

1. State of residence

For the purpose of firearms purchases, the person's state of residence is the state in which the person is present and where the individual has an intention of making a home. 27 CFR § 478.11.

> **EXAMPLE:**
> John maintains a home in Virginia. John travels to Kentucky on a hunting, fishing, business, or other type of trip. John does not become a resident of Kentucky by reason of such trip.

2. What if a person maintains a home in two states?

If a person maintains a home in two (or more) states and resides in those states for periods of the year, he or she may, during the period of time the person actually resides in a particular state, purchase a firearm in that state. However, simply owning property in another state does not qualify a person as a resident of that state so as to purchase a firearm in that state. To meet the residency requirements, a person must actually maintain a home in a state which includes an intention to make a particular state a residence. *See* 27 CFR § 478.11. This issue may ultimately be a fact question with evidence of residency being things like a driver's license, insurance records, and recurring expenses in the state, as well as other things related to making a particular state a person's residence.

> **EXAMPLE:**
>
> Alice maintains a home in Virginia and a home in Kentucky. Alice resides in Virginia except for weekends or the summer months of the year and in Kentucky for the weekends or the summer months of the year. During the time that Alice actually resides in Virginia, Alice is a resident of Virginia, and during the time that Alice actually resides in Kentucky, Alice is a resident of Kentucky.

3. Members of the Armed Forces

A member of the Armed Forces on active duty is a resident of the state in which his or her permanent duty station is located. If a member of the Armed Forces maintains a home in one state and the member's permanent duty station is in a nearby state to which he or she commutes each day, then the member has two states of residence and may purchase a firearm in either the state where the duty station is located or the state where the home is maintained. *See* 18 U.S.C. § 921(b). (*See also* ATF FAQs on residency at www.atf.gov).

4. Immigrant aliens

Persons who are legally present in the United States are residents of the state in which they reside and where they intend to make a home. Such persons, provided they meet all other requirements and are not otherwise prohibited from purchasing a firearm, are lawfully permitted to purchase a firearm.

> **EXAMPLE A:**
>
> Mary, an alien, travels to the United States on a three-week vacation to Virginia. Mary does not have a state of residence in Virginia because Mary does not have the intention of making a home in Virginia while on vacation. This is true regardless of the length of the vacation.

> **EXAMPLE B:**
>
> Paul, an alien, travels to the United States to work for three years in Virginia. Paul rents a home in Virginia, moves his personal possessions into the home, and his family resides with him in the home. Paul intends to reside in Virginia during the three-year period of his employment. Paul is a resident of Virginia.

VII. BUYING, SELLING, AND TRANSFERRING THROUGH AN FFL

A. Basic procedures

Persons purchasing firearms through dealers must comply with all legal requirements imposed by federal law. These include both paperwork and appropriate background checks or screenings to ensure that the purchaser is not prohibited from the purchase or possession of a firearm under federal law.

When purchasing through a dealer, the first thing a prospective buyer will do is select a firearm. Once a selection has been made, the prospective purchaser is required to show proper identification and complete ATF Form 4473. This form requires the applicant, under penalty of law, to provide accurate identifying information, as well as answer certain questions in order to establish whether a person may legally purchase a firearm. The information provided on Form 4473 is then provided to NICS for processing and approval in order to proceed with the transfer (however, no NICS background check may be required if the transferee is legally exempt for reasons such as possessing a state-issued firearms license or permit). An FFL dealer can submit the check to NICS either by telephone or through the online website and only after the FFL completes all of these steps successfully is a purchaser/transferee allowed to take possession of the firearm.

B. What is Form 4473?

ATF Form 4473 is the ATF's form known as a Firearms Transaction Record which must be completed when a person purchases a firearm from an FFL dealer. *See* 27 CFR § 478.124. Form 4473 requires the applicant to provide their name, address, birth date, state of residence, and other information including a government-issued photo identification. The form also contains information blanks to be filled in including the NICS background check transaction number; the make, model, and serial number of the firearm to be purchased; and a series of questions that a person must answer. *See* 27 CFR § 478.124(c). This series of questions and the corresponding answers help determine a firearm purchaser's eligibility under federal law. Once the form is completed, the prospective purchaser will sign the form and attest that the information provided is truthful and accurate under penalty of federal law. This means that if you lie or make false statements on this form, the Feds can and will prosecute you for a crime!

Likewise, the dealer must also sign the Form 4473 and retain it for at least 20 years. The ATF is permitted to inspect, as well as receive a copy of the Form 4473 from the dealer both during audits and during the course of a criminal investigation. The 4473 records must be surrendered to the ATF in the event the FFL dealer retires or ceases business.

C. How are background checks administered when purchasing a firearm?

1. NICS: National Instant Criminal Background Check System

Background checks by dealers when transferring firearms are completed through the Virginia State Police Firearms Transaction Center, which operates in conjunction with the National Instant Criminal Background Check System (or NICS), if required, prior to the transfer of a firearm from an FFL dealer to a non-dealer. When the prospective purchaser/transferee's information is given to NICS, the system will check the applicant against at least three different databases containing various types of records. Applicants are checked against the records maintained by the Interstate Identification Index ("III") which contains criminal history records, the National Crime Information Center ("NCIC") which contains records including warrants and protective orders, as well as the NICS Index which contains records of individuals who are prohibited from purchasing or possessing firearms under either federal or state law. In addition, if the applicant is not a United States Citizen, the application is processed for an Immigration Alien Query ("IAQ") through the Department of Homeland Security's Immigration and Customs Enforcement Division.

2. Responses from NICS

NICS responses to background checks come in three basic forms: proceed, delay, or deny. The "proceed" response allows for the transfer to be completed. The "delay" response means that the transfer may not legally proceed. If the dealer receives a response of "delay," NICS has three business days to research the applicant further. If the dealer has not received a notice that the transfer is denied after the three business days, then the transfer may proceed. "Deny" means the transfer should not take place; a transferee's options after a "deny" are discussed below.

3. What transactions require background checks under federal law?

A background check is required before each and every sale or other transfer of a firearm from an FFL to a non-licensee unless an exception is provided under the law. For every transaction that requires a background check, the purchaser/transferee must also complete ATF Form 4473. This includes:

- The sale or trade of a firearm;
- The return of a consigned firearm;
- The redemption of a pawned firearm;
- The loan or rental of a firearm for use off of an FFL's licensed premises; and
- Any other non-exempt transfer of a firearm.

PRACTICAL LEGAL TIP

Thinking about pawning a firearm for a little emergency cash? Be sure you are eligible to purchase a firearm when you redeem your pawn ticket. Since most pawn shops are FFL dealers, you will need to complete an ATF Form 4473 and pass a NICS background check simply to get your own firearm out of pawn. –Gilbert

4. What transactions do not require a background check?

A background check is not required under the following circumstances:

- The sale or transfer of a firearm where the transferee presents a valid state permit/license that allows the transferee to carry a firearm from the state where the FFL is located and the state permit/license is recognized by the ATF as a qualifying alternative to the background check requirement;
- The transfer of a firearm from one FFL to another FFL;
- The return of a repaired firearm to the person from whom it was received;
- The sale of a firearm to a law enforcement agency or a law enforcement officer for official duties if the transaction meets

the specific requirements of 27 CFR § 478.134 including providing a signed certification from a person in authority on agency letterhead stating that the officer will use the firearm in official duties and where a records check reveals the officer does not have any misdemeanor convictions for domestic violence;
- The transfer of a replacement firearm of the same kind and type to the person from whom a firearm was received;
- The transfer of a firearm that is subject to the National Firearms Act if the transfer was pre-approved by the ATF.

Note: About half of handgun licenses and permits qualify as an alternative to the NICS background check requirement as long as the license or permit was issued within five years of the date of the transfer. A complete permit chart for all states is available on the ATF's website. Bureau of Alcohol, Tobacco, Firearms and Explosives. (2021). Permanent Brady Permit Chart. [online] Available at: https://www.atf.gov/rules-and-regulations/permanent-brady-permit-chart [Accessed 2 February 2021].

5. If a person buys multiple handguns, a dealer must report that person to the ATF

Under federal law, FFLs are required to report to the ATF any sale or transfer of two or more pistols, revolvers, or any combination of pistols and revolvers totaling two or more to an unlicensed (non-FFL) individual that takes place at one time or during any five consecutive business days. *See* 18 U.S.C. § 923(g)(3). This report is made to the ATF on Form 3310.4 and is completed in triplicate with the original copy sent to the ATF, one sent to the designated state police or local law enforcement agency in the jurisdiction where the sale took place, and one retained by the dealer and held for no less than five years.

VIII. WHAT IF I'M DENIED THE RIGHT TO PURCHASE A FIREARM?

A. If I am denied the right to purchase, how do I appeal?

Persons who believe they have been erroneously denied or delayed a firearm transfer based on a match to a record returned by NICS may request an appeal of their "deny" or "delay" decision. All appeal inquiries must be submitted to the NICS Section's Appeal Service Team ("AST") in writing, either via mail or online on the FBI's website at www.fbi.gov. An appellant must provide their complete name, complete mailing address, and NICS Transaction Number. For persons appealing a delayed transaction, a fingerprint card is required and must be submitted with the appeal, although the fingerprint card is merely recommended on appeals for denied applications. This may seem counterintuitive, but it is required per the FBI's website.

B. What if my gun purchase from a firearm dealer is denied?

Any individual that is denied the purchase, trade, exchange, or pawn redemption of a firearm shall be provided a Virginia Firearms Transaction Program Brochure that explains options the individual may pursue if he believes he is not prohibited by federal or Virginia law from purchasing or possessing a firearm.

A denied individual may:
- Contact the VSP Firearms Transaction Center ("FTC") to discuss the ineligible determination and/or to provide additional information deemed pertinent to the final determination of eligibility. Fingerprint comparison may be necessary in some instances, and may support the issuance of a Unique Firearms Identification Number to facilitate future purchase approvals.
- Review the criminal history record and request correction of the record if the record is found to be in error, pursuant to

Va. Code § 9.1-132, provided that any such action is initiated within 30 days of the denial. Obtain a copy of the Virginia criminal history record by completing a Criminal History Record Request on VSP Form SP-167.
- Exercise the right to institute a civil action pursuant to Va. Code § 9.1-135, provided that any such action be initiated within 30 days of the denial.
- Elect to direct the challenge to the accuracy of a record, in writing, to: FBI, NICS Operations Center, Criminal Justice Information Services Division, 1000 Custer Hollow Road, Module C-3, Clarksburg, West Virginia 26306. Electronic appeal requests can be made through the NICS Appeal website at http://www.fbi.gov/nics-appeals. This appeal process is authorized by 28 CFR 25.10.

Should you decide to appeal the denial of a firearm purchase, it is important that you are sure you are not prohibited. If you file an appeal alleging you are not prohibited when in fact you are prohibited, the appeal may be used as a further basis for prosecution. In this situation the appeal will be additional evidence against you to support charges for making false statements when obtaining a criminal history check required for the transfer of firearms under Va. Code § 18.2-308.2:2(k). This crime is punishable by up to 10 years imprisonment.

C. What if I keep getting erroneously delayed or denied when I am attempting to buy a firearm?
Apply for a Unique Personal Identification Number ("UPIN") that is designed to solve this issue. Some individuals may have a name which is common enough (or happens to be flagged for other reasons) that it causes undue delays or denials in the background

check verification process through NICS. For that reason, NICS maintains the Voluntary Appeal File database ("VAF") which allows any applicant to apply by submitting an appeal request and then obtain a UPIN. A person who has been cleared through the VAF and received a UPIN is able to use their UPIN when completing Form 4473 in order to help avoid further erroneous denials or extended delays. A person can obtain a UPIN by following the procedures outlined on the FBI's website at www.fbi.gov.

IX. ADDITIONAL CONSIDERATIONS IN FIREARMS PURCHASING AND POSSESSION LAWS

A. How can I legally purchase a firearm from someone in another state?

Any individual who wishes to purchase a firearm from a resident of another state must complete the transaction through an FFL. Sellers or transferors are legally authorized to facilitate a private transaction or transfer by shipping the firearm to the purchaser's FFL in the recipient/buyer's state, where the FFL will complete the transfer process. It is a federal crime to sell or transfer a firearm between persons who are residents of different states, or where a transfer takes place in a state other than the transferee/transferor's singular state of residence.

B. Can I purchase firearms on the internet?

Yes. However, all legal requirements for a transfer must be followed. If the buyer and seller are both residents of the same state, then the two may conduct a private sale (if allowed under state law) so long as all other legal issues are satisfied (see our earlier discussion on disqualifications to purchasing and possessing firearms in this chapter). However, if buyer and seller are not residents of the same state, the transaction can only be legally facilitated through an FFL.

C. Shipping firearms

1. Can I ship my firearm through the United States Postal Service ("USPS")?

Long guns: yes. Handguns: no. However, under federal law, a non-licensed individual may not transfer (and this would include shipping to someone) a firearm to a non-licensed resident (non-FFL) of another state. However, a non-licensed individual may mail a long gun to a resident of his or her own state, and they may also mail a long gun to an FFL of another state. To that end, the USPS recommends that long guns be mailed via registered mail and that the packaging used to mail the long gun be ambiguous so as to not identify the contents. Handguns are not allowed to be mailed via USPS. *See* 18 U.S.C. §§ 1715, 922(a)(3), 922(a)(5), and 922(a)(2)(A). Rather, handguns must be shipped using a common or contract carrier (*e.g.*, UPS or FedEx).

2. Shipping handguns and other firearms through a common or contract carrier

Under federal law, a non-licensed individual may ship a firearm (including a handgun) by a common or contract carrier (*e.g.*, UPS or FedEx) to a resident of his or her own state, or to an FFL in another state. However, it is illegal to ship any firearm to a non-FFL in another state. It is a requirement that the carrier be notified that the shipment contains a firearm; however, carriers are prohibited from requiring any identifying marks on the package which may be used to identify the contents as containing a firearm. *See* 18 U.S.C. §§ 922(a)(2)(A), 922(a)(3), 922(a)(5), 922(e), 27 CFR 478.31 and 478.30.

3. Can I ship my firearm to myself for use in another state?

Yes. In accordance with the law as described in the preceding section, a person may ship a firearm to himself or herself in care of another person in another state where he or she intends to hunt or engage in other lawful activity, so long as it is legal to possess the firearm in both the starting state and destination state. Finally, the package should be addressed to the owner, and persons other than the owner should not open the package and take possession of the firearm.

4. Can a moving company move my firearms?

Yes, a person who lawfully possesses firearms may transport or ship the firearms interstate when changing the person's state of residence so long as the person complies with the requirements for shipping and transporting firearms as outlined earlier. *See* 18 U.S.C. § 922(e) and 27 CFR § 478.31. However, certain NFA items such as destructive devices, machine guns, short-barreled shotguns or rifles, and so forth require approval from the ATF before they can be moved interstate. *See* 18 U.S.C. § 922(a)(4) and 27 CFR § 478.28. It is important that the person seeking to move the firearms also checks state and local laws where the firearms will be relocated to ensure that the movement of the firearms into the new state does not violate any state law or local ordinance. Va. Code § 18.2-295 requires every machine gun in Virginia to be registered with the Department of State Police within 24 hours after its acquisition.

D. May I loan my firearm to another person?

There is no prohibition under Virginia law on loaning a firearm to another person, so long as the person receiving the firearm may lawfully possess one. Additionally, federal law allows the loan or rental of a firearm even to a resident of another state so long as the person receiving the weapon is not prohibited from possessing it, and the loan or rental is for "temporary use for a lawful sporting purpose." *See* 18 USC § 922(a)(5) and 18 USC § 922(d).

E. What happens to my firearms when I die?

Depending on the manner in which a person leaves his or her estate behind, firearms may be bequeathed in a customary manner like other personal property. However, firearms held in an estate are still subject to the laws of transfer and possession. Thus, careful consideration needs to be given in estate planning with consideration for the firearms laws of both the jurisdiction in which the estate is located as well as the jurisdiction in which the recipient is located. An interesting exception to FFL transfers, firearms passed by bequest or intestate succession (dying without a will) do not need to go through an FFL, including interstate transfers. *See* 18 U.S.C. § 922(a)(3).

F. What happens if a firearm is stolen?

A stolen firearm can be a headache no gun owner wants to deal with. However, if the proper steps are taken, the risks associated with the loss of a firearm can be minimized. Once a firearm goes missing, it can be prudent to contact a lawyer to ensure that during the reporting process criminal liability is not inadvertently created. Virginia law requires reporting a lost or stolen firearm to the Department of State Police within 48 hours after such person discovers the loss or theft or is informed by a person with personal knowledge of the loss or theft. The law enforcement agency shall enter such report information into the National Crime Information Center maintained by the Federal Bureau of Investigation. The provisions of this subsection shall not apply to the loss or theft of an antique firearm as defined in Va. Code § 18.2-308.2:2.

The benefit of this reporting is that no person who, in good faith, reports a lost or stolen firearm will be held criminally or civilly liable for any damages from acts or omissions resulting from the loss or theft. This subsection shall not apply to any person who makes a report in violation of Va. Code § 18.2-461. A violation of this provision is punishable by a civil fine of $250.

X. AMMUNITION: THE LAW OF PURCHASING AND POSSESSION
A. Who is legally prohibited from purchasing ammunition under federal law?

Under federal law, there are six primary situations where a person is prohibited from buying, selling, or possessing ammunition (beyond armor-piercing ammunition, which was discussed in Chapter 5).

(1) Under 18 U.S.C. § 922(b)(1), it is unlawful for a person to sell long gun ammunition to a person under the age of 18;

(2) Under 18 U.S.C. § 922(b)(1), it is unlawful for a person to sell handgun ammunition to a person under the age of 21;

(3) Under 18 U.S.C. § 922(x)(2)(B), it is unlawful for a juvenile to possess handgun ammunition;

(4) Under 18 U.S.C. § 922(d), it is unlawful to sell ammunition to a person who is prohibited from purchasing firearms;

(5) Under 18 U.S.C. § 922(g), it is unlawful for a person who is disqualified from purchasing or possessing firearms to possess firearm ammunition if such ammunition has moved in interstate commerce (which is nearly all ammunition); and

(6) Under 18 U.S.C. § 922(h), it is unlawful for a person who is employed by a person who is disqualified from purchasing or possessing ammunition to possess or transport ammunition for the disqualified individual.

For the statutes that involve juveniles, there are a couple of notable exceptions to the law. First, the law against selling handgun ammunition to a juvenile and possession of handgun ammunition by a juvenile does not apply to a temporary transfer of ammunition or to the possession or use of ammunition if the handgun and ammunition are possessed and used by the juvenile in the course of employment, in the course of ranching or farming-related activities at the residence of the juvenile (or on property used for ranching or farming at which the juvenile, with the permission of the property owner or lessee, and is performing activities related to the operation of the farm or ranch), target practice, hunting, or a course of instruction in the safe and lawful use of a handgun. The law also does not apply to the temporary transfer to or use of ammunition by a juvenile if the juvenile has been provided with prior written consent by his or her parent or guardian who is not prohibited by federal, state, or local law from possessing firearms. *See* 18 U.S.C. § 922(x)(3).

Second, the law against selling ammunition to juveniles does not apply to juveniles who:
1) are members of the Armed Forces of the United States or the National Guard who possess or are armed with a handgun in the line of duty;
2) receive ammunition by inheritance; or
3) possess ammunition in the course of self-defense or defense of others in the residence of the juvenile or a residence in which the juvenile is an invited guest.

B. Virginia law

Virginia law does not require a license to purchase, possess, or sell ammunition nor is there a minimum age for possessing ammunition; however, federal law imposes a minimum age. Virginia law does make it illegal for certain classes of individuals to possess and transport ammunition. Va. Code § 18.2-308.2(A) makes it illegal to knowingly and intentionally possess or transport ammunition by any person:

- Convicted of a felony;
- Adjudicated delinquent as a juvenile 14 years of age or older at the time of the offense of murder, kidnapping, robbery by the threat or presentation of firearms, or rape; or
- Who is under the age of 29 and was found guilty as a juvenile (14 years of age or older) of a delinquent act which would be a felony if committed by an adult.

A violation of this statute is a felony punishable by up to five years in prison and a $2,500 fine. However, Virginia law does not prohibit other individuals ineligible to possess firearms under state law from possessing ammunition.

The prohibitions of this section shall not apply to:
 (i) any person carrying out his duties as a member of the Armed Forces of the United States or of the National Guard of Virginia or of any other state,
 (ii) any law enforcement officer in the performance of his duties,
 (iii) any person who has been pardoned or whose political disabilities have been removed pursuant to Article V, Section 12 of the Constitution of Virginia provided the Governor, in the document granting the pardon or removing the person's political disabilities, may expressly place conditions upon the reinstatement of the person's right to ship, transport, possess, or receive firearms,
 (iv) any person whose right to possess firearms or ammunition has been restored under the law of another state subject to conditions placed upon the reinstatement of the person's right to ship, transport, possess, or receive firearms by such state, or
 (v) any person adjudicated delinquent as a juvenile who has completed a term of service of no less than two years in the

Armed Forces of the United States and, if such person has been discharged from the Armed Forces of the United States, received an honorable discharge and who is not otherwise prohibited.

In addition to ammunition in general, Va. Code § 18.2-308.3 makes it unlawful for any person to knowingly use or attempt to use restricted firearm ammunition such as KTW bullets or French Arcanes while committing or attempting to commit a crime. A violation of this law is a felony punishable by up to 10 years in prison.

C. Can a person be disqualified from purchasing ammunition if they are disqualified from purchasing firearms?

Yes. Under federal law 18 U.S.C. § 922(g), it is unlawful for a person who is disqualified from purchasing or possessing firearms to purchase ammunition if the ammunition has moved in interstate commerce. Since nearly all ammunition or ammunition components move through interstate commerce in one form or another, this disqualification includes essentially all ammunition.

D. Can a person purchase ammunition that is labeled "law enforcement use only"?

Yes. Although some handgun ammunition is sold with a label "law enforcement use," such a label has no legal meaning and is only reflective of a company policy or a marketing strategy.

➤ CHAPTER SEVEN ◂

WHEN CAN I LEGALLY USE MY GUN: PART I
UNDERSTANDING THE LAW OF JUSTIFICATION
SOME BASIC LEGAL CONCEPTS

I. INTRODUCTION AND OVERVIEW

When a person can legally use a gun for self-defense in Virginia is a critically important legal issue for every law-abiding gun owner. A failure to understand or misapplication of the Virginia self-defense law can get a lot of good folks in serious trouble! The purpose of this chapter is to educate the gun owner on when a gun may and may not be legally used for self-defense in Virginia.

II. IGNORANCE OF THE LAW IS NO EXCUSE!

The Virginia self-defense law is a law of necessity that provides excellent protection for those who need to use force to defend themselves from an attacker, including deadly force. The amount of force used to defend oneself must not be excessive. It must be proportional and reasonable in relation to the perceived threat. Thus, you generally cannot use deadly force to shoot and kill someone for starting a fight by punching you in the face and call it self-defense. You can certainly defend yourself, but your self-defense must always be proportional to your attacker's actions. If you know and follow the law, then you have put yourself in the best possible situation to preserve your legal rights and to defend yourself. Remember, ignorance of the law holds no weight in a courtroom!

III. FORCE VS. DEADLY FORCE

The use of force is permitted for self-defense. Force can be defined as "[t]he impetus of power; physical power or strength exerted against a person or thing," and deadly force is any force that endangers human life or causes great bodily harm. It is very important to know and understand the difference between force and deadly force, because going on the offensive with excessive force is no longer self-defense.

If a person uses force when no force is legally allowed, then that use of force will not be legally justified. Likewise, if a person uses deadly force when the law only allows for the use of force, then that use of deadly force will not be legally justified. Justification is a sufficient or acceptable legal excuse or explanation for an act that is otherwise unlawful.

Force and deadly force can be applied with or without the use of a weapon. The weapon could be a gun, a knife, or items not originally intended to be a weapon such as a baseball bat, a hammer, or a lead pipe. Many items can be used to cause injury or death under certain circumstances. How the weapon or item is being used is the key.

A. Deadly weapon defined

A deadly weapon is any tool likely to produce death or great bodily harm from the manner in which it is used. In determining whether a weapon is regarded as deadly, more weight is given to the manner in which the weapon is used than to the inherent character of the instrument. Although the term "deadly weapon" is not defined by Virginia code, the court has proclaimed that "there are deadly weapons such as a loaded pistol, a dirk, or an axe, which the court may pronounce as a matter of law a 'deadly weapon.' On the other hand, a weapon may not be per se deadly, yet the vicious and cruel use of it may be the determinative factor in pronouncing it deadly." *Pannill v. Commonwealth*, 185 Va. 244, 253, 38 S.E.2d 457, 462 (1946), Additionally, Virginia Model Jury Instruction No. 18.850 defines deadly weapon as: "A deadly weapon is any object or instrument, not part of the human body, that is likely to cause death or great bodily injury because of the manner and under the circumstances in which it is used."

Any firearm is by design a tool that has the ability to deliver deadly force. The firing of a gun is considered a use of deadly force because it endangers human life and can cause great bodily harm. Death is not a requirement for the use of force to be considered deadly force. Additionally, a gun may be used without being fired. Two other common uses are displaying a gun in self-defense to scare off an attacker or using the butt of a pistol in self-defense. It is critically important for the gun owner to understand both when and how he or she may legally use a gun for self-defense.

B. Use-of-force continuum

A use-of-force continuum is a standard that provides guidelines as to how much force may be used in a specific situation. The use-of-force continuum is a common practice in law enforcement, but it carries useful lessons for civilians as well. The purpose of a use-of-force continuum model is to clarify the complex subject of use of force. Any use-of-force continuum generally has many levels of force. The circumstances of the attack or altercation will determine what level of force, if any, would be appropriate. Keep in mind that an altercation can quickly change and that one may move from one part of the continuum to another in a matter of seconds.

There is no single universally accepted use-of-force continuum model; however, we have provided an example use-of-force continuum that can assist gun owners in understanding the various levels of force. Understanding various levels of acceptable force is naturally crucial because some circumstances will justify the use of deadly force, where others may only justify either no force or a lower level of force. The use of excessive force or the unlawful use of force can get a lot of good folks into trouble with the law.

1. Verbal communication–force does not have to be physical.
Use of calm, nonthreatening language, such as "Stop," "Get off me," "Don't touch me," "Leave me alone," "Get off my property" or "I do not want to get into a fight with you" would likely be the first step of any use-of-force continuum. Increasing the volume and repeating the command while sounding as assertive as possible may be necessary to gain compliance. Additionally, if you are in a public place you may attract the attention of onlookers, who could help you and support the facts down the road. If the attacker keeps approaching you after you give multiple loud verbal warnings to stay away, you will have additional support for you contention that you were threatened.

2. Bodily force

Using bodily force would be considered more force than a verbal command but would generally be considered less force than using a weapon.

3. Less-than-deadly force: use of less-lethal technologies

a) Blunt impact – Use of a baton, club, stick or staff. There are countless objects that can be used to fight off an attacker. Some objects are considered non-deadly weapons and are specifically designed for such a purpose, while in other cases an object can become improvised from its intended use and become a weapon. Caution: Consider how the object or weapon is being used because it is possible for virtually any item to become a deadly weapon based on its use.

b) Chemical – Use of pepper spray. Pepper spray, also known as oleoresin capsicum or OC, is made from the same naturally-occurring chemical that makes chili peppers hot, but at concentrations much higher. Pepper spray is legal in Virginia and can be used to disable an attacker long enough for you to get to safety if you are in a threatening situation where you need to defend yourself.

c) Conducted electrical devices – Use of a taser. The use of a taser is not intended to be fatal, but that does not mean the weapon cannot cause death.

d) Brandishing of a firearm – The pointing or holding of any firearm in a manner to reasonably induce fear in the mind of another is a threat to use deadly force. If the use of self-defense is justified or excused, then you can brandish your gun to defend yourself. Justifiable and excusable self-defense will be discussed in the next section.

4. Deadly force: firing of a gun

The firing of a gun is only permitted where there is imminent danger of death or serious bodily harm.

IV. SELF-DEFENSE MUST BE EITHER "JUSTIFIED" OR "EXCUSED"

Under what circumstances is it lawful to use deadly force against another person in Virginia for self-defense? In Virginia, the legal use of self-defense can either be justifiable self-defense or excusable self-defense.

A. Justifiable self-defense: not at fault

If you are without fault in provoking or bringing on the fight, and you reasonably fear that you are in imminent danger of being killed or in imminent danger of great bodily harm, and you use no more force than is reasonably necessary to protect yourself from the perceived harm, under the circumstances as they appear to you, then your use of deadly force in self-defense is legally justified. Virginia Model Jury Instruction No. 33.800. *See* also *Bell v. Commonwealth*, 66 Va. App. 479, 788 S.E.2d 272 (2016).

1. Stand your ground

"Stand your ground" is a common term that means a person has no legal duty to retreat before using self-defense if legally justified. Virginia is a stand your ground state, which means that if you did not start the fight or provoke the incident in any way, then you can stand your ground and defend yourself against your attacker without having to retreat. *See* Virginia Model Jury Instruction 33.800 and Instruction No. 52.510. See also *Bell v. Commonwealth*, 66 Va. App. 479, 788 S.E.2d 272 (2016).

On the other hand, if you are partially at fault in starting the fight or confrontation, then Virginia law requires you to retreat as far as you safely can before you are permitted to use what is called excusable self-defense, which we will discuss later.

2. Is your fear sufficiently reasonable?

The test of whether your fear was sufficiently reasonable to justify acting in self-defense is based upon your subjective point of view rather than the reaction of an ordinary person to similar circumstances. Additionally, the perceived danger must be imminent and must be manifested by an overt act. The overt act requirement is the court's way of saying that at a bare minimum, for a fear to be considered reasonable, you must be able to point to something other than the other party's words alone to establish your fear. Many other states require that your fear must be both subjectively real and objectively reasonable before a killing will be justified or excused; however, the Supreme Court of Virginia has expressly rejected any objective component in Virginia's test. *McGhee v. Commonwealth*, 219 Va. 560, 248 S.E.2d 808 (1978) citing *Harper v. Commonwealth*, 196 Va. 723, 731, 85 S.E.2d 249, 254 (1955). Nevertheless, it is critically important that your fear is reasonable because there have been cases where the accused in fact feared death or serious bodily harm, but the fear was unreasonable. Unreasonable fear will not entitle you to your claim of self-defense; rather, it would merely reduce the killing from murder to manslaughter.

3. Imminent danger

The existence of imminent danger is determined from your point of view at the time you used deadly force to defend yourself. Whether imminent danger existed will depend on the facts and circumstances of each particular case. Threats or words alone will not justify the taking of a life prior to an overt act. The "bare fear" of serious bodily injury, or even death, however well-grounded, will not justify the taking of human life. *Stoneman v. Commonwealth*, 66 Va. 887 (1874). There must also be some overt act indicative of imminent danger at the time. In other words, you must wait until some overt act is done until the danger becomes imminent. Additionally, you must be able to articulate in as much detail as possible that the assailant acted in a manner that either threatened your life or safety – you cannot simply say that you feared the assailant; you must be able to describe the threatening conduct.

In the context of a self-defense plea, "imminent danger" is defined as an immediate, real threat to one's safety There must be some menacing act presenting peril and the act must be of such a character as to afford a reasonable ground for believing there is a design to do some serious bodily harm, and imminent danger of carrying such design into immediate execution. The requirement of an overt act indicative of imminent danger ensures that the most extreme recourse, the killing of another human being, will be used only in situations of necessity. The plea of self-defense is a plea of necessity, and the necessity must be shown to exist or there must be shown such reasonable apprehension of the immediate danger, by some overt act, as to amount to the creation of necessity. *Couture v. Commonwealth*, 51 Va. App. 239, 656 S.E.2d 425 (2008).

4. Justifiable self-defense examples
Reading about the law can be confusing.

Below are some examples that demonstrate the concept of justifiable self-defense. These are general examples. In the real world, there will likely be numerous detailed factors under the totality of the circumstances that will be considered when determining whether self-defense was justified.

> **EXAMPLE:**
>
> One busy day at his job, David is working quietly at his desk when he hears an angry voice yell out, "I hate this company, and I'm going to kill every one of you!" About that time, David spots a machete in a deranged-looking stranger's hand. The stranger turns toward David with an evil look. David, fearing he is about to be struck with a machete and killed, draws a gun from his desk, points it at the attacker, and shouts, "Stop, drop the weapon, or I will shoot." As the man rushes toward David with the machete raised, David fires two shots at the attacker, killing him.

Will David's use of deadly force be justified?

If the prosecution had sufficient evidence to believe that David's use of force was unlawful, then David could find himself accused of killing the attacker in this hypothetical. In that case, it would be up to the judge or jury hearing the case and sitting in judgment to determine if David's claim of self-defense was justified. However, in this example, it is unlikely that David would be arrested and stand trial for the killing of the stranger.

The facts demonstrate that David was in fear and was in imminent danger from the deranged stranger who was a second away from seriously injuring or killing David with a machete while yelling, "I am going to kill every one of you" and ignoring David's demand to "Stop, drop the weapon, or I will shoot." David does not appear to be at fault here in any way; thus, he can stand his ground and defend himself. David first used force with his verbal command then quickly transitioned to the use of deadly force by firing his gun. Remember, the type of force that is justified can change quickly along the use-of-force continuum, and it is permissible to skip lower levels of force and immediately use deadly force if the circumstances permit. Therefore, David would likely be legally justified in using deadly force to defend himself. Keep in mind, however, that if David discharged the second shot after the attacker had fallen, he still may be in a situation where he is prosecuted. The likely argument from the prosecutor would be that one shot was justified to stop the threat, but that after the attacker was falling, a second shot was not justified.

> **EXAMPLE:**
>
> Jane is out jogging one evening. A white van pulls up alongside her and a masked man pointing a gun at her jumps out of the van, grabs Jane, and attempts to drag her into his van. A freaked-out Jane manages to pull out her Glock pistol and fires a lone shot at the attacker, killing the attacker.

Was Jane's use of deadly force justified?

Under these circumstances, Jane became the victim of an attempted abduction by an armed attacker. Jane can stand her ground and defend herself because she was without fault in provoking the incident. Her fear or being "freaked out" would likely be viewed as reasonable. The masked man pointing a gun while attempting to abduct Jane created an imminent danger of Jane either being killed or suffering great bodily harm. Jane immediately used deadly force to defend herself without first attempting to use less than lethal force. Was Jane required to first use a lower level of force before using deadly force? No. Jane's use of deadly force to defend herself would likely be considered justified.

> **EXAMPLE:**
>
> Billy is walking to his car after leaving the grocery store when three individuals with baseball bats confront him in the parking lot and surround him in an aggressive manner. Billy fears that he is about to get beat up by the individuals with bats. Billy draws his gun and clearly demands that the aggressors leave him alone, at which point they all flee from the scene.

Has Billy used deadly force by showing his gun? No. The display of the gun is a use of force but not a use of deadly force. It is pretty clear that Billy is the victim of an assault that is about to get worse. Billy's production of a weapon was a use of force in self-defense to scare off his attackers. A person can legally "display" a gun in self-defense when the use of force is legally justified—not just when the use of deadly force is justified! Caution: If a self-defense claim involving the display of a gun is not valid and the use of force is not justified, then the gun owner could be charged with the criminal violation of brandishing a firearm according to Va. Code § 18.2-282.

> **EXAMPLE:**
>
> Tina is on her way home from work. She stops by a local convenience store for some bread and milk. As she enters the store, a masked man suddenly approaches her with a knife, grabs her by the arm, places the knife alongside her body, and demands all of her money. Tina, scared, shaken, fearing for her life and remembering her training, opens her purse and manages to pull out her .357 revolver. She fires her gun and kills the masked robber.

Remember, every killing will be thoroughly investigated by the authorities. Ideally, Tina would not even be arrested under these circumstances. She was permitted to stand her ground and defend herself. Her fear was more than reasonable that she was in imminent danger of being killed or suffering great bodily harm from the masked robber who held her at knifepoint, and she used no more force than was reasonably necessary to protect herself.

What if the altercation is less clear?

> **EXAMPLE:**
>
> Hank, a 66-year-old disabled man, works downtown. He has to park four blocks from his company's office building and walk through some rough parts of town in order to get to work. One day on Hank's walk to work after parking his car, a panhandler suddenly appears in front of him and says, "Hey, man—give me some money!" Hank, feeling very frightened and intimidated, ignores the panhandler and keeps walking. The panhandler gets louder and more aggressive, demanding, "Hey, man! I said give me some money!" Hank now becomes extremely concerned for his safety. About that time, Hank makes a wrong turn into an alley where he is cornered. He again hears, "HEY, MAN! I SAID GIVE ME SOME MONEY!" When Hank turns around, he sees the panhandler, now very aggressive, with something in his hand.

Is the panhandler just being annoying, or is Hank about to be attacked?

The panhandler neither verbally threatened Hank nor did he ever physically touch him. All the panhandler said was "Give me some money"; he didn't even demand all of Hank's money—just some. Do robbers ever demand just *some* money? What if Hank took out his legally concealed-carry pistol and fired it at the panhandler to defend himself? Would Hank be justified in his use of deadly force against the panhandler for self-defense under these circumstances? Would Hank's claim that he was fearful of the panhandler and that he believed he was in imminent danger of being killed or suffering serious bodily harm be reasonable? Would it be reasonably necessary for Hank to use deadly force to protect himself under the circumstances?

The authorities might believe that Hank used excessive force against the panhandler and charge him with a crime regardless of whether the panhandler was struck by the bullet or not. What if the object in the panhandler's hand was actually a weapon and he raised it up in the air as he was moving aggressively toward Hank? What if the panhandler outweighed Hank by 75 pounds and was a foot taller? What if Hank's sworn testimony was that he was in fear for his safety, had seen the panhandler acting violently on the same street many times in the past, and was about to be robbed? Hank would certainly be able to claim self-defense, but as we have said repeatedly now, it would be up to the judge or jury to decide if Hank's use of deadly force for self-defense was justified.

The point of this example is not to answer the question of whether Hank's use of deadly force was justified. The point is to demonstrate that it can sometimes be difficult to assess a situation and that the circumstances of an encounter can quickly change. Always remember, if you are without fault in provoking the fight, and (1) you reasonably fear, under the circumstances as they appear to you, that you are in imminent danger of being killed or that you are in imminent danger of great bodily harm; and (2) you use no more force, under the circumstances as they appear to you, than was reasonably necessary to protect yourself from the perceived harm, then the use of deadly force for self-defense is legally justified.

5. "Castle Doctrine"

The Castle Doctrine concept originated in England where it was said that an Englishman's home is his castle and that if you are attacked in your own home, you need not retreat, but may stand your ground and defend yourself. Many people think that the Castle Doctrine means that you can legally shoot any stranger you find in your house. That is not the case in Virginia and to do so could likely be a use of excessive deadly force.

In Virginia, there is no statutory castle law that has been created by the legislature. In fact, the legislature has previously considered and rejected laws that would codify the Castle Doctrine. However, the courts in Virginia have recognized the concept of the Castle Doctrine on many occasions. In one noteworthy case, the Supreme Court of Virginia discussed the Defense of the Castle in 1922 in *Fortune v. Commonwealth*, 112 S.E. 861 (Va. 1922), a case that did not even involve an attack inside the home.

The Virginia Supreme Court went on to explain that you are not required to retreat if assaulted in your house or on the curtilage, but you may stand your ground and use such means as are absolutely necessary to repel your assailant from your house or to prevent your attacker's forcible entry. The curtilage of a house is the land immediately surrounding it. Remember, you are actually defending yourself and your family and not merely defending your real estate. Defense of others will be discussed in the next chapter.

The defense does not apply to ejecting visitors, guests, or those who have an implied license. In those instances, you are limited to reasonable force in ejecting the visitor, guest, or implied licensee. On the other hand, if your visitor attacks you and you are without fault, then you may stand your ground and use justifiable self-defense. However, if you are at fault in starting or provoking the fight in your home, then you would only be able to claim excusable self-defense, which we discuss in the next section. Excusable self-defense requires that you retreat before you can claim self-defense.

> **EXAMPLE:**
>
> Harry the homeowner and his family live in a peaceful Richmond neighborhood. One night after everyone has gone to bed and all the lights have been turned down, Harry hears a strange noise downstairs at his back door. He grabs his 12-gauge Remington shotgun and goes to the back door to investigate. At his back door, he finds a large man, 6 foot 5, 275 pounds, with an angry look on his face and a with a crowbar wedged within the doorframe of the back door in the process of prying open the door. Harry, with his Remington shotgun pointed at the man, makes his presence known by repeatedly shouting, "Stop! Get out of here! I have already called the police. I am going to shoot you if you come any closer." The man ignores Harry and within seconds breaks the door open. Harry fires off a blast from his Remington shotgun at the man. The man dies instantly.

Was Harry's use of deadly force absolutely necessary?

Is Harry's use of force justified?

As we previously explained, any killing will be thoroughly investigated by the law enforcement community and any dispute regarding the lawfulness of his actions will be determined by the judge or jury. However, if Harry reasonably feared that he was in imminent danger of being killed or suffering great bodily harm from the intruder, then it seems pretty clear that he would be justified in his use of deadly force in this example. Harry used lower levels of force when he verbally commanded multiple times "Stop! Get out of here! I have already called the police. I am going to shoot you if you come any closer" along with pointing his shotgun at the attacker. What else could Harry have reasonably done to protect himself from the perceived harm presented by a large, angry man intruding into his house who failed to heed his warning and kept charging an armed Harry? Note: Every situation is different, and the circumstances are critically important to every use-of-force incident.

> **EXAMPLE:**
>
> Harriett is a student and lives alone in busy Northern Virginia in an apartment complex. She works part time as a lifeguard at the local swimming pool. One afternoon Harriett comes home to her apartment after her lifeguard shift at the pool to find a strange-looking man jumping out of her apartment window holding her new expensive flat-screen television. Harriett quickly runs to the window, draws her .380 pistol, and fires it at the fleeing man running through the apartment parking lot because she cannot afford to buy a new television. Harriett's shot strikes and injures the man, but Harriett recovers her expensive television.

Is Harriett's use of deadly force justified?

Probably not. As we previously discussed, the firing of a gun is considered the use of deadly force even if nobody dies. The Castle Doctrine allows for the use of deadly force if absolutely necessary to keep out aggressors, which would include Harriett's apartment. In this example, the man holding Harriett's television is more of a thief than an aggressor; besides, he was in the apartment parking lot when Harriett fired her gun.

Additionally, the facts are clear that Harriett was neither fearing for her life in any way nor was she in imminent danger of being killed or suffering serious bodily injury. Harriett seemed pretty focused on saving her expensive television. A person has no right to use deadly force or the threat of deadly force solely to defend personal property. In the next chapter, we discuss defense of personal property in more detail.

B. Excusable self-defense: at fault

The self-defense law is different if you are partially at fault for starting the fight or confrontation. Excusable self-defense requires that you must retreat as far as you safely can before you can legally use deadly force to defend yourself.

If you are at least some degree at fault, or if you had a hand in provoking or bringing on the fight, but you:
  (1) retreat as far as you safely can under the circumstances in a good-faith attempt to abandon the fight;
  (2) you make known your desire for peace by word or act;
  (3) you reasonably fear, under the circumstances as they appear to you, that you are in imminent danger of being killed or that you are in imminent danger of great bodily harm; and
  (4) you use no more force, under the circumstances as they appear to you, than was reasonably necessary to protect yourself from the perceived harm, then your use of deadly force in self-defense is legally excused.

Keep in mind that the language from the court is very broad when considering who provoked the conflict. If you played any part in bringing about the conflict, your best bet may be to simply retreat if possible.

1. Provocation/retreat

What does it mean to provoke an attack? One who uses provoking language or incites a fight or follows the other combatant from a prior altercation has lost his claim of justifiable self-defense. In essence, a person cannot effectively "bait" another person into a violent confrontation and then claim justifiable self-defense.

The accused must be without fault "in the minutest degree" to claim justifiable self-defense. However, what if a person who started or provoked a fight soon realizes they bit off more than they can chew? Under the law, that person may be able to claim excusable self-defense if that person can retreat and communicate his or her desire to abandon the encounter. If, after a person abandons, or attempts to abandon, the encounter he or she started or provoked, and the other combatant who was provoked pursues and uses unlawful force against the provocateur, then the provocateur would be permitted to use force in self-defense.

2. Excusable self-defense examples

These are general examples. In the real world, there will likely be numerous detailed factors under the totality of the circumstances that the judge or jury sitting in judgment will consider when determining whether the use of self-defense was excused.

EXAMPLE:

> Dave is at a bar when he notices another man checking out his girlfriend. Dave tells the other man, "Take a hike or you'll regret it" and slightly shoves the admirer. The other man responds by punching Dave in the face. Dave, who didn't really want a confrontation, holds both his hands up in surrender and says, "I don't want any more trouble!" as he starts to exit the bar. However, the other man pulls out a knife and lunges at Dave just as he is exiting through the bar's front door and shouts, "Take that!"

Would Dave be legally permitted to fight back and defend himself? What if Dave pulled out a pistol and shot and killed the knife-wielding attacker as he was exiting the bar? Would this use of deadly force be excusable self-defense?

In this scenario, Dave clearly started or provoked the encounter. Dave would not be permitted to stand his ground and claim self-defense. The law of excusable self-defense would require that Dave retreat.

Would Dave's use of deadly force at the end of the encounter be legally excused? Possibly. Dave's walking away from the admirer while attempting to exit the bar and stating "I don't want any more trouble!" would likely be sufficient as a retreat to abandon the fight and to communicate that Dave's desire was for peace. The remaining questions deal with whether Dave reasonably feared he was in imminent danger of being killed or suffering great bodily injury and whether he used no more force than was reasonably necessary to protect himself. In some instances, it can be unclear if a person can stand their ground and defend themselves or if they are required to first retreat before using force in self-defense.

> **EXAMPLE:**
>
> Police respond to a two-car collision in a parking lot. When the police arrive on the scene, they discover that the collision sparked a violent road-rage incident between the two drivers. At the scene, one of the drivers is lying dead on the ground from bullet wounds with a tire iron beside him. The other driver was Stan the shooter. Stan claimed that the other driver became irate after the collision, was verbally abusive, threatened him, and aggressively came toward him with the tire iron raised in his hand.
>
> Stan made a statement to the police, which included an admission that he was in fear for his life and that he fired two shots at the other driver in self-defense. Stan is a 45-year-old man with no previous criminal record. The physical evidence recovered at the scene of the collision makes it unclear who was the true victim of the encounter, but one investigator thinks Stan is lying. There are no other witnesses. Stan is now a suspect in a murder investigation. Assume Stan is ultimately arrested, indicted, and stands trial for murder and claims self-defense.

Will Stan's use of deadly force be justified or excused?

Was he entitled to stand his ground and defend himself, or was he required to retreat because he was at least partially at fault in bringing on the fight?

Was his fear reasonable?

Was he in imminent danger of being killed or suffering a serious bodily injury?

Was his use of force proportional and reasonable under the circumstances?

At trial, the prosecution's case would be strongest if they could prove that Stan was at least partially at fault in starting the road-rage altercation and that he was not entitled to stand his ground and claim self-defense without first retreating. There seems to be no indication of an attempt by Stan to retreat. The prosecution will also likely present testimony from investigators. The prosecution may also argue that Stan's claimed fear was unreasonable and that his use of deadly force was excessive and unnecessary. In Stan's defense, his lawyers will have the burden of producing at least "some evidence" at trial to support his self-defense claim that he was not at fault in provoking the fight, that he reasonably feared he was in imminent danger of being killed or suffering great bodily harm, and that he used no more force under the circumstances than was reasonably necessary to protect himself from the other driver's attack in order for the court to consider his claim of self-defense. Either way, it would be up to the judge or jury hearing the case to determine if Stan's use of deadly force was justified. If the court were to determine that Stan was partially at fault in provoking the fight and that he did not retreat before using deadly force, then the killing would not be excused and Stan would be found guilty of killing the other driver.

C. Federal self-defense laws

Virginia is home to several national parks, national forests and national wildlife refuges. The federal law determines what amount of force, if any, is permitted for self-defense on federal property. Federal law recognizes the common law defense of self-defense.

Under federal law, the use of force is justified when a person reasonably believes that force is necessary for self-defense against the immediate use of unlawful force. However, a person must use no more force than appears reasonably necessary under the circumstances. Force likely to cause death or great bodily injury is justified in self-defense only if a person reasonably believes such force is necessary to prevent death or great bodily harm.

V. WARNING SHOTS

A warning shot is an intentional gunshot often made with the firearm pointed in the air with the intent not to harm one's adversary, but to subdue or scare off an attacker. The purpose of firing warning shots is to warn or intimidate an opponent and to showcase one's capability or will to act if provoked. They are intended to convince a potentially hostile force to withdraw or cease its actions. This is a sufficiently aggressive act to demand attention and alert those nearby that they might be shot if directions are not followed.

Warning shots are not recommended and will almost always get you in trouble because a shot fired into the air or in some other direction has the ability to strike an unintended target or ricochet. Warning shots are commonly portrayed in movies and television as a good idea, and people like to mimic what they see in movies and on TV!

As we have previously discussed, the firing of a gun is considered the use of deadly force; thus, you'd better make sure that the use of deadly force is lawful under the circumstances. Every law-abiding gun owner needs to know that willfully discharging a firearm in a public place in Virginia can lead to criminal prosecution unless such firing is considered justifiable or excusable self-defense.

Furthermore, given that a warning shot will be considered deadly force, you will expose yourself to a potential argument from the prosecution, that to be justified in using deadly force, the threat has to be immediate. If the threat was truly immediate, how did you have time to be aiming the gun any direction except at the threat? For all of these reasons, we strongly recommend against warning shots.

VI. BRANDISHING

Brandishing is a commonly charged crime in Virginia. Brandishing is a Class 1 misdemeanor (meaning it is punishable by up to a year in jail and a fine of up to $2,500), unless occurring on school grounds, or within 1,000 feet of a school (at which point it becomes a Class 6 felony). Brandishing is defined by Va. Code § 18.2-282 as:

> "Hold(ing) or brandish(ing) any firearm or any air or gas operated weapon or any object similar in appearance, whether capable of being fired or not, in such manner as to reasonably induce fear in the mind of another or hold a firearm or any air or gas operated weapon in a public place in such a manner as to reasonably induce fear in the mind of another of being shot or injured. However, this section shall not apply to any person engaged in excusable or justifiable self-defense."

A couple of points seem to get people in trouble with this statute. Far too frequently, people charged with brandishing attempt to defend themselves by saying, "I didn't even point it at him." This is normally an ineffective defense. While self-defense is a defense to brandishing, claiming that you did not point the firearm is not necessarily a defense. The law punishes conduct with a firearm if you put another person in fear while holding the gun, even if you did not point it. For this reason, before you reach or put your hands on a firearm at all, you need to make sure you have a valid self-defense reason for doing so. A valid self-defense reason means you are in a situation where you are faced with the imminent threat of the unlawful application of physical force. While you must have justification before brandishing a firearm, that justification might arise in situations where the use of deadly force is not yet justified. However, Virginia case law has made it clear that brandishing solely in defense of property is never justified. In addition, Va. Code § 18.2-433.2 prohibits paramilitary activity and makes it a Class 5 felony if a person brandishes a firearm while assembled with one or more persons for the purpose of and with the intent to intimidate any person or group of persons.

VII. MUTUAL COMBAT

Mutual combat is a fight wherein both parties mutually fight upon equal terms. In some instances, mutual combat can lead to death. Killing another during such an activity is manslaughter. If you agree to a fight, then you cannot claim justifiable self-defense because you are at fault in entering into the fight. Likewise, you cannot claim excusable self-defense because you did not abandon the fight and retreat.

EXAMPLE:

Andy and Dwight are at the local sports bar watching football on television. The two strike up a conversation about their favorite teams making it to the Super Bowl. After a few minutes, the two become engaged in a heated argument about whose favorite football team will win the Super Bowl. In the heat of the argument, Andy calls Dwight a derogatory name and Dwight asks if Andy

> wants to take it outside. Andy agrees, and they both begin fist fighting in the parking lot. Shortly after they begin fighting, the police show up and arrest both of them for assault and battery.

Will either Andy or Dwight be able to defend against their assault and battery criminal cases with a claim of self-defense?

Not likely. Both appear to be at fault in starting or provoking the fight, neither attempted to retreat, and both parties agreed to the fight. If a person agrees to engage in using force against another person, then that person cannot later claim that they fought back in self-defense!

VIII. RIGHT TO RESIST UNLAWFUL ARREST

Unfortunately, there are instances where police officers exceed their authority and attempt to make an unlawful arrest. If this is the case, the use of reasonable force in self-defense is justified. However, it is important to note that it can be extremely difficult to know at the time of the arrest whether the arrest is lawful or unlawful. Caution: If you use force to resist an arrest by police and the courts later determine that the arrest was lawful, then you may find yourself in violation of the resisting arrest and/or obstruction of justice laws. Questioning a policeman's authority to arrest during the actual arrest is a very slippery slope. In most situations it is best to be cooperative with law enforcement, and fight the issue out in court later if you are wrongfully arrested. The old saying often holds true, that "roadside lawyers always lose their case."

IX. THE VIRGINIA CRIMINAL TRIAL

Virginia uses a two-tiered trial court system comprising trial courts "not of record" and trial courts "of record." Courts "not of record" are called district courts and courts "of record" are called circuit courts. Misdemeanor trials are typically held in the district courts unless the defendant appeals a district court conviction to the circuit court or if there is a direct indictment by the prosecuting attorney. The defendant has an automatic right to appeal any district court misdemeanor conviction to the circuit court for a new trial. There is no right to a trial by jury in the district courts. A district court judge hears the case and imposes the sentence in the event of a conviction.

Felony trials must be held in the circuit court. The right to trial by jury can only be carried out in the circuit court. Virginia is one of the few jurisdictions in the United States in which the jury recommends the sentence in the event of a conviction. In a Virginia jury trial, the jury must first decide if the defendant is guilty or not guilty. If the jury finds the defendant not guilty, then the defendant is set free. If the jury finds the defendant guilty, then the jury will immediately begin the sentencing phase of the trial where the jury will recommend a sentence. The judge must ratify or affirm the jury's sentence.

In Virginia, a judge can lower or reduce a jury's sentence if appropriate, but the judge cannot increase the jury's sentence. In most instances, judges do not view it as their role to impede or step on the toes of a jury's sentence, and jury sentences are often ratified.

1. Defendant's right to testify at trial
The Fifth Amendment to the U.S. Constitution provides that no person shall be compelled in any criminal case to be a witness against himself. At trial, the prosecution can neither call the

defendant as a witness nor comment on the defendant's failure to testify. The decision to testify or not is exclusively the privilege of the defendant.

In many self-defense cases, the defendant will have to testify in his trial about his fear and that he had no other choice but to act the way he did when he used force to defend himself. However, in some cases, it may be a trial tactic for the defendant not to testify because it prevents the prosecution from examining the defendant under oath and on the witness stand. Once the defendant takes the witness stand, he will be subject to cross-examination by the prosecuting attorney, which can severely alter the outcome of the trial based on the circumstances of the case and the credibility of the defendant.

2. Burden of proof

In criminal cases, the state attorneys or prosecutors have the burden of proof. This means that it is the state's responsibility to present enough evidence to prove the defendant committed a crime. The burden of proof the prosecutor bears is a standard called "beyond a reasonable doubt." It is the highest level of proof used in the American justice system.

Self-defense is an affirmative defense. An affirmative defense is a set of facts or some evidence produced by the defendant after the prosecution rests its case, which if believed by the judge or jury sitting in judgment, defeats or mitigates the legal consequences of the defendant's otherwise unlawful conduct. However, in self-defense cases, the defendant has the burden of coming forward with or producing self-defense evidence. The prosecution is required to prove the alleged offense beyond a reasonable doubt but is not required to disprove self-defense beyond a reasonable doubt. The defendant should be acquitted only if the self-defense evidence raises a doubt as to his guilt by justifying or excusing his actions under the circumstances.

3. Necessary evidence and jury instruction

The defendant must put forth "some evidence" at trial that he reasonably feared he was in imminent danger of being killed or suffering serious bodily injury, and that he used no more force than necessary to defend himself under the circumstances as they appeared to him.

In a jury trial, if there is evidence in the record to support the defendant's theory of self-defense, then the trial judge must properly instruct the jury on the law. If the evidence is in conflict, then the judge is to instruct the jury on the law as it relates to theories of the case for both the prosecution and the defense. Thus, the judge must instruct the jury on both theories of the case to guide the jury in its deliberations as to the law applicable to the case, depending upon how the jury decides the facts. The jury, as the finder of fact, has the right to reject evidence its believes to be untrue and accept evidence it believes to be true. Finally, it is up to the judge or jury hearing the case to decide whether the defendant is either guilty of the crime alleged or should be found not guilty because the use of force in self-defense was either justified or excused.

> CHAPTER EIGHT <

WHEN CAN I LEGALLY USE MY GUN: PART II
DEFENSE OF OTHERS
Understanding When Force And Deadly Force Can Be Legally Used To Defend Another Person

I. INTRODUCTION AND OVERVIEW

In addition to self-defense, every law-abiding gun owner needs to also know when they can use their gun to defend another person. For many people, the choice to carry a firearm may be more about protecting loved ones than about defending themselves. With mass killings regularly being seen on the news, there is a valid perception that gun owners need to be prepared not only to defend themselves but also to defend those around them from criminals bent on causing harm. However, failure to understand the law can quickly get good folks in serious trouble!

II. DEFENSE OF OTHERS IN VIRGINIA

Defense of others is an affirmative defense just like self-defense that was discussed in the previous chapter. In Virginia, you may defend another person, even a stranger, but generally there is no duty to render aid unless there is some special relationship such as a business proprietor and an invitee or an innkeeper and a guest. This means that if there is a threat, generally speaking, you have no obligation to help. In many cases, the best thing to do may be to simply flee. If you do decide to involve yourself in the situation, the amount of force used to defend another must not be excessive and must be reasonable in relation to the harm threatened. The defense of another against an aggressor also includes the use of deadly force if necessary under the circumstances. Deadly force is justified in the defense of another party when you reasonably believe that the person you are defending is not at fault in provoking the conflict and is in imminent danger of being killed or suffering great bodily harm based on the circumstances. However, if you reasonably believe that the party you are defending was at fault in provoking the conflict but sufficiently retreated, and that they are still in imminent danger of being killed or suffering great bodily harm based on the circumstances, then your use of deadly force in defense of another would be excusable.

It is important to note that whether the defended person was in fact free from fault is largely legally irrelevant to the defense so long as your interpretation of which party needed assistance was reasonable. The reason is based on the principle that one should not be convicted of a crime for attempting to protect another victim from a violent assault. The policy of the law is to encourage individuals to come to the aid of perceived victims of assault.

> **EXAMPLE:**
>
> Elliott is taking a stroll one evening in the downtown section of Richmond when he hears cries for help emanating from a nearby alley. Elliott runs to the alley and finds a masked man beating Drew's head with a baseball bat and yelling repeatedly, "Give me all your money!" Elliott runs up closer to find blood everywhere as the man standing over Drew continues the beatdown. Drew is not armed with a weapon. Elliott draws his holstered pistol and shouts repeatedly, "Stop, drop the bat!" Elliott believes that Drew is about to be killed. Elliott fires two shots into the back of the masked man, killing him instantly. Elliott neither knew the masked man nor Drew, and had never seen either one of them in his life. There were no other witnesses.

Was Elliott justified in using deadly force to defend Drew? As we have previously stated, any death will be thoroughly investigated by the law enforcement community and any dispute as to what happened will be determined by a judge or jury hearing the case.

Even though Elliott shot the masked man in the back, it seems pretty clear that Elliott would be justified in his use of deadly force to defend Drew. First, did Elliott reasonably believe that Drew was not at fault? There are no facts to suggest that Elliott could have possibly believed Drew was in any way at fault in provoking this incident. Because of this, it is irrelevant whether Drew was actually at fault or how the confrontation with the masked man started. It is therefore likely that Elliott's reasonable belief that Drew was not at fault would be determined as lawful.

Second, was Drew in imminent danger of being killed or suffering serious bodily injury? Drew was being severely beaten in the head with a baseball bat, and as any reasonable person would know, being beaten in the head with a baseball bat is a surefire way to either suffer serious bodily injury or even die. Additionally, it seemed as if Drew had already suffered serious bodily injuries to the head, and that according to Elliott it looked like Drew would die if Elliott did not do something.

> **EXAMPLE:**
>
> Mark is walking up to the entrance of his favorite local bar when he sees Spencer pointing a gun at Eric's face at close range and yelling, "I told you not to mess with me!" Mark, thinking Eric may get shot, quickly rushes up to Spencer and demands that he put the gun down. When Spencer fails to do so after a second request, Mark shoots and kills him. Mark has never seen either Spencer or Eric in his life.

In this example, Eric has a gun pointed in his face. As we previously discussed, this is considered a threat of deadly force by Spencer. Eric is in imminent danger of being killed or suffering serious bodily injury. This example becomes less clear than the last example with respect to whether Mark, the defender, reasonably believed that the person being defended, Eric, was free from fault.

Was Eric at fault in instigating the incident? Maybe. Maybe not, but it does not matter because Eric's fault is legally irrelevant. Was there any way for Mark to reasonably believe that Eric was at fault in any way in bringing about the conflict? Mark really has no way of knowing whether Eric was in any way at fault in this example except for one clue when Spencer yelled, "I told you not to mess with me!" However, just because Spencer yelled this does not necessarily put Mark on notice that Eric was at fault in starting the incident. Spencer's statement could have been a result of a misunderstanding or an overreaction to something Eric did inside the bar that Spencer did not like.

In this example, the judge or jury may have difficulty determining Mark's defense of others claim based on his reasonable belief regarding Eric's fault. Some might be satisfied that Mark reasonably believed that Eric was free from fault, while others may disagree. When the penalty for a conviction in a situation such as this could be a lengthy term of imprisonment, the smart move may be to not roll the dice by getting involved, or at least not use deadly force.

> CHAPTER NINE ◄

WHEN CAN I LEGALLY USE MY GUN: PART III
DEFENSE AGAINST ANIMALS

I. DEFENSE AGAINST ANIMALS

The Virginia cruelty to animals law pursuant to Va. Code § 3.2-6570 states in part that it is a criminal offense to cruelly or unnecessarily beat, maim, mutilate, or kill any animal. However, there are many exceptions to this law where you can kill an animal if the killing is in self-defense, is in defense of others, or is to defend property from an attacking or nuisance animal.

A. Self-defense against an animal attack and defense of others against an animal attack

The law of self-defense and defense of others applies when defending against an animal attack. We previously discussed the law of self-defense in Virginia at length in Chapter 7.

> **EXAMPLE:**
>
> Wendy the walker is taking a casual afternoon walk by herself near her home in her friendly suburban retirement community. Suddenly, a pit bull dog manages to escape its fenced property and runs toward Wendy. The dog is aggressively barking, growling, and showing its teeth as it is directly approaching Wendy in a very rapid pace with its ears pulled back. Wendy quickly starts to distance herself from the dog, attempting to create as much space as possible, but it is impossible to outrun the dog. The dog, is now two to three seconds from Wendy's position as she begins to frantically scream at the dog to stay away. Wendy is 65 years old, weighs 110 pounds, and legally carries a pistol with her concealed handgun permit.

What is Wendy to do? Does the dog have to actually bite Wendy first before she can use deadly force to defend herself? What would *you* do?

> **EXAMPLE CONTINUED:**
>
> Wendy fires two quick shots at the dog at the last second based on her training from her local self-defense instructor. The dog later dies from a gunshot wound.

Was Wendy's use of deadly force in self-defense justified? As we have said, events like this will be thoroughly investigated by the law enforcement community. If the law enforcement community believes that Wendy used excessive force, then it may charge her with cruelty to animals. It would then be up to the judge or jury hearing the case to determine if Wendy reasonably feared, under the circumstances as they appeared to her, that she was in imminent danger of being killed or that she was in imminent danger of great bodily harm, and that she used no more force, under the circumstances as they appeared to her, than was reasonably necessary to protect herself from the perceived harm.

Every case is different. Some judges, jurors, and prosecutors may take the position that Wendy's fear was unreasonable. Some may take the position that Wendy's force was excessive and that she should have tried kicking the dog first before using deadly force. Others may believe that what Wendy did was justified. The purpose of this example is to bring awareness to a common scenario and educate the law-abiding gun owner that they are permitted to use deadly force to defend against an animal attack, just as if defending against an attack from a person, but that use of force must still be justified. We often remind people that there are many juries out there that like dogs more than they like humans. In addition to the potential for criminal charges, the killing of someone's beloved pet, even in a defensive scenario, brings about the risk of civil suits, which will be discussed in greater detail in Chapter 15.

As we previously discussed, federal law determines what amount of force, if any, is permitted in self-defense and defense of others regarding attacks on federal property such as national parks, national forests and national wildlife refuges. In accordance with the principles of self-defense, deadly force can only be used against animals while on federal land when you reasonably believe that the animal poses an imminent threat of death or serious bodily injury to yourself or another. This remains true even when the animal is protected by federal law. Federal statutes expressly allow for the use of deadly force against endangered species and other protected classifications when such force is used in self-defense and defense of others.

B. Defense of property against an animal attack

Property can be categorized as real property or personal property. Land and any improvements on the land would be considered real property. Personal property is generally considered movable, as opposed to real property. Livestock, such as cattle and fowl, and domestic animals, such as cats and dogs, are considered personal property.

1. Defending personal property from an animal attack

The Supreme Court of Virginia, *Willeroy v. Commonwealth*, 181 Va. 779, 27 S.E.2d 211 (1943), has stated that the owner of personal property in the form of livestock, domestic animals, or fowl, has the right to defend them from injury or destruction from an animal attack, but the extent of the defense will depend on the circumstances and necessities of the particular case. The use of force must be reasonably or properly exercised to make it lawful and justifiable.

Each disputed incident involving the killing of an attacking animal will be a question for the judge or jury sitting in judgment to decide. Would a man of ordinary prudence reasonably believe that it was necessary for him to kill the attacking animal to protect his property? There is no hard and fast rule, but such a killing is illegal if the property can be reasonably protected without a killing.

The Code of Virginia, Va. Code § 3.2-6552, has further defined what action may be taken against dogs endangering livestock or poultry. Any person who finds a dog in the act of killing or injuring livestock or poultry shall have the right to kill such dog on sight as shall any owner of livestock or his agent finding a dog chasing livestock on land utilized by the livestock when the circumstances show that such chasing is harmful to the livestock.

It is important to exercise caution when using force against any animal because an excessive use of force under the circumstances against any animal resulting in an unnecessary beating or death could trigger a cruelty to animals arrest. Along those lines, there is one very important provision of the cruelty to animals law that all property owners must know. The homeowner is entitled to a rare presumption in defense of his dog or cat. If a dog or cat is attacked on its owner's property by a dog so as to cause injury or death, the owner of the injured dog or cat may use all reasonable and necessary force against the dog at the time of the attack to protect his dog or cat. Such owner is presumed to have taken necessary and appropriate action to defend his dog or cat and is not in violation of the animal cruelty statute.

Federal law does not allow for the use of deadly force against a federally protected animal in order to defend property. If a protected animal is harming your property, including livestock, you may not use deadly force to prevent such harm. The appropriate measure is to either contact the Virginia Department of Game and Inland Fisheries or the U.S. Fish and Wildlife Service, which we discuss in more detail momentarily. Under federal regulations, permits authorizing the killing of the protected animal causing property damage may be issued. If no such permits are issued, the property owner may not kill the animal. The killing of a protected animal, when not in self-defense or pursuant to a lawful permit, is a violation of federal law, which carries both civil and criminal penalties.

2. Defending real property from animals
In some instances, various kinds of wildlife animals can either

cause damage to, become a nuisance to, or interfere with the enjoyment of a residential homeowner's real property. This can often be seen with wild animals digging through one's garden or trash or banging and pecking into the side of the home to name a few examples. Commercial businesses, agricultural entities, and other various types of property owners can also experience damage to real property.

The cruelty to animals law pursuant to Va. Code § 3.2-6570(D) shall not prohibit authorized wildlife management activities or hunting, fishing, or trapping as regulated under the Code of Virginia. Caution: There are various wildlife animals that are protected from wildlife management activities, hunting, or fishing under federal and state law.

The best recommendation for the Virginia property owner experiencing wildlife animal nuisance issues to property that are not posing a direct threat to human life, livestock, fowl, or domestic animals as we have previously discussed in detail would be to contact the Virginia Department of Wildlife Resources ("VDWR").

The Virginia Department of Wildlife Resources and the U.S. Fish and Wildlife Service investigate, enforce, and regulate wildlife, among other responsibilities. Law enforcement officers of VDWR carry the official title of Conservation Police Officer (formerly known as Game Warden) and are also cross-designated as Deputy U.S. Fish and Wildlife Special Agents to investigate violations of federal wildlife laws.

The VDWR publishes a list of wildlife animals on its website with detailed instructions on how to prevent and resolve issues with wildlife animals. There are too many wildlife animals with exceptions ranging from bears to groundhogs to go into great detail. Some animals like groundhogs and coyotes are considered nuisance species and can be killed by the property owner at any time. Other animals are considered endangered species that are protected by law, and killing them would be illegal, which we just discussed in the last section. Contact the VDWR to make sure you understand the law relative to the wildlife animal you are having an issue with before you decide to kill the animal.

PRACTICAL LEGAL TIP

Beware! Using deadly force against a dog or cat that is only digging in your flower bed or getting into your garbage may not be justified, even under the doctrine of necessity. –Gilbert

In some instances, the wildlife animal at issue may be damaging fruit trees, crops, livestock, personal property, or creating a hazard. In cases like this, you should contact your local Game Warden at the VDWR and apply for a kill permit to be issued. The Game Warden will come and investigate to determine if the wildlife animal is responsible for the alleged damage. The Game Warden may issue the landowner a kill permit that will allow the landowner to kill the wildlife animal when found on the property where the damage occurred. The Virginia Department of Wildlife Resources has created a form called the "Commercial Nuisance Animal Permit." Individuals with a permit must fill out an annual report form, due January 10th of each year, of animals that they have captured, euthanized, released on-site, or relocated. Note that the permit does allow for immediate dispatch or killing of these animals when necessary.

However, there are exceptions, and the permit does not apply to all animals. For example, the permittee may not capture, possess, transport, or kill companion animals, including domestic dogs and cats that are owned or feral. Further, the permit does not apply to state or federal threatened or endangered species, protected bird species, black bears, white-tailed deer, and wild turkeys.

PRACTICAL LEGAL TIP

It is possible that you may be authorized to kill select animals on your private property without a permit if you have a hunting license and the animal is killed during hunting season. Still, be sure to consult with the VDWR to ensure that your actions are legal. –Gilbert

For more in-depth information about the permit and the animals to which it applies, please visit https://dwr.virginia.gov/forms-download/PERM/PERM-nuisance.pdf.

C. Federal law defenses

The federal law, in a comprehensive fashion, has actually had the foresight to specifically provide that a person may kill an animal protected by federal law in self-defense, such as the regulations concerning the Mexican gray wolf in 50 CFR § 17.84(k)(3)(xii), or the grizzly bear in 50 CFR § 17.40(b)(i)(B). Unlike some state statutes, this makes federal law clear and comprehendible. Therefore, if you are carrying a firearm in a national park (*See* Chapter 13), and you find yourself face to face with a grizzly bear, you will have a legal defense for protecting yourself.

➤ CHAPTER TEN ◄

WHEN CAN I LEGALLY USE MY GUN: PART IV
UNDERSTANDING WHEN DEADLY FORCE
Can Be Used To Protect Property

The defense of property is completely different from self-defense or defense of others because this defense does not involve the protection of human life. This defense applies where you are only defending your property and not defending yourself or another person.

I. CAN I USE DEADLY FORCE TO PROTECT MY PROPERTY?

You can never use deadly force to solely defend your property. An easy example would be that you cannot shoot someone in the back while they are running across your yard with your television. Likewise, you can never threaten the use of deadly force solely, such as brandishing a firearm, to defend your property. On the other hand, you may use as much force as reasonably necessary, such as using your hands in a proper manner so as to protect your property as long as you do not commit an assault and battery or a breach of the peace. In trespassing cases, the landowner has the right to order a trespasser to leave his property, and, if the trespasser refuses to leave, then the landowner may lay hands on the trespasser in a proper manner solely to expel him from the property. The landowner cannot commit an assault and battery for the purpose of expelling the trespasser. If the landowner does commit an assault and battery, then the trespasser has the right to strike in defense. A good recommendation is to always call the authorities anytime your property is in jeopardy.

How much force is reasonably necessary to protect my property?

EXAMPLE:

> Harry the homeowner lives on a busy street in the oceanfront area of Virginia Beach. Harry looks out his window and sees a person standing in the middle of his front lawn. Harry yells at the fellow to get out of his yard. The fellow on the lawn does not respond. Harry rushes out to confront the fellow and demands that he immediately leave his lawn.

What degree of force may Harry use to remove the trespasser? This fellow does not belong on the property and is clearly a trespasser. Harry can issue multiple warnings that this fellow is trespassing and that he must immediately exit the property. Harry may also use a "come-along" escort technique with his hands to remove this trespasser from his lawn. Both of these actions would be considered lower levels of force that we discussed in the example use-of-force continuum in Chapter 7 that the law allows. Harry would not be permitted to assault the fellow or commit a breach of peace by doing something like starting a fight. Sometimes the best thing may be to call the police for assistance. This often surprises people but is critical for them to understand. One of the fastest ways to be charged with a crime is to defend property with force or the threat of force through brandishing a firearm.

> **EXAMPLE:**
>
> Mike sees Todd taking a walk on his farmland. Mike immediately runs up to Todd with a shotgun in his hands and yells at Todd to get off his property. Todd is startled and freezes in his tracks. Mike then shoots Todd and kills him.

Mike was neither permitted to threaten the use of deadly force nor actually use deadly force to defend his farmland from a trespasser. However, Mike would have been able to use proper force as a landowner to order Todd the trespasser to leave and to employ proper force if Todd the trespasser refused to leave provided no breach of peace or assault is committed. It is highly likely that Mike will be charged with a crime for killing Todd.

> **EXAMPLE:**
>
> One day, looking for a shortcut through the neighborhood, Tom hops a fence and is walking across open property to reach the street on the other side of the property. Tom is now a trespasser. Phil the property owner verbally confronts Tom. Tom tries to explain that he meant no harm and was just taking a shortcut. However, Phil becomes irate and cocks his gun, aims it at Tom, and says, "I'm going to kill you!"

Is Phil's brandishing of his gun and his threat to use deadly force permissible? No. As we previously discussed, Virginia law considers brandishing a firearm an assault and an excessive use of force solely to defend property.

Now let us take the example one step further.

> **EXAMPLE:**
> Tom is scared out of his mind as he looks down the barrel of Phil's shotgun. The two are about 20 feet apart. Tom, hearing Phil's threat to kill him, draws his own firearm and fires two shots, killing Phil.

Is Tom justified to use deadly force to defend against Phil's brandishing of a firearm and threat to kill? Yes, if Tom reasonably fears that he is in imminent danger of being killed or suffering serious bodily injury and he uses no more force than is necessary under the circumstances as they appear to him, then he can defend himself from Phil's threat to use deadly force. Tom was not at fault in provoking the fight; thus, he can stand his ground and defend himself from Phil's illegal brandishing of a gun.

Here, Phil is threatening deadly force against Tom, who appears to be a non-threating trespasser. As previously discussed, brandishing a firearm is illegal if solely defending property. In some instances, a defense of property can quickly become self-defense.

> **EXAMPLE:**
>
> Assume that when Phil verbally confronts Tom about Tom's trespassing that it is done in a very calm, non-threatening manner without the display of weapons of any kind, and it is Tom who becomes irate and hostile. Additionally, it is Tom, in a rage, who pulls out a knife and attempts to stab Phil in the chest. Phil then draws his gun and fires it at Tom, killing him instantly.

Was Phil's use of force justified? Phil's verbal confrontation ordering Tom to exit the property is lawful in his defense of his property. Tom's reaction and use of force with the knife changes the encounter. Phil can now use more force for self-defense than the law would have allowed if he were merely protecting property. Remember the justified self-defense requirements we discussed in the previous chapter: If you are without fault in provoking the fight, you reasonably fear that you are in imminent danger of being killed or are in imminent danger of great bodily harm, and you use no more force than is reasonably necessary to protect yourself from the perceived harm, under the circumstances as they appear to you, then you can stand your ground and use deadly force.

Was Phil at fault in any way? Was his fear reasonable? Was he in imminent danger of being killed or suffering serious bodily injury? Did Phil use more force that reasonably necessary?

It seems pretty clear that Phil was well within the law to defend his property, and a verbal request asking Tom to leave would not be viewed as an excessive use of force. Additionally, it seems pretty clear that Tom's actions triggered Phil's self-defense rights. Phil's use of his gun was for self-defense, not to defend his property. Phil was not at fault in provoking the incident, so he is entitled to stand his ground and defend himself. It also seems clear that Phil's use of his gun against an irate knife-wielding attacker would be viewed as reasonable under the circumstances.

PRACTICAL LEGAL TIP

If you use your firearm for defensive purposes, the first number you should call is 911. But keep your call brief: You only need to tell the operator that you have been the victim of a crime, where you are located, and some identifying information. After that, hang up! You are not required to remain on the line, and doing so could cause you problems later. Remember, all 911 calls are recorded and operators are trained to gather as much information as possible. No matter how justified you are in your use of a firearm, something you say on a 911 call may become a real headache later at trial. —Gilbert

> CHAPTER ELEVEN <

WHAT CRIMES CAN I BE CHARGED WITH WHEN MY USE OF DEADLY FORCE IS NOT JUSTIFIED?

I. INTRODUCTION AND OVERVIEW

Now it's time to give a brief summary of where you'll find yourself in legal trouble if you don't meet the elements of justification as we've discussed throughout this book. This chapter describes some of the crimes involving the use of deadly force or a firearm, and where relevant provisions may be found in Virginia law.

II. CRIMES AGAINST PERSONS

When a person uses force or deadly force, it is specifically directed at a particular individual or individuals, the criminal aggressors. In the event that the investigators do not believe that this force or deadly force is justified, this can lead to criminal charges for crimes against persons.

A. Murder

The most severe crime that a person can be charged with for using deadly force is murder. Murder in Virginia is divided into capital murder under Va. Code § 18.2-31, and first or second degree murder under Va. Code § 18.2-32. Murder involves the willful, deliberate, and premeditated unlawful killing of another, and is graded differently depending on factors surrounding the killing, such as age of the victim, motivation for the crime, and method of killing. Depending on how a murder charge is graded, it can be punished by death (capital murder), life in prison (first degree murder), or up to 40 years imprisonment (second degree murder).

B. Manslaughter

Manslaughter is divided into categories of either voluntary or involuntary. Voluntary manslaughter is often charged when an intentional killing occurs but without premeditation. Often voluntary manslaughter is charged when a killing occurs in the heat of passion, or during mutual combat. Voluntary manslaughter may also be charged when a killing occurs during an act of self-defense that "went too far." Voluntary manslaughter is a Class 5 felony punishable by up to 10 years imprisonment.

Involuntary manslaughter occurs when someone shows a "reckless disregard for human life." Often involuntary manslaughter is charged when someone is killed during something like a drunk driving accident. Involuntary manslaughter could also be charged if someone was killed by a stray bullet from a gun owner who was not using proper safety precautions when target shooting. Involuntary manslaughter is a Class 5 felony punishable by up to 10 years imprisonment.

C. Malicious Wounding

Malicious wounding is very similar to what is called aggravated assault in most other states. The statute governing malicious wounding can be found at Va. Code § 18.2-51 which makes it a crime to "maliciously shoot, stab, cut, or wound any person or by any means cause him bodily injury, with the intent to maim, disfigure, disable, or kill." Malicious wounding is typically charged as a Class 3 felony and is punishable by up to 20 years imprisonment. If such act is done unlawfully, but not maliciously, however, the offender will be charged with a Class 6 felony, punishable by up to five years imprisonment.

D. Assault and battery

Virginia's assault and battery law can be found at Va. Code § 18.2-57. The definitions of assault and battery in Virginia are consistent with the common law definitions of the respective terms. An assault is generally described as "well-founded fear or apprehension of harm, combined with an intent to instill that fear," while a battery consists of making unwanted or unlawful physical contact with someone. In Virginia, any person who commits a simple assault or assault and battery is generally guilty of a Class 1 misdemeanor. However, if a person intentionally selects the person against whom an assault and battery resulting in bodily injury is committed because of his "race, religious conviction, gender, disability, gender identity, sexual orientation, color, or national origin, the person is guilty of a Class 6 felony, and the penalty upon conviction shall include a term of confinement of at least six months." Finally, if any person commits an assault or an assault and battery against a certain class of individual, such as a judge or law enforcement officer, then there could a heightened penalty.

E. Reckless handling of firearms

Reckless handling of firearms while hunting is codified as a crime at Va. Code § 18.2-56.1. This crime makes it illegal to handle recklessly any firearm so as to endanger the life, limb, or property of any person. Any person violating this section shall be guilty of a Class 1 misdemeanor. If someone is harmed by your conduct, with the result of serious bodily injury, you may be charged with a Class 6 felony.

F. Shooting from vehicles so as to endanger persons

Va. Code § 18.2-286.1 makes it a crime for any person who, while in or on a motor vehicle, intentionally discharges a firearm so as to create the risk of injury or death to another person or thereby cause another person to have a reasonable apprehension of injury or death shall be guilty of a Class 5 felony. Because the law specifies in or on a motor vehicle, this law applies equally to discharging a firearm from a motorcycle or ATV in a manner that creates the risk of injury or death to other persons.

III. CRIMES AGAINST SOCIETY

Many crimes do not have a particular victim, but rather are charged as crimes committed against society.

A. Brandishing

Brandishing can be found at Va. Code § 18.2-282. It is unlawful in Virginia to "point, hold or brandish any firearm or any air or gas operated weapon or any object similar in appearance, whether capable of being fired or not, in such manner as to reasonably induce fear in the mind of another or hold a firearm or any air or gas operated weapon in a public place in such a manner as to reasonably induce fear in the mind of another of being shot or injured." While self-defense can be used as a successful defense against a brandishing charge, brandishing is often charged based on the subjective fear of the "victim(s)." Case law in Virginia makes it clear that brandishing can never be justified solely in defense of property.

B. Discharging firearms or missiles within or at building or dwelling house

Virginia law found at Va. Code § 18.2-279 makes it unlawful to maliciously discharge a firearm within any building when occupied by one or more persons in such a manner as to endanger the life or lives of such person or persons, or maliciously shoot at, or maliciously throw any missile at or against any dwelling house or other building when occupied by one or more persons, whereby the life or lives of any such person or persons may be put in peril. The person so offending is guilty of a Class 4 felony. In the event of the death of any person, resulting from such malicious shooting or throwing, the person so offending is guilty of murder in the second degree. However, if the homicide was willful, deliberate, and premeditated, the offender is guilty of murder in the first degree.

If any such act is done unlawfully, but not maliciously, the person so offending is guilty of a Class 6 felony; and, in the event of the death of any person resulting from such unlawful shooting or throwing, the person so offending is guilty of involuntary manslaughter. Furthermore, if any person willfully discharges a firearm within or shoots at any school building whether occupied or not, he is guilty of a Class 4 felony.

C. Willfully discharging firearms in public places

Virginia law found at § 18.2-280 makes it a crime to discharge a firearm in a public place. This crime occurs when any person willfully discharges or causes to be discharged any firearm in any street in a city or town, or in any place of public business or place of public gathering. If someone is injured by the discharge, this crime will be charged as a Class 6 felony. If no injury occurs the discharge will be charged as a Class 1 misdemeanor. Other locations where criminal liability (Class 4 felony) will attach to the discharge of a firearm include on the grounds or in the buildings of elementary, middle, or high schools unless the person discharging the weapon is engaged in a program or curriculum sponsored by or conducted with permission of a public, private, or religious school. Furthermore, if any person willfully discharges or causes to be discharged any firearm upon any public property within 1,000 feet of the property line of any public, private, or religious elementary, middle, or high school property they will be charged with a Class 4 felony, unless engaged in lawful hunting.

IV. THE AFTERMATH

When a person has found themselves in the position where they were forced to defend themselves with a firearm, what should they do to help increase the chances that the police investigation will exonerate them and implicate the aggressive law breaker?

1. Make sure that the threat is contained or neutralized;
2. Return your firearm to safekeeping;
3. Call 911 and tell them you (or another person) have been the victim of a crime. Give the operator your location and description. Avoid giving any unnecessary information, and

avoid telling them you shot someone. It may be wise to suggest an ambulance is needed. Then hang up with 911.
4. Call the U.S. LawShield Emergency Hotline and follow the instructions your program attorney gives you;
5. Wait for the police and do not touch any evidence;
6. If directed by your attorney, provide the police only simple details of the crime against you;
7. Be careful of police questions and always be ready to invoke your right to silence and your right to counsel at any time.

> CHAPTER TWELVE <

LAW OF HANDGUN CARRY: PART I
THE CONCEALED HANDGUN PERMIT
Qualifications, Requirements, Appeals, And Regulations

Virginia is a "shall issue" state, which means that a Virginia concealed handgun permit ("CHP") shall be issued upon application unless the applicant is otherwise disqualified. An issued CHP or de facto CHP must be carried by the CHP holder if he or she is carrying a concealed handgun and must be displayed with a photoidentification issued by a government agency of the Commonwealth or by the United States Department of Defense or United States State Department upon demand by a law enforcement officer.

PRACTICAL LEGAL TIP

Even if you do not plan to carry a concealed weapon, I recommend you get a CHP. Having the appropriate license makes transporting a handgun lawfully much easier within the Commonwealth, and you never know when you might want to transport a weapon. –Gilbert

Virginia has two types of CHPs: a CHP for residents and a CHP for non-residents. Virginia resident CHPs are issued by the circuit court of the county or city in which the applicant resides. Non-resident CHPs are issued by the Virginia State Police ("VSP"). Va. Code § 18.2-308.016 grants retired law enforcement an exception to the CHP requirement, which allows for concealed carry with a CHP if certain procedures are followed.

I. APPLICATION FOR RESIDENT CHP PROCESS

Any person 21 years of age or older may apply in writing to the clerk of the circuit court of the county or city in which he or she resides, or if he is a member of the United States Armed Forces, the county or city in which he or she is domiciled, for a five-year permit to carry a concealed handgun. There is no requirement as to the length of time an applicant for a CHP must have been a resident or domiciliary of the county or city where he or she resides. It is suggested that the applicant check with the circuit court where they reside for any local procedures. Questions specific to completion of the application, residency, or acceptable proof of handgun competency should be directed to the court.

PRACTICAL LEGAL TIP

You do not have to be a Virginia resident to obtain a Virginia Concealed Handgun Permit. Many residents of other states apply for and receive a non-resident CHP.
–Gilbert

A. Documentation of proof of handgun competency

To obtain either a resident or non-resident CHP, the court shall require proof that the applicant has demonstrated competence with a handgun. Beginning January 1, 2021, the demonstration of competence with a handgun has to occur in person, and no online classes will suffice. The applicant may demonstrate such competence in person by one of the following:

- Completing any hunter education or hunter safety course approved by the Department of Game and Inland Fisheries or a similar agency of another state;
- Completing any National Rifle Association firearms safety or training course;
- Completing any firearms safety or training course or class available to the general public offered by a law enforcement agency, junior college, college, or private or public institution or organization or firearms training school utilizing instructors certified by the National Rifle Association or the Department of Criminal Justice Services;
- Completing any law enforcement firearms safety or training course or class offered for security guards, investigators, special

deputies, or any division or subdivision of law enforcement or security enforcement;
- Presenting evidence of equivalent experience with a firearm through participation in organized shooting competition or current military service or proof of an honorable discharge from any branch of the armed services;
- Obtaining or previously having held a license to carry a firearm in this Commonwealth or a locality thereof, unless such license has been revoked for cause;
- Completing any in-person firearms training or safety course or class conducted by a state-certified or National Rifle Association-certified firearms instructor;
- Completing any governmental police agency firearms training course and qualifying to carry a firearm in the course of normal police duties; or
- Completing any other firearms training which the court deems adequate.

A photocopy of a certificate of completion of any of the courses or classes; an affidavit from the instructor, school, club, organization, or group that conducted or taught such course or class attesting to the completion of the course or class by the applicant; or a copy of any document which shows completion of the course or class or evidences participation in firearms competition shall constitute evidence of qualification under this subsection.

No applicant shall be required to submit to any additional demonstration of competence, nor shall any proof of demonstrated competence expire.

B. Fees and issuance of the CHP

The court shall charge a fee of $10 for the processing of an application or issuing of a permit. Local law enforcement agencies may charge a fee not to exceed $35 to cover the cost of conducting an investigation. The VSP may charge a fee not to exceed $5 to cover the cost associated with processing the application. The total amount of the charges may not exceed $50, and payment may be made by any method accepted by the court. Certain classes of individuals are exempt from this fee. The court shall issue the permit within 45 days of receipt of the completed application unless it appears that the applicant is disqualified.

C. CHP is not issued within 45 days

If the court has not issued the permit or determined that the applicant is disqualified within 45 days of the date of receipt noted on the application, then the clerk shall certify on the application that the 45-day period has expired and send a copy of the certified application to the applicant. The certified application shall serve as a de facto permit, which shall expire 90 days after issuance, and shall be recognized as a valid concealed handgun permit when presented with a valid government-issued photo identification until the court issues a five-year permit or finds the applicant to be disqualified. If the applicant is found to be disqualified after the de facto permit is issued, the applicant shall surrender the de facto permit to the court and the disqualification shall be deemed a denial of the permit and a revocation of the de facto permit. If the applicant is later found by the court to be disqualified after a five-year permit has been issued, the permit shall be revoked.

D. CHP renewal

Persons who previously have held a Virginia resident permit shall be issued, upon application, a new five-year permit unless there is good cause shown for refusing to reissue a permit. The same fees and time constraints apply in the instance of renewal. Persons who previously have been issued a concealed handgun permit are not required to appear in person to apply for a new five-year permit; the application for the new permit may be submitted via the United States mail. The circuit court that receives the application shall promptly notify the applicant if the application is incomplete or if the fee submitted is incorrect.

If the new five-year permit is issued while an existing permit remains valid, the new five-year permit shall become effective upon the expiration date of the existing permit, provided that the application is received by the court at least 90 days but no more than 180 days prior to the expiration of the existing permit.

If a permit holder is a member of the Virginia National Guard, Armed Forces of the United States, or the Armed Forces reserves of the United States, and his five-year permit expires during an active-duty military deployment outside of the permittee's county or city of residence, such permit shall remain valid for 90 days after the end date of the deployment. In order to establish proof of continued validity of the permit, such a permittee shall carry with him and display, upon request of a law enforcement officer, a copy of the permittee's deployment orders or other documentation from the permittee's commanding officer that order the permittee to travel outside of his county or city of residence and that indicate the start and end date of such deployment.

E. Change of address and replacement CHPs

The clerk of a circuit court that issued a valid CHP shall, upon presentation of the valid CHP and proof of a new address of residence by the CHP holder, issue a replacement CHP specifying the CHP holder's new address. The total amount assessed for processing a replacement CHP due to a change of address shall not exceed $10, with such fees to be paid in one sum to the person who accepts the information for the replacement CHP. Obtaining a replacement CHP solely because of a change of address within the state is not required but may be prudent to avoid unnecessary confusion.

The clerk of a circuit court that issued a valid CHP shall, upon submission of a notarized statement by the CHP holder that the CHP was lost or destroyed or that the CHP holder has undergone a legal name change, issue a replacement CHP. The replacement CHP shall have the same expiration date as the CHP that was lost, destroyed, or issued to the CHP holder under a previous name. The clerk shall issue the replacement CHP within 10 business days of receiving the notarized statement and may charge a fee not to exceed $5.

F. Denied CHP applications

Only a circuit court judge may deny issuance of a CHP to a Virginia resident or domiciliary who has applied for a CHP pursuant to Va. Code § 18.2-308.04. Any order denying issuance of a CHP shall state the basis for the denial of the CHP and shall provide notice in writing to the applicant that the CHP application was denied along with notice that the applicant may request a hearing to appeal the decision to deny issuance of the CHP.

If you receive what you believe to be a wrongful denial of a CHP, you must act rapidly. The applicant may appeal a denied CHP application within 21 days to the circuit court. The court shall place the matter on the docket for an oral hearing. The applicant may be represented by counsel, but counsel shall not be appointed, and the rules of evidence shall apply. The final order of the court shall include the court's findings of fact and conclusions of law.

Any applicant denied a CHP in circuit court may present a petition for review to the Virginia Court of Appeals. The petition for review shall be filed within 60 days of the expiration of the time for requesting a hearing pursuant to Va. Code § 18.2-308.08(C) or if a hearing was requested, then within 60 days of the entry of the final order of the circuit court following the hearing. The petition shall be accompanied by a copy of the original papers filed in the circuit court, including a copy of the order of the circuit court denying the CHP. According to Va. Code § 17.1-410 B, the decision of the Virginia Court of Appeals shall be final. If the decision to deny the CHP is reversed on appeal, then taxable costs incurred by the applicant shall be paid by the Commonwealth.

G. Revocation or suspension of a CHP

Any CHP holder convicted of an offense that would disqualify that person from obtaining a CHP or who makes a materially false statement in a CHP application shall forfeit his CHP and surrender it to the court. Persons disqualified from obtaining a CHP are discussed later in section III of this chapter.

Any CHP holder who has a felony charge pending or a charge of any assault, assault and battery, sexual battery, discharging a firearm, brandishing a firearm, or stalking may have the CHP suspended by the court before which such charge is pending or by the court that issued the CHP.

The court shall revoke the CHP of any individual who has been adjudicated legally incompetent, mentally incapacitated, incapacitated, or any individual who has been involuntarily admitted to a facility or ordered to mandatory outpatient treatment as explained in Va. Code § 18.2-308.1:3 or to any individual who was the subject of a temporary detention and subsequently agreed to voluntary admission.

Any CHP holder who becomes subject to a protective order pursuant to Va. Code § 18.2-308.1:4 shall be prohibited from carrying any concealed firearm and shall surrender his CHP to the court entering the order for the duration of any protective order.

Any CHP holder who is convicted of being under the influence of alcohol or illegal drugs while carrying a handgun in a public place shall have his CHP revoked. Such person shall be ineligible to apply for a CHP for a period of five years.

II. APPLICATION FOR NON-RESIDENT CHP PROCESS

Non-residents of Virginia who are 21 years of age or older may apply in writing to the VSP for a five-year permit to carry a concealed handgun. The application shall be made under oath before a notary or other person qualified to take oaths on a form provided by the VSP requiring only that information necessary to determine eligibility for the permit. Every applicant for a non-resident CHP shall submit two photographs of a type and kind specified by the VSP for inclusion on the CHP and shall submit fingerprints on a card provided by the VSP for the purpose of obtaining the applicant's state or national criminal history record. The applicant shall submit to fingerprinting by his local or state law enforcement agency using the provided VSP fingerprint cards. The applicant must provide a legible photocopy of a valid photo ID issued by a governmental agency. The VSP may charge a fee not to exceed $100 to cover the cost of the background check and issuance of the CHP.

A Virginia non-resident CHP may be necessary for residents of other states who have a license or permit issued from a state that Virginia law does not recognize as valid for purposes of carrying a concealed firearm in Virginia. We will discuss the reciprocity of the CHP later in this chapter.

A. Documentation of proof of handgun competency

Proper documentation regarding proof of handgun competency was previously discussed in section A of this chapter. The same documentation applies to non-resident applicants as Virginia resident applicants except that the VSP, as opposed the court, may deem other training as adequate.

B. Non-resident CHP renewal

The renewal process is identical to the processes and costs associated with the original permit with the exception of proof of competence with a handgun. New photos and fingerprint impressions will be required. It is suggested that all renewal application packages be submitted at least 60 days prior to expiration of the existing permit. Request a packet for the renewal process by contacting the VSP Firearms Transaction Center at nonrespermit@vsp.virginia.gov.

C. Change of address

Non-resident CHP holders are requested to notify the VSP Firearms Transaction Center ("FTC") of changes of address. Notification may be made in writing to the FTC at P.O. Box 85141, Richmond, VA, 23285-5141 or nonrespermit@vsp.virginia.gov, and must include the CHP file number or a photocopy of the CHP. A change of address card will be provided to the non-resident CHP holder to be retained with the original non-resident CHP.

D. Replacement non-resident CHP

A replacement non-resident CHP may be requested in writing addressed to the FTC at P.O. Box 85141, Richmond, VA 23285-5141. All requests for replacement must include a cashier's check or money order in the amount of $5 made payable to the VSP, a photograph, and one of the following:
- The non-resident CHP file number;
- A photocopy of the non-resident CHP; and
- A photocopy of a valid photo-ID issued by a governmental agency.

A replacement non-resident CHP will have the same expiration date as the permit originally issued.

III. DISQUALIFIED INDIVIDUALS INELIGIBLE TO OBTAIN A CHP

Va. Code § 18.2-308.09 lists individuals who are disqualified from obtaining either a Virginia resident CHP or a Virginia non-resident CHP as follows:

- An individual who was acquitted of any felony and most misdemeanor criminal offenses as explained in Va. Code § 18.2-308.1:1 by reason of insanity and committed to the custody of Behavioral Health and Developmental Services, or who has pursuant to Va. Code § 18.2-308.1:2 been adjudicated legally incompetent, mentally incapacitated, incapacitated, or has been involuntarily admitted to a facility or ordered to mandatory outpatient treatment as explained in Va. Code § 18.2-308.1:3 or who was the subject of a temporary detention and subsequently agreed to voluntary admission. Additionally those subject to a substantial risk protection order pursuant to Va. Code § 18.2-308.1:6 who are ineligible to possess a firearm are disqualified from obtaining a CHP. Finally, anyone who is on the "Virginia Voluntary Do Not Sell List" pursuant to Va. Code § 18.2-308.1:7 or has been convicted of a misdemeanor crime of domestic violence pursuant to Va. Code § 18.2-308.1:8 is prohibited from obtaining a CHP. These disqualifications also apply to substantially similar laws of the United States or any other state.

- An individual who is subject to a restraining order or to a protective order and is prohibited from purchasing or transporting a firearm pursuant to Va. Code § 18.2-308.1:4.
- An individual who has been convicted of a felony; or an individual who was once adjudicated delinquent as a juvenile at 14 years of age or older at the time of the offense for the offenses of either murder, kidnapping, robbery by the threat or presentation of a firearm, or rape; or an individual under the age of 29 who was once adjudicated delinquent as a juvenile at 14 years of age or older at the time of the offense for a delinquent act which would be a felony if committed by an adult, whether such conviction or adjudication occurred under the laws of Virginia, another state, the District of Columbia, or the United States or any

territory thereof unless such individual may now lawfully possess or carry a firearm after successfully petitioning the applicable circuit court.
- An individual who has been convicted of two or more misdemeanors within the five-year period immediately preceding the CHP application, if one of the misdemeanors was a Class 1 misdemeanor, but the judge shall have the discretion to deny a CHP for two or more misdemeanors that are not Class 1 misdemeanors. Traffic infractions and misdemeanors set forth in the Motor Vehicle Code pursuant to Title 46.2, such as reckless driving, shall not be considered for purposes of this disqualification.
- An individual who is addicted to, or is an unlawful user or distributor of, marijuana, synthetic cannabinoids, or any controlled substance.
- An individual who has been convicted of driving under the influence or a substantially similar local ordinance, or of public drunkenness, or of a substantially similar offense under the laws of any other state, the District of Columbia, the United States, or its territories within the three-year period immediately preceding the CHP application, or who is a habitual drunkard as determined pursuant to Va. Code § 4.1-333.
- An alien other than an alien lawfully admitted for permanent residence in the United States.
- An individual who has been discharged from the Armed Forces of the United States under dishonorable conditions.
- An individual who is a fugitive from justice.
- An individual who the court finds, by a preponderance of the evidence, based on specific acts by the CHP applicant, is likely to use a weapon unlawfully or negligently to

endanger others. The sheriff, chief of police, or attorney for the Commonwealth may submit to the court a sworn, written statement indicating that, in the opinion of such sheriff, chief of police, or attorney for the Commonwealth, based upon a disqualifying conviction or upon the specific acts set forth in the statement, the CHP applicant is likely to use a weapon unlawfully or negligently to endanger others. The statement of the sheriff, chief of police, or the attorney for the Commonwealth shall be based upon personal knowledge of such individual or of a deputy sheriff, police officer, or assistant attorney for the Commonwealth of the specific acts, or upon a written statement made under oath before a notary public of a competent person having personal knowledge of the specific acts.

- An individual who has been convicted of any assault, assault and battery, sexual battery, discharging of a firearm or brandishing of a firearm within the three-year period immediately preceding the CHP application.
- An individual who has been convicted of stalking.
- An individual whose previous convictions or adjudications of delinquency were based on an offense that would have been at the time of conviction a felony if committed by an adult under the laws of any state, the District of Columbia, the United States, or its territories. For purposes of this disqualifier, only convictions occurring within 16 years following the later of the date of (i) the conviction or adjudication or (ii) release from any incarceration imposed upon such conviction or adjudication shall be deemed to be "previous convictions." Disqualification under this subdivision shall not apply to an individual with previous adjudications of delinquency who has completed a term of service of no less than two years in

the Armed Forces of the United States and, if such person has been discharged from the Armed Forces of the United States, received an honorable discharge.
- An individual who has a felony charge pending or a charge of any assault, assault and battery, sexual battery, discharging of a firearm, brandishing of a firearm, or stalking pending.
- An individual who has received mental health treatment or substance abuse treatment in a residential setting within five years prior to the date of his CHP application.
- An individual who was found guilty of any criminal offense set forth in Title 18.2, Chapter 7, Article 1 of the Code of Virginia, which includes drug and drug-related offenses, or of a criminal offense of illegal possession or distribution of marijuana or any controlled substance, under the laws of any state, the District of Columbia, or the United States or its territories within the three-year period immediately preceding the CHP application.
- An individual whose first drug offense was disposed of pursuant to Va. Code § 18.2-251 or the substantially similar law of any other state, the District of Columbia, or the United States or its territories within the three-year period immediately preceding the CHP application.

IV. CHP RECIPROCITY

CHP reciprocity is the recognition or honoring of a concealed carry license or permit that was issued by another state. In 2015, the Virginia Attorney General announced that Virginia would be terminating CHP reciprocity agreements with 25 states. This caused quite a stir to say the least. In the end, Virginia did not terminate its CHP reciprocity agreements. We mention this because CHP reciprocity agreements are subject to change at any time due to the nature of politics. Before traveling it is always a good idea to confirm the other state's recognition or lack thereof regarding your Virginia resident or non-resident CHP if you will be traveling through another state and expect that the other state will recognize your Virginia CHP.

Effective July 1, 2016, the holder of a valid CHP issued by another state may carry a concealed handgun in Virginia provided that:

- The holder of such permit or license is at least 21 years of age;
- The permit or license holder carries a photo identification issued by a government agency of any state or by the U.S. Department of Defense or U.S. Department of State;
- The holder displays the permit or license and such identification upon demand by a law enforcement officer;
- The issuing authority maintains the means for instantaneous verification of the validity of all such permits or licenses issued within that state accessible 24 hours a day; and
- The permit or license holder has not previously been denied a CHP in Virginia nor had a Virginia concealed handgun permit revoked.

> CHAPTER THIRTEEN ◄

LAW OF HANDGUN CARRY: PART II
WHAT, HOW, AND WHERE
You Can Legally Carry With A Concealed Handgun Permit

I. INTRODUCTION

We have previously discussed that the constitutional right to bear arms is not an absolute right, that certain classes of individuals are prohibited from purchasing and possessing firearms, and that the government has the authority to regulate firearms under certain circumstances. In this chapter, we discuss the law of open carry, concealed carry, and where the federal and Virginia law regulates the possession, carrying, and transportation of firearms on certain premises.

II. VIRGINIA IS AN OPEN CARRY STATE

A person's right to carry a firearm openly is considered universal in Virginia, subject to definite and limited restrictions upon certain locations and classifications of individuals. If you are at least 18 years old, and not otherwise prohibited from possessing a firearm, then you may openly carry a loaded firearm in public without a license or a concealed handgun permit ("CHP"); however, there are exceptions.

Open carry on private property is different. Any private party can either regulate or ban firearms on their property, even property leased from the government. If a private property owner or responsible person asks an open carry individual to leave, then that individual must leave or he may be prosecuted for trespassing pursuant to Va. Code § 18.2-119, which is punishable by up to 12 months in jail and a $2,500 fine. A firearm may also be openly carried in either a personal, private motor vehicle or vessel if the firearm is openly and plainly visible. Questions of at what point a firearm is "concealed" can become questions of fact that are decided by a judge or jury. Often this analysis asks whether a weapon is "hidden from common observation."

An additional exception for carrying a firearm in a car or on a boat without a CHP allows possession of a loaded handgun by "any person who may lawfully possess a firearm and is carrying a handgun while in a personal, private motor vehicle or vessel and such handgun is secured in a container or compartment in the vehicle or vessel." A 2012 opinion from then-Attorney General Kenneth T. Cuccinelli stands for the proposition that when a firearm is otherwise lawfully stored in a glove box, center console, or other container in a vehicle "such storage tool need not be locked."

If you plan on carrying a loaded handgun in a center console or glove box, be certain that it is actually latched. A 2021 Virginia Supreme Court decision in *Myers v. Commonwealth* 857 S.E.2d 805 Va. (2021) extended this "secure container" in a personal vehicle exception further, by finding that a zipped-up backpack on the passenger floorboard of a car constituted a "secure container." If you plan to carry in this matter without a CHP, you must be extremely careful, as this exception to the general prohibition on concealed carry without a permit is fact specific, and as soon as you get out of the vehicle with the weapon in the backpack, it is likely a concealed weapon to which no exception applies.

Va. Code § 15.2-915.2 creates an open carry exception for loaded shotguns and rifles in vehicles traveling on public highways. This law allows for any county or city to pass an ordinance that makes it unlawful for any person to transport, possess, or carry a loaded shotgun or loaded rifle in any vehicle on any public street, road, or highway within such locality. However, this section shall neither apply to law-enforcement or military personnel in the performance of their lawful duties nor to any person who reasonably believes that a loaded rifle or shotgun is necessary for his personal safety in the course of his employment or business. Any violation of such ordinance shall be punishable by a fine of not more than $100.

Va. Code § 18.2-287.4 creates another open carry exception regarding the carrying of a loaded assault firearm in public in certain jurisdictions. This law states that it is unlawful for any person to carry a loaded assault firearm on or about his person on any public street, road, alley, sidewalk, public right-of-way, or in any public park or any other place of whatever nature that is open to the public in the cities of Alexandria, Chesapeake, Fairfax, Falls

Church, Newport News, Norfolk, Richmond, or Virginia Beach or in the counties of Arlington, Fairfax, Henrico, Loudoun, or Prince William. A violation of this section is a misdemeanor punishable by up to 12 months in jail and a $2,500 fine. However, this does not apply to any person having a valid CHP, law-enforcement, licensed security guards, military personnel in the performance of their lawful duties, to any person actually engaged in lawful hunting, or lawful recreational shooting activities at an established shooting range or shooting contest. There are other exceptions that limit a person's ability to open carry that we will also discuss in this chapter along with firearm restrictions that prohibit all firearms from various premises.

III. LAW OF CONCEALED CARRY OF A FIREARM

Concealed carry of a firearm is significantly more restrictive than open carry of a firearm. Concealed carry of a firearm refers to the practice of carrying a firearm in a concealed or hidden manner, either on one's person or in close proximity. Va. Code § 18.2-308(A) defines the law of concealed carry, as it relates to a firearm, as any person who carries about his person any pistol, revolver, or other weapon designed or intended to propel a missile of any kind by action of an explosion of any combustible material, hidden from common observation. Hidden from common observation includes when the firearm is observable, but is of such a deceptive appearance as to disguise the firearm's true nature. A first violation of this law is a misdemeanor punishable by up to 12 months in jail and/or a $2,500 fine. Second and third violations of this law are felonies and are punishable by up to five and 10 years in prison, respectively, both with fines of up to $2,500. Law enforcement will also confiscate the firearm for a violation.

Concealed carry of any firearm is permissible for a limited number of very specific reasons as determined by the Virginia State Legislature. If one of these specific reasons to carry a concealed firearm does not apply to you, then you may only carry a concealed handgun with a CHP if not otherwise prohibited by law or the owner of private property.

The following are allowed to carry any concealed firearm without a CHP if not otherwise prohibited by law:
- Any person while in his own place of abode or on the curtilage;
- Any person while in his own place of business;
- Any person who may lawfully possess a firearm and is carrying a handgun while in a personal, private motor vehicle or vessel and such handgun is secured in a container or compartment in the vehicle or vessel;
- Any law-enforcement officer or retired law-enforcement officer pursuant to Va. Code § 18.2-308.016;
- Any person who is at, or going to or from, an established shooting range, provided that the weapons are unloaded and securely wrapped while being transported;
- Any enrolled participant of a firearms training course who is at, or going to or from, a training location, provided that the weapons are unloaded and securely wrapped while being transported;
- Any regularly enrolled member of a weapons collecting organization who is at, or going to or from, a bona fide weapons exhibition, provided that the weapons are unloaded and securely wrapped while being transported;
- Any person carrying such weapons between his place of abode and a place of purchase or repair, provided the weapons are unloaded and securely wrapped while being transported;

- Any person actually engaged in lawful hunting, as authorized by the Department of Game and Inland Fisheries, under inclement weather conditions necessitating temporary protection of his firearm from those conditions, provided that possession of a handgun while engaged in lawful hunting shall not be construed as hunting with a handgun if the person hunting is carrying a valid concealed handgun permit;
- Any attorney for the Commonwealth or assistant attorney for the Commonwealth;
- Any judge of the Commonwealth;
- Certain individuals while in the discharge of their official duties or while in transit to or from such duties as follows:
    - carriers of the United States mail;
    - officers or guards of any state correctional institution;
    - conservators of the peace;
    - noncustodial employees of the Department of Corrections designated to carry weapons by the Director of the Department of Corrections pursuant to Va. Code § 53.1-29; and
    - Harbormaster of the City of Hopewell.

IV. FIREARM PROHIBITIONS BY PREMISES

Federal law and Virginia law prohibit firearms from being possessed on certain premises. Generally, premises are land and buildings together considered as a property. However, the legal definition of premises can vary based on the law that is restricting or banning the firearm. As we will see, the law completely bans the possession of all firearms on certain premises, but there are some exceptions where it is lawful to either open carry or carry a handgun with a CHP.

A. Private property

As we previously discussed, any private party can ban the open carry of firearms on its property. A private party can also ban the carrying of a concealed handgun with a CHP. The Second Amendment acts as a restraint on government, not private parties.

B. Restaurants and clubs that serve alcoholic beverages

Va. Code § 18.2-308.012 states that no person who carries a concealed handgun with a CHP onto the premises of any restaurant or club (as defined in Va. Code § 4.1-100 that has an Alcoholic Beverage Control license to sell and serve alcoholic beverages on-premises) may consume an alcoholic beverage while on the premises. A violation of this section is a misdemeanor punishable by six months in jail and/or a $1,000 fine. This law does not apply to law enforcement. What does all of that mean? A CHP holder may carry their concealed handgun into a restaurant or club as long as they don't drink a sip of alcohol!

Remember, as we previously discussed in Chapter 12, any CHP holder who is convicted for being under the influence of alcohol or illegal drugs while carrying such handgun in a public place shall have his CHP revoked. Such person shall be ineligible to apply for a CHP for a period of five years.

C. Place of employment

A private employer may prohibit firearms in the workplace and may ban firearms on its private property. Such a prohibition includes storing a firearm in one's vehicle at a place of employment if there is a company policy or signage prohibiting firearms on the premises. It is recommended that all gun owners understand their employer's position on firearms before taking any firearm into their place of employment.

A locality employer may adopt workplace rules that restrict or prohibit firearms. However, no locality employer shall adopt any workplace rule that prevents an employee of that locality from storing at that locality's workplace a lawfully possessed firearm and ammunition in a locked private motor vehicle.

Federal and state employees are prohibited from possessing firearms in their government building workplaces unless an exception applies.

D. Courts and government buildings

1. Courthouses

Va. Code § 18.2-283.1 states that it is unlawful for any person to possess a firearm or to transport a firearm into any courthouse. A violation of this section is a misdemeanor punishable by up to 12 months in jail and a $2,500 fine. However, this section shall not apply to law enforcement and other officials including any police officer, sheriff, law-enforcement agent or official, conservation police officer, conservator of the peace, magistrate, court officer, judge, or city or county treasurer while in the conduct of such person's official duties.

2. Virginia buildings

Beginning July 1st, 2021, and pursuant to Va. Code § 18.2-283.2, firearms are prohibited within the following locations:

- (i) the Capitol of Virginia;
- (ii) Capitol Square and the surrounding area;
- (iii) any building owned or leased by the Commonwealth or any agency thereof; or
- (iv) any office where employees of the Commonwealth or any agency thereof are regularly present for the purpose of performing their official duties.

Capitol Square and the surrounding area means "(i) the grounds, land, real property, and improvements in the City of Richmond bounded by Bank, Governor, Broad, and Ninth Streets, and the sidewalks of Bank Street extending from 50 feet west of the Pocahontas Building entrance to 50 feet east of the entrance of the Capitol of Virginia." This restriction appears aimed to prevent groups like Virginia Citizens Defense League from carrying firearms during what had previously been an annual lobby day event at the state capitol in Richmond. A violation of the law is punishable as a Class 1 misdemeanor. The restriction specifically does not apply to:

"(i) any retired law-enforcement officer qualified pursuant to subsection C of § 18.2-308.016 who is visiting a gun range owned or leased by the Commonwealth;

(ii) any of the following employees authorized to carry a firearm while acting in the conduct of such employee's official duties:
  (a) a bail bondsman as defined in § 9.1-185,
  (b) an employee of the Department of Corrections or a state juvenile correctional facility,
  (c) an employee of the Department of Conservation and Recreation, or
  (d) an employee of the Department of Wildlife Resources;

(iii) any individual carrying a weapon into a courthouse who is exempt under § 18.2-283.1;

(iv) any property owned or operated by a public institution of higher education;

(v) any state park; or

(vi) any magistrate acting in the conduct of the magistrate's official duties."

Firearms are also prohibited in Virginia state government executive branch offices and workplace facilities, such as the Department of Motor Vehicles ("DMV"), Alcohol Beverage Control ("ABC") retail stores, and any Department of Corrections facility. This prohibition does not apply to law-enforcement officers, authorized security personnel, or military personnel, when such individuals are authorized to carry a firearm in accordance with their duties, and when they are carrying the firearm within that authority. It also does not apply to state employees where the employee's position requires carrying a concealed firearm. This concealed carry regulation also does not apply to individuals who are on public hunting lands and are engaged in lawful hunting activities according to the Virginia Department of Wildlife Resources' Hunting and Trapping regulations found in 4VAC15. A state institution of higher education is exempt from this regulation if the institution has implemented its own policies or regulations governing firearms.

As we previously discussed, a locality may adopt workplace rules that restrict or prohibit firearms at the workplace. Additionally, any local or regional jail or juvenile detention facility may adopt and enforce a firearms ordinance.

Finally, as previously discussed, any locality may adopt an ordinance that prohibits the possession, carrying, or transportation of any firearms, ammunition, or components or combination thereof (i) in any building, or part thereof, owned or used by such locality, or by any authority or local governmental entity created or controlled by the locality, for governmental purposes; (ii) in any public park owned or operated by the locality, or by any authority or local governmental entity created or controlled by the locality; (iii) in any recreation or community center facility operated by the locality, or by any authority or local governmental entity created or controlled by the locality; or (iv) in any public street, road, alley, or sidewalk or public right-of-way or any other place of whatever nature that is open to the public and is being used by or is adjacent to a permitted event or an event that would otherwise require a permit. In buildings that are not owned by a locality, or by any authority or local governmental entity created or controlled by the locality, such ordinance shall apply only to the part of the building that is being used for a governmental purpose and when such building, or part thereof, is being used for a governmental purpose.

E. Preschools, elementary, middle, and high schools

Firearms are restricted in public, parochial, and private schools according to federal and Virginia law. Va. Code § 18.2-308.1 prohibits anyone from knowingly possessing any firearm while such person is upon:

i. any public, private or religious preschool, elementary, middle or high school, including buildings and grounds;

ii. that portion of any property open to the public and then exclusively used for school-sponsored functions or extracurricular activities while such functions or activities are taking place; or

iii. any school bus owned or operated by any such school.

The portion of Va. Code § 18.2-308.1 that applies to private or religious preschools specifically applies only during the operating hours of such private or religious preschool and do not apply to any person (a) whose residence is on the property of a private or religious preschool and (b) who possesses a firearm or other weapon prohibited under this section while in his residence.

A violation of this section by unlawfully possessing a firearm on school property is a felony punishable by up to five years in prison and a $2,500 fine. However, this section does not apply to:
  i. a person who has a valid CHP and possesses a concealed handgun while in a motor vehicle in a parking lot, traffic circle, or other means of vehicular ingress or egress to the school;
  ii. any law-enforcement officer; however, Va. Code 18.2 § 308.1(e) specifically does not apply the law-enforcement officer exemption to a special conservator of peace appointed pursuant to § 19.2-13;
  iii. an unloaded firearm that is in a closed container;
  iv. unloaded shotguns or rifles in or upon a motor vehicle in a firearms rack in or upon a motor vehicle; or
  v. an armed security officer hired by a child day care center or a private or religious school for the protection of students and employees as authorized by such school.

Additionally, beginning July 1, 2021, and pursuant to Va. Code § 22.1-131.1, a school board may "deem any building or property that it owns or leases where employees of such school board are regularly present for the purpose of performing their official duties, outside of school zones, as that term is defined in 18 U.S.C. § 921, as a gun-free zone and may prohibit any individual from knowingly purchasing, possessing, transferring, carrying, storing, or transporting firearms, ammunition, or components or combination thereof while such individual is upon such property." Even when a school board makes a building it owns or uses a gun-free zone, exceptions exist for:
  (i) any law-enforcement officer;
  (ii) any retired law-enforcement officer qualified to carry firearms pursuant to subsection C of § 18.2-308.016;

(iii) any individual who possesses an unloaded firearm that is in a closed container in or upon a motor vehicle or an unloaded shotgun or rifle in a firearms rack in or upon a motor vehicle; or

(iv) any individual who has a valid concealed handgun permit and possesses a concealed handgun while in a motor vehicle in a parking lot, traffic circle, or other means of vehicular ingress to or egress from the school board property.

Under federal law the Gun-Free School Zones Act ("GFSZA") prohibits any person from knowingly possessing a firearm that has moved in or otherwise affects interstate or foreign commerce at a place the individual knows, or has reasonable cause to believe, is a school zone. The GFSZA also prohibits any person from knowingly, or with reckless disregard for the safety of another, discharging or attempting to discharge a firearm that has moved in or otherwise affects interstate or foreign commerce at a place the person knows is a school zone. The GFSZA defines "school zone" as: 1) in, or on the grounds of, a public, parochial or private school; or 2) within a distance of 1,000 feet from the grounds of a public, parochial or private school.

Exceptions to the possession prohibition include:
- If the individual possessing the firearm has a Virginia issued CHP;
- Where the firearm is:
  - unloaded and in a locked container or locked firearms rack on a motor vehicle; or
  - unloaded and possessed while traversing school premises for the purpose of gaining access to public or private lands open to hunting, if the entry on school premises is authorized by school authorities.

Exceptions to both the possession and discharge bans include:
- Possession of a firearm on private property not part of school grounds;
- Where the firearm is possessed for use in a program approved by a school held in the school zone, or in accordance with a contract entered into between a school and the individual or an employer of the individual; or
- Where the firearm is possessed or used by a law enforcement officer acting in his or her official capacity.

The GFSZA requires each local elementary or secondary educational agency requesting financial assistance from the state educational agency charged with receiving and distributing federal funds to expel any student for bringing a firearm to school or possessing a firearm at school, to include school-sponsored events and activities, even those held off school grounds. The chief administering officer of a local educational agency is allowed to modify an expulsion for a student, in writing, on a case-by-case basis.

Furthermore, the GFSZA provides that a state may allow a local educational agency that has expelled a student from the student's regular school setting to provide an alternative educational setting, but a referral to the criminal justice or juvenile delinquency system is required. The exception to the GFSZA permits firearm possession where the firearm is lawfully stored inside a locked vehicle on school property, or where the gun is possessed for an activity approved and authorized by the local educational agency, if the agency has adopted appropriate safeguards to ensure student safety.

F. Universities and colleges

Private universities, like any other owner of private property, may restrict or ban firearms on their property. The Second Amendment acts as a restraint on government, not private parties. It is recommended that all gun owners review a private university's firearm policy before taking any firearm onto any private university's property.

According to Virginia Attorney General Opinion 78 (2006), a public university cannot generally prohibit firearms on campus. However, a public university can prohibit students and university employees from carrying firearms on campus, even if those individuals hold a CHP, since specific statutes grant a public university authority to regulate the conduct of students and university employees.

The Supreme Court of Virginia has held that a public university can regulate and restrict the possession and carrying of firearms inside public campus buildings and at campus events. The Court pointed out that such a regulation was tailored, restricting weapons only in those places where people congregate and are most vulnerable. Individuals could still carry or possess weapons on the open grounds of the university, and in other places on campus not enumerated in the regulation.

Most of the public universities and colleges in Virginia have very similar weapons regulations, which include prohibitions to the carrying of firearms and weapons in school buildings and at school events. Each university or college's weapons policy is published in the Virginia Administrative Code under Title 8 by the respective institution.

G. Place of religious worship

Va. Code § 18.2-283 states that it is illegal for any person to carry any firearm without a good and sufficient reason to a place of worship while a meeting for religious purposes is being held at such place. A violation of this section is a misdemeanor punishable by a maximum $250 fine. Personal protection is considered to be a good and sufficient reason to carry a firearm. However, a place of worship can choose to ban guns on its property. Keep in mind, a church situated on school grounds will likely continue to be off limits for those carrying a firearm even when school is not in session. It is recommended that all gun owners understand their place of worship's position on firearms before taking any firearm into their place of worship.

H. Child day center facilities

Firearms are prohibited in child day centers, often called child day care facilities. Child-care facilities must be licensed by the Department of Social Services.

The portion of Va. Code § 18.2-308.1 that applies to child day centers specifically applies only during the operating hours of such child day center and do not apply to any person (a) whose residence is on the property of a child day center and (b) who possesses a firearm or other weapon prohibited under this section while in his residence.

In this situation firearms shall be stored, unloaded in a locked container, compartment, or cabinet, and apart from ammunition. Ammunition shall be stored in a locked container, compartment, or cabinet during the family day home's hours of operation. If a key is used to lock the container, compartment, or cabinet, the key shall be inaccessible to children.

It is also important to understand that the law defines "child day centers" as a facility "defined in § 63.2-100, that is licensed in accordance with the provisions of Chapter 17 (§ 63.2-1700 et seq.) of Title 63.2 and is not operated at the residence of the provider or of any of the children." Often child-care facilities set up at churches are not licensed, and therefore do not fit the definition of a "child day center" for purposes of this law.

Va. Code § 15.2-914 states that certain localities based on their form of government may regulate the possession and storage of firearms, ammunition, or components or combination thereof at child-care facilities so long as such regulation remains no more extensive in scope than comparable state regulations applicable to family day homes. It is recommended that all gun owners understand their child-care facility's position on firearms before taking any firearm into their child-care facility.

I. National forests, parks and wildlife refuges, and state lands

1. National parks, wildlife refuges, and Virginia state parks

Possession of a firearm in a national park or national wildlife refuge is lawful if in compliance with the law of the State in which the federal land is located. Thus, an individual can open carry a firearm on these federal lands located in Virginia because open carry is lawful. Note: This does not grant an individual the ability to possess a firearm inside a federal building. The law of open carry applies to Virginia state parks just like any other public location that is not otherwise restricted. Concealed carry is also permissible on these lands with a CHP, if not otherwise prohibited from possessing a firearm.

2. National forests and land owned or managed by the Department of Game and Inland Fisheries

4VAC15-40-60 states that it shall be unlawful to possess any firearm that is loaded and uncased or dismantled on all national forests, Virginia Department of Wildlife Resources-owned lands, and on other lands managed by VDWR under a cooperative agreement. It is also unlawful to possess or transport any loaded firearm in or on any vehicle at any time on VDWR-owned lands. However, this prohibition shall neither prohibit the possession, transport and use of loaded firearms by employees of the VDWR while engaged in the performance of their authorized and official duties, nor shall it prohibit possession and transportation of loaded concealed handguns where the individual possesses a CHP, nor at archery and shooting ranges. Hunting regulations differ. It is recommended that hunters refer to all applicable hunting laws and regulations.

3. Hog Island Wildlife Management Area

4VAC15-40-120 states that it is unlawful to possess at any time a gun which is not unloaded and cased or dismantled on that portion of the Hog Island Wildlife Management Area bordering on the James River and lying north of the Surry Nuclear Power Plant, except while hunting deer or waterfowl in conformity with a special permit issued by the department.

4. Buggs Island

4VAC15-40-140 states that it is unlawful to possess a loaded gun on Buggs Island or to shoot over or have a loaded gun upon the water on Gaston Reservoir (Roanoke River) from a point beginning at High Rock and extending to the John H. Kerr Dam.

J. Federal property

A state license or permit to carry a handgun is a product of state law and conveys no rights to the permit holder that have been recognized under federal law. However, in certain instances, the federal government recognizes these state rights on certain federal property.

1. Federal buildings: firearms are prohibited

> **FIREARMS PROHIBITED IN FEDERAL FACILITIES**
> **18 U.S.C. § 930(a)**
>
> Whoever knowingly possesses or causes to be present a firearm or other dangerous weapon in a federal facility (other than a federal court facility), or attempts to do so, shall be fined under this title or imprisoned not more than one year, or both.

Under this statute, a "federal facility" refers to any building or part of a building that is owned or leased by the federal government and is a place where federal employees are regularly present for the purpose of performing their official duties. *See* 18 U.S.C. § 930(g)(1). However, this statute does not apply to "the lawful performance of official duties by an officer, agent, or employee of the United States, a State, or a political subdivision thereof, who is authorized by law to engage in or supervise the prevention, detection, investigation, or prosecution of any violation of law," nor does it apply to federal officials or members of the armed forces who are permitted to possess such a firearm by law, or the lawful carrying of a firearm incident to hunting or "other lawful purposes." 18 U.S.C. § 930(d). This statute does not govern the possession of a firearm in a federal court facility.

2. National parks

> **FIREARMS IN NATIONAL PARKS**
> **16 U.S.C. §1a-7b (2012); 54 U.S.C. § 104906 (2012)**
>
> Federal law allows possession of firearms in national parks and wildlife refuges so long as the person is not otherwise prohibited by law from possessing the firearm, and the possession of the firearm is in compliance with the law of the state in which the national park or wildlife refuge is located.

Recognized license and permit holders are permitted to carry in national parks in states where their license or permit is recognized but not in buildings within the park, such as ranger stations because these are federal buildings. Under federal law, for firearms purposes, all federal parks are subject to the state law of the state in which the park is located. *See* 16 U.S.C. § 1a-7b.

3. VA hospitals: firearms prohibited

> **FIREARMS PROHIBITED AT VETERANS AFFAIRS HOSPITALS**
> **38 CFR § 1.218(a)(13)**
>
> No person while on property shall carry firearms, other dangerous or deadly weapons, or explosives, either openly or concealed, except for official purposes.

One place where many law-abiding license and permit holders fall victim is at the VA Hospital. The VA Hospital system is governed by federal law, which prohibits the carrying of any firearm while on VA property. This includes the parking lot, sidewalks, and any other area which is the property of the VA.

Under federal law, 38 CFR § 1.218(a)(13) states that "no person while on property shall carry firearms, other dangerous or deadly weapons, or explosives, either openly or concealed, except for official purposes." The "official purposes" refers specifically to the VA Hospital police. The area where this specific law gets good people in trouble is that the Department of Veterans Affairs has its own set of laws and guidelines and is not controlled strictly by the Gun Control Act and the general provisions regarding the prohibition of firearms on federal property. The VA law is much more restrictive, and many veterans have found themselves in trouble when they valet-park their vehicles and the valet discovers a handgun in the console, in the door storage area, or lying on the seat in a shoulder or belt holster. How rigidly this law is enforced is determined by the individual hospital administrators as described in 38 CFR § 1.218(a); however, regardless of how strictly the law is enforced, firearms are still prohibited and the VA police are very aggressive in enforcing the law.

4. United States Post Offices: firearms prohibited

FIREARMS PROHIBITED AT POST OFFICES
39 CFR § 232.1(I)

Notwithstanding the provisions of any other law, rule or regulation, no person while on postal property may carry firearms, other dangerous or deadly weapons, or explosives, either openly or concealed, or store the same on postal property, except for official purposes.

Under this regulation, firearms or other deadly weapons are prohibited on postal property, which includes not only the building, but also all property surrounding the building where a post office is located. This includes the parking lot (*e.g.*, a person's vehicle where a firearm may be stored), as well as the sidewalks and walkways. Earlier in this chapter, we mentioned that parking lots, sidewalks, walkways, and other related areas are generally not included when discussing the premises of a location where the carrying of a weapon is prohibited by law. Like the VA Hospital, United States Post Offices are another exception to this rule. In 2013, there was a decision by a United States district court addressing this issue in Colorado which allowed a license holder to bring his firearm into the parking lot of the Avon, Colorado, Post Office. However, in 2015 that case was reversed on appeal by the United States Tenth Circuit Court of Appeals. In 2016, the United States Supreme Court let the Tenth Circuit Court's ruling stand by refusing to review the decision. It should be noted that the United States Tenth Circuit ruling only applies to the states within its jurisdiction, and therefore the district court's initial ruling striking down the U.S. Post Office's rule had no legal bearing on the prohibition against possessing firearms on United States Post Office property in most states.

5. Army Corps of Engineers property: firearms prohibited

> **FIREARMS PROHIBITED AT PARKS, FORESTS, AND PUBLIC PROPERTY OF THE CORPS OF ENGINEERS 36 CFR § 327.13(a)**
>
> The possession of loaded firearms, ammunition, loaded projectile firing devices, bows and arrows, crossbows, or other weapons is prohibited.

Under this regulation, loaded firearms, ammunition, and other projectile firing devices are generally prohibited on U.S. Army Corps of Engineers ("USACE") property. This applies to property owned and managed by the USACE, including bodies of water, but does not include easements or other rights of way that USACE may have near a project site (*e.g.*, private or state-owned shoreline near a USACE lake). Simply put, if the USACE does not own the property in whole, then the prohibition on the possession and carrying of firearms will not apply under this regulation. Unfortunately, these boundaries and ownership are oftentimes unclear. To be safe, be on the lookout for signs prohibiting the possession of these items and contact the office of the USACE project site for clarification. *See* 36 CFR § 327.30(d).

The exception to this general prohibition falls into the hands of USACE "District Commanders." The prohibition against the possession of loaded firearms, ammunition, loaded projectile firing devices, bows and arrows, crossbows, or other weapons does not apply if "written permission has been received from the district commander." Additionally, the following evidence suggests that this exception may be used more often than you would think. *See* 36 CFR § 327.13(a)(4).

On May 14, 2018, the Chief of Operations and Regulatory Division Directorate of Civil Works promulgated a memorandum providing guidance on firearm possession requests. The memorandum explained that the primary consideration in determining whether a request is granted should be based on whether possession would interfere, impede, or disrupt the use of a project, or otherwise impair safety; however, district commanders have complete discretion. As part of the memorandum, an example permission letter was provided with instructions on requirements the District Commander must impose if granting such a request.

If such permission to possess a loaded firearm is granted, district commanders are required to impose the following conditions:
1) possession must be in full compliance with federal, state and local laws and will be revoked upon any violation of law that renders possession of a firearm illegal;
2) the individual must have a state-issued weapons permit, valid (including by reciprocal agreement) in the state where the project is located;
3) the authorization to carry a firearm may only be for carrying it concealed;
4) the authorization must require the individual to carry a copy of the Corps permission letter and the state-issued firearm carry permit at all times while on Corps property, and the individual must be required to present a copy of the documents when requested by a law enforcement or Corps official;
5) the authorization must clearly specify at which Corps projects the authorization applies. The authorization must also specify where on the project the firearm can be carried; and
6) the authorization must specify a definite period of time for which it is valid.

6. Military bases and installations: firearms generally prohibited
Military bases and installations are treated much like the VA Hospital and United States Post Offices in that they have, and are governed by, a separate set of rules and regulations with respect to firearms on the premises of an installation or base and are generally prohibited. Military installations are governed by the federal law under Title 32 of the Code of Federal Regulations. Moreover, the

sections covering the laws governing and relating to military bases and installations are exceedingly numerous. There are, in fact, sections which are dedicated to only certain bases such as 32 CFR § 552.98 which only governs the possessing, carrying, concealing, and transporting of firearms on Fort Stewart/Hunter Army Airfield.

V. TRAVELING ACROSS STATE LINES WITH FIREARMS

Many people vacation and travel outside of their home state. Naturally, no one wants to travel unarmed if they can help it, but, unfortunately, not every state shares the same views on gun ownership. This is especially true in the northeast corner and west coast of the United States. How then does a person pass through states that have restrictive firearms laws? For example, how does a person legally pass through a state that prohibits the possession of a handgun without a license from that state? The answer: Safe Passage legislation.

A. Federal law: qualifying for "Safe Passage"

Traveling across state lines with a firearm means that a person may need to use the provisions of the federal law known as the "Safe Passage" provision. Federal law allows individuals who are legally in possession of firearms in their state (the starting point of traveling) to travel through states that are not as friendly. This protection is only available under federal law to transport such firearms across state lines for lawful purposes, as long as they comply with the requirements of the Firearm Owners Protection Act, 18 U.S.C. § 926A, nicknamed the "Safe Passage" provision. The first requirement to qualify for the federal "Safe Passage" provision is that throughout the duration of the trip through the anti-firearm state, the firearm must be unloaded and locked in the trunk, or locked in a container that is out of reach or not readily accessible from the passenger compartment. The ammunition also must be locked in the trunk or a container. Note that for the storage of both firearms and ammunition, the glove box and center console compartment are specifically not allowed under the statute.

B. "Safe Passage" requires legal start to legal finish

To get protection under federal law, a gun owner's journey must start and end in states where the traveler's possession of the firearm is legal; for instance, a person traveling with their Glock 17 starting in Virginia and ending in Vermont. Even though a person must drive through New York or Massachusetts to get to Vermont, as long as the person qualifies under the "Safe Passage" provision then they may legally pass through. However, if the starting point was Virginia and the ending point was New York (a place where the handgun would be illegal), there is no protection under the federal law. Safe passage requires legal start and legal finish.

Although traveling across state lines naturally invokes federal law, it is important to remember that whenever a person finally completes their journey and reaches their destination state, the laws of that state control the possession, carrying, and use of the firearm. Federal law does not make it legal or provide any protection for possession of a firearm that is illegal under the laws of the destination state (*i.e.*, the end state of your travels).

C. What is the definition of "traveling" for the "Safe Passage" provision?

The final requirement for protection under the federal law is that individuals MUST be "traveling" while in the firearm-hostile state. The legal definition of "traveling" is both murky and narrow. The "Safe Passage" provision protection has been held in courts to be limited to situations that strictly relate to traveling and nothing more. Traveling is a term that is not defined in the federal statute; however, it has received treatment in the courts that is indicative of what one can expect. Generally speaking, if a person stops somewhere for too long they cease to be "traveling" and, therefore, lose their protection under the "Safe Passage" provision. How long this time limit is has not been determined either statutorily or by case law with any definitiveness.

While stopping for gas or restroom breaks may not disqualify a person from the "traveling" protection, any stop for an activity not directly related to traveling could be considered a destination and thus you would lose the legal protection. For example, in Chicago anyone in the city for more than 24 hours is not considered to be traveling under local policy. In an actual case, stopping for a brief nap in a bank parking lot in New Jersey caused a Texan driving back home from Maine to lose the "traveling" protection. *See Reininger v. New Jersey*, No. 14–5486–BRM, 2018 WL 3617962 (D.N.J. July 30, 2018). He received five years in prison for possession of weapons that are illegal under New Jersey law. Of course, if the driver would have made it to Allentown, Pennsylvania, he would have been safe. The moral of the story is to travel through these gun-unfriendly States as fast as you can (without breaking the speed limit, of course)!

D. Protection under federal law does not mean protection from prosecution in unfriendly states

To make matters even worse for firearms travelers, even if a person qualifies for protection under the federal "Safe Passage" provision, New Jersey and New York seem quite proud to treat this protection as an affirmative defense. This means that someone can be arrested even though they met all of the requirements of the federal statute. Then, they would have to go to court to assert this defense. In other words, while a person could beat the rap, they will not beat the ride! This becomes even more troublesome in the instance of someone who is legally flying with their firearm, and then due to flight complications, must land in New Jersey or New York, as travelers in this position have been arrested or threatened with arrest.

Once again, the "Safe Passage" provision only applies while a person is traveling; as soon as they arrive at their destination and cease their travels, the laws of that state control a person's actions. Remember: Check all applicable state firearms laws before you leave for your destination!

A good recommendation is to carry a copy of 18 U.S.C. § 926A of the federal code with you because not all law enforcement officers may be familiar with this law.

VI. AIR TRAVEL WITH A FIREARM

A. How do I legally travel with a firearm as a passenger on a commercial airline?

It is legal to travel with firearms on commercial airlines so long as the firearms transported are unloaded and in a locked, hard-sided container as checked baggage. Under federal law, the container must be completely inaccessible to passengers. Further, under U.S. Homeland Security rules, firearms, ammunition and firearm parts, including firearm frames, receivers, clips, and magazines, are prohibited in carry-on baggage. Finally, "Realistic replicas of firearms are also prohibited in carry-on bags and must be packed in checked baggage. Rifle scopes are permitted in carry-on and checked bags."

Va. Code § 18.2-287.01 states that it is unlawful for any person to possess a firearm inside or transport a firearm into any air carrier airport terminal in Virginia. A violation of this section is a misdemeanor punishable by up to 12 months in jail, a $2,500 fine, and forfeiture of the firearm.

The Virginia Citizens Defense League lists the following as air carrier airports:
- Reagan National;
- Charlottesville Regional;
- Dulles International;
- Lynchburg Municipal;
- Norfolk International;
- Richmond International Richmond;
- Roanoke Regional;
- Shenandoah Valley Regional; and
- Newport News Williamsburg International.

This section shall not apply to law enforcement or to any passenger of an airline who, to the extent otherwise permitted by law, transports a lawful firearm, or ammunition into or out of an air carrier airport terminal for the sole purposes, respectively, of (i) presenting such firearm or ammunition to U.S. Customs agents in advance of an international flight, in order to comply with federal law; (ii) checking such firearm, weapon, or ammunition with his luggage; or (iii) retrieving such firearm or ammunition from the baggage claim area.

1. Firearms must be inaccessible

Federal law makes it a crime subject to fine, imprisonment for up to 10 years, or both, if a person "when on, or attempting to get on, an aircraft in, or intended for operation in, air transportation or intrastate air transportation, has on or about the individual or the property of the individual a concealed dangerous weapon that is or would be accessible to the individual in flight." 49 U.S.C. § 46505(b). Additionally, under 49 U.S.C. § 46303(a) "[a]n individual who, when on, or attempting to board, an aircraft in, or intended for operation in, air transportation or intrastate air transportation, has on or about the individual or the property of the individual a concealed dangerous weapon that is or would be accessible to the individual in flight is liable to the United States Government for a civil penalty of not more than $10,000 for each violation."

2. Firearms must be checked in baggage

The following guidelines are provided by the TSA for traveling with firearms on airlines: You may transport unloaded firearms in a locked hard-sided container as checked baggage only. Declare the firearm and/or ammunition to the airline when checking your bag at the ticket counter. The container must completely secure the firearm from being accessed. Locked cases that can be easily opened are not permitted. Be aware that the container the firearm was in when purchased may not adequately secure the firearm when it is transported in checked baggage.

FIREARMS
- When traveling, comply with the laws concerning possession of firearms as they vary by local, state and international governments.
- If you are traveling internationally with a firearm in checked baggage, please check the U.S. Customs and Border Protection website for information and requirements prior to travel.

- Declare each firearm each time you present it for transport as checked baggage. Ask your airline about limitations or fees that may apply.
- Firearms must be unloaded and locked in a hard-sided container and transported as checked baggage only. As defined by 49 CFR 1540.5, a loaded firearm has a live round of ammunition, or any component thereof, in the chamber or cylinder or in a magazine inserted in the firearm. Only the passenger should retain the key or combination to the lock unless TSA personnel request the key to open the firearm container to ensure compliance with TSA regulations. You may use any brand or type of lock to secure your firearm case, including TSA-recognized locks.
- Firearm parts, including magazines, clips, bolts, and firing pins, are prohibited in carry-on baggage, but may be transported in checked baggage.
- Replica firearms, including firearm replicas that are toys, may be transported in checked baggage only.
- Rifle scopes are permitted in carry-on and checked baggage.

Warning: United States Code, Title 18, Part 1, Chapter 44, firearm definition includes: any weapon (including a starter gun) which will, or is designed to, or may readily be converted to expel a projectile by the action of an explosive; the frame or receiver of any such weapon; any firearm muffler or firearm silencer; and any destructive device. As defined by 49 CFR 1540.5 a loaded firearm has a live round of ammunition, or any component thereof, in the chamber or cylinder or in a magazine inserted in the firearm.

AMMUNITION
- Ammunition is prohibited in carry-on baggage, but may be transported in checked baggage.

- Firearm magazines and ammunition clips, whether loaded or empty, must be securely boxed or included within a hard-sided case containing an unloaded firearm. Read the requirements governing the transport of ammunition in checked baggage as defined by 49 CFR 175.10 (a)(8).
- Small arms ammunition, including ammunition not exceeding .75 caliber and shotgun shells of any gauge, may be carried in the same hard-sided case as the firearm.

Transportation Security Administration. (2021). Transporting Firearms and Ammunition. [online] Available at: https://www.tsa. gov/travel/transporting-firearms-and-ammunition [Accessed 2 February 2021].

B. May I have a firearm while operating or as a passenger in a private aircraft that does not leave the state?
Generally, yes. For purposes of state law, a private aircraft is treated like any other motorized vehicle. For that reason, legal possession is determined on a state-by-state basis. For more information concerning firearms in vehicles, see our earlier discussion in this chapter under Sections II and III.

C. May I have a firearm in a private aircraft that takes off from one state and lands in another?
In situations where a private aircraft is taking off from one state and landing in another, the law will simply view this as traveling interstate with firearms. Where no other statutes apply to the person's flight, the person will be subject to the provisions of 18 U.S.C. § 926A regarding the interstate transportation of a firearm: "any person who is not otherwise prohibited by this chapter from transporting, shipping, or receiving a firearm shall be entitled to

transport a firearm for any lawful purpose from any place where he may lawfully possess and carry such firearm to any other place where he may lawfully possess and carry such firearm if, during such transportation the firearm is unloaded, and neither the firearm nor any ammunition being transported is readily accessible or is directly accessible from the passenger compartment of such transporting vehicle."

This statute allows a person to transport firearms between states subject to the following conditions: The person can lawfully possess the firearm at his or her points of departure and arrival, and the firearm remains unloaded and inaccessible during the trip. However, what if the person holds a handgun license or permit and wants to carry a handgun between states? Fortunately, 18 U.S.C. § 927 states that Section 926A does not preempt applicable state law. Thus, if a person can lawfully carry a weapon in the state in which he or she boards the aircraft and in the state in which he or she lands, the license or permit holder is not subject to the unloaded and inaccessible restrictions of Section 926A, unless, of course, there are stops in more restrictive states.

For operations of private aircraft within one state, a person will only be subject to the laws of the state within which he or she is operating. The person will need to review their state's statutes to determine whether they impose any restrictions on possession of firearms within non-secure areas of airports. The person will also need to be familiar with the airports he or she will be visiting to determine whether each airport has any restrictions (*e.g.*, posting to prohibit carrying a firearm, *etc.*).

PRACTICAL LEGAL TIP

To avoid inadvertently bringing a firearm into an airport, use your range bag as a dedicated range bag, and never put firearms in bags that you use as travel bags.
–Gilbert

VII. FREQUENTLY ASKED QUESTIONS
1. Can I carry my gun in a hospital or polling place?

Virginia has no laws prohibiting firearms in hospitals. However, beginning July 1, 2021, and pursuant to Va. Code § 24.2-604 it is unlawful to knowingly possess a firearm within 40 feet of a building operating as or containing a polling place. This prohibition explicitly does not apply to:

(i) any law-enforcement officer or any retired law-enforcement officer qualified pursuant to subsection C of § 18.2-308.016;

(ii) any person occupying his own private property that falls within 40 feet of a polling place; or

(iii) an armed security officer, licensed pursuant to Article 4 (§ 9.1-138 et seq.) of Chapter 1 of Title 9.1, whose employment or performance of his duties occurs within 40 feet of any building, or part thereof, used as a polling place.

Furthermore, some hospitals are operated by public university institutions or on private property and may have policies that restrict firearms or weapons.

2. Can I keep a loaded handgun in my glove box even if I do not have a CHP?

Yes. Va. Code § 18.2-308(C)(8) states that it is lawful for any person to carry a handgun while in a personal, private motor vehicle that is secured in a container or compartment in the vehicle, provided that person may lawfully possess a firearm.

3. Can I carry my gun into a nightclub or bar?

It depends. An owner of private property may ban firearms from the property. If there is no private property weapons ban, then an individual may open carry a firearm. If a handgun is lawfully being carried concealed by a CHP holder, and there is no private property weapons ban, then the handgun may be lawfully carried while concealed as long as the CHP holder does not consume alcohol. It is important to note that guns and alcohol don't mix.

4. Can I carry my handgun concealed with my CHP to a professional or collegiate sporting event or to an amusement park?

It depends. An owner of private property may ban firearms from the property. A public university or college may also ban open carry and concealed carry by CHP holders at sporting events. Make sure you understand the public university or college firearms policy before you attempt to carry a firearm to a collegiate sporting event. The policy for students and employees is sometimes different than the policy for visitors.

5. Must I tell a police officer that I have a concealed handgun in the car if pulled over for a traffic violation?

No. Va. Code § 18.2-308.01 only requires that you provide your CHP along with proper identification to law enforcement upon demand. However, sometimes it may be wise to advise the police officer of a firearm being in the vehicle for safety reasons. It is important to note that the CHP files are linked to the Department of Motor Vehicles database; thus, an alert police officer may be aware of a possible firearm being in the vehicle during the traffic stop. If the police officer locates a firearm during the traffic stop, then expect a brief investigation into the lawfulness of your firearm possession before being released from the traffic stop.

6. Can I carry my handgun while in a local county or city park?
Possibly. While Virginia law does not outright ban possession of firearms in local, county, or city parks, Va. Code § 15.2-915 allows local government to regulate firearms "in any public park owned or operated by the locality, or by any authority or local governmental entity created or controlled by the locality, or in any recreation or community center facility operated by the locality, or by any authority or local governmental entity created or controlled by the locality."

7. May I keep a handgun in my vehicle if there are children in the vehicle?
Firearm safety is very important, especially when children are involved. However, there is no simple answer to this question. The answer will depend on various circumstances. Va. Code § 18.2-56.2 states that it is unlawful for any person to recklessly leave a loaded, unsecured firearm in such a manner as to endanger the life or limb of any child under 14 years old. Additionally, it is also unlawful for any person to knowingly authorize a child under 12 years of age to use a firearm except when the child is under the supervision of an adult.

8. May I travel with a firearm in the cabin of a private aircraft?
It depends. First, it is important to note that an "air carrier terminal" as defined in Va. Code §18.2-287.01 usually refers to a commercial airport with commercial airlines, not to airports that engage in general aviation with non-commercial private aircraft. Nevertheless, private pilots and their passengers typically access the aircraft in or near the hanger and never enter a terminal. Confirm with your airports to make sure you are not in violation. Second, the law of open carry and concealed carry with or without a CHP would apply if traveling in Virginia.

> CHAPTER FOURTEEN ◄

RESTORATION OF FIREARMS RIGHTS: THE LAW OF PARDONS AND EXPUNGEMENTS

I. IS IT POSSIBLE TO RESTORE A PERSON'S RIGHT TO BEAR ARMS?

What happens after a person has been convicted of a crime, and is it possible to later clear their name and/or criminal record? If possible, then what is the process for removing a conviction and restoring a person's right to purchase and possess firearms? This chapter will explain how a person under very limited circumstances can have arrest records, criminal charges, and even criminal convictions removed or nullified. But a word of caution: Success in this arena may be rare. Further, each state has different rules concerning these issues, as well as a completely different set of rules under federal law. Before we begin a meaningful discussion, it is important to explain two terms and concepts: clemency and expunction. A small point about terminology: Many states use the word "expunction" and federal law uses the word "expungement" to refer to the same process; therefore these words are usually used interchangeably.

A. What is clemency?

Clemency is the action the government, usually the chief executive (*e.g.*, the president on the federal level or a governor on the state level), takes in forgiving or pardoning a crime or canceling the penalty of a crime, either wholly or in part. Clemency can include: full pardons after a conviction, full pardons after completion of deferred adjudication community supervision, conditional pardons, pardons based on innocence, commutations of a sentence, emergency medical reprieves, and family medical reprieves. Clemency can be granted at both the federal and state level.

B. What is an expunction?

An expunction is the physical act of destroying or purging government criminal records, unlike sealing which is simply hiding the records from the public. Under certain circumstances, a person may have their criminal record either expunged or sealed.

PRACTICAL LEGAL TIP

While our intention is to provide you with as much information as possible as to how you can have your firearms rights restored if you are convicted of a crime, it's also important to make sure you are aware of how rarely pardons, expunctions, and restorations of firearms rights are granted. While it's certainly worth the effort to apply for a pardon in the event you receive one, be careful not to get your hopes up, because pardons are seldom granted.
– Gilbert

II. FEDERAL LAW

A. Presidential pardon

Under Article II, Section 2 of the U.S. Constitution, the president of the United States has the power "to grant reprieves and pardons for offenses against the United States, except in cases of impeachment." The president's power to pardon offenses has also been interpreted to include the power to grant conditional pardons, commutations of sentences, conditional commutations of sentences, remission of fines and forfeitures, respites, and amnesties. However, the president's clemency authority only extends to federal offenses; the president cannot grant clemency for a state crime.

1. How does a person petition for federal clemency or a pardon?

Under federal law, a person requesting executive clemency must petition the president of the United States and submit the petition to the Office of the Pardon Attorney in the Department of Justice. The Office of the Pardon Attorney can provide petitions and other required forms necessary to complete the application for clemency. *See* 28 CFR § 1.1. Petition forms for commutation of sentence may also be obtained from the wardens of federal penal institutions. In addition, a petitioner applying for executive clemency with respect to military offenses should submit his or her petition directly to the Secretary of the military branch that had original jurisdiction over the court-martial trial and conviction of the petitioner.

The Code of Federal Regulations requires an applicant to wait five years after the date of the release of the petitioner from confinement, or in a case where no prison sentence was imposed, an applicant is required to wait five years after the date of conviction prior to submitting a petition for clemency. The regulation further states that "generally, no petition should be submitted by a person who is on probation, parole, or supervised release." 28 CFR § 1.2. With that in mind, the president can grant clemency at any time, whether an individual has made a formal petition or not. For example, President Gerald Ford granted a full and unconditional pardon to former President Richard Nixon prior to any indictment or charges being filed related to his involvement in Watergate.

2. What should a petition for clemency include?

Petitions for executive clemency should include the information required in the form prescribed by the United States Attorney General. This includes information:

1) that the person requesting clemency must state specifically the purpose for which clemency is sought, as well as attach any and all relevant documentary evidence that will show how clemency will support that purpose;
2) that discloses any arrests or convictions subsequent to the federal crime for which clemency is sought;

3) that discloses all delinquent credit obligations (whether disputed or not), all civil lawsuits to which the applicant is a party (whether plaintiff or defendant), and all unpaid tax obligations (whether local, state, or federal); and
4) that includes three character affidavits from persons not related to the applicant by blood or marriage.

In addition, acceptance of a presidential pardon generally carries with it an admission of guilt. For that reason, a petitioner should include in his or her petition a statement of the petitioner's acceptance of responsibility, an expression of remorse, and atonement for the offense. All of the requirements are contained in 28 CFR §§ 1.1-1.11.

3. What happens after a petition for executive clemency is submitted?

All petitions for federal clemency are reviewed by the Office of the Pardon Attorney in the Department of Justice. A non-binding recommendation on an application is made to the president. Federal regulations also provide for guidelines and requirements to notify victims of the crimes, if any, for which clemency is sought. The president will either grant or deny a pardon. There are no hearings held on the petition, and there is no appeal of the president's decision.

4. What is the effect of a presidential pardon?

A pardon is the forgiveness of a crime and the cancellation of the penalty associated with that crime. While a presidential pardon will restore various rights lost as a result of the pardoned offense, it will not expunge the record of your conviction. This means that even if a person is granted a pardon, the person must still disclose their conviction on any form where such information is required, although the person may also disclose the fact that the offense for which they were convicted was pardoned.

B. Expungement of federal convictions
1. No law exists for general federal expungement
Congress has not provided federal legislation that offers any comprehensive authority or procedure for expunging criminal offenses. There exist only statutes that allow expungement in certain cases for possession of small amounts of controlled substances and, interestingly, a procedure to expunge DNA samples of certain members of the military who were wrongfully convicted. Because there is no statutory guidance, federal courts have literally made up the rules and procedures themselves, often coming to different conclusions. Some federal court circuits have stated they have no power to expunge records. However, other federal courts have indicated that they do have the power to expunge. For example, the federal Fifth Circuit has held that under certain limited circumstances, federal courts may order expungement both of records held by other branches of the government (*e.g.*, executive branch), and its own court records. *See Sealed Appellant v. Sealed Appellee*, 130 F.3d 695 (5th Cir. 1997). The Supreme Court has passed on hearing cases that would have resolved the split between the circuits. This issue remains legally murky.

2. Possible procedure for federal expungement
There are no statutory guidelines for how to seek an expungement under federal law; however, the place to start would be to file a motion with the federal court that issued the conviction a person wants to have expunged. However, federal judges very rarely grant these types of motions. Some circuits have adopted a balancing test

to decide if a record held by the court may be expunged. The court weighs the interests of the government in keeping open, unredacted records against the injury to the individual of maintaining a criminal record. The same court, however, has acknowledged that "expungement is 'exceedingly narrow' and is granted only in exceptional circumstances." The court explained, "the government cannot and should not be forced to rewrite history" every time a wrongfully accused wants his record expunged. *Sealed Appellant v. Sealed Appellee*, 130 F.3d 695 (5th Cir. 1997). Some of the areas where expungement has worked are in incidents of extreme police misconduct, or where the conviction is being misused against the person. Unless there exist compelling reasons, a federal judge is highly unlikely to grant expungement.

3. Expungement for drug possession: statutory authority
Under a federal law entitled "Special probation and expungement procedures for drug possessors," certain persons are allowed to request a federal court to issue an expungement order from all public records. 18 U.S.C. § 3607. Congress intended this order to restore the person to the status he or she "occupied before such arrest or institution of criminal proceedings." 18 U.S.C. § 3607(c). In order to qualify for the expungement, you must have been under the age of 21 when you were convicted, you must have no prior drug offenses, and your conviction must have been for simple possession of a small amount of a controlled substance.

4. How does a person have firearms rights restored under federal law?
Under the Gun Control Act of 1968, a person who has received a Presidential pardon is not considered convicted of a crime preventing the purchase and possession of firearms subject to all

other federal laws. *See* 18 U.S.C. §§ 921(a)(20)(B) and (a)(33)(B)(ii). In addition, persons who had a conviction expunged or set aside, or who have had their civil rights restored, are not considered to have been convicted for purposes of the GCA "unless the pardon, expungement, or restoration of civil rights expressly provides the person may not ship, transport, possess, or receive firearms." 18 U.S.C. §§ 921(a)(20)(B) and (a)(33)(B)(ii).

The GCA also provides the United States Attorney General with the authority to grant relief from firearms disabilities where the Attorney General determines that the person is not likely to act in a manner dangerous to the public safety and where granting relief would not be contrary to the public interest. 18 U.S.C. § 925(c). The Attorney General has delegated this authority to the ATF. Unfortunately, the ATF reports that it has been prohibited from spending any funds in order to investigate or act upon applications from individuals seeking relief from federal firearms disabilities. This means that until the ATF's prohibition has been lifted, a person's best—and most likely—option to have their firearms rights restored is through a Presidential pardon. *See* www.atf.gov.

III. VIRGINIA LAW

How an individual will restore his right to purchase, possess, or transport a firearm will depend on how the right to purchase, possess, or transport a firearm was lost in the first place. As we discussed in Chapter 6, it is unlawful to purchase, possess, or transport a firearm as follows, if an individual:

- Was convicted of a felony;
- Was convicted of any misdemeanor crime of domestic violence;

- Was adjudicated delinquent of an offense which would be a felony if committed by an adult;
- Was either acquitted of a felony or certain Class 1 and Class 2 misdemeanors as outlined in Va. Code § 18.2-308.1:1 by reason of insanity and committed to the custody of the Commissioner of Behavioral Health and Developmental Services;
- Was adjudicated incompetent or incapacitated; or,
- Was involuntarily admitted to a facility or ordered to mandatory outpatient treatment or who was the subject of a temporary detention order and subsequently agreed to voluntary admission as outlined in Va. Code § 18.2-308.1:3.

An individual adjudicated delinquent as a juvenile of an offense which would be a felony if committed by an adult who has served for at least two years in the U.S. Armed Forces, and received an honorable discharge if no longer serving, is not required to seek a pardon because they are not prohibited from possessing a firearm or ammunition pursuant to Va. Code § 18.2-308.2(A).

Individuals serving in law enforcement, the Armed Forces of the United States, the National Guard of Virginia or of any other state who would otherwise not be permitted to possess or transport a firearm or ammunition are not required to petition the circuit court for restoration or seek a pardon from the governor if their possession or transportation of a firearm or ammunition is in the performance of their duties.

If a felony conviction from another state disqualified an individual from possessing or transporting a firearm, but that other state restored that individual's firearm rights, then that individual does not need to also have firearm rights restored in Virginia.

A. Petition the court

1. Criminal convictions

In cases involving a felony conviction or a juvenile's adjudication of delinquency for an offense which would have been a felony if committed by an adult, the governor must first restore the individual's civil rights before a petition to restore firearm rights can be filed with the circuit court. Virginia residents file their petition in the circuit court where they reside, and non-residents file their petition in the circuit court where they were last convicted.

The circuit court shall conduct a hearing if requested. The circuit court may, in its discretion and for good cause shown, grant such petition and issue a permit that would allow the convicted felon or adjudicated delinquent the right to possess, transport, or carry a firearm or ammunition. The statute does not state specific factors for the circuit court to consider, but the circuit court "may" grant the petition for "good cause shown." There is no statutory time limit on when one may apply to restore their rights after serving a sentence, but courts understandably seem to be more lenient with the restoration of rights after substantial time has passed since the underlying conviction without the applicant finding themselves in any other criminal trouble.

2. Insanity, incompetence, incapacitation, treatment

The following individuals can petition the general district court in the city or county in which they reside to restore firearm rights:

- Any individual acquitted of a criminal offense by reason of insanity upon discharge from custody;
- Any individual whose competency or capacity has been restored; or

- Any individual following release from involuntary admission to a facility, or release from an order of mandatory outpatient treatment, or release from a voluntary admission following a temporary detention order.

The general district court shall conduct a hearing if requested. Any individual denied relief by the general district court may petition the circuit court for a *de novo* review of the denial. There is not a time limit on when the application for restoration of rights may be completed, and in fact one may petition the court for restoration immediately following release from a facility after an involuntary commitment. While each case is evaluated based on the specific facts surrounding it, the prevailing wisdom is that allowing substantial time to pass without issues after release from an involuntary commitment is critical to a successful petition to restore firearm rights.

It is important to recognize that pursuant to 18.2-308.1:3 that even someone who appeals an involuntary commitment and prevails on appeal will still be prohibited from possessing firearms. Such a prohibition will continue unless and until a restoration of firearms rights is granted in general district court.

B. Governor pardon

Virginia governors only consider pardons for exceptional situations because they are reluctant to substitute their judgment for that of the courts. However, any individual may submit a petition for a pardon, but such petition must provide substantial evidence of such exceptional circumstances in order to justify a pardon. All petitions for a pardon are processed by the Secretary of the Commonwealth and require a Virginia Pardon Petition Questionnaire.

A governor's pardon is not necessarily a victory for the individual applicant's restoration of firearm rights because the governor may expressly place conditions upon the reinstatement of the person's right to ship, transport, possess, or receive firearms.

There are three types of governor pardons: simple, conditional, and absolute:

1. A simple pardon is a statement of official forgiveness. It does not expunge or remove a criminal conviction from the record, but it often serves as a means for the petitioner to advance in employment, education, and self-esteem;
2. A conditional or medical pardon is available only to people who are currently incarcerated. It is usually granted for early release and involves certain conditions. There must be extraordinary circumstances for an inmate to be considered for such a pardon; and
3. An absolute pardon is rarely granted because it is based on the belief that the petitioner was unjustly convicted and is innocent. An absolute pardon is the only form of executive clemency that would allow for a petition to the circuit court to have the underlying conviction expunged or removed from both the criminal record and public record.

If the petition is denied, then the petitioner has no right of appeal but may reapply after a two-year period.

An individual convicted of a Virginia misdemeanor domestic violence offense cannot possess a firearm according to federal law. This is an instance where a state conviction has triggered a loss of firearm rights under federal law. Such an individual cannot petition a Virginia circuit court for restoration of firearm rights according to Va. Code § 18.2-308.2(C). Such an individual cannot be pardoned by the President of the United States. The only remedy for such an individual would be a pardon from the governor.

C. Expungement of a Virginia criminal case

Criminal convictions in Virginia can be expunged only in certain scenarios. Not every state allows expungement. If you were convicted in a state other than Virginia, you must consult the state where the conviction occurred to determine eligibility. The following instances allow for a Virginia expungement:

- Individuals who have been found innocent of the alleged offense;
- Individuals whose criminal cases were later dropped, not prosecuted, nolle prosequi by the Commonwealth Attorney, or were otherwise disposed of without a finding of guilt; or
- Individuals who were granted an absolute pardon by the governor.

In addition, Virginia allows for "sealing" of public records in certain scenarios. Sealing prevents the public from seeing certain low level felony and misdemeanor convictions. To be eligible for "sealing" under Virginia law, you must have been conviction free for a number of years (the exact number depends on the offense which you wish to have sealed), and have never been convicted of a Class 1 or Class 2 felony. Virginia Code § 19.2-392.12.

A petition to expunge the criminal record is filed in the circuit court that disposed of the case.

> CHAPTER FIFTEEN ◄

I'M BEING SUED FOR WHAT? CIVIL LIABILITY IF YOU HAVE USED YOUR GUN

I. WHAT DOES IT MEAN TO BE SUED?

The term "lawsuit" refers to one party's assertion in a written filing with a court that another party has violated the law. In the context of firearms, typically the party suing has been injured and wants a ruling or judgment from the court stating that the party was injured and entitling the party to money.

It is important to note that an individual's irresponsible or wrongful conduct can result in both criminal liability and civil liability. In general, civil liability differs from criminal liability in that a civil wrong does not subject the responsible or liable party to incarceration or punishment for a crime. The so-called trial of the century involving O.J. Simpson is a prime example. Mr. Simpson was arrested for murder and prosecuted criminally, but was found not to be criminally liable or found to be not guilty of the crimes alleged because the jury believed that the prosecution did not prove its case "beyond a reasonable doubt." However, Mr. Simpson was later sued civilly for wrongful death. The civil jury found him to be civilly liable for his wrongful actions by the "preponderance of the evidence" and awarded money damages to the plaintiffs. "Beyond a reasonable doubt" and "preponderance of the evidence" are the standards of proof that determine criminal liability and civil liability, respectively.

A. What is a civil claim or lawsuit?

A civil "lawsuit" or "suit" refers to the actual filing of written paperwork with a court (1) asserting that another party violated the law, and (2) seeking some type of redress. A "claim" can exist without the filing of a lawsuit. A claim is simply the belief or assertion that another party has violated the law. Many parties have claims they never assert, or sometimes parties informally assert the claim in hopes of resolving the disputes without the filing of a lawsuit. Also, another term commonly used is "tort" or "tort claim." A tort is a civil claim arising out of a wrongful act, not including a breach of contract or trust that results in injury to another's person, property, reputation, or the like. The claims described below are all tort claims.

B. Criminal liability versus civil liability

Criminal liability is the responsibility for a crime or an offense against the state. An individual will be criminally liable for a crime if the prosecution proves beyond a reasonable doubt that the individual commited the alleged criminal act with the required intent. Criminal liabilty and the use of a firearm for self-defense was discussed in Chapter 7. Justifiable and excusable self-defense negate criminal liability.

A criminal prosecution is an action brought by the government to punish an individual for committing a crime against the public or the state, and to deter others from committing similar crimes. The public policy is that a violation of any criminal law harms the public in general and not just a particular person or victim. Therefore, it is the government's job and not the individual victim's job to prosecute a criminal case. The victim will of course always be a key witness to the prosecution's case. The lawyer for the government is called the prosecutor and the individual alleged to have committed the crime is called the defendant. Penalties for criminal liabilty may include a criminal conviction, incarceration, court fines, and victim restitution. Restitution in the criminal justice system means payment by the defendant to the victim for the harm caused by the defendant's wrongful acts. Courts have the authority to order the convicted defendant to pay restitution to the victim as part of their sentence.

A civil lawsuit may be filed by any individual, corporation, or trust. The person or entity that files the civil lawsuit with the court is called the plaintiff. The plaintiff, or his lawyer, prosecutes a civil lawsuit against the defendant. The government can also initiate a civil lawsuit. For example, if an individual were to shoot a county propane tank and cause a fire, then the county could sue that individual civilly to recover for those damages. The party being sued is called the defendant. However, the defendant is permitted to file either cross-claims or counterclaims against the plaintiff. There is no criminal prosecutor in a civil case and there are no criminal penalites associated with a civil lawsuit.

C. Standards of proof

The level of certainty and the degree of evidence necessary to establish proof in either a criminal case or a civil lawsuit is referred to as the standard of proof. In a criminal case, the standard of proof is "beyond a reasonable doubt." This is the highest standard of proof that must be met in any trial. The prosecution's evidence in a criminal case must prove the defendant's guilt beyond a reasonable doubt such that no other logical explanation can be derived from the facts except that the defendant committed the alleged crime. If there is any reasonable uncertainty of guilt based on the evidence presented, then the defendant cannot be convicted. Legal authorities who venture to assign a numerical value to "beyond a reasonable doubt" place it in the certainty range of 98 or 99 percent.

In a civil lawsuit, the standard of proof is "preponderance of the evidence." A preponderance of the evidence is a much lower standard than the criminal standard of beyond a reasonable doubt. Legal authorities who venture to assign a numerical value to a "preponderance of the evidence" place it in the certainty range of as little as 51 percent. This means that the party who presents the greater weight of credible evidence or whose evidence demonstrates that something "more likely occurred than not" will prevail. It does not mean the party with the most exhibits or greater number of witnesses will prevail. One highly credible witness can prevail over the testimony of a dozen biased, shady witnesses.

EXAMPLE:

John mistakes a utility meter reader in the back alley of his Northern Virginia condo for a burglar. The meter reader has a disheveled appearance, a tool bag, and looks to be snooping around John's condo. John fires a shot without warning and injures the meter reader.

Possible criminal liability: Virginia prosecutors could bring various criminal charges against John for his shooting and injuring the meter reader. Any criminal case would have to be proved "beyond a reasonable doubt." A conviction could trigger imprisonment, a fine, and/or restitution to the meter reader for the injuries sustained.

Possible civil liability: The meter reader could file a civil lawsuit against John alleging that John was responsible for the harm caused and damages suffered due to his civil wrong. The meter reader would be required to prove his civil lawsuit allegations by a "preponderance of the evidence." A civil lawsuit could be filed whether or not there was a criminal case.

PRACTICAL LEGAL TIP

Because civil cases require a much lower standard of proof than criminal cases, there are often situations where criminal charges are not brought, but an individual is still sued for their actions. –Gilbert

D. Parallel proceedings

As a general rule, parallel proceedings is a term that can refer to two actions, one civil and one criminal, both arising out of the same set of facts that proceed either simultaneously or successively against the same party.

> **EXAMPLE:**
>
> Phil and Jeremy become involved in a road-rage incident, and a physical altercation follows. Phil shoots and wounds Jeremy. Can Phil be criminally prosecuted by the government and sued civilly by Jeremy at the same time?

Yes. Virginia criminal prosecutions and civil cases arising out of the same set of facts can proceed simultaneously, although it is rare. Typically, the Virginia criminal prosecution proceeds first and the civil case, if one is filed at all, is filed after the criminal case is finalized. However, there is no bar to pursuing a civil action during a pending criminal prosecution.

> **EXAMPLE:**
>
> Phil and Jeremy become involved in a road-rage incident, and a physical altercation follows. Phil shoots and wounds Jeremy. Phil is criminally prosecuted by the government for assaulting Jeremy. Phil pleads not guilty, but is convicted for assaulting Jeremy. After the criminal case, Jeremy sues Phil civilly for his injuries in an attempt to collect monetary damages. Can Phil's guilty verdict be used as evidence in the civil trial?

No. In Virginia, a criminal verdict of either guilt or innocence cannot be used as evidence in a later civil trial. However, Phil's plea in the criminal case and any statements or testimony he made about the incident could be used in the civil trial.

> **EXAMPLE:**
>
> Phil and Jeremy become involved in a road-rage incident, and a physical altercation follows. Phil shoots and wounds Jeremy. Phil is arrested and criminally prosecuted for assaulting Jeremy. Phil pleads guilty.

Phil's admission of guilt by way of his guilty plea may be used as evidence to prove liability in a later civil action brought by Jeremy.

Caution: The primary area where a civil case can impact a criminal case and vice versa is the potential for overlapping use of evidence and testimony. A party's statement, or under oath admission, in one case can almost always be used in the other case.

E. *Res Judicata* and collateral estoppel

Res judicata is Latin for the legal doctrine that bars "claims" that have been previously finally adjudicated by a trial court from being pursued further by the same parties in a subsequent trial court. *Collateral estoppel* is the doctrine that bars "issues" that have been finally adjudicated by a trial court from being further pursued by the same parties in a subsequent trial court. However, the truth of any facts or disposition determined in a previous criminal trial are neither admissible in a subsequent civil trial nor does it bar a later civil trial. In layman's terms, the government and the civil plaintiff are not the same "person," which is why two legal actions, one civil and one criminal, against the same defendant for actions arising from the same act are permissible.

Note: An appeal from a trial court to an appellate court neither violates the doctrine of res judicata nor the doctrine of collateral estoppel. The purpose of the appellate court is to review the prior trial and to determine if the trial court correctly applied the law.

F. Red flag laws

Starting July 1, 2020, Virginia has an emergency substantial risk order and substantial risk order law (commonly called red flag laws), which allow for the confiscation of firearms from someone whom the courts deem to be an immediate threat to themselves or others.

The law provides that an attorney for the Commonwealth or law-enforcement officer may petition a magistrate or a circuit court, general district court, or juvenile and domestic relations district court judge to issue an emergency substantial risk order. If the judge or magistrate finds that there is probable cause to believe that a person poses a substantial risk of personal injury to himself or others in the near future by such person's possession or acquisition of a firearm, the judge will issue an *ex parte* emergency substantial risk order.

When such an order is issued, it prohibits the person who is subject to the order from purchasing, possessing, or transporting a firearm for the duration of the order. In determining whether probable cause for the issuance of an order exists, the judge or magistrate considers any relevant evidence, including any recent act of violence, force, or threat as defined in § 19.2-152.7:1 by such person directed toward another person or toward himself. No petition should be filed unless an independent investigation has been conducted by law enforcement that determines that grounds for the petition exist.

If an order is issued, it should contain a statement (i) informing the person who is subject to the order of the requirements and penalties under § 18.2-308.1:6, including that it is unlawful for such person to purchase, possess, or transport a firearm for the duration of the order and that such person is required to surrender his concealed handgun permit if he possesses such permit, and (ii) advising such person to voluntarily relinquish any firearm within his custody to the law-enforcement agency that serves the order.

Upon service of an emergency substantial risk order, the person who is subject to the order is given the opportunity to voluntarily relinquish any firearms in his possession. The law-enforcement agency that executed the emergency substantial risk order shall take custody of all firearms that are voluntarily relinquished by such person. The law-enforcement agency that takes into custody a firearm pursuant to the order shall prepare a written receipt containing the name of the person who is subject to the order and the manufacturer, model, condition, and serial number of the firearm and shall provide a copy thereof to such person. Nothing in the subsection precludes a law-enforcement officer from later obtaining a search warrant for any firearms if the law-enforcement officer has reason to believe that the person who is subject to an emergency substantial risk order has not relinquished all firearms in his possession.

The emergency order is effective for 14 days after it is issued but may be extended by a subsequent substantial risk-order hearing.

Because these orders are issued *ex parte*, they are issued without you ever having the opportunity to defend yourself against the allegations forming the basis for the order prior to your weapons being seized. Only subsequent to the seizure will an individual subject to the order be able to defend themselves in court. Any hearing challenging the emergency substantial risk order will follow the civil rules of procedure. The person subject to the order may be represented by counsel but will have no right to counsel. This means that while the state will be represented by the Commonwealth Attorney's office, you must retain private counsel in order to have an attorney present.

II. WHAT MIGHT YOU BE SUED FOR? GUN-RELATED CLAIMS IN CIVIL COURTS

Civil liability involving a firearm can occur as the result of either an intentional, unintentional, or accidental shooting. A wrongful shooting that creates civil liability due to either an intentional or unintentional wrongful act is commonly referred to as a tort. A tort is nothing more than a civil wrong.

An intentional tort is a category of torts that results from an intentional, purposeful, and/or deliberate wrongful act. There is no requirement that the wrongful act be done with either a hostile intent or a desire to do serious harm. An unintentional or accidental shooting due to carelessness is called a negligent tort.

A. Intentional torts

An intentional tort that results in an injury after the use of a firearm may range from a minor assault to a wrongful death. An assault is an act intended to cause either harmful or offensive contact with another person or apprehension of such contact that creates a reasonable apprehension of an imminent battery in another person's mind. A battery is an unwanted touching that is neither consented to, excused, nor justified. There are many instances where the law-abiding gun owner's use of a firearm can be classified as an intentional tort of assault and battery. However, it is important to note that justified self-defense negates civil liability due to intentional tort allegations. Caution: Intentional tort conduct that creates civil liability may also be a crime.

EXAMPLE:

Bill is driving through an unfamiliar part of downtown Richmond and comes to a stop at a red light. Martha is standing next to his passenger window at the traffic light screaming that he cut her off in traffic, but taking no action to indicate she intends to harm Bill or do anything besides verbally lodge her complaints. In response, Bill points his gun at Martha, says, "You're dead!" and fires his gun but misses.

Bill has likely committed an intentional tort of civil assault. Bill may also face a criminal prosecution. He knowingly threatened Martha with imminent bodily injury with no legal justification.

EXAMPLE:

Bill is driving through an unfamiliar part of downtown Richmond and comes to a stop at a red light. Martha is standing next to his passenger window at the traffic light screaming that he cut her off in traffic, but taking no action to indicate she intends to harm Bill or do anything besides verbally lodge her complaints. A startled Bill fires a shot at Martha to make her go away and hits her in the leg.

Bill has likely committed an intentional tort of assault and battery. Bill may also face a criminal prosecution. He intended to and did cause serious bodily injury to Martha with no legal justification. Therefore, a civil jury would likely find Bill liable and financially responsible for Martha's injuries.

> **EXAMPLE:**
>
> Bill is driving through an unfamiliar part of downtown Richmond and comes to a stop at a red light. Martha is standing next to his passenger window at the traffic light screaming that he cut her off in traffic, but taking no action to indicate she intends to harm Bill or do anything besides verbally lodge her complaints. A startled Bill fires a shot at Martha to make her go away, but Martha is hit in the head and dies.

Martha's heirs or surviving family members will be able to bring a wrongful death civil lawsuit against Bill for his intentional tort of battery that killed Martha. Bill will also likely face a criminal prosecution for killing Martha. In Virginia, an individual is civilly liable for his wrongful acts if they caused an individual's death.

> **EXAMPLE:**
>
> Emily fears she is about to be attacked in a grocery store parking lot by Randall. Randall follows her step-by-step through the parking lot and stops right next to Emily's car. Emily draws her .380, points it directly at Randall and tells him to "stay right there while I call the police." Randall does not move. Emily keeps the gun pointed at Randall until the police arrive. When the police arrive, they determine that Randall was an out-of-uniform grocery store employee tasked with rounding up the grocery carts in the parking lot and was no threat to Emily.

Emily has likely committed an intentional tort of false imprisonment when she held Randall at gunpoint. Emily may also be criminally prosecuted. False imprisonment occurs when an individual is detained or restrained without consent by another, and without the legal right to do so.

B. Negligence

An unintentional or negligent tort is called negligence. Negligence is the legal term for careless behavior that causes or contributes to an accident. In the context of firearms, an individual has a duty to exercise reasonable or ordinary care with their firearms. However, reasonable or ordinary care is a relative term and varies with the nature and character of the situation to which it is applied. There are various types of firearm discharges that could create civil liability due to the law abiding gun owner's negligence. Hunting accidents, cleaning accidents, and the mishandling of a gun are common events associated with a civil liability negligence lawsuit. It is important to note that the mere discharge of a firearm is not automatically negligent. The amount or degree of diligence and caution which is necessary to constitute reasonable or ordinary care depends upon the circumstances and the particular surroundings of each specific case, which is ultimately decided by the judge or jury if there is a dispute. The test is that degree of care which an ordinarily prudent person would exercise under the same or similar circumstances to avoid injury to another. An individual may be considered negligent and civilly liable whenever he had a duty to act carefully and failed to do so.

In Virginia, there are three levels of negligence. The first level, sometimes called "simple negligence," was just described above. The second level is "gross negligence." The difference between simple negligence and gross negligence is one of degree. However, gross negligence is not typically relevant to a civil lawsuit alleging negligent use of a firearm unless there is a special legal relationship. The third level of negligence is "willful and wanton negligence," which is conduct defined as acting consciously in disregard of another person's rights or acting with reckless indifference to the consequences, with the defendant aware, from his knowledge of existing circumstances and conditions, that his conduct probably would cause injury to another. If the plaintiff establishes willful and wanton negligence, then the plaintiff may be entitled to an additional monetary award not available in simple negligence cases.

EXAMPLE:

Jessica has practiced her target shooting at a private range on her country property in Southwest Virginia for 20 years without incident. Jessica shoots toward an area where she has never seen another person, and she believes the range of her guns cannot reach her property line. One day, a neighbor is hit by a shot and injured as he is strolling through the woods just along the other side of Jessica's property. The neighbor later files a civil lawsuit against Jessica for his injuries.

Jessica might be civilly liable for simple negligence if a jury determines that a reasonably prudent person would have acted differently, tested the range of her guns, or built a different type of backstop or berm, *etc.*

EXAMPLE:

Jessica has received several complaints over the years about bullets leaving her property from the private shooting range and hitting her neighbor's property. She received other reports that neighbors often walked in the area. Nevertheless, Jessica ignores the complaints and continues her target practice as usual. One day while target shooting, her bullet leaves her property and hits her neighbor, causing an injury. The neighbor files a civil lawsuit against Jessica for the injuries.

Jessica may very well be civilly liable for willful and wanton negligence if the jury finds she consciously disregarded another person's rights or was acting with reckless indifference to the consequences, being aware, from her knowledge of existing circumstances and conditions, that her conduct would probably cause injury to another. She continued to shoot in the same area without taking any safety measures such as building a backstop or berm after she was advised multiple times that her shots were reaching the neighbor's property and that there were people in the same area.

> **EXAMPLE:**
> Jessica's shot killed the neighbor. The neighbor's surviving family members or heirs file a civil lawsuit against Jessica for wrongful death.

Jessica did not intend to shoot anyone, but if the jury hearing the case believed that the killing was due to her negligence, then she may be liable for damages causes by the neighbor's wrongful death.

C. Negligent entrustment

Civil liability under the doctrine of negligent entrustment requires that the owner of the firearm used to inflict the injury knew, or had reasonable cause to know, that he was entrusting the firearm to a third person who was likely to use it in a manner that would cause injury to others.

EXAMPLE:

Steve lost his way in Craig County and drove his car onto property belonging to Betty and Frank. Frank fired a rifle at Steve's vehicle and injured Steve when a bullet fragment grazed his head. Betty had previously received the rifle that Frank used from her grandfather five years before the incident of Frank shooting Steve. Betty placed the rifle with other possessions upon receiving it and never touched it thereafter. Betty was not present when Frank fired the rifle at Steve. Frank was prohibited from possessing a firearm due to an incident 10 years earlier that resulted in a felony conviction. Betty knew about Frank's prior incident and conviction, but never instructed Frank not to use the rifle and did not keep the rifle in a manner which would prevent Frank from having access to it. There was no evidence that Betty ever either permitted Frank to use the rifle or prohibited him from doing so. Frank had a previous altercation with trespassers, but no firearms were involved in that incident. Steve files a civil lawsuit against Betty, the owner of the rifle, for negligent entrustment of a firearm.

Did Betty negligently entrust her rifle to Frank? Will Betty be civilly liable to Steve in his negligent entrustment of a firearm lawsuit? The answer to both of these questions is no. Betty did not negligently entrust her firearm to Frank and will not be civilly liable to Steve for negligent entrustment of a firearm according to the Supreme Court of Virginia.

Negligent entrustment cases require evidence of express permission, evidence of a pattern of conduct supporting implied permission, or evidence of knowledge that the firearm would be used notwithstanding explicit instructions to the contrary.

In this example, the evidence that Betty "entrusted" the rifle to Frank is insufficient. There is no evidence that Betty expressly permitted Frank to use the rifle. There is no affirmative act or pattern of action establishing implied permission. Nor is the evidence sufficient to show that Betty knew, or should have known, that regardless of her actions, if Frank had access to the rifle, he would use it to harm others. Betty's knowledge of a single incident a decade ago involving Frank's use of a firearm is insufficient as a matter of law to support a finding that she should have known that Frank would take the rifle and injure another. The rifle was on the premises for five years without incident. The prior altercation with trespassers did not involve a firearm. There was no habit or pattern of conduct which supports a finding that Betty knew or should have known that Frank would engage in dangerous or reckless handling of her rifle. Betty's failure to keep a gun under lock and key, or failure to otherwise prohibit Frank from using the rifle, does not support a finding that she negligently entrusted the rifle to him under the facts of this example.

D. Parental liability

Educated and responsible gun-owning parents understand that they have a duty to supervise their children and to take proper measures in order to safeguard firearms from their children. Unfortunately, there may be instances where a child is able to access a parent's firearm and cause an injury. If such an event were to happen, then the parent would generally not be civilly liable for the civil wrong or tort of the minor child. This is also true even if the parent is careless or negligent in his supervision of the child that engages in the tortious conduct. An exception may be in situations involving negligent entrustment as discussed above. However, the minor child is civilly liable for his own civil wrongs or torts. There is a statutory exception that provides for parental civil liability for up to $2,500 in damages to public or private property when the child's destruction of or damage to property was willful or malicious.

Parents also need to be aware of Va. Code § 18.2-56.2, which is a criminal law that punishes those who allow children access to firearms. This statute makes it a misdemeanor criminal offense for any person to recklessly leave a loaded, unsecured firearm in such a manner as to endanger the life or limb of any child under the age of 14. A violation is punishable by up to a year imprisonment and a fine of up to $2,500. It is also a misdemeanor criminal offense for any person to knowingly authorize a child under the age of 12 to use a firearm except when the child is under the supervision of an adult. A violation is punishable with a maximum fine of $2,500 and incarceration of up to 12 months.

A violation of Va. Code § 18.2-56.2 may create civil liability on a negligence per se theory. The violation of a statute constitutes negligence per se, and if such negligence is the cause of an injury, then it will support a recovery for damages for such injury. The question of whether such conduct is negligence per se and was the cause of an injury is usually a question of fact for the judge or jury hearing the case to determine.

EXAMPLE:
Jon and his father go bird hunting one day in the Virginia countryside. Jon, 17 years old, has been hunting since he was 11 years old and has taken several firearms training courses. Jon accidentally discharges his rifle and injures another person.

It is highly unlikely that Jon's father will be civilly liable for the injury in the accidental discharge of Jon's shotgun.

Note: There is no minimum age to possess a rifle in Virginia; however, there may be criminal liability with recklessly leaving a child under the age of 14 in possession of a rifle.

> **EXAMPLE:**
>
> Gordon, 12 years old, and his father, Glen, go to the firing range together for the first time to shoot Glen's Glock. Gordon has never handled a gun or taken a firearms training course. Gordon repeatedly fires the Glock into the ceiling and the floor. The firing range asks Glen and Gordon to leave the range. Glen and Gordon leave the first firing range and immediately go to a second firing range across the street with no additional instruction or training for Gordon. Gordon shoots and injures another person with Glen's Glock at the second firing range. The injured person files a civil lawsuit against Glen for negligent entrustment of a firearm.

Did Glen negligently entrust his Glock to Gordon? Will Glen be civilly liable for his negligent entrustment of his Glock to Gordon?

Glen expressly permitted Gordon to use his Glock at both firing ranges. It is likely that a jury hearing a case like this example would find that Glen should have known that Gordon was engaging in dangerous and reckless conduct at the first range and that to immediately keep shooting at the second range without any training would likely injure another person. Glen will likely be civilly liable for the injuries caused at the second firing range due to his negligent entrustment of the Glock to Gordon.

Note: Va. Code § 18.2-309 states that it is illegal for anyone to furnish a handgun to any minor and Va. Code § 18.2-308.7 states that it is illegal for anyone under the age of 18 to knowingly and intentionally possess a handgun. However, an exception to such possession by a minor is if he is accompanied by an adult at a lawful shooting range.

> **EXAMPLE:**
>
> Bobby, a 14-year-old boy, does not like his neighbor. One day, he retrieves the family 12-gauge shotgun and decides to shoot the neighbor's fence. Bobby's parents know nothing about this behavior, and Bobby has never had trouble with a firearm in the past. As a result of the shooting, a number of pickets from the fence were destroyed, three windows were broken, and numerous pockmarks were left in the brick façade of the home. Can the neighbor file a civil lawsuit against Bobby's parents and seek recovery for the damages from Bobby's parents?

The neighbor can file a civil lawsuit against Bobby's parents pursuant to Va. Code § 8.01-44 for the damage to their private property. The owner of any private property may institute a civil action and recover from the parents of a minor who is living with his parents for damages suffered by reason of the willful or malicious destruction of, or damage to, such property by the minor, but no more than $2,500 may be recovered from the parents. Any recovery from the parents of the minor shall not preclude the neighbor from full recovery from the minor except to the amount of the recovery already paid by the parents.

E. Contributory negligence

Virginia is known as a "pure contributory negligence" state, which means that plaintiffs who are contributorily negligent or contributed to the accident at all are completely barred from any recovery. This means that if the jury thinks the plaintiff is even 1% at fault, then the plaintiff cannot recover. Technically, contributory negligence is considered an affirmative defense to the plaintiff's negligence lawsuit, but it requires the defendant to present evidence and prove by a preponderance of the evidence that the plaintiff contributed to the accident.

F. Civil liability and lost or stolen firearms

One of the big concerns for any gun owner is what to do when a weapon turns up missing. Virginia law addresses this situation at Va. Code § 18.2-287.5. The law requires that when a firearm is lost or stolen from a person who lawfully possessed it, that such person shall report the loss or theft to any local law-enforcement agency or the Department of State Police within 48 hours after such person discovers the loss or theft or is informed by a person with personal knowledge of the loss or theft.

A violation of this law is punishable by a civil penalty of not more than $250. However, there is additional risk associated with a lost or stolen weapon. Should you fail to report a lost or stolen weapon, and the weapon later be associated with a crime, it is likely the police will consider you as a suspect.

Va. Code § 18.2-287.5 provides additional protection for a person who, in good faith, reports a lost or stolen firearm. If the report is made as required, the law prevents you from being criminally or civilly liable for any damages from acts or omissions resulting from the loss or theft. This subsection shall not apply to any person who makes a report in violation of Va. Code § 18.2-461 (false reports).

It is also important to recognize that the protection against criminal and civil liability protects you against charges or suits that arise from conduct after you make the report. This does not shield you from criminal or civil liability for actions that may have occurred before the report. For this reason, if you discover a missing firearm, it can be important to speak with a qualified attorney before making a timely report.

III. THE VIRGINIA CIVIL TRIAL: AN OVERVIEW

A civil lawsuit in the context of an incident involving the use of a firearm is typically a plaintiff's attempt to secure financial compensation for injuries allegedly caused by the wrongful actions of the defendant. As we have discussed, any use of a firearm creates the possibility of civil liability, regardless of what happens with any criminal case. If a civil plaintiff alleges to have been injured as the result of the defendant's wrongful actions in the use of a firearm, then a civil lawsuit can be filed against the defendant upon the payment of a filing fee. The filing of a civil lawsuit by the plaintiff, no matter how frivolous, must still be taken seriously and defended by the defendant. The process can take significant time, money, and legal energy, even for the most frivolous of cases. It is important to understand that the mere filing of a civil lawsuit by the plaintiff does not mean the plaintiff will succeed. The plaintiff must prove his case by a preponderance of the evidence in order to win his lawsuit.

A. Statute of limitations

The statute of limitations is a doctrine in Virginia (and almost every other jurisdiction) that requires a civil lawsuit to be filed within a certain period of time after the incident. If the plaintiff does not file his civil lawsuit within the statute of limitations period, then he is forever barred from bringing that civil case against the defendant. There are a number of issues relating to when the statute of limitations period begins, but for the most part, the time period will start to run immediately after the incident. The statute of limitations can vary by legal claim, but most limitation periods range between one and four years. In Virginia, the statute of limitations period that will apply to a civil lawsuit involving a firearm is two years. Assault and battery, negligence, wrongful death, and false imprisonment claims all provide two-year statutory limitation periods.

B. Proximate cause

One basic concept that is important to most civil claims, and is usually required to recover damages, is "proximate cause." Virtually every tort claim will require the plaintiff to prove that their damages were proximately caused by the defendant. "Proximate cause" is defined as cause that was a substantial factor in bringing about an event and without which the event would not have occurred. This concept is much discussed and has few bright-line tests.

For a gun owner, the most obvious cases of proximate cause are pulling the trigger on a firearm and hitting the aimed-at person or thing. The law will hold that your action proximately caused whatever physical damage the bullet did to persons or property. But what about those circumstances where the use of the gun is too far removed from the damages claimed? This is where the doctrine of proximate cause will cut off liability. If the damage is too far removed from the act of firing the gun, then it cannot be a proximate cause of the damage.

EXAMPLE:

Anthony is cleaning his AR-15 one night in his apartment and is negligent in his handling of the rifle. Anthony has a negligent discharge, the bullet goes through the wall of his apartment and strikes his neighbor Ray in the leg. Ray, obviously in pain, received prompt medical care from his wife, Gail, and made a speedy recovery. Ray and Gail both file civil lawsuits against Anthony to recover monetary damages.

In this example, it is clear that Anthony's negligence "proximately caused" damages for things like Ray's medical bills, hospital stay, and perhaps even lost wages. But what if Gail claims that because of her having to treat Ray's wounds, she missed a big job interview, lost out on a big raise in pay, and that she wants Anthony to pay that as a component of damages? The law would hold that Gail likely could not recover damages for her lost raise in pay because the loss would not be "proximately caused" by the sued-upon action. To put it another way, it is reasonably foreseeable that the negligent discharge of a firearm will cause medical bills for someone struck by a bullet. Therefore, this is recoverable. However, the law would say that the loss of a possible job opportunity for the wife who treated the person who was actually shot is not a reasonably foreseeable consequence of negligently discharging a firearm.

C. Damages

Damages are awarded by the judge or jury deciding the case. Damages typically come in the form of money to be paid to the plaintiff as compensation for a loss or injury if the plaintiff proves his case. However, the plaintiff is required to also prove his damages. It is possible that the defendant is 100% at fault or liable for the plaintiff's injury, but no damages are awarded to the plaintiff because the plaintiff failed to prove damages by a preponderance of the evidence. For example, a plaintiff who seeks reimbursement for medical expenses, but has no evidence that they ever went to a doctor or hospital, will very unlikely be able to recover those medical expenses.

Damages are categorized into compensatory (or actual) damages, and punitive damages. Compensatory damages are further categorized into special damages and general damages. Special damages are economic losses such as loss of earnings, property damage, and medical expenses. General damages are noneconomic damages such as pain and suffering and emotional distress. Punitive damages are not awarded in order to compensate the plaintiff, but are awarded to punish the defendant and warn others. Punitive damages are recoverable if the plaintiff pleads and proves either an intentional tort or willful and wanton negligence.

IV. INSURANCE
A. Homeowners insurance

With few exceptions, almost every homeowners insurance policy excludes coverage for intentional acts. The act of using your firearm in self-defense is almost always an intentional act. You intended to stop the threat. Plaintiffs' attorneys will very likely assert a negligence claim against a homeowner in an attempt to fall within the coverage and negotiate a settlement with the insurance carrier. However, at the end of the day, if the only evidence is that you intentionally shot the plaintiff because you intended to stop a threat, it is likely that any policy with an intentional act exclusion will not provide coverage for any damages awarded.

B. Auto insurance

Scores of cases around the country exist where the parties allege that a gun incident is covered by automobile insurance merely because the use of the firearm occurs in the auto or involves an auto. Almost universally, courts have held that these incidents are not covered under insurance policies merely because the discharge occurs in a car or involves a car.

In order for automobile insurance coverage to apply, the injury must arise from the "use" of a motor vehicle as a motor vehicle. There must be a causal connection between the use of the motor vehicle and the injury. This connection is shown if the injury is the natural and reasonable consequence of the motor vehicle's use. There is no coverage if the injury results from something wholly disassociated from, independent of, and remote from the motor vehicle's normal employment.

EXAMPLE:

Justin is cleaning his 9mm handgun in his car. Justin has an automobile insurance policy. Justin's gun discharges and severely injures his passenger.

In this example, Justin's automobile insurance policy will not likely cover the injuries of the passenger. For an injury to fall within the "use" coverage of an automobile policy:

1) the accident must have arisen out of the inherent nature of the automobile;
2) the accident must have arisen within the natural territorial limits of an automobile;
3) the actual use must not have terminated; and

4) the automobile must not merely contribute to cause the condition which produces the injury, but must itself produce injury.

PRACTICAL LEGAL TIP

One of the biggest mistakes people make is ignoring a lawsuit. If you get sued, you must answer! Otherwise you may lose on a legal concept called default judgment.
–Gilbert

> CHAPTER SIXTEEN ◄

BEYOND FIREARMS: KNIVES, BLACKJACKS, NUNCHUCKS, THROWING STARS, AND TASERS

I. INTRODUCTION

A person's right to carry a firearm openly is considered universal in Virginia, subject to definite and limited restrictions upon certain premises and classifications of individuals. The right to open carry another weapon is no different just because it is not a firearm. The Code of Virginia's weapon regulation deals primarily with certain weapons it deems dangerous when either carried concealed or taken upon certain premises. As we have previously discussed, it is always important to remember that a private party is free to regulate or ban weapons on their property.

II. WEAPONS REGULATED BY VA. CODE § 18.2-308

Va. Code § 18.2-308 makes it unlawful for any person to carry certain weapons concealed about their person if hidden from common observation. A weapon shall be deemed to be hidden from common observation when it is observable, but is of such deceptive appearance as to disguise the weapon's true nature. As discussed in Chapter 13, section III, the same exceptions applying to concealed handguns carried without a CHP also apply to regulated weapons listed in Va. Code § 18.2-308. There is no prohibition to open carry any of these listed weapons unless otherwise prohibited by law. The weapons that are illegal to carry concealed are as follows:

- Any dirk, bowie knife, switchblade knife, ballistic knife, machete, razor, slingshot, spring stick, metal knucks, or blackjack;
- Nun chahka, nun chuck, nunchaku, shuriken, fighting chain or any flailing instrument consisting of two or more rigid parts connected in such a manner as to allow them to swing freely;
- Throwing star, oriental dart, or any disc, of whatever configuration, having at least two points or pointed blades which is designed to be thrown or propelled; or
- Any weapon of like kind as enumerated above.

A violation is a misdemeanor punishable by 12 months in jail and/or a $2,500 fine. A violation by a convicted felon or person adjudicated delinquent of a delinquent act which would be a felony if committed by an adult is a felony punishable by up to five years in prison and/or a $2,500 fine. A second violation is a felony punishable by up to five years in prison and/or a $2,500 fine. A third or subsequent violation is also a felony, but punishable by up to 10 years in prison.

Brass Knuckles

Bowie Knife

Throwing Star

Dirk

Nunchucks

The Code of Virginia only defines the following weapons in Va. Code § 18.2-308:

- a "ballistic knife" is any knife with a detachable blade that is propelled by a spring-operated mechanism; and,

- a "spring stick" is a spring-loaded metal stick activated by pushing a button that rapidly and forcefully telescopes the weapon to several times its original length.

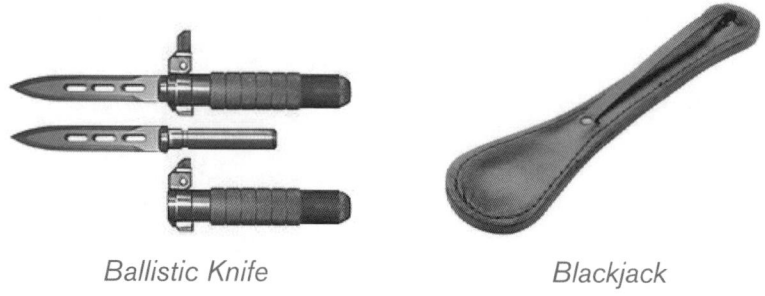

Ballistic Knife   Blackjack

The following weapons listed in Va. Code § 18.2-308 are not defined by the Code of Virginia, but have been defined by the courts:

- a "dirk" is a long straight-bladed dagger formerly carried by Scottish Highlanders or is a short sword formerly worn by British junior naval officers;
- a "bowie knife" is a large hunting knife adapted for knife-fighting and common in western frontier regions and having a guarded handle and a strong single-edge blade typically 10 to 15 inches long with its back straight for most of its length and then curving concavely and sometimes in a sharpened edge to the point;
- a "switchblade knife" is a pocket knife having the blade spring-operated so that pressure on a release catch causes it to fly open.
- a "machete" is defined as a type of knife, albeit a large one, that, like other knives, is capable of being used as both a tool and a weapon.

Caution: Virginia has a law that makes the sale or distribution of certain weapons illegal. Va. Code § 18.2-311 makes it illegal to sell, give, exhibit for sale, or possess with an intention to sell a blackjack, brass or metal knucks, a throwing star, a switchblade knife, or a ballistic knife. A violation is a misdemeanor punishable by a maximum fine of $250.

It is not unlawful to simply possess a blackjack or other weapon listed in the statute, but it is unlawful to possess such weapons with an intent to sell them. The law is made more complicated for lawful possessors of such weapons due to language in the statute that makes possession *prima facie* evidence of an intent to sell the weapon. This essentially means that the mere possession of such weapon is evidence that you had an intent to sell the weapon.

PRACTICAL LEGAL TIP

The simple possession of a blackjack, brass knuckles, throwing star, switchblade knife, or ballistic knife, while legal, can still trigger an arrest or criminal charge by the police because the wording of the law presumes that possession includes an intention to sell. This is a unique situation that in many ways seems to imply a presumption of guilt. −Gilbert

Does that mean an individual is in violation of this law that appears intended to stop the sale and/or distribution of such weapons for mere possession? No. Such an individual would have various valid defenses to such an allegation as long as the possession was not otherwise unlawful, but mere possession could allow a law enforcement officer to charge you with a crime. Va. Code § 18.2-311.

On a related note, Va. Code § 18.2-309 makes it unlawful to sell, barter, give, or furnish any dirk, switchblade knife, or bowie knife to a minor. Such an offense is a misdemeanor punishable by 12 months in jail and/or a $2,500 fine.

III. STUN WEAPONS

Va. Code § 18.2-308.1 defines a stun weapon as any device that emits a momentary or pulsed output, which is electrical, audible, optical, or electromagnetic in nature and which is designed to temporarily incapacitate a person. Stun weapons are also commonly referred to as stun guns, stun batons, or tasers. It is legal to open carry and conceal carry a stun weapon unless otherwise prohibited by law due to premises prohibitions or a felony conviction. While stun weapons are generally prohibited on school property, Va. Code § 18.2-308.1 allows someone with a valid concealed handgun permit to possess a stun gun while in a motor vehicle in a parking lot, traffic circle, or other means of vehicular ingress or egress to the school. Someone without a valid concealed handgun permit may possess a stun weapon on school property if it is in a secured container in a vehicle.

Handheld "Stun Gun"

Cartridge Taser

It is unlawful for any person convicted of a felony or adjudicated delinquent of a delinquent act which would be a felony if committed by an adult to knowingly and intentionally possess or transport any stun weapon. A violation is a felony punishable by up to five years in prison and/or a $2,500 fine. However, there is an exception that allows such persons to possess a stun weapon in their residence or on their curtilage.

Use of a stun weapon would be considered a use of force and the same standards of self-defense as discussed in Chapter 7 would apply.

IV. OTHER WEAPONS
A. Chemical weapons

As a general rule, pepper spray may be carried in Virginia. However, federal property is governed by federal law. It is recommended to contact either the federal agency or property you may visit if you will be carrying pepper spray to ensure you are in compliance with any federal regulations. Additionally, there are two chemical weapon sections in the Code of Virginia that you should be aware of when carrying pepper spray.

Va. Code § 18.2-312 states that it is unlawful to release tear gas, mustard gas, phosgene gas, or other noxious or nauseating gases or mixtures of chemicals designed to produce vile, injurious, or nauseating odors or gases that results in bodily injury. A violation is a felony punishable by up to five years in prison and/or a $2,500 fine. A violation if done maliciously is a felony punishable by five to 20 years in prison and a maximum fine of $100,000. Members of law enforcement are exempt if chemical weapons are used in the performance of their official duties.

Va. Code § 18.2-52 states that it is unlawful to cause any other person bodily injury by means of any acid, lye, or other caustic substance or agent or use of any explosive or fire. A violation is a felony punishable by up to five years in prison and/or a $2,500 fine. A violation if done maliciously is punishable by five to 30 years in prison and a maximum fine of $100,000.

B. Crossbow and bow and arrow

It is unlawful to discharge a crossbow or bow and arrow in or across any road, or within the right-of-way thereof, or in a street of any city or town. A violation is a misdemeanor punishable by a fine of up to $250. Military personnel and law enforcement officers are exempt if in performance of their lawful duties.

C. Spring gun

It is unlawful for any person to set or fix in any manner any firearm or other deadly weapon so that it may be discharged or activated by a person coming in contact with any string, wire, spring, or any other contrivance attached thereto or designed to activate such weapon remotely. A violation is a felony punishable by up to five years in prison and/or a $2,500 fine.

D. Nails, tacks, *etc.* on a highway

No person shall throw or deposit or cause to be deposited upon any highway any glass bottle, glass, nail, tack, wire, can, or any other substance likely to injure any person or animal, or damage any vehicle upon such highway. A violation is a misdemeanor punishable by up to 12 months in jail and/or a $2,500 fine. This law does not apply to law enforcement in the discharge of official duties while using any device designed to deflate tires.

A caltrop is a weapon made up of two or more sharp nails arranged in a way that one always points up from a stable base. In ancient times, caltrops were used as a way to slow the advance of horses, war elephants, camels, and human troops and were used as early as 331 B.C. Today, caltrops (pictured below) are used to deflate automobile tires.

Caltrops

E. Pointing a laser at law enforcement

It is unlawful for any person to intentionally project a point of light from a laser or a beam of light from any device that simulates a laser at a law enforcement officer engaged in the performance of his public duties. A violation is a misdemeanor punishable by six months in jail and/or a $1,000 fine.

F. Bricks, bottles, rocks, and ball bearings

The Code of Virginia also states that it is illegal to unlawfully or maliciously throw or shoot any "missile" against any motor vehicle, dwelling house, building, train, vessel, watercraft, or other vehicle when occupied by one or more persons. The Code of Virginia does not define missile. However, the courts have defined a missile to be various items such as bricks, bottles, rocks, and ball bearings. Essentially, any object that can be hurled can meet the definition of a missile for purposes of these laws. A violation is a felony punishable by incarceration and a fine. The amount of incarceration and any fine depends upon whether the missile was thrown or shot unlawfully or maliciously, and whether any person died.

V. PROHIBITED PREMISES FOR REGULATED WEAPONS

A. Public, private, and religious child day centers and preschools, elementary, middle, and high schools

Va. Code § 18.2-308.1 permits a pocket knife with a folding metal blade of less than 3 inches on school property. However, it is unlawful to knowingly possess any of the regulated weapons from Va. Code § 18.2-308 and/or a stun weapon upon:

a) the property of any public, private or religious child day center, preschool, elementary, middle, or high school, including buildings and grounds;
b) that portion of any property open to the public and then exclusively used for school-sponsored functions or extracurricular activities while such functions or activities are taking place; or
c) any school bus owned or operated by any such school.

The restriction on weapons in a child day center and private or religious preschool provisions of this section: (i) shall apply only during the operating hours of such child day center or private or religious preschool; and (ii) shall not apply to any person (a) whose residence is on the property of a child day center or a private or religious preschool and (b) who possesses a firearm or other weapon prohibited under this section while in his residence.

A violation is a misdemeanor punishable by up to 12 months in jail and/or a $2,500 fine. Exceptions include:

- Persons who possess such weapon or weapons as a part of the school's curriculum or activities;
- A person possessing a knife customarily used for food preparation or service and is using it for such purpose;
- Persons who possess such weapon or weapons as a part of any program sponsored or facilitated by either the school or any organization authorized by the school to conduct its programs either on or off the school premises;
- Law-enforcement and licensed security officers;
- Any person who possesses a knife or blade which he uses customarily in his trade;
- A person who possesses a knife having a metal blade, in or upon a motor vehicle;
- Any person who possesses a stun weapon in a secured container within a motor vehicle; and
- Any person with a valid concealed handgun permit who possesses a concealed handgun or stun weapon while in a motor vehicle in a parking lot, traffic circle, or other means of vehicular ingress and egress to the school.

B. Virginia courthouses

Va. Code § 18.2-283.1 makes it unlawful for any person to possess in a courthouse or transport into a courthouse any of the regulated weapons from Va. Code § 18.2-308 and/or a stun weapon. A violation is a misdemeanor, will result in the weapon being seized by law enforcement, and is punishable by up to 12 months in jail and/or a $2,500 fine. The provisions of this law do not apply to law enforcement, a magistrate, a court officer, judge, or city/county treasurer while in the conduct of such person's official duties.

C. Place of worship

Va. Code § 18.2-283 states that a person may not carry any bowie knife, dagger, or other dangerous weapon, without good and sufficient reason, to a place of worship while a meeting for religious purposes is being held at such place. A violation is a misdemeanor punishable by a maximum $250 fine. Personal protection is considered to be a good and sufficient reason to carry a weapon. However, a place of worship can choose to ban weapons on its property. It is recommended to understand the place of worship's position on weapons before taking any weapon into a place of worship. You should also consider if your church has a school, licensed day care, or preschool affiliated with it, and whether your church would constitute school grounds.

D. Airports

Va. Code § 18.2-287.01 states that it is unlawful for any person to possess or transport into any air carrier airport terminal any of the regulated weapons from Va. Code § 18.2-308, stun weapons, and other dangerous weapon or explosives. A violation is a misdemeanor, results in forfeiture of the weapon, and is punishable by up to 12 months in jail and/or a $2,500 fine.

E. Federal courts, buildings, and facilities

18 U.S.C. Code § 930 states that it is unlawful to knowingly possesses a dangerous weapon in a federal facility or federal courthouse or to cause a dangerous weapon to be present in a federal facility or federal courthouse. A "dangerous weapon" is defined as a weapon, device, instrument, material, or substance, animate or inanimate, that is used for, or is readily capable of, causing death or serious bodily injury, except that such term does not include a pocket knife with a blade of less than 2½ inches in length.

A violation can result in imprisonment for up to one year and/or a fine when committed in federal facilities and up to two years and/or a fine when committed in federal courthouses. The penalties increase if such an act was done in the commission of a crime or resulted in the killing of a person.

Exceptions are permitted for those in the lawful performance of official duties by an officer, member, agent, or employee of the United States, a State, or a political subdivision thereof, or the lawful carrying of other dangerous weapons in a federal facility incident to hunting or other lawful purposes.

F. Universities and colleges

Private universities, like any other owners of private property, may restrict or ban weapons on their property. The Second Amendment acts as a restraint on government, not private parties. It is recommended to review a private university's weapons policy before taking any weapon onto any private university's property.

Most of the public universities and colleges in Virginia have very similar weapons regulations, which include prohibitions to the carrying of firearms and weapons in school buildings and at school events. Each university or college's weapons policy is published in the Virginia Administrative Code under Title 8, which we discuss below.

1. George Mason University

Virginia Administrative Code, Title 8, Agency 35, Chapter 60, cited as 8VAC35-60, states that it is prohibited for any person, except law enforcement, to possess or carry any weapon on university property in academic buildings, administrative office buildings, student residence buildings, dining facilities, or while attending sporting, entertainment, or educational events.

A weapon is defined as any pistol, revolver, or other weapon designed or intended to propel a missile of any kind, or any dirk, bowie knife, switchblade knife, ballistic knife, razor slingshot, spring stick, metal knucks, blackjack, or any flailing instrument consisting of two or more rigid parts connected in such manner as to allow them to swing freely, which may be known as nun chahka, nun chuck, nunchaku, shuriken, or fighting chain, or any disc, of whatever configuration, having at least two points or pointed blades that is designed to be thrown or propelled and that may be known as throwing star or oriental dart.

2. Virginia Tech

8VAC105-20 states that university employees, students, and volunteers are prohibited from carrying, maintaining, or storing a firearm or weapon on any university property. Any visitor or other third party attending a sporting, entertainment, or educational event or visiting an academic or administrative office building, dining facility, or residence hall is prohibited from carrying, maintaining, or storing a firearm or weapon on any university facility, even if the owner has a valid CHP. This prohibition also applies to all events on campus where people congregate in any public or outdoor areas.

8VAC105-20-30 outlines various exceptions such as for law enforcement purposes and for those employees who reside in university-owned houses. These types of employees are permitted to keep personal firearms on these premises. However, this exception does not extend to employees living in university residence halls.

A weapon is defined as any instrument of combat, or any object not designed as an instrument of combat but carried for the purpose of inflicting or threatening bodily injury. Examples include but are not limited to: (i) firearms; (ii) knives with fixed blades or pocket knives with blades longer than 4 inches; (iii) razors or metal knuckles; (iv) blackjacks, foils, or hatchets; (v) bows and arrows; (vi) nun chahkas; (vii) stun weapons; or (viii) any explosive or incendiary device. Stun weapon is defined as any device that emits a momentary or pulsed output that is electrical, audible, optical, or electromagnetic in nature and that is designed to temporarily incapacitate a person.

3. College of William and Mary

8VAC115-20 states that it is prohibited for any person, except law enforcement or authorized personnel, to possess or carry any weapon on university property in academic buildings, administrative buildings, student residence and student life buildings, or dining or athletic facilities, or while attending an official university event, such as an athletic, academic, social, recreational, or educational event, or on vessels that are university property.

A weapon is defined as any firearm or any other weapon listed in Va. Code § 18.2-308.

4. James Madison University

8VAC45-10 states that it is prohibited for any person, except law enforcement, to possess or carry any weapon on university property in any buildings or any outdoor area to which access is restricted to members of the university community and invited guests, or while attending any university events or university-sanctioned events.

A weapon is defined as any firearm or any other weapon listed in Va. Code § 18.2-308.

5. Longwood University

8VAC50-20 states that it is prohibited for any person, except law enforcement, to possess or carry any weapon on university property in academic buildings, administrative office buildings, student resident buildings, or dining facilities or while attending sporting, entertainment, or educational events.

Weapons are defined similarly to any other weapon listed in Va. Code § 18.2-308.

6. Old Dominion University

8VAC65-10 states that it is prohibited for any person, except law enforcement, to possess or carry any weapon on university property in academic buildings, administrative office buildings, student residence buildings, or dining facilities, or while attending sporting, entertainment, or educational events.

Weapon means: (i) firearms; (ii) knives, machetes, straight razors, spring sticks, metal knucks, or blackjacks; (iii) any flailing instrument consisting of two or more rigid parts connected in such a manner as to allow them to swing freely, which may be known as a nun chahka, nun chuck, nunchaku, shuriken, or fighting chain; (iv) any disc, of whatever configuration having at least two points or pointed blades, that is designed to be thrown or propelled and that may be known as a throwing star or oriental dart; and (v) any electrical conduction weapon including tasers.

Weapon does not mean knives used for domestic purposes, pen or folding knives with blades less than 3 inches in length, or box cutters and utility knives kept or carried for use in accordance with the purpose intended by the original seller.

7. Radford University

8VAC75-20 states that university employees, students, and volunteers are prohibited from carrying, maintaining, or storing a firearm or weapon on any university property. Any visitor or other third party attending a sporting, entertainment, or educational event, or visiting an academic or administrative office building, dining facility, or residence hall, is prohibited from carrying, maintaining, or storing a firearm or weapon on any university facility, even if the owner has a valid CHP. This prohibition also applies to all events on campus where people congregate in any public or outdoor areas. Exceptions include the Chief of the Radford University Police Department authorizing a student or employee on a case-by-case basis in writing to store a firearm that would normally be prohibited.

Firearms are defined as any gun, rifle, pistol, or handgun designed to fire any projectile including but not limited to bullets, BBs, pellets, or shots, including paintballs, regardless of the propellant used.

Weapons are defined as any instrument of combat, or any object not designed as an instrument of combat but carried for the purpose of inflicting or threatening bodily injury. Examples include but are not limited to firearms, knives with fixed blades or pocket knives with blades longer than 4 inches, razors, metal knuckles, blackjacks, hatchets, bows and arrows, nun chahkas, foils, stun weapons, or any explosive or incendiary device. Stun weapon is defined as any device that emits a momentary or pulsed output that is electrical, audible, optical, or electromagnetic in nature and that is designed to temporarily incapacitate a person.

8. Richard Bland College

8VAC115-30 states that it is prohibited for any person, except law enforcement, to possess or carry any weapon on college property in academic buildings, administrative buildings, student residence and student life buildings, or dining or athletic facilities, or while attending an official college event, such as an athletic, academic, social, recreational, or educational event, or on vessels that are college property.

A weapon is defined as any firearm or any other weapon listed in Va. Code § 18.2-308.

9. University of Mary Washington

8VAC55-10 states that it is prohibited for any person, except law enforcement, to possess or carry any weapon on university property in academic buildings, administrative office buildings, student residence buildings, dining facilities, or athletic facilities or while attending sporting, entertainment, or educational events.

Weapons are defined similarly to any other weapon listed in Va. Code § 18.2-308.

10. University of Virginia

8VAC85-20 states that it is prohibited for any university student, faculty, employee, trainee, or volunteer, except law enforcement, to possess, store, or use any weapon on university property. The possession, storage, or use of any weapon is prohibited by the general public or visitors, except law-enforcement, on university property in academic, administrative, athletic, entertainment, or student residence buildings, child care or dining facilities, or the University Medical Center, or while attending sporting, entertainment, or educational activities. Exceptions can be made in various circumstances as outlined in 8VAC85-20-30(D).

Weapons are defined similarly to any other weapon listed in Va. Code § 18.2-308.

11. Virginia Commonwealth University

8VAC90-60 states that it is prohibited for any person, except law enforcement, to possess or carry any weapon on university property in academic buildings, administrative office buildings, medical venues, clinics, laboratories, research facilities, student residence buildings, and dining facilities; or while attending sporting, entertainment, or educational events.

Weapons are defined similarly to any other weapon listed in Va. Code § 18.2-308.

12. Virginia Military Institute

8VAC100-10 states that it is prohibited for any person, except law enforcement, to possess or carry any weapon on institute property, to include academic buildings, administrative office buildings, support buildings, military training facilities, athletic facilities, barracks or any structure designated for cadet housing, or dining facilities, or while attending sporting, entertainment, or educational events. The prohibition would not apply to those activities falling under the Reserve Officer Training Corps programs, NCAA rifle teams, Trap and Skeet Club, VMI Firing Range(s) or Marksmanship Club, or other official institute club or other activities.

Weapons are defined similarly to any other weapon listed in Va. Code § 18.2-308.

13. Virginia State University

8VAC110-10 states that it is prohibited for university employees, students, and volunteers to carry, maintain, or store a firearm or weapon on any university property. Any visitor or other third party attending a sporting, entertainment, or educational event, or visiting an academic or administrative office building, dining facility, or residence hall is prohibited from carrying, maintaining, or storing a firearm or weapon on any university facility, even if the owner has a valid CHP. This prohibition also applies to all events on.campus where people congregate in any public or outdoor areas.

8VAC110-10-30 outlines exceptions to this prohibition, which state that an employee may possess or carry a firearm if the employee is residing in university-owned houses and is permitted to keep personal firearms on the premises. However, this exception does not extend to employees living in university residence halls.

Firearms are defined as any gun, rifle, pistol, or handgun designed to fire any projectile including but not limited to bullets, BBs, pellets, or shots, including paintballs, regardless of the propellant used.

Weapons are defined as any instrument of combat, or any object not designed as an instrument of combat but carried for the purpose of inflicting or threatening bodily injury. Examples include but are not limited to firearms, knives with fixed blades or pocket knives with blades longer than 4 inches, razors, metal knuckles, blackjacks, hatchets, bows and arrows, nun chahkas, foils, stun weapons, or any explosive or incendiary device. "Stun weapon" is defined as any device that emits a momentary or pulsed output that is electrical, audible, optical, or electromagnetic in nature and that is designed to temporarily incapacitate a person.

14. Christopher Newport University

Unauthorized possession, storage, or control of weapons, firearms and ammunition by students on university property is prohibited. This includes storage in vehicles on campus as well as in the residence halls.

A firearm is defined as any gun, rifle, pistol, or handgun designed to fire bullets, BBs, pellets, or shot regardless of the propellant used. Other weapons include any instrument of combat, or any object not designed as an instrument of combat but carried for the purpose of inflicting or threatening bodily injury. Examples include, but are not limited to, knives with fixed blades or pocket knives with blades longer than 4 inches, razors, metal knuckles, blackjacks, hatchets, bows and arrows, nunchakus, foils, or explosives and incendiary devices.

Hazardous chemicals, which could pose a health risk, are also prohibited from the campus. This includes chemicals which, when combined with other substances, could be hazardous or present a danger to others.

15. Norfolk State University

The unauthorized possession, carrying, maintaining, storage, control, brandishing, or use of firearms and weapons, or any reasonable facsimiles thereof by students, faculty, staff, transient personnel, invitees or any other third parties, except law enforcement, while on University property or on University controlled sites, and at

University-sponsored activities, services or programs, even if the owner has a valid CHP is prohibited.

This prohibition includes the unauthorized storage of firearms and weapons in vehicles on campus and in residential halls. This policy prohibits all concealed weapons and unauthorized possession of realistic replicas of weapons. There are various narrow exceptions to this policy.

A firearm is defined as any device that can be used as a weapon and that is designed to fire either single or multiple projectiles propelled at high velocity regardless of the type of propellant used. A firearm includes, but is not limited to any gun, rifle, air-gun, pistol, cannon, or handgun designed to fire bullets, BBs, pellets, balls, air, spears, flares, tranquilizers, darts, shots (including paintballs), or any other projectile, whether loaded or unloaded, and the ammunition for any such device.

A weapon is defined as, but is not limited to, any instrument of combat or any object that is used, designed to be used, or intended to be used by the possessor to inflict death or bodily injury to any person, or for the purpose of threatening or intimidating any person with death or bodily injury. Examples of weapons include, but are not limited to, knives with fixed blades, pocket knives, dirks, switchblades, butterfly knives, firearms, ammunition, explosives or other incendiary devices, box cutters, razors, broken bottles, metal knuckles, blackjacks, bows and arrows, billy clubs, night sticks, bludgeons, slingshots, machetes, hatchets, nun chukkas, foils, chains, swords, ice picks, stun weapons, acid and other corrosive chemicals. The unauthorized possession of realistic replicas of weapons is prohibited. The possession, carrying, use and brandishing of a potentially harmful object(s) in a situation where there is no reasonable use for it and/or when such object(s) is used to intimidate, cause death or serious bodily injury, or to threaten another with death or serious bodily injury will be considered a violation of this policy. Examples include, but are not limited to, steak knives, butcher knives, tools, hammers, shovels, and any other potentially harmful object or implement.

16. Virginia Community Colleges

8VAC95-10 states that it is prohibited for any person to possess or carry any weapon on college property in academic buildings, administrative office buildings, student centers, child care centers, dining facilities, and places of like kind where people congregate, or while attending any sporting, entertainment, or educational events. However, this prohibition neither applies to law enforcement nor to possession of a weapon when stored securely inside the vehicle of properly permitted students and employees.

Weapons are defined similarly to any other weapon listed in Va. Code § 18.2-308.

"Weapon" does not mean knives or razors used for domestic purposes, pen or folding knives with blades less than 3 inches in length, or knives of like kind carried for use in accordance with the purpose intended by the original seller.

> CHAPTER SEVENTEEN <

THE NATIONAL FIREARMS ACT &
THE VIRGINIA UNIFORM MACHINE GUN ACT
SILENCERS, SHORT-BARRELED WEAPONS, AND MACHINE GUNS

Can an individual legally own a silencer or suppressor, short-barreled shotgun, short-barreled rifle, machine gun, or destructive device? The short answer is yes, so long as the item is legal under state law and all NFA regulations are satisfied. The National Firearms Act ("NFA") and the Virginia Uniform Machine Gun Act regulate machine guns. The NFA also regulates silencers or suppressors, short-barreled shotguns and rifles, and destructive devices. These firearms are illegal to purchase or possess without possessing the proper paperwork and a tax stamp. In this chapter, we will discuss both Acts, the purpose behind the NFA, what firearms and other items are regulated, and the process and procedure for legally possessing weapons that are subject to each Act's provisions.

I. VIRGINIA UNIFORM MACHINE GUN ACT

A. Registration of a machine gun

Va. Code § 18.2-295 requires every machine gun in Virginia to be registered with the Virginia State Police ("VSP") within 24 hours after its acquisition. A Certificate of Registration is issued upon receipt of a completed Machine Gun Registration Application and is valid as long as the registrant information remains the same. The transferor of the machine gun is required to immediately notify the VSP Superintendent of the transfer in writing with the name and address of the transferee along with the date of the transfer.

The VSP must be notified promptly of any change of information pertaining to the registration, such as change of address, telephone number, *etc.*, to initiate receipt of an updated registration. Failure to either give the required notification to the VSP or to keep and/or produce a Certificate of Registration for inspection is a misdemeanor punishable by a fine of up to $500.

B. Possession or use of a machine gun

The possession of a machine gun for a purpose manifestly not aggressive or offensive, for scientific purposes, or possessed as a curiosity, ornament, or keepsake is lawful. Possession or use of a machine gun shall be presumed to be for an offensive or aggressive purpose when:

    (1) the machine gun is on premises not owned or rented as a *bona fide* permanent residence or business occupancy by the possessor of the machine gun;

(2) the machine gun is in the possession of, or used by, a person who has been convicted of a crime of violence in any federal or state court of record;
(3) the machine gun has not been registered as required by Va. Code § 18.2-295; or
(4) empty or loaded shells which have been or are susceptible of use in the machine gun are found in the immediate vicinity.

Unlawful possession or use of a machine gun for an offensive or aggressive purpose is a felony punishable by up to 10 years in prison and a fine of up to $100,000. Possession or use of a machine gun in the perpetration or attempted perpetration of a crime of violence is a felony punishable by up to imprisonment for life and a fine of up to $100,000.

Caution: The language of Va. Code § 18.2-292 has a presumption that merely being in the same room or vehicle where a machine gun is located would be sufficient evidence for the prosecution that an individual was in legal possession of said machine gun. Additionally, Va. Code § 18.2-292 presumes certain types of conduct to meet the legal definition of possessing or using a machine gun for an offensive or aggressive purpose. Legal presumptions can be rebutted with defense motions, evidence, and arguments, but make no mistake, the language of the Uniform Machine Gun Act is written to greatly favor the prosecution in any case involving a machine gun.

II. WHAT IS THE NATIONAL FIREARMS ACT?

The National Firearms Act was enacted in 1934 in response to gangster crimes. Prior to the Act's passage, any person could go to the local hardware store and purchase a Thompson Submachine

Gun or shorten the barrel on their rifle or shotgun. President Franklin D. Roosevelt pushed for the passage of the NFA in an attempt to diminish a gangster's ability to possess and carry dangerous and/or easily concealable firearms, such as machine guns and short-barreled rifles and shotguns.

The NFA requires both the registration of and tax on the manufacture and transfer of certain firearms. The law created a tax of $200 on the transfer of the following firearms: short-barreled shotguns, short-barreled rifles, machine guns, silencers, and destructive devices. The tax is only $5 for firearms that are classified as "Any Other Weapons" or AOWs. Back in 1934, a $200 tax was the approximate equivalent to about $3,500 today!

Five years after the NFA's passage, the Supreme Court held in *United States v. Miller* that the right to bear arms can be subject to federal regulation. Miller defended himself against the government, stating that the NFA infringed upon his constitutional right to bear arms under the Second Amendment. While the Court agreed that the Constitution does guarantee a right to bear arms, it held that the right does not extend to every firearm. See *United States v. Miller*, 307 U.S. 174 (1939).

III. WHAT FIREARMS DOES THE NFA REGULATE?
A. Short-barreled or "sawed-off" rifles and shotguns

In order to be legal, short-barreled shotguns and rifles must be registered, and a tax paid on the firearm. What is a short-barreled shotgun? Under federal law, short-barreled shotguns have one or more barrels less than 18 inches in length and the overall length of the shotgun is less than 26 inches. What is a short-barreled rifle? It is any rifle with one or more barrels less than 16 inches in length, and the overall length of the rifle is less than 26 inches. *See* 27 CFR 478.11. The Virginia definition of a short-barreled rifle or shotgun is essentially the same, but the firearms are referred to as being "sawed off."

In order to be legal under the NFA, short-barreled shotguns and rifles must be registered, and a tax paid on the firearm. Short-barreled shotguns and rifles are typically purchased from a FFL that deals in NFA items. However, such firearms are very popular for individuals to build and/or modify on their own. This is legal if the individual has properly registered the firearm to be modified into a short-barreled firearm with the ATF and paid the tax before it is modified. Once approved, an individual may alter or produce a short-barreled firearm and must engrave legally required information on the receiver of the firearm such as manufacturer, location, *etc*.

Va. Code § 18.2-303.1 states that possession of a "sawed-off" shotgun or "sawed-off" rifle is lawful if possessed in compliance with federal law, for scientific purposes, or not usable as a firing weapon but possessed as a curiosity, ornament, or keepsake. However, unlawful possession or use of a "sawed-off" rifle or shotgun is a felony punishable by up to 10 years or life in prison, depending on whether such firearm is used in a crime of violence. Law enforcement and military are exempt from this provision.

B. Stabilizing braces

The most common type of rifle that is manufactured or modified into a short-barreled rifle ("SBR") is the AR-style sporting rifle. The AR can also be manufactured as a pistol. An AR-style SBR and an AR-style pistol appear very similar. The key difference between the two is that the SBR has a shoulder stock and the pistol does not. However, the AR pistol will have a "buffer tube" extending from the back of the receiver to compensate for the firearm's recoil. In recent years it has become a trend that some manufacturers and DIY firearm hobbyists will attach a device to this buffer tube called an "arm brace" or "stabilizing brace." This is an accessory, typically made of plastic and Velcro, that wraps around the shooter's forearm, enabling him or her to have better aim and recoil control. When the arm brace was first developed, it had the appearance of a telescoping shoulder stock. Attaching a shoulder stock to a traditional handgun or AR-style pistol with a barrel length under 16 inches turns the handgun into an NFA weapon, which is only allowed upon the approval of a Form 1. Many manufacturers of these stabilizing braces have sought preapproval from the ATF's Firearms Technology Industry Services Branch to confirm that their devices did not turn AR pistols into SBRs. In a somewhat confusing series of letters and statements, the ATF has taken the position that the stabilizing brace, when used as manufactured and intended, does not make an AR pistol into an SBR or AOW. Keep in mind, this interpretation could change at any time.

However, if an individual installing and using the brace made any alterations with the intent to use it as a shoulder stock, such as adding padding or taping the sides of the brace together, and they did not get approval with a Form 1 and pay the $200 tax, they could be subject to prosecution for illegally making an NFA weapon. Further, if a person does affix a stabilizing brace to a pistol, a vertical foregrip cannot be added because the ATF has determined that this addition alters the character of the firearm so that it is no longer a pistol (since it is not designed to be fired with one hand).

C. Personal defense firearms

Recently, a weapon came into the market that is designed as a personal defense firearm utilizing shotgun rounds. Mossberg was the first manufacturer to produce such a weapon, the Shockwave. This market now includes the Remington TAC-14 and the Black Aces Tactical Pro Series S Semiautomatic. These firearms have barrels that are shorter than the 18 inches required for a non-NFA shotgun. However, the ATF has determined that these firearms are not short-barreled shotguns (because of their "bird's head" stock which is not designed to be fired from the shoulder). As such, these firearms fall outside the NFA regulations. *See* Chapter 5.

D. Machine guns

Machine guns are illegal under federal law. However, if the requirements of the NFA are satisfied, machine guns may be legally owned by individuals. First, what is a machine gun? Federal law defines a machine gun as "any weapon which shoots, is designed to shoot, or can be readily restored to shoot, automatically more than one shot, without manual reloading, by a single function of the trigger. The term shall also include the frame or receiver of any such weapon, any part designed and intended solely and exclusively, or combination of parts designed and intended, for use in converting a weapon into a machine gun, and any combination of parts from which a machine gun can be assembled if such parts are in the possession or under the control of a person." 27 CFR § 478.11. As a result of this definition, the individual metal components that make up a whole machine gun, such as a full-auto sear, individually meet the federal definition of machine gun. The parts for the machine gun do not have to be assembled.

It is illegal to manufacture a new machine gun for private ownership. Because of a federal law that effectively disallows private ownership (not military, police department, *etc.*) of any machine gun manufactured after May 19, 1986, the machine guns available for private ownership are limited to the legally registered machine guns that existed prior to May 19, 1986. Thus, the private market is very limited and prices, as a result, are very high.

Bump stocks

Bump stocks are a rifle accessory that harness the energy of the recoil to assist the shooter in pulling the trigger as soon as it resets. This device does not alter the mechanical operation of the rifle; it still fires only one round for each trigger pull. The bump stock became controversial after the October 1, 2017, shooting at an outdoor concert in Las Vegas. Politicians and the media immediately declared that these devices allow a semi-automatic rifle to fire as rapidly as a machine gun. Many of them erroneously stated that a bump stock "turns a rifle into a machine gun." Bills were filed in Congress which did not pass, but ultimately in 2018, the Department of Justice, through the ATF, issued a final rule banning bump stocks by way of regulation. This was done in spite of an ATF determination in 2010 that bump stocks did not modify a semi-automatic rifle to make it an NFA-regulated machine gun. This new rule specifically defined bump stocks as "machineguns" under federal law. This effectively renders all such devices illegal to possess under federal law, since any lawful machine gun must have been in existence and properly registered under the National Firearms Act as of May 19, 1986, decades before the bump stock was invented. In crafting the new rule, the ATF reasoned that bump stocks allow the shooter to produce fully automatic fire while continuously applying pressure to the trigger.

Virginia also criminalized possession of bump stocks by outlawing trigger activators in § Va. Code 18.2-308.5:1. This code section criminalizes possession of any "device designed to allow a semi-automatic firearm to shoot more than one shot with a single pull of the trigger by harnessing the recoil energy of any semi-automatic firearm to which it is affixed so that the trigger resets and continues firing without additional physical manipulation of the trigger by the shooter."

Along with the Virginia law banning trigger activators, the ATF's new rule mandated that all bump stocks must be destroyed or surrendered to the ATF by March 26, 2019. Afterward, it became a federal felony to possess a bump stock. This crime is classified as a violation of 18 U.S.C. § 922(o)—illegal possession of a machinegun. If convicted of such a crime, you could face up to 10 years in federal prison and up to a $250,000 fine for each bump stock in your possession. Immediately following the passage of this rule, Second Amendment advocacy groups and individuals across the United States began litigation. However, no court has issued a nationwide preliminary injunction against the final rule going into effect while its constitutionality is litigated.

E. Firearm suppressors

What is a suppressor? It is just a muffler for a firearm and is legal if all NFA requirements are met. In legal terms, a firearm suppressor is defined in 27 CFR § 478.11 as "any device for silencing, muffling, or diminishing the report of a portable firearm, including any combination of parts, designed or redesigned, and intended for use in assembling or fabricating a firearm silencer or firearm muffler, and any part intended only for use in such assembly or fabrication."

Firearm suppressors are very practical instruments. They are great for hunting and recreational shooting not only because they suppress gunshots in a way so as to not alarm other animals being hunted, but also because they lessen the impact on the shooter's ears. However, firearm owners should be carefully aware that the definition of a suppressor is very broad. Suppressors do not need to be items manufactured specifically for use as a suppressor. There are some ordinary, everyday items that could be easily converted into a suppressor such as a water bottle or an automotive oil filter. Possession of otherwise legal items when used or modified to be used as a suppressor is illegal. In 2017, the Hearing Protection Act, which sought to remove silencers from regulation under the NFA and treat them as common firearms, died in Congress. At the time of writing this book, this act has yet to be considered by either the House of Representatives or the Senate.

To further complicate matters, in 2019, in response to a mass shooting where a suppressor was used, a bill banning them was introduced in Congress. This bill was not passed into law.

F. Destructive devices

The term "destructive device" is a legal term given to certain firearms, objects, and munitions that are illegal under the NFA.

DESTRUCTIVE DEVICES – PART A
27 CFR § 478.11

Any explosive, incendiary, or poison gas (1) bomb, (2) grenade, (3) rocket having a propellant charge of more than 4 ounces, (4) missile having an explosive or incendiary charge of more than one-quarter ounce, (5) mine, or (6) device similar to any of the devices described in the preceding paragraphs of this definition.

DESTRUCTIVE DEVICES – PART B
27 CFR § 478.11

Any type of weapon (other than a shotgun or shotgun shell which the Director finds is generally recognized as particularly suitable for sporting purposes) by whatever name known which will, or which may be readily converted to, expel a projectile by the action of an explosive or other propellant, and which has any barrel with a bore of more than one-half inch in diameter.

DESTRUCTIVE DEVICES – PART C
27 CFR § 478.11

Any combination of parts either designed or intended for use in converting any destructive device described in [part] (A) and (B) of this section and from which a destructive device may be readily assembled.

The "destructive devices" as defined in the statute are effectively broken down into three categories: explosive devices, large caliber weapons, and parts easily convertible into a destructive device.

The first portion of the definition of a destructive device deals with explosive, incendiary, and poison gas munitions. The definition specifies that any explosive, incendiary, or poison gas bomb, grenade, mine, or similar device is a destructive device. In addition, the definition includes a rocket having a propellant charge of more than four ounces and a missile (projectile) having an explosive or incendiary charge of more than one-quarter ounce. These topics and the regulations thereof are beyond the scope of this book's discussion.

The second section of the definition addresses large-caliber weapons and states that any type of weapon that has a bore of more than one-half inch in diameter, is a destructive device with the exception of shotguns (and shotgun shells) that are suitable for sporting purposes. Thus, any caliber in a rifle or handgun more than .50 inches or 50 caliber is classified as a destructive device. Shotguns are exempt from this prohibition on size unless the ATF rules it is not for "sporting purposes."

How do you know if a shotgun is suitable for sporting purposes? The ATF keeps a list, and has issued rulings classifying specific shotguns as destructive devices because they are not considered to be particularly "suitable for sporting purposes" including the USAS-12, Striker-12, Streetsweeper, and 37/38mm Beanbags. The ATF does not provide any specific definition of what constitutes being "suitable for sporting purposes," nor does it specify the methodology by which it determines what makes a particular shotgun suitable for sporting purposes. Ultimately, one will have to check with the ATF lists to see whether a particular shotgun with a larger bore-diameter is classified as a destructive device or not.

Finally, a destructive device does not need to be a completed and assembled product to fall under the federal definition and regulation under the NFA. Much like machine guns, if a person possesses parts that can be readily assembled into a destructive device, then whether or not the device has actually been constructed is irrelevant—by law it's already a destructive device.

Although these firearms, munitions, and devices are prohibited by the law on its face pursuant to the NFA, a person may nevertheless receive permission to possess them so long as they possess the correct legal authorization.

G. "Any Other Weapons" or AOWs

The AOW category under the NFA pertains to firearms and weapons that may not fit the traditional definition of some of the firearms discussed elsewhere in this book due to the way in which they are manufactured or modified. Under federal law, an AOW is "any weapon or device capable of being concealed on the person from which a shot can be discharged through the energy of an explosive, a pistol or revolver having a barrel with a smooth bore designed or redesigned to fire a fixed shotgun shell, weapons with combination shotgun and rifle barrels 12 inches or more, less than 18 inches in length, from which only a single discharge can be made from either barrel without manual reloading, and shall include any such weapon which may be readily restored to fire. Such term shall not include a pistol or a revolver having a rifled bore, or rifled bores, or weapons designed, made, or intended to be fired from the shoulder and not capable of firing fixed ammunition." 26 U.S.C. § 5845(e).

1. Concealable weapons and devices

Weapons that are capable of being concealed from which a shot can be discharged are AOWs. This includes such weapons as a pen gun, knife gun, wallet gun, or umbrella gun.

Pen Gun

Knife Gun

Umbrella Gun

Wallet Gun

2. Pistols and revolvers having a smooth-bore barrel for firing shotgun shells

Pistols and revolvers which have a smooth bore (no rifling) that are designed to shoot shotgun ammunition are defined as an AOW. The ATF cites firearms such as the H&R Handy Gun or the Ithaca Auto & Burglar Gun as firearms which fall under the AOW category. Note: Handguns with partially rifled barrels such as The Judge do not fall under this category due to the rifling of the barrel.

H&R Handy Gun

Ithaca Auto & Burglar Gun

3. Weapons with barrels 12 inches or longer and lengths 18 inches or shorter

The definition of AOW also includes any weapon which has a shotgun or rifle barrel of 12 inches or more but is 18 inches or less in overall length from which only a single discharge can be made from either barrel without manual reloading. The ATF identifies the "Marble Game Getter" as the firearm most commonly associated with this definition (excluding the model with an 18-inch barrel and folding shoulder stock).

4. Pistols and revolvers with vertical handgrips

If a pistol is modified with a vertical grip on the front, it will now be legally classified as an AOW and require registration and a paid tax. Note, vertical grips are readily available and are legal to own as long as they are not placed on a handgun. The definition of a handgun is a weapon which is intended to be fired by one hand, the addition of the vertical foregrip makes it so the weapon now is intended to be fired using two hands. This modification changes the weapon from a handgun to an AOW and is now a prohibited weapon without the proper documentation. It is not an SBR or SBS because it cannot be fired from the shoulder. *See* 26 U.S.C. § 5845(e).

H. Antique firearms

Firearms that are defined by the NFA as "antique firearms" are not regulated by the NFA. The NFA definition of antique firearm is found in 26 U.S.C. § 5845(g) as "any firearm not designed or redesigned for using rimfire or conventional centerfire ignition with fixed ammunition and manufactured in or before 1898 (including any matchlock, flintlock, percussion cap, or similar type of ignition system or replica thereof, whether actually manufactured before or after the year 1898) and also any firearm using fixed ammunition manufactured in or before 1898, for which ammunition is no longer manufactured in the United States and is not readily available in the ordinary channels of commercial trade." Under this statute, and for NFA purposes, the only firearms that are antiques are firearms which were both actually manufactured in or before 1898 and ones for which fixed ammunition is no longer manufactured in the United States and is not readily available in the ordinary channels of commercial trade.

With this in mind, the ATF states in its NFA guidebook that "it is important to note that a specific type of fixed ammunition that has been out of production for many years may again become available due to increasing interest in older firearms. Therefore, the classification of a specific NFA firearm as an antique can change if ammunition for the weapon becomes readily available in the ordinary channels of commerce."

I. NFA curio firearms and relics

Under federal law, curios or relics are defined in 27 CFR § 478.11 as "firearms which are of special interest to collectors by reason of some quality other than is associated with firearms intended for sporting use or as offensive or defensive weapons." Persons who collect curios or relics may do so with a special collector's license, although one is not required. The impact of an NFA item being classified as a curio or relic, however, is that it allows the item to be transferred interstate to persons possessing a collector's license. The collector's license does not allow the individual to deal in curios or relics, nor does it allow the collector to obtain other firearms interstate as those transactions still require an FFL.

To be classified as a curio or relic, federal law states that the firearm must fall into one of the following three categories:
1) firearms which were manufactured at least 50 years prior to the current date, but not including replicas thereof;
2) firearms which are certified by the curator of a municipal, state, or federal museum which exhibits firearms to be curios or relics of museum interest; or
3) any other firearms which derive a substantial part of their monetary value from the fact that they are novel, rare, bizarre, or because of their association with some historical figure, period, or event.

See 27 CFR § 478.11.

The ATF maintains a list of firearms that are classified as curios or relics.

J. How can some after-market gun parts make your firearm illegal?

A number of companies manufacture and sell gun products or parts that alter the appearance or utility of a firearm (*i.e.,* shoulder stocks, forward hand grips, *etc.*). However, some of these after-market products can actually change the firearm you possess from one type of a weapon to another type of weapon for legal purposes, whether you realize it or not. As a result, many individuals make the modifications to their firearms thinking that because there was no special process for purchasing the accessory, any modification would be in compliance with the law. Unfortunately, this is not always the case. Consider the example of short-barreled uppers for AR-15s: selling, buying, or possessing AR-15 "uppers" with barrels less than 16 inches is legal. However, it is illegal to put the upper on a receiver of an AR-15 because this would be the act of manufacturing a short-barreled rifle and is legally prohibited. This is equally true of vertical foregrips on a handgun. Vertical foregrips are legal to buy or possess; however, if you actually install one on a handgun, you have manufactured an AOW, and it is illegal, unless registered and a tax paid.

PRACTICAL LEGAL TIP

Many people choose to purchase NFA items like machine guns with a gun trust to avoid potential issues with passing the weapon on through their estate, and to avoid possible possession complications for others who they wish to include in the trust.
–Gilbert

IV. PROCESS AND PROCEDURE FOR OBTAINING NFA FIREARMS

A. Who can own and possess an NFA firearm?

Any person may own and possess an NFA firearm as long as they are legally not disqualified to own or possess firearms, and live in a state that allows possession of NFA items. The ATF also allows for a non-person legal entity to own these items, such as corporations, partnerships, and trusts, *etc*. On July 13, 2016, a new rule went into effect modifying the process for filing for a transfer or manufacture of an NFA weapon.

B. Steps for buying or manufacturing NFA items

Whether a person is buying or making (manufacturing) an NFA firearm, there are several steps in the process. The transfer or manufacture of an NFA firearm requires the filing of an appropriate form with the ATF, payment of any federally mandated tax, approval of the transfer or making by the ATF, and registration of the firearm to the transferee or maker. Only after these steps have occurred may a buyer legally take possession of the NFA item, or may a person legally assemble or manufacture the NFA item. In this section, we will walk through the process, step by step, of: (1)

purchasing an NFA item that already exists; and (2) manufacturing an NFA firearm.

Steps for buying an existing NFA item (for example, a suppressor):
1. select and purchase the item (suppressor) from a transferor who is usually an FFL dealer who is authorized to sell NFA weapons;
2. assemble appropriate paperwork: ATF Form 4 (*See* Appendix B), fingerprints on an FBI Form FD-258, a passport-size photograph, and a payment for the tax of $200;
   a. If the buyer is an individual they must notify the Chief Law Enforcement Officer of their city or county of residence by delivering the CLEO copy of ATF Form 4;
   b. If the buyer is a corporation or trust, each "responsible person" of the corporation or trust must complete an ATF Form 5320.23 (*See* Appendix B), including fingerprints and a passport photograph, and must notify the Chief Law Enforcement Officer of their city or county of residence by delivering to them the CLEO copy of ATF Form 5320.23;
3. submit paperwork, fingerprints, and tax to the ATF for review and approval;
4. ATF sends approval (tax stamp affixed to Form 4) to the transferor; and then
5. transferor notifies the buyer to pick up the suppressor.

Steps for manufacturing an NFA item (such as a short-barreled rifle):
1. select the item to manufacture or modify, *i.e.*, short-barreled AR-15;
2. assemble appropriate paperwork: ATF Form 1 (*See* Appendix B), fingerprints on an FBI Form FD-258, a passport-size photograph, and a payment for the tax ($200);

a. If the maker is an individual they must notify the Chief Law Enforcement Officer of the city or county of their residence by delivering the CLEO copy of ATF Form 1;
b. If the maker is a corporation or trust, each "responsible person" of the corporation or trust must complete an ATF Form 5320.23 (*See* Appendix B), including fingerprints and a passport photograph, and must notify the Chief Law Enforcement Officer of their city or county of residence by delivering to them the CLEO copy of ATF Form 5320.23;
3. the "Applicant" submits paperwork and tax to the ATF for review and approval;
4. ATF sends approval (tax stamp affixed to Form 1); and then
5. the short-barreled AR-15 may be legally assembled, *i.e.*, put upper with a barrel length of less than 16 inches on a lower receiver, *etc*. The item must now be engraved and identified.

When purchasing an NFA firearm from a dealer, the dealer is required to have the purchaser fill out ATF Form 4473 when the purchaser goes to pick up the item from the dealer.

C. How must an NFA item be engraved and identified if I make it myself?

Once you receive ATF approval to manufacture your own NFA item (such as the short-barreled AR-15 in the previous section), federal law requires that you engrave, cast, stamp, or otherwise conspicuously place or cause to be engraved, cast, stamped, or placed on the frame, receiver, or barrel of the NFA item the following information:

1. the item's serial number;
2. the item's model (if so designated);
3. caliber or gauge;
4. the name of the owner whether individual, corporation, or trust; and
5. the city and state where the item was made.

This information must be placed on the item with a minimum depth of .003 inch and in a print size no smaller than 1/16 inch. *See* 27 CFR § 479.102.

D. Which way should I own my NFA item? Paperwork requirements for individuals, trusts, or business entities to own NFA items

Form 4 and Form 1 are the appropriate paperwork that must be assembled and submitted to the ATF under the NFA and varies depending on whether an individual, or a legal entity such as a trust, corporation, or partnership, is purchasing or manufacturing the NFA item. The paperwork generally starts either with an ATF Form 4 used for purchasing an existing item, or an ATF Form 1 which is used if a person wishes to manufacture a new NFA item. All relevant portions of the forms must be completed. Both Form 4 and Form 1 have a requirement that a Chief Law Enforcement Officer for the city or county where the applicant lives must be given their copy of the ATF Form.

Who is a Chief Law Enforcement Officer who must be notified? For the purposes of ATF Form 4 or Form 1, and the responsible person questionnaire, ATF Form 5320.23, the Chief Law Enforcement Officer is considered to be the chief law enforcement officer who has jurisdiction where the transferor, the applicant, and any "responsible persons" are located. These persons include "the Chief of Police; the Sheriff; the Head of the State Police; or a State or local district attorney or prosecutor."

Photograph and fingerprints are required for individual applicants and "responsible persons." If an individual is purchasing or manufacturing an NFA item, the applicant must submit an appropriate photograph and their fingerprints. An entity such as a trust or corporation must designate "responsible persons" who are allowed to have access to use and possess an NFA weapon. As of July 13, 2016, corporations and trusts must submit the appropriate documents showing its existence, such as the trust or corporate formation documents, the ATF responsible person questionnaire, fingerprints, and passport photographs of these persons.

"Responsible persons" of trusts, partnerships, associations, companies, or corporations, are defined as "any individual who possesses, directly or indirectly, the power or authority to direct the management and policies of the trust or entity to receive, possess, ship, transport, deliver, transfer or otherwise dispose of a firearm for, or on behalf of, the trust or legal entity." *See* ATF Form 1, Instructions. Further, with regard to NFA trusts, responsible persons are defined in the following way: "those persons with the power or authority to direct the management and policies of the trust includes any person who has the capability to exercise such power and possesses, directly or indirectly the power or authority under any trust instrument, or under State law, to receive, possess, ship, transport, deliver, transfer, or otherwise dispose of a firearm for, or on behalf of the trust." The ATF Form 5320.23 provides examples of responsible persons, including, "settlors/grantors, trustees, partners, members, officers, directors, board members, or owners." Persons who are not "responsible persons" are "the beneficiary of a trust, if the beneficiary does not have the capability to exercise the enumerated powers or authorities."

E. Why are trusts so popular to own NFA items?

There are three major reasons trusts are very popular to own NFA items: paperwork, control, and ease of ownership. A trust is a legal entity that can hold property.

A major reason for having a trust own an NFA item is that it makes owning and using the NFA item easier if more than one person wishes to use the item. If an individual owns the item, then only the individual can possess it. On the other hand, if the item is owned by a trust, all trustees, including co-trustees, are able to possess and use the items contained in the trust. Therefore, co-trustees may be added or removed as necessary.

Further, unlike other entities such as corporations, LLCs, *etc.*, a trust requires no filings with a government to create, which saves expenses. Further, these expense savings continue because there are no continuing government fees or compliance requirements. Thus, trusts are one of the best ways currently to own an NFA item.

F. The tax stamp

Once the ATF has an applicant's materials in hand, they will be reviewed and checked by NFA researchers and an examiner. The application will then either be approved or denied. A denial will be accompanied by an explanation of why the application was denied and how to remedy it, if possible. If the application is approved, the examiner will affix a tax stamp on one of the submitted Form 1 or Form 4 and send the newly stamped form to the applicant.

This tax stamp on the appropriate form is a person's evidence of compliance with the NFA's requirements and is a very important document. A copy should always be kept with the NFA item.

G. What documents should I have with me when I am in actual possession of my suppressor, short-barreled firearm, or other NFA item?

If you have an NFA item, it is a good idea to have the proper documentation with you to prove that you legally possess the item. As of 2015, the law states it is a crime to be in possession of an unregistered NFA item, which means the police officer will need reasonable suspicion of your failure to register in order to detain you to determine the status of your item. Reasonable suspicion is a very low standard to meet. It is good advice that if you are in possession of your suppressor, short-barreled firearm, destructive device, or if you are lucky enough, your machine gun—have your paperwork showing you are legal, or it may be a long day with law enforcement. To show you are legal, always keep a copy of your ATF Form 4 or Form 1 (whichever is applicable) with the tax stamp affixed for every NFA item in your possession, personal identification, and if the item is held in a trust or corporation, a copy of the trust or articles of incorporation, and the authorization for your possession. Care should be given to make sure these documents name the individual so as to show legal ownership, *i.e.*, trust and/or amendments showing the person is a co-trustee or an officer of the corporation.

Practically, individuals should not carry around the original documents as they could be destroyed by wear and tear, rain, or be misplaced, effectively destroying the required evidence of compliance. Photocopies of the stamp and any other pertinent documents are generally enough to satisfy inquisitive law enforcement officials. The more technologically advanced may take pictures on their phone or other mobile device, or even upload them to a cloud database. Keep in mind that if the phone dies or the cloud cannot be reached, and you have no way to access the documents, your proof is gone and you may have a very bad day ahead of you! We recommend keeping photocopies of the ATF Form with the tax stamp affixed and appropriate documents with the NFA weapon to avoid any problems with technology.

H. Is the paperwork necessary?

Yes. As a practical matter, you will want to keep your NFA paperwork with each item, giving you the ability to prove compliance under the National Firearms Act quickly. Without documentation, theoretically, a law enforcement official could detain you to inquire about your item's registration status. From there, they could very easily develop probable cause that the NFA item is unregistered because most state law enforcement officials cannot access the ATF's database of registered items. Once probable cause has been developed, an officer may make a lawful arrest. This is a long way of saying that it is a good idea to keep your paperwork with you to prove compliance!

› APPENDICES ‹

APPENDIX A:
Selected Virginia Statutes

> **NOTICE**
>
> This appendix contains the legislative changes of the 2021 Virginia Legislature so it is updated as of July 1st, 2021

CODE OF VIRGINIA

TITLE 3.2. AGRICULTURE, ANIMAL CARE, AND FOOD CHAPTER 65. COMPREHENSIVE ANIMAL CARE ARTICLE 6. AUTHORITY OF LOCAL GOVERNING BODIES

§ 3.2-6552. DOGS KILLING, INJURING, OR CHASING LIVESTOCK OR POULTRY.

A. It shall be the duty of any animal control officer or other officer who may find a dog in the act of killing or injuring livestock or poultry to seize or kill such dog forthwith whether such dog bears a tag or not. Any person finding a dog committing any of the depredations mentioned in this section shall have the right to kill such dog on sight as shall any owner of livestock or his agent finding a dog chasing livestock on land utilized by the livestock when the circumstances show that such chasing is harmful to the livestock. Any court shall have the power to order the animal control officer or other officer to kill any dog known to be a confirmed livestock or poultry killer, and any dog killing poultry for the third time shall be considered a confirmed poultry killer. The court, through its contempt powers, may compel the owner, custodian, or harborer of the dog to produce the dog.

B. Any animal control officer who has reason to believe that any dog is killing livestock or poultry shall be empowered to seize such dog solely for the purpose of examining such dog in order to determine whether it committed any of the depredations mentioned herein. Any animal control officer or other person who has reason to believe that any dog is killing livestock, or committing any of the depredations mentioned in this section, shall apply to a magistrate serving the locality wherein the dog may be, who shall issue a warrant requiring the owner or custodian, if known, to appear before a general district court at a time and place named therein, at which time evidence shall be heard. If it shall appear that the dog is a livestock killer, or has committed any of the depredations mentioned in this section, the district court shall order that the dog be (i) killed or euthanized immediately by the animal control officer or other officer designated by the court or (ii) removed to another state that does not border on the Commonwealth and prohibited from returning to the Commonwealth. Any dog ordered removed from the Commonwealth that is later found in the Commonwealth shall be ordered by a court to be killed or euthanized immediately.

C. Notwithstanding the provisions of subsection B, if it is determined that the dog has killed or injured only poultry, the district court may, instead of ordering killing, euthanasia, or removal to another state pursuant to this section, order either (a) that the dog be transferred to another owner whom the court deems appropriate and permanently fitted with an identifying microchip registered to that owner or (b) that the dog be fitted with an identifying microchip registered to the owner and confined indoors or in a securely enclosed and locked structure of sufficient height and design to prevent the dog's escape; direct contact with the dog by minors, adults, or other animals; or entry by minors, adults, or other animals. The structure shall be designed to provide the dog with shelter from the elements of nature. When off its owner's property, any dog found to be a poultry killer shall be kept on a leash and muzzled in such a manner as not to cause injury to the dog or interfere with its vision or respiration, but so as to prevent it from biting a person or another animal.

TITLE 3.2. AGRICULTURE, ANIMAL CARE, AND FOOD CHAPTER 65. COMPREHENSIVE ANIMAL CARE ARTICLE 9. CRUELTY TO ANIMALS

§ 3.2-6570. CRUELTY TO ANIMALS; PENALTY.

A. Any person who (i) overrides, overdrives, overloads, ill-treats, or abandons any animal, whether belonging to himself or another; (ii) tortures any animal, willfully inflicts inhumane injury or pain not connected with bona fide scientific or medical experimentation on any animal, or cruelly or unnecessarily beats, maims, mutilates, or kills any animal, whether belonging to himself or another; (iii) deprives any animal of necessary food, drink, shelter, or emergency veterinary treatment; (iv) sores any equine for any purpose or administers drugs or medications to alter or mask such soring for the purpose of sale, show, or exhibition of any kind, unless such administration of drugs or medications is within the context of a veterinary client-patient relationship and solely for therapeutic purposes; (v) ropes, lassoes, or otherwise obstructs or interferes with one or more legs of an equine in order to intentionally cause it to trip or fall for the purpose of engagement in a rodeo, contest, exhibition, entertainment, or sport unless such actions are in the practice of accepted animal husbandry or for the purpose of allowing veterinary care; (vi) willfully sets on foot, instigates, engages in, or in any way furthers any act of cruelty to any animal; (vii) carries or causes to be carried by any vehicle, vessel or otherwise any animal in a cruel, brutal, or inhumane manner, so as to produce torture or unnecessary suffering; or (viii) causes any of the above things, or being the owner of such animal permits such acts to be done by another is guilty of a Class 1 misdemeanor.

In addition to the penalties provided in this subsection, the court may, in its discretion, require any person convicted of a violation of this subsection to attend an anger management or other appropriate treatment program or obtain psychiatric or psychological counseling. The court may impose the costs of such a program or counseling upon the person convicted.

B. Any person who (i) tortures, willfully inflicts inhumane injury or pain not connected with bona fide scientific or medical experimentation, or cruelly and unnecessarily beats, maims, mutilates or kills any animal whether belonging to himself or another; (ii) sores any equine for any purpose or administers drugs or medications to alter or mask such soring for the purpose of sale, show, or exhibit of any kind, unless such administration of drugs or medications is under the supervision of a licensed veterinarian and solely for therapeutic purposes; (iii) ropes, lassoes, or otherwise obstructs or interferes with one or more legs of an equine in order to intentionally cause it to trip or fall for the purpose of engagement in a rodeo, contest, exhibition, entertainment, or sport unless such actions are in the practice of accepted animal husbandry or for the purpose of allowing veterinary care; (iv) maliciously deprives any companion animal of necessary food, drink, shelter or emergency veterinary treatment; (v) instigates, engages in, or in any way furthers any act of cruelty to any animal set forth in clauses (i) through (iv); or (vi) causes any of the actions described in clauses (i) through (v), or being the owner of such animal permits such acts to be done by another; and has been within five years convicted of a violation of this subsection or subsection A, is guilty of a Class 6 felony if the current violation or any previous violation of this subsection or subsection A resulted in the death of an animal or the euthanasia of an animal based on the recommendation of a licensed veterinarian upon determination that such euthanasia was necessary due to the condition of the animal, and such condition was a direct result of a violation of this subsection or subsection A.

C. Nothing in this section shall be construed to prohibit the dehorning of cattle conducted in a reasonable and customary manner.

D. This section shall not prohibit authorized wildlife management activities or hunting, fishing or trapping as regulated under other titles of the Code of Virginia, including Title 29.1, or to farming activities as provided under this title or regulations adopted hereunder.

E. It is unlawful for any person to kill a domestic dog or cat for the purpose of obtaining the hide, fur or pelt of the dog or cat. A violation of this subsection is a Class 1 misdemeanor. A second or subsequent violation of this subsection is a Class 6 felony.

F. Any person who (i) tortures, willfully inflicts inhumane injury or pain not connected with bona fide scientific or medical experimentation, or cruelly and unnecessarily beats, maims, or mutilates any dog or cat that is a companion animal whether belonging to him or another and (ii) as a direct result causes serious bodily injury to such dog or cat that is a companion animal, the death of such dog or cat that is a companion animal, or the euthanasia of such animal on the recommendation of a licensed veterinarian upon determination that such euthanasia was necessary due to the condition of the animal is guilty of a Class 6 felony. If a dog or cat is attacked on its owner's property by a dog so as to cause injury or death, the owner of the injured dog or cat may use all reasonable and necessary force against the dog at the time of the attack to protect his dog or cat. Such owner may be presumed to have taken necessary and appropriate action to defend his dog or cat and shall therefore be presumed not to have violated this subsection. The provisions of this subsection shall not overrule § 3.2-6540, 3.2-6540.1, or 3.2-6552.

For the purposes of this subsection, "serious bodily injury" means bodily injury that involves substantial risk of death, extreme physical pain, protracted and obvious disfigurement, or protracted loss or impairment of the function of a bodily member, organ, or mental faculty.

G. Any person convicted of violating this section may be prohibited by the court from possession or ownership of companion animals.

TITLE 9.1. COMMONWEALTH PUBLIC SAFETY
CHAPTER 1. DEPARTMENT OF CRIMINAL JUSTICE SERVICES
ARTICLE 3. CRIMINAL JUSTICE INFORMATION SYSTEM

§ 9.1-132. INDIVIDUAL'S RIGHT OF ACCESS TO AND REVIEW AND CORRECTION OF INFORMATION.

A. Any individual who believes that criminal history record information is being maintained about him by the Central Criminal Records Exchange (the "Exchange"), or by the arresting law-enforcement agency in the case of offenses not required to be reported to the Exchange, shall have the right to inspect a copy of his criminal history record information at the Exchange or the arresting law-enforcement agency, respectively, for the purpose of ascertaining the completeness and accuracy of the information. The individual's right to access and review shall not extend to any information or data other than that defined in § 9.1-101.

B. The Board shall adopt regulations with respect to an individual's right to access and review criminal history record information about himself reported to the Exchange or, if not reported to the Exchange, maintained by the arresting law-enforcement agency. The regulations shall provide for (i) public notice of the right of access; (ii) access to criminal history record information by an individual or an attorney-at-law acting for an individual; (iii) the submission of identification; (iv) the places and times for review; (v) review of Virginia records by individuals located in other states; (vi) assistance in understanding the record; (vii) obtaining a copy for purposes of initiating a challenge to the record; (viii) procedures for investigation of alleged incompleteness or inaccuracy; (ix) completion or correction of records if indicated; and (x) notification of the individuals and agencies to whom an inaccurate or incomplete record has been disseminated.

C. If an individual believes information maintained about him is inaccurate or incomplete, he may request the agency having custody or control of the records to purge, modify, or supplement them. Should the agency decline to so act, or should the individual believe the agency's decision to be otherwise unsatisfactory, the individual may make written request for review by the Board. The Board or its designee shall, in each case in which it finds prima facie basis for a complaint, conduct a hearing at which the individual may appear with counsel, present evidence, and examine and cross-examine witnesses. The Board shall issue written findings and conclusions. Should the record in question be found to be inaccurate or incomplete, the criminal justice agency maintaining the information shall purge, modify, or supplement it in accordance with the findings and conclusions of the Board. Notification of purging, modification, or supplementation of criminal history record information shall be promptly made by the criminal justice agency maintaining the previously inaccurate information to any individuals or agencies to which the information in question was communicated, as well as to the individual who is the subject of the records.

D. Criminal justice agencies shall maintain records of all agencies to whom criminal history record information has been disseminated, the date upon which the information was disseminated, and such other record matter for the number of years required by regulations of the Board.

E. Any individual or agency aggrieved by any order or decision of the Board may appeal the order or decision in accordance with the Administrative Process Act (§ 2.2-4000 et seq.).

§ 9.1-135. CIVIL REMEDIES FOR VIOLATION OF THIS CHAPTER

A. Any person may institute a civil action in the circuit court of the jurisdiction in which the Board has its administrative headquarters, or in the jurisdiction in which any violation is alleged to have occurred:
1. For actual damages resulting from violation of this article or to restrain any such violation, or both.
2. To obtain appropriate equitable relief against any person who has engaged, is engaged, or is about to engage in any acts or practices in violation of Chapter 23 (§ 19.2-387 et seq.) of Title 19.2, this chapter or rules or regulations of the Board.

B. This section shall not be construed as a waiver of the defense of sovereign immunity.

TITLE 15.2. COUNTIES, CITIES AND TOWNS
CHAPTER 9. GENERAL POWERS OF LOCAL GOVERNMENTS
ARTICLE 1. PUBLIC HEALTH AND SAFETY; NUISANCES

§ 15.2-914. REGULATION OF CHILD-CARE SERVICES AND FACILITIES IN CERTAIN COUNTIES AND CITIES.

§ 15.2-914. (Effective until July 1, 2021) Regulation of child-care services and facilities in certain counties and cities.

Any (i) county that has adopted the urban county executive form of government, (ii) city adjacent to a county that has adopted the urban county executive form of government, or (iii) city which is completely surrounded by such county may by ordinance provide for the regulation and licensing of persons who provide child-care services for compensation and for the regulation and licensing of child-care facilities. "Child-care services" means provision of regular care, protection and guidance to one or more children not related by blood or marriage while such children are separated from their parent, guardian or legal custodian in a dwelling not the residence of the child during a part of the day for at least four days of a calendar week. "Child-care facilities" includes any commercial or residential structure which is used to provide child-care services.

Such local ordinance shall not require the regulation or licensing of any child-care facility that is licensed by the Commonwealth and such ordinance shall not require the regulation or licensing of any facility operated by a religious institution as exempted from licensure by § 63.2-1716.

Except as otherwise provided in this section, such local ordinances shall not be more extensive in scope than comparable state regulations applicable to family day homes. Such local ordinances may regulate the possession and storage of firearms, ammunition, or components or combination thereof at child-care facilities and may be more extensive in scope than comparable state statutes or regulations applicable to family day homes. Local regulations shall not affect the manner of construction or materials to be used in the erection, alteration, repair or use of a residential dwelling.

Such local ordinances may require that persons who provide child-care services shall provide certification from the Central Criminal Records Exchange and a national criminal background check, in accordance with §§ 19.2-389 and 19.2-392.02, that such persons have not been convicted of any offense involving the sexual molestation of children or the physical or sexual abuse or rape of a child or any barrier crime defined in § 19.2-392.02, and such ordinances may require that persons who provide child-care services shall provide certification from the central registry of the Department of Social Services that such persons have not been the subject of a founded complaint of abuse or neglect. If an applicant is denied licensure because of any adverse information appearing on a record obtained from the Central Criminal Records Exchange, the national criminal background check, or the Department of Social Services, the applicant shall be provided a copy of the information upon which that denial was based.

§ 15.2-914. (Effective July 1, 2021) Regulation of child-care services and facilities in certain counties and cities.

Any (i) county that has adopted the urban county executive form of government, (ii) city adjacent to a county that has adopted the urban county executive form of government, or (iii) city which is completely surrounded by such county may by ordinance provide for the regulation and licensing of persons who provide child-care services for compensation and for the regulation and licensing of child-care facilities. "Child-care services" means provision of regular care, protection and guidance to one or more children not related by blood or marriage while such children are separated from their parent, guardian or legal custodian in a dwelling not the residence of the child during a part of the day for at least four days of a calendar week. "Child-care facilities" includes any commercial or residential structure which is used to provide child-care services. Such local ordinance shall not require the regulation or licensing of any child-care facility that is licensed by the Commonwealth and such ordinance shall not require the regulation or licensing of any facility operated by a religious institution as exempted from licensure by § 22.1-289.031.

Except as otherwise provided in this section, such local ordinances shall not be more extensive in scope than comparable state regulations applicable to family day homes. Such local ordinances may regulate the possession and storage of firearms, ammunition, or components or combination thereof at child-care facilities and may be more extensive in scope than comparable state statutes or regulations applicable to family day homes. Local regulations shall not affect the manner of construction or materials to be used in the erection, alteration, repair or use of a residential dwelling.

Such local ordinances may require that persons who provide child-care services shall provide certification from the Central Criminal Records Exchange and a national criminal background check, in accordance with §§ 19.2-389 and 19.2-392.02, that such persons have not been convicted of any offense involving the sexual molestation of children or the physical or sexual abuse or rape of a child or any barrier crime defined in § 19.2-392.02, and such ordinances may require that persons who provide child-care services shall provide certification from the central registry of the Department of Social Services that such persons have not been the subject of a founded complaint of abuse or neglect. If an applicant is denied licensure because of any adverse information appearing on a record obtained from the Central Criminal Records Exchange, the national criminal background check, or the Department of Social Services, the applicant shall be provided a copy of the information upon which that denial was based.

§ 15.2-915. CONTROL OF FIREARMS; APPLICABILITY TO AUTHORITIES AND LOCAL GOVERNMENTAL AGENCIES.

§ 15.2-915. Control of firearms; applicability to authorities and local governmental agencies.

A. No locality shall adopt or enforce any ordinance, resolution, or motion, as permitted by § 15.2-1425, and no agent of such locality shall take any administrative action, governing the purchase, possession, transfer, ownership, carrying, storage, or transporting of firearms, ammunition, or components or combination thereof other than those expressly authorized by statute. For purposes of this section, a statute that does not refer to firearms, ammunition, or components or combination thereof shall not be construed to provide express authorization.

Nothing in this section shall prohibit a locality from adopting workplace rules relating to terms and conditions of employment of the workforce. However, no locality shall adopt any workplace rule, other than for the purposes of a community services board or behavioral health authority as defined in § 37.2-100, that prevents an employee of that locality from storing at that locality's workplace a lawfully possessed firearm and ammunition in a locked private motor vehicle. Nothing in this section shall prohibit a law-enforcement officer, as defined in § 9.1-101, from acting within the scope of his duties.

The provisions of this section applicable to a locality shall also apply to any authority or to a local governmental entity, including a department or agency, but not including any local or regional jail, juvenile detention facility, or state-governed entity, department, or agency.

B. Any local ordinance, resolution, or motion adopted prior to July 1, 2004, governing the purchase, possession, transfer, ownership, carrying, or transporting of firearms, ammunition, or components or combination thereof, other than those expressly authorized by statute, is invalid.

C. In addition to any other relief provided, the court may award reasonable attorney fees, expenses, and court costs to any person, group, or entity that prevails in an action challenging (i) an ordinance, resolution, or motion as being in conflict with this section or (ii) an administrative action taken in bad faith as being in conflict with this section.

D. For purposes of this section, "workplace" means "workplace of the locality."

E. Notwithstanding the provisions of this section, a locality may adopt an ordinance that prohibits the possession, carrying, or transportation of any firearms, ammunition, or components or combination thereof (i) in any building, or part thereof, owned or used by such locality, or by any authority or local governmental entity created or controlled by the locality, for governmental purposes; (ii) in any public park owned or operated by the locality, or by any authority or local governmental entity created or controlled by the locality; (iii) in any recreation or community center facility operated by the locality, or by any authority or local governmental entity created or controlled by the locality; or

(iv) in any public street, road, alley, or sidewalk or public right-of-way or any other place of whatever nature that is open to the public and is being used by or is adjacent to a permitted event or an event that would otherwise require a permit. In buildings that are not owned by a locality, or by any authority or local governmental entity created or controlled by the locality, such ordinance shall apply only to the part of the building that is being used for a governmental purpose and when such building, or part thereof, is being used for a governmental purpose.

Any such ordinance may include security measures that are designed to reasonably prevent the unauthorized access of such buildings, parks, recreation or community center facilities, or public streets, roads, alleys, or sidewalks or public rights-of-way or any other place of whatever nature that is open to the public and is being used by or is adjacent to a permitted event or an event that would otherwise require a permit by a person with any firearms, ammunition, or components or combination thereof, such as the use of metal detectors and increased use of security personnel.

The provisions of this subsection shall not apply to the activities of (i) a Senior Reserve Officers' Training Corps program operated at a public or private institution of higher education in accordance with the provisions of 10 U.S.C. § 2101 et seq. or (ii) any intercollegiate athletics program operated by a public or private institution of higher education and governed by the National Collegiate Athletic Association or any club sports team recognized by a public or private institution of higher education where the sport engaged in by such program or team involves the use of a firearm. Such activities shall follow strict guidelines developed by such institutions for these activities and shall be conducted under the supervision of staff officials of such institutions.

F. Notice of any ordinance adopted pursuant to subsection E shall be posted (i) at all entrances of any building, or part thereof, owned or used by the locality, or by any authority or local governmental entity created or controlled by the locality, for governmental purposes; (ii) at all entrances of any public park owned or operated by the locality, or by any authority or local governmental entity created or controlled by the locality; (iii) at all entrances of any recreation or community center facilities operated by the locality, or by any authority or local governmental entity created or controlled by the locality; and (iv) at all entrances or other appropriate places of ingress and egress to any public street, road, alley, or sidewalk or public right-of-way or any other place of whatever nature that is open to the public and is being used by or is adjacent to a permitted event or an event that would otherwise require a permit.

§ 15.2-915.2. REGULATION OF TRANSPORTATION OF A LOADED RIFLE OR SHOTGUN.

The governing body of any county or city may by ordinance make it unlawful for any person to transport, possess or carry a loaded shotgun or loaded rifle in any vehicle on any public street, road, or highway within such locality. Any violation of such ordinance shall be punishable by a fine of not more than $100. Conservation police officers, sheriffs and all other law-enforcement officers shall enforce the provisions of this section. No ordinance adopted pursuant to this section shall be enforceable unless the governing body adopting such ordinance so notifies the Director of the Department of Wildlife Resourcesby registered mail prior to May 1 of the year in which such ordinance is to take effect.

The provisions of this section shall not apply to duly authorized law-enforcement officers or military personnel in the performance of their lawful duties, nor to any person who reasonably believes that a loaded rifle or shotgun is necessary for his personal safety in the course of his employment or business.

TITLE 16.1. COURTS NOT OF RECORD
CHAPTER 11. JUVENILE AND DOMESTIC RELATIONS DISTRICT COURTS ARTICLE 4. IMMEDIATE CUSTODY, ARREST, DETENTION AND SHELTER CARE

§ 16.1-253. PRELIMINARY PROTECTIVE ORDER.
A. Upon the motion of any person or upon the court's own motion, the court may issue a preliminary protective order, after a hearing, if necessary to protect a child's life, health, safety or normal development pending the final determination of any matter before the court. The order may require a child's parents, guardian, legal custodian, other person standing in loco parentis or other family or household member of the child to observe reasonable conditions of behavior for a specified length of time. These conditions shall include any one or more of the following:
1. To abstain from offensive conduct against the child, a family or household member of the child or any person to whom custody of the child is awarded;
2. To cooperate in the provision of reasonable services or programs designed to protect the child's life, health or normal development;
3. To allow persons named by the court to come into the child's home at reasonable times designated by the court to visit the

child or inspect the fitness of the home and to determine the physical or emotional health of the child;
4. To allow visitation with the child by persons entitled thereto, as determined by the court;
5. To refrain from acts of commission or omission which tend to endanger the child's life, health or normal development;
6. To refrain from such contact with the child or family or household members of the child, as the court may deem appropriate, including removal of such person from the residence of the child. However, prior to the issuance by the court of an order removing such person from the residence of the child, the petitioner must prove by a preponderance of the evidence that such person's probable future conduct would constitute a danger to the life or health of such child, and that there are no less drastic alternatives which could reasonably and adequately protect the child's life or health pending a final determination on the petition; or
7. To grant the person on whose behalf the order is issued the possession of any companion animal as defined in § 3.2-6500 if such person meets the definition of owner in § 3.2-6500.

B. A preliminary protective order may be issued ex parte upon motion of any person or the court's own motion in any matter before the court, or upon petition. The motion or petition shall be supported by an affidavit or by sworn testimony in person before the judge or intake officer which establishes that the child would be subjected to an imminent threat to life or health to the extent that delay for the provision of an adversary hearing would be likely to result in serious or irremediable injury to the child's life or health. If an ex parte order is issued without an affidavit being presented, the court, in its order, shall state the basis upon which the order was entered, including a summary of the allegations made and the court's findings. Following the issuance of an ex parte order the court shall provide an adversary hearing to the affected parties within the shortest practicable time not to exceed five business days after the issuance of the order.

C. Prior to the hearing required by this section, notice of the hearing shall be given at least 24 hours in advance of the hearing to the guardian ad litem for the child, to the parents, guardian, legal custodian, or other person standing in loco parentis of the child, to any other family or household member of the child to whom the protective order may be directed and to the child if he or she is 12 years of age or older. The notice provided herein shall include (i) the time, date and place for the hearing and (ii) a specific statement of the factual circumstances which allegedly necessitate the issuance of a preliminary protective order.

D. All parties to the hearing shall be informed of their right to counsel pursuant to § 16.1-266.

E. At the hearing the child, his or her parents, guardian, legal custodian or other person standing in loco parentis and any other family or household member of the child to whom notice was given shall have the right to confront and cross-examine all adverse witnesses and evidence and to present evidence on their own behalf.

F. If a petition alleging abuse or neglect of a child has been filed, at the hearing pursuant to this section the court shall determine whether the allegations of abuse or neglect have been proven by a preponderance of the evidence. Any finding of abuse or neglect shall be stated in the court order. However, if, before such a finding is made, a person responsible for the care and custody of the child, the child's guardian ad litem or the local department of social services objects to a finding being made at the hearing, the court shall schedule an adjudicatory hearing to be held within 30 days of the date of the initial preliminary protective order hearing. The adjudicatory hearing shall be held to determine whether the allegations of abuse and neglect have been proven by a preponderance of the evidence. Parties who are present at the hearing shall be given notice of the date set for the adjudicatory hearing and parties who are not present shall be summoned as provided in § 16.1-263. The adjudicatory hearing shall be held and an order may be entered, although a party to the hearing fails to appear and is not represented by counsel, provided personal or substituted service was made on the person, or the court determines that such person cannot be found, after reasonable effort, or in the case of a person who is without the Commonwealth, the person cannot be found or his post office address cannot be ascertained after reasonable effort.

Any preliminary protective order issued shall remain in full force and effect pending the adjudicatory hearing.

G. If at the preliminary protective order hearing held pursuant to this section the court makes a finding of abuse or neglect and a preliminary protective order is issued, a dispositional hearing shall be held pursuant to § 16.1-278.2. The court shall forthwith, but in all cases no later than the end of the business day on which the order was issued, enter and transfer electronically to the Virginia Criminal Information Network the respondent's identifying information and the name, date of birth, sex, and race of each protected person provided to the court. A copy of the preliminary protective order containing any such identifying information shall be forwarded forthwith to the primary law-enforcement agency responsible for service and entry of protective orders. Upon receipt of the order by the primary law-enforcement agency, the agency shall forthwith verify and enter any modification as necessary to the identifying information and other appropriate information required by the Department of State Police into the Virginia Criminal Information Network established and maintained by the Department of State Police pursuant to Chapter 2 (§ 52-12 et seq.) of Title 52 and the order shall be served forthwith on the allegedly abusing person in person as provided in § 16.1-264 and due return made to the court. However, if the order is issued by the circuit court, the clerk of the circuit court shall forthwith forward an attested copy of the order containing the respondent's identifying information and the name, date of birth, sex, and race of each protected person provided to the court to the primary law-enforcement agency providing service and entry of protective orders and upon receipt of the order, the primary law-enforcement agency shall enter the name of the person subject to the order and other appropriate information required by the Department of State Police into the Virginia Criminal Information Network established and maintained by the Department pursuant to Chapter 2 (§ 52-12 et seq.) of Title 52 and the order shall be served forthwith upon the allegedly abusing person in person as provided in § 16.1-264. Upon service, the agency making service shall enter the date and time of service and other appropriate information required by the Department of State Police into the Virginia Criminal Information Network and make due return to the court. The preliminary order shall specify a date for the dispositional hearing. The dispositional hearing shall be scheduled at the time of the hearing pursuant to this section, and shall be held within 60 days of this hearing. If an adjudicatory hearing is requested pursuant to subsection F, the dispositional hearing shall nonetheless be scheduled at the hearing pursuant to this section. All parties present at the hearing shall be given notice of the date and time scheduled for the dispositional hearing; parties who are not present shall be summoned to appear as provided in § 16.1-263.

H. Nothing in this section enables the court to remove a child from the custody of his or her parents, guardian, legal custodian or other person standing in loco parentis, except as provided in § 16.1278.2, and no order hereunder shall be entered against a person over whom the court does not have jurisdiction.

I. Neither a law-enforcement agency, the attorney for the Commonwealth, a court nor the clerk's office, nor any employee of them, may disclose, except among themselves, the residential address, telephone number, or place of employment of the person protected by the order or that of the family of such person, except to the extent that disclosure is (i) required by law or the Rules of the Supreme Court, (ii) necessary for law-enforcement purposes, or (iii) permitted by the court for good cause.

J. Violation of any order issued pursuant to this section shall constitute contempt of court.

K. The court shall forthwith, but in all cases no later than the end of the business day on which the order was issued, enter and transfer electronically to the Virginia Criminal Information Network the respondent's identifying information and the name, date of birth, sex, and race of each protected person provided to the court. A copy of the preliminary protective order containing any such identifying information shall be forwarded forthwith to the primary law-enforcement agency responsible for service and entry of protective orders. Upon receipt of the order by the primary law-enforcement agency, the agency shall forthwith verify and enter any modification as necessary to the identifying information and other appropriate information required by the Department of State Police into the Virginia Criminal Information Network established and maintained by the Department pursuant to Chapter 2 (§ 52-12 et seq.) of Title 52 and the order shall be served forthwith on the allegedly abusing person in person as provided in § 16.1-264 and due return made to the court. However, if the order is issued by the circuit court, the clerk of the circuit court shall forthwith forward an attested copy of the order containing the respondent's identifying information and the name, date of birth, sex, and race of each protected person provided to the court to the primary law-enforcement agency providing service and entry of protective orders and upon receipt of the order, the primary law-enforcement agency shall enter the name of the person subject to the order and other appropriate information required by the Department of State Police into the Virginia Criminal Information Network established and maintained by the Department pursuant to Chapter 2 (§ 52-12 et seq.) of Title 52 and the order shall be served forthwith on the allegedly abusing person in person as provided in § 16.1-264. Upon service, the agency making service shall enter the date and time of service and other appropriate information required by the Department of State Police into the Virginia Criminal Information Network and make due return to the court. The preliminary order shall specify a date for the full hearing.

Upon receipt of the return of service or other proof of service pursuant to subsection C of § 16.1-264, the clerk shall forthwith forward an attested copy of the preliminary protective order to the primary law-enforcement agency and the agency shall forthwith verify and enter any modification as necessary into the Virginia Criminal Information Network as described above. If the order is later dissolved or modified, a copy of the dissolution or modification order shall also be attested, forwarded forthwith to the primary law-enforcement agency responsible for service and entry of protective orders, and upon receipt of the order by the primary law-enforcement agency, the agency shall forthwith verify and enter any modification as necessary to the identifying information and other appropriate information required by the Department of State Police into the Virginia Criminal Information Network as described above and the order shall be served forthwith and due return made to the court.

L. No fee shall be charged for filing or serving any petition or order pursuant to this section.

§ 16.1-253.1. PRELIMINARY PROTECTIVE ORDERS IN CASES OF FAMILY ABUSE; CONFIDENTIALITY.

A. Upon the filing of a petition alleging that the petitioner is or has been, within a reasonable period of time, subjected to family abuse, the court may issue a preliminary protective order against an allegedly abusing person in order to protect the health and safety of the petitioner or any family or household member of the petitioner. The order may be issued in an ex parte proceeding upon good cause shown when the petition is supported by an affidavit or sworn testimony before the judge or intake officer. If an ex parte order is issued without an affidavit or a completed form as prescribed by subsection D of § 16.1-253.4 being presented, the court, in its order, shall state the basis upon which the order was entered, including a summary of the allegations made and the court's findings. Immediate and present danger of family abuse or evidence sufficient to establish probable cause that family abuse has recently occurred shall constitute good cause. Evidence that the petitioner has been subjected to family abuse within a reasonable time and evidence of immediate and present danger of family abuse may be established by a showing that (i) the allegedly abusing person is incarcerated and is to be released from incarceration within 30 days following the petition or has been released from incarceration within 30 days prior to the petition, (ii) the crime for which the allegedly abusing person was convicted and incarcerated involved family abuse against the petitioner, and (iii) the allegedly abusing person has made threatening contact with the petitioner while he was incarcerated, exhibiting a renewed threat to the petitioner of family abuse.

A preliminary protective order may include any one or more of the following conditions to be imposed on the allegedly abusing person:
1. Prohibiting acts of family abuse or criminal offenses that result in injury to person or property.
2. Prohibiting such contacts by the respondent with the petitioner or family or household members of the petitioner as the court deems necessary for the health or safety of such persons.
3. Granting the petitioner possession of the premises occupied by the parties to the exclusion of the allegedly abusing person; however, no such grant of possession shall affect title to any real or personal property.

4. Enjoining the respondent from terminating any necessary utility service to a premises that the petitioner has been granted possession of pursuant to subdivision 3 or, where appropriate, ordering the respondent to restore utility services to such premises.
5. Granting the petitioner and, where appropriate, any other family or household member of the petitioner, exclusive use and possession of a cellular telephone number or electronic device. The court may enjoin the respondent from terminating a cellular telephone number or electronic device before the expiration of the contract term with a third-party provider. The court may enjoin the respondent from using a cellular telephone or other electronic device to locate the petitioner.
6. Granting the petitioner temporary possession or use of a motor vehicle owned by the petitioner alone or jointly owned by the parties to the exclusion of the allegedly abusing person; however, no such grant of possession or use shall affect title to the vehicle.
7. Requiring that the allegedly abusing person provide suitable alternative housing for the petitioner and any other family or household member and, where appropriate, requiring the respondent to pay deposits to connect or restore necessary utility services in the alternative housing provided.
8. Granting the petitioner the possession of any companion animal as defined in § 3.2-6500 if such petitioner meets the definition of owner in § 3.2-6500.
9. Any other relief necessary for the protection of the petitioner and family or household members of the petitioner.

B. The court shall forthwith, but in all cases no later than the end of the business day on which the order was issued, enter and transfer electronically to the Virginia Criminal Information Network the respondent's identifying information and the name, date of birth, sex, and race of each protected person provided to the court. A copy of a preliminary protective order containing any such identifying information shall be forwarded forthwith to the primary law-enforcement agency responsible for service and entry of protective orders. Upon receipt of the order by the primary law-enforcement agency, the agency shall forthwith verify and enter any modification as necessary to the identifying information and other appropriate information required by the Department of State Police into the Virginia Criminal Information Network established and maintained by the Department pursuant to Chapter 2 (§ 52-12 et seq.) of Title 52 and the order shall be served forthwith on the allegedly abusing person in person as provided in § 16.1-264 and due return made to the court. However, if the order is issued by the circuit court, the clerk of the circuit court shall forthwith forward an attested copy of the order containing the respondent's identifying information and the name, date of birth, sex, and race of each protected person provided to the court to the primary law-enforcement agency providing service and entry of protective orders and upon receipt of the order, the primary law-enforcement agency shall enter the name of the person subject to the order and other appropriate information required by the Department of State Police into the Virginia Criminal Information Network established and maintained by the Department pursuant to Chapter 2 (§ 52-12 et seq.) of Title 52 and the order shall be served forthwith on the allegedly abusing person in person as provided in § 16.1-264. Upon service, the agency making service shall enter the date and time of service and other appropriate information required by the Department of State Police into the Virginia Criminal Information Network and make due return to the court. The preliminary order shall specify a date for the full hearing. The hearing shall be held within 15 days of the issuance of the preliminary order, unless the court is closed pursuant to § 16.1-69.35 or 17.1-207 and such closure prevents the hearing from being held within such time period, in which case the hearing shall be held on the next day not a Saturday, Sunday, legal holiday, or day on which the court is lawfully closed. If such court is closed pursuant to § 16.1-69.35 or 17.1-207, the preliminary protective order shall remain in full force and effect until it is dissolved by such court, until another preliminary protective order is entered, or until a protective order is entered. If the respondent fails to appear at this hearing because the respondent was not personally served, or if personally served was incarcerated and not transported to the hearing, the court may extend the protective order for a period not to exceed six months. The extended protective order shall be served forthwith on the respondent. However, upon motion of the respondent and for good cause shown, the court may continue the hearing. The preliminary order shall remain in effect until the hearing. Upon request after the order is issued, the clerk shall provide the petitioner with a copy of the order and information regarding the date and time of service. The order shall further specify that either party may at any time file a motion with the court requesting a hearing to dissolve or modify the order. The hearing on the motion shall be given precedence on the docket of the court. Upon petitioner's motion to dissolve the preliminary protective order, a dissolution order may be issued ex parte by the court with or without a hearing. If an ex parte hearing is held, it shall be heard by the court as soon as practicable. If a dissolution order is issued ex parte, the court shall serve a copy of such dissolution order on respondent in conformity with §§ 8.01-286.1 and 8.01-296.

Upon receipt of the return of service or other proof of service pursuant to subsection C of § 16.1-264, the clerk shall forthwith forward an attested copy of the preliminary protective order to the primary law-enforcement agency, and the agency shall forthwith verify and enter any modification as necessary into the Virginia Criminal Information Network as described above. If the order is later dissolved or modified, a copy of the dissolution or modification order shall also be attested, forwarded forthwith to the primary law-enforcement agency responsible for service and entry of protective orders, and upon receipt of the order by the primary law-enforcement agency, the agency shall forthwith verify and enter any modification as necessary to the identifying information and other appropriate information required by the Department of State Police into the Virginia Criminal Information Network as described above and the order shall be served forthwith and due return made to the court.

C. The preliminary order is effective upon personal service on the allegedly abusing person. Except as otherwise provided in § 16.1-253.2, a violation of the order shall constitute contempt of court.

D. At a full hearing on the petition, the court may issue a protective order pursuant to § 16.1-279.1 if the court finds that the petitioner has proven the allegation of family abuse by a preponderance of the evidence.

E. Neither a law-enforcement agency, the attorney for the Commonwealth, a court nor the clerk's office, nor any employee of them, may disclose, except among themselves, the residential address, telephone number, or place of employment of the person protected by the order or that of the family of such person, except to the extent that disclosure is (i) required by law or the Rules of the Supreme Court, (ii) necessary for law-enforcement purposes, or (iii) permitted by the court for good cause.

F. As used in this section, "copy" includes a facsimile copy.

G. No fee shall be charged for filing or serving any petition or order pursuant to this section.

H. Upon issuance of a preliminary protective order, the clerk of the court shall make available to the petitioner information that is published by the Department of Criminal Justice Services for victims of domestic violence or for petitioners in protective order cases.

§ 16.1-253.4. EMERGENCY PROTECTIVE ORDERS AUTHORIZED IN CERTAIN CASES; PENALTY.

A. Any judge of a circuit court, general district court, juvenile and domestic relations district court or magistrate may issue a written or oral ex parte emergency protective order pursuant to this section in order to protect the health or safety of any person.

B. When a law-enforcement officer or an allegedly abused person asserts under oath to a judge or magistrate, and on that assertion or other evidence the judge or magistrate (i) finds that a warrant for a violation of § 18.2-57.2 has been issued or issues a warrant for violation of § 18.2-57.2 and finds that there is probable danger of further acts of family abuse against a family or household member by the respondent or (ii) finds that reasonable grounds exist to believe that the respondent has committed family abuse and there is probable danger of a further such offense against a family or household member by the respondent, the judge or magistrate shall issue an ex parte emergency protective order, except if the respondent is a minor, an emergency protective order shall not be required, imposing one or more of the following conditions on the respondent:

1. Prohibiting acts of family abuse or criminal offenses that result in injury to person or property;
2. Prohibiting such contacts by the respondent with the allegedly abused person or family or household members of the allegedly abused person, including prohibiting the respondent from being in the physical presence of the allegedly abused person or family or household members of the allegedly abused person, as the judge or magistrate deems necessary to protect the safety of such persons;
3. Granting the family or household member possession of the premises occupied by the parties to the exclusion of the respondent; however, no such grant of possession shall affect title to any real or personal property; and
4. Granting the petitioner the possession of any companion animal as defined in § 3.2-6500 if such petitioner meets the definition of owner in § 3.2-6500.

When the judge or magistrate considers the issuance of an emergency protective order pursuant to clause (i), he shall presume that there is probable danger of further acts of family abuse against a family or household member by the respondent unless the presumption is rebutted by the allegedly abused person.

C. An emergency protective order issued pursuant to this section shall expire at 11:59 p.m. on the third day following issuance. If the expiration occurs on a day that the court is not in session, the emergency protective order shall be extended until 11:59 p.m. on the next day that the juvenile and domestic relations district court is in session. When issuing an emergency protective order under this section, the judge or magistrate shall provide the protected person or the law-enforcement officer seeking the emergency protective order with the form for use in filing petitions pursuant to § 16.1-253.1 and written information regarding protective orders that shall include the telephone numbers of domestic violence agencies and legal referral sources on a form prepared by the Supreme Court. If these forms are provided to a law-enforcement officer, the officer may provide these forms to the protected person when giving the emergency protective order to the protected person. The respondent may at any time file a motion with the court requesting a hearing to dissolve or modify the order issued hereunder. The hearing on the motion shall be given precedence on the docket of the court.

D. A law-enforcement officer may request an emergency protective order pursuant to this section and, if the person in need of protection is physically or mentally incapable of filing a petition pursuant to § 16.1-253.1 or 16.1-279.1, may request the extension of an emergency protective order for an additional period of time not to exceed three days after expiration of the original order. The request for an emergency protective order or extension of an order may be made orally, in person or by electronic means, and the judge of a circuit court, general district court, or juvenile and domestic relations district court or a magistrate may issue an oral emergency protective order. An oral emergency protective order issued pursuant to this section shall be reduced to writing, by the law-enforcement officer requesting the order or the magistrate on a preprinted form approved and provided by the Supreme Court of Virginia. The completed form shall include a statement of the grounds for the order asserted by the officer or the allegedly abused person.

E. The court or magistrate shall forthwith, but in all cases no later than the end of the business day on which the order was issued, enter and transfer electronically to the Virginia Criminal Information Network the respondent's identifying information and the name, date of birth, sex, and race of each protected person provided to the court or magistrate. A copy of an emergency protective order issued pursuant to this section containing any such identifying information shall be forwarded forthwith to the primary law-enforcement agency responsible for service and entry of protective orders. Upon receipt of the order by the primary law-enforcement agency, the agency shall forthwith verify and enter any modification as necessary to the identifying information and other appropriate information required by the Department of State Police into the Virginia Criminal Information Network established and maintained by the Department pursuant to Chapter 2 (§ 52-12 et seq.) of Title 52 and the order shall be served forthwith upon the respondent and due return made to the court. However, if the order is issued by the circuit court, the clerk of the circuit court shall forthwith forward an attested copy of the order containing the respondent's identifying information and the name, date of birth, sex, and race of each protected person provided to the court to the primary law-enforcement agency providing service and entry of protective orders and upon receipt of the order, the primary law-enforcement agency shall enter the name of the person subject to the order and other appropriate information required by the Department of State Police into the Virginia Criminal Network established and maintained by the Department pursuant to Chapter 2 (§ 52-12 et seq.) of Title 52 and the order shall be served forthwith on the respondent. Upon service, the agency making service shall enter the date and time of service and other appropriate information required by the Department of State Police into the Virginia Criminal Information Network and make due return to the court. One copy of the order shall be given to the allegedly abused person when it is issued, and one copy shall be filed with the written report required by subsection D of § 19.2-81.3. The judge or magistrate who issues an oral order pursuant to an electronic request by a law-enforcement officer shall verify the written order to determine whether the officer who reduced it to writing accurately transcribed the contents of the oral order. The original copy shall be filed with the clerk of the juvenile and domestic relations district court within five business days of the issuance of the order. If the order is later dissolved or modified, a copy of the dissolution or modification order shall also be attested, forwarded forthwith to the primary law-enforcement agency responsible for service and entry of protective orders, and upon receipt of the order by the primary law-enforcement agency, the agency shall forthwith verify and enter any modification as necessary to the identifying information and other appropriate information required by the Department of State Police into the Virginia Criminal Information Network as described above and the order shall be served forthwith and due return made to the court. Upon request, the clerk shall provide the allegedly abused person with information regarding the date and time of service.

F. The availability of an emergency protective order shall not be affected by the fact that the family or household member left the premises to avoid the danger of family abuse by the respondent.

G. The issuance of an emergency protective order shall not be considered evidence of any wrongdoing by the respondent.

H. As used in this section, "law-enforcement officer" means (i) any full-time or part-time employee of a police department or sheriff's office which is part of or administered by the Commonwealth or any political subdivision thereof and who is responsible for the prevention and detection of crime and the enforcement of the penal, traffic, or highway laws of the Commonwealth; (ii) any member of an auxiliary police force established pursuant to § 15.2-1731; and (iii) any special conservator of the peace who meets the certification requirements for a law-enforcement officer as set forth in § 15.2-1706. Part-time employees are compensated officers who are not full-time employees as defined by the employing police department or sheriff's office.

I. Neither a law-enforcement agency, the attorney for the Commonwealth, a court nor the clerk's office, nor any employee of them, may disclose, except among themselves, the residential address, telephone number, or place of employment of the person protected by the order or that of the family of such person, except to the extent that disclosure is (i) required by law or the Rules of the Supreme Court, (ii) necessary for law-enforcement purposes, or (iii) permitted by the court for good cause.

J. As used in this section:
"Copy" includes a facsimile copy.

"Physical presence" includes (i) intentionally maintaining direct visual contact with the petitioner or (ii) unreasonably being within 100 feet from the petitioner's residence or place of employment.

K. No fee shall be charged for filing or serving any petition or order pursuant to this section.

L. Except as provided in § 16.1-253.2, a violation of a protective order issued under this section shall constitute contempt of court.

M. Upon issuance of an emergency protective order, the clerk of court shall make available to the petitioner information that is published by the Department of Criminal Justice Services for victims of domestic violence or for petitioners in protective order cases.

TITLE 16.1. COURTS NOT OF RECORD
CHAPTER 11. JUVENILE AND DOMESTIC RELATIONS DISTRICT COURTS ARTICLE 9. DISPOSITION

§ 16.1-278.2. ABUSED, NEGLECTED, OR ABANDONED CHILDREN OR CHILDREN WITHOUT PARENTAL CARE.

A. Within 60 days of a preliminary removal order hearing held pursuant to § 16.1-252 or a hearing on a preliminary protective order held pursuant to § 16.1-253, a dispositional hearing shall be held if the court found abuse or neglect and (i) removed the child from his home or (ii) entered a preliminary protective order. Notice of the dispositional hearing shall be provided to the child's parent, guardian, legal custodian, or other person standing in loco parentis in accordance with § 16.1-263. The hearing shall be held and a dispositional order may be entered, although a parent, guardian, legal custodian, or person standing in loco parentis fails to appear and is not represented by counsel, provided personal or substituted service was made on the person, or the court determines that such person cannot be found, after reasonable effort, or in the case of a person who is without the Commonwealth, the person cannot be found or his post office address cannot be ascertained after reasonable effort. Notice shall also be provided to the local department of social services, the guardian ad litem and, if appointed, the court-appointed special advocate.

If a child is found to be (a) abused or neglected; (b) at risk of being abused or neglected by a parent or custodian who has been adjudicated as having abused or neglected another child in his care; or (c) abandoned by his parent or other custodian, or without parental care and guardianship because of his parent's absence or physical or mental incapacity, the juvenile court or the circuit court may make any of the following orders of disposition to protect the welfare of the child:

1. Enter an order pursuant to the provisions of § 16.1-278;
2. Permit the child to remain with his parent, subject to such conditions and limitations as the court may order with respect to such child and his parent or other adult occupant of the same dwelling;
3. Prohibit or limit contact as the court deems appropriate between the child and his parent or other adult occupant of the same dwelling whose presence tends to endanger the child's life, health or normal development. The prohibition may exclude any such individual from the home under such conditions as the court may prescribe for a period to be determined by the court but in no event for longer than 180 days from the date of such determination. A hearing shall be held within 150 days to determine further disposition of the matter that may include limiting or prohibiting contact for another 180 days;
4. Permit the local board of social services or a public agency designated by the community policy and management team to place the child, subject to the provisions of § 16.1-281, in suitable family homes, child-caring institutions, residential

facilities, or independent living arrangements with legal custody remaining with the parents or guardians. The local board or public agency and the parents or guardians shall enter into an agreement which shall specify the responsibilities of each for the care and control of the child. The board or public agency that places the child shall have the final authority to determine the appropriate placement for the child.

Any order allowing a local board or public agency to place a child where legal custody remains with the parents or guardians as provided in this section shall be entered only upon a finding by the court that reasonable efforts have been made to prevent placement out of the home and that continued placement in the home would be contrary to the welfare of the child; and the order shall so state.

5. After a finding that there is no less drastic alternative, transfer legal custody, subject to the provisions of § 16.1-281, to any of the following:
    a. A person with a legitimate interest subject to the provisions of subsection A1;
    b. A child welfare agency, private organization or facility that is licensed or otherwise authorized by law to receive and provide care for such child; however, a court shall not transfer legal custody of an abused or neglected child to an agency, organization or facility out of the Commonwealth without the approval of the Commissioner of Social Services; or
    c. The local board of social services of the county or city in which the court has jurisdiction or, at the discretion of the court, to the local board of the county or city in

which the child has residence if other than the county or city in which the court has jurisdiction. The local board shall accept the child for care and custody, provided that it has been given reasonable notice of the pendency of the case and an opportunity to be heard. However, in an emergency in the county or city in which the court has jurisdiction, the local board may be required to accept a child for a period not to exceed 14 days without prior notice or an opportunity to be heard if the judge entering the placement order describes the emergency and the need for such temporary placement in the order. Nothing in this section shall prohibit the commitment of a child to any local board of social services in the Commonwealth when the local board consents to the commitment. The board to which the child is committed shall have the final authority to determine the appropriate placement for the child.

Any order authorizing removal from the home and transferring legal custody of a child to a local board of social services as provided in this section shall be entered only upon a finding by the court that reasonable efforts have been made to prevent removal and that continued placement in the home would be contrary to the welfare of the child; and the order shall so state.

A finding by the court that reasonable efforts were made to prevent removal of the child from his home shall not be required if the court finds that (i) the residual parental rights of the parent regarding a sibling of the child have previously been involuntarily terminated; (ii) the parent has been convicted of an offense under the laws of the Commonwealth or a substantially similar law of any other state, the United States, or any foreign jurisdiction that constitutes murder or voluntary manslaughter, or a felony attempt, conspiracy, or solicitation to commit any such offense, if the victim of the offense was a child of the parent, a child with whom the parent resided at the time such offense occurred, or the other parent of the child; (iii) the parent has been convicted of an offense under the laws of the Commonwealth or a substantially similar law of any other state, the United States, or any foreign jurisdiction that constitutes felony assault resulting in serious bodily injury or felony bodily wounding resulting in serious bodily injury or felony sexual assault, if the victim of the offense was a child of the parent or a child with whom the parent resided at the time of such offense; or (iv) on the basis of clear and convincing evidence, the parent has subjected any child to aggravated circumstances, or abandoned a child under circumstances that would justify the termination of residual parental rights pursuant to subsection D of § 16.1-283.

As used in this section:
"Aggravated circumstances" means torture, chronic or severe abuse, or chronic or severe sexual abuse, if the victim of such conduct was a child of the parent or child with whom the parent resided at the time such conduct occurred, including the failure to protect such a child from such conduct, which conduct or failure to protect (i) evinces a wanton or depraved indifference to human life or (ii) has resulted in the death of such a child or in serious bodily injury to such a child.

"Chronic abuse" or "chronic sexual abuse" means recurring acts of physical abuse that place the child's health, safety and well-being at risk.

"Serious bodily injury" means bodily injury that involves substantial risk of death, extreme physical pain, protracted and obvious disfigurement, or protracted loss or impairment of the function of a bodily member, organ or mental faculty.

"Severe abuse" or "severe sexual abuse" may include an act or omission that occurred only once but otherwise meets the definition of "aggravated circumstances."

6. Transfer legal custody pursuant to subdivision 5 of this section and order the parent to participate in such services and programs or to refrain from such conduct as the court may prescribe; or
7. Terminate the rights of the parent pursuant to § 16.1-283. A1. Any order transferring custody of the child to a person with a legitimate interest pursuant to subdivision A 5 a shall be entered only upon a finding, based upon a preponderance of the evidence, that such person is one who, after an investigation as directed by the court, (i) is found by the court to be willing and qualified to receive and care for the child; (ii) is willing to have a positive, continuous relationship with the child; (iii) is committed to providing a permanent, suitable home for the child; and (iv) is willing and has the ability to protect the child from abuse and neglect; and the order shall so state. The court's order transferring custody to a person with a legitimate interest should further provide for, as appropriate, any terms or conditions which would promote the child's interest and welfare; ongoing provision of social services to the child and the child's custodian; and court review of the child's placement.

B. If the child has been placed in foster care, at the dispositional hearing the court shall review the foster care plan for the child filed in accordance with § 16.1-281 by the local department of social services, a public agency designated by the community policy and management team which places a child through an agreement with the parents or guardians where legal custody remains with the parents or guardians, or child welfare agency.

C. Any preliminary protective orders entered on behalf of the child shall be reviewed at the dispositional hearing and may be incorporated, as appropriate, in the dispositional order.

D. A dispositional order entered pursuant to this section is a final order from which an appeal may be taken in accordance with § 16.1-296.

§ 16.1-279.1. PROTECTIVE ORDER IN CASES OF FAMILY ABUSE.

A. In cases of family abuse, including any case involving an incarcerated or recently incarcerated respondent against whom a preliminary protective order has been issued pursuant to § 16.1-253.1, the court may issue a protective order to protect the health and safety of the petitioner and family or household members of the petitioner. A protective order issued under this section may include any one or more of the following conditions to be imposed on the respondent:
1. Prohibiting acts of family abuse or criminal offenses that result in injury to person or property;
2. Prohibiting such contacts by the respondent with the petitioner or family or household members of the petitioner as the court deems necessary for the health or safety of such persons;

3. Granting the petitioner possession of the residence occupied by the parties to the exclusion of the respondent; however, no such grant of possession shall affect title to any real or personal property;
4. Enjoining the respondent from terminating any necessary utility service to the residence to which the petitioner was granted possession pursuant to subdivision 3 or, where appropriate, ordering the respondent to restore utility services to that residence;
5. Granting the petitioner and, where appropriate, any other family or household member of the petitioner, exclusive use and possession of a cellular telephone number or electronic device. The court may enjoin the respondent from terminating a cellular telephone number or electronic device before the expiration of the contract term with a third-party provider. The court may enjoin the respondent from using a cellular telephone or other electronic device to locate the petitioner;
6. Granting the petitioner temporary possession or use of a motor vehicle owned by the petitioner alone or jointly owned by the parties to the exclusion of the respondent and enjoining the respondent from terminating any insurance, registration, or taxes on the motor vehicle and directing the respondent to maintain the insurance, registration, and taxes, as appropriate; however, no such grant of possession or use shall affect title to the vehicle;
7. Requiring that the respondent provide suitable alternative housing for the petitioner and, if appropriate, any other family or household member and where appropriate, requiring the respondent to pay deposits to connect or restore necessary utility services in the alternative housing provided;

8. Ordering the respondent to participate in treatment, counseling or other programs as the court deems appropriate;
9. Granting the petitioner the possession of any companion animal as defined in § 3.2-6500 if such petitioner meets the definition of owner in § 3.2-6500; and
10. Any other relief necessary for the protection of the petitioner and family or household members of the petitioner, including a provision for temporary custody or visitation of a minor child.

A1. If a protective order is issued pursuant to subsection A, the court may also issue a temporary child support order for the support of any children of the petitioner whom the respondent has a legal obligation to support. Such order shall terminate upon the determination of support pursuant to § 20-108.1.

B. The protective order may be issued for a specified period of time up to a maximum of two years. The protective order shall expire at 11:59 p.m. on the last day specified or at 11:59 p.m. on the last day of the two-year period if no date is specified. Prior to the expiration of the protective order, a petitioner may file a written motion requesting a hearing to extend the order. Proceedings to extend a protective order shall be given precedence on the docket of the court. If the petitioner was a family or household member of the respondent at the time the initial protective order was issued, the court may extend the protective order for a period not longer than two years to protect the health and safety of the petitioner or persons who are family or household members of the petitioner at the time the request for an extension is made. The extension of the protective order shall expire at 11:59 p.m. on the last day specified or at 11:59 p.m. on the last day of the two-year period if no date is specified. Nothing herein shall limit the number of extensions that may be requested or issued.

C. A copy of the protective order shall be served on the respondent and provided to the petitioner as soon as possible. The court, including a circuit court if the circuit court issued the order, shall forthwith, but in all cases no later than the end of the business day on which the order was issued, enter and transfer electronically to the Virginia Criminal Information Network the respondent's identifying information and the name, date of birth, sex, and race of each protected person provided to the court and shall forthwith forward the attested copy of the protective order containing any such identifying information to the primary law-enforcement agency responsible for service and entry of protective orders. Upon receipt of the order by the primary law-enforcement agency, the agency shall forthwith verify and enter any modification as necessary to the identifying information and other appropriate information required by the Department of State Police into the Virginia Criminal Information Network established and maintained by the Department pursuant to Chapter 2 (§ 52-12 et seq.) of Title 52 and the order shall be served forthwith upon the respondent and due return made to the court. Upon service, the agency making service shall enter the date and time of service and other appropriate information required by the Department of State Police into the Virginia Criminal Information Network and make due return to the court. If the order is later dissolved or modified, a copy of the dissolution or modification order shall also be attested, forwarded forthwith to the primary law-enforcement agency responsible for service and entry of protective orders, and upon receipt of the order by the primary law-enforcement agency, the agency shall forthwith verify and enter any modification as necessary to the identifying information and other appropriate information required by the Department of State Police into the Virginia Criminal Information Network as described above and the order shall be served forthwith and due return made to the court.

D. Except as otherwise provided in § 16.1-253.2, a violation of a protective order issued under this section shall constitute contempt of court.

E. The court may assess costs and attorneys' fees against either party regardless of whether an order of protection has been issued as a result of a full hearing.

F. Any judgment, order or decree, whether permanent or temporary, issued by a court of appropriate jurisdiction in another state, the United States or any of its territories, possessions or Commonwealths, the District of Columbia or by any tribal court of appropriate jurisdiction for the purpose of preventing violent or threatening acts or harassment against or contact or communication with or physical proximity to another person, including any of the conditions specified in subsection A, shall be accorded full faith and credit and enforced in the Commonwealth as if it were an order of the Commonwealth, provided reasonable notice and opportunity to be heard were given by the issuing jurisdiction to the person against whom the order is sought to be enforced sufficient to protect such person's due process rights and consistent with federal law. A person entitled to protection under such a foreign order may file the order in any juvenile and domestic relations district court by filing with the court an attested or exemplified copy of the order. Upon such a filing, the clerk shall forthwith forward an attested copy of the order to the primary law-enforcement agency responsible for service and entry of protective orders which shall, upon receipt, enter the name of the person subject to the order and other appropriate information required by the Department of State Police into the Virginia Criminal Information Network established and maintained by the Department pursuant to Chapter 2 (§ 52-12 et seq.) of Title 52. Where practical, the court may transfer information electronically to the Virginia Criminal Information Network.

Upon inquiry by any law-enforcement agency of the Commonwealth, the clerk shall make a copy available of any foreign order filed with that court. A law-enforcement officer may, in the performance of his duties, rely upon a copy of a foreign protective order or other suitable evidence which has been provided to him by any source and may also rely upon the statement of any person protected by the order that the order remains in effect.

G. Either party may at any time file a written motion with the court requesting a hearing to dissolve or modify the order. Proceedings to dissolve or modify a protective order shall be given precedence on the docket of the court. Upon petitioner's motion to dissolve the protective order, a dissolution order may be issued ex parte by the court with or without a hearing. If an ex parte hearing is held, it shall be heard by the court as soon as practicable. If a dissolution order is issued ex parte, the court shall serve a copy of such dissolution order on respondent in conformity with §§ 8.01-286.1 and 8.01-296.

H. As used in this section:
"Copy" includes a facsimile copy; and "Protective order" includes an initial, modified or extended protective order.

I. Neither a law-enforcement agency, the attorney for the Commonwealth, a court nor the clerk's office, nor any employee of them, may disclose, except among themselves, the residential address, telephone number, or place of employment of the person protected by the order or that of the family of such person, except to the extent that disclosure is (i) required by law or the Rules of the Supreme Court, (ii) necessary for law-enforcement purposes, or (iii) permitted by the court for good cause.

J. No fee shall be charged for filing or serving any petition or order pursuant to this section.

K. Upon issuance of a protective order, the clerk of the court shall make available to the petitioner information that is published by the Department of Criminal Justice Services for victims of domestic violence or for petitioners in protective order cases.

TITLE 18.2. CRIMES AND OFFENSES GENERALLY CHAPTER 1. IN GENERAL
ARTICLE 3. CLASSIFICATION OF CRIMINAL OFFENSES AND PUNISHMENT

§ 18.2-10. PUNISHMENT FOR CONVICTION OF FELONY; PENALTY.
The authorized punishments for conviction of a felony are:
  (a) For Class 1 felonies, death, if the person so convicted was 18 years of age or older at the time of the offense and is not determined to be mentally retarded pursuant to § 19.2-264.3:1.1, or imprisonment for life and, subject to subdivision (g), a fine of not more than $100,000. If the person was under 18 years of age at the time of the offense or is determined

to be mentally retarded pursuant to § 19.2-264.3:1.1, the punishment shall be imprisonment for life and, subject to subdivision (g), a fine of not more than $100,000.

(b) For Class 2 felonies, imprisonment for life or for any term not less than 20 years and, subject to subdivision (g), a fine of not more than $100,000.

(c) For Class 3 felonies, a term of imprisonment of not less than five years nor more than 20 years and, subject to subdivision (g), a fine of not more than $100,000.

(d) For Class 4 felonies, a term of imprisonment of not less than two years nor more than 10 years and, subject to subdivision (g), a fine of not more than $100,000.

(e) For Class 5 felonies, a term of imprisonment of not less than one year nor more than 10 years, or in the discretion of the jury or the court trying the case without a jury, confinement in jail for not more than 12 months and a fine of not more than $2,500, either or both.

(f) For Class 6 felonies, a term of imprisonment of not less than one year nor more than five years, or in the discretion of the jury or the court trying the case without a jury, confinement in jail for not more than 12 months and a fine of not more than $2,500, either or both.

(g) Except as specifically authorized in subdivision (e) or (f), or in Class 1 felonies for which a sentence of death is imposed, the court shall impose either a sentence of imprisonment together with a fine, or imprisonment only. However, if the defendant is not a natural person, the court shall impose only a fine.

For any felony offense committed (i) on or after January 1, 1995, the court may, and (ii) on or after July 1, 2000, shall, except in cases in which the court orders a suspended term of confinement of at least six months, impose an additional term of not less than six months nor more than three years, which shall be suspended conditioned upon successful completion of a period of post-release supervision pursuant to § 19.2-295.2 and compliance with such other terms as the sentencing court may require. However, such additional term may only be imposed when the sentence includes an active term of incarceration in a correctional facility.

For a felony offense prohibiting proximity to children as described in subsection A of § 18.2-370.2, the sentencing court is authorized to impose the punishment set forth in that section in addition to any other penalty provided by law.

§ 18.2-11. PUNISHMENT FOR CONVICTION OF MISDEMEANOR.

The authorized punishments for conviction of a misdemeanor are:
- (a) For Class 1 misdemeanors, confinement in jail for not more than twelve months and a fine of not more than $2,500, either or both.
- (b) For Class 2 misdemeanors, confinement in jail for not more than six months and a fine of not more than $1,000, either or both.
- (c) For Class 3 misdemeanors, a fine of not more than $500.
- (d) For Class 4 misdemeanors, a fine of not more than $250.

For a misdemeanor offense prohibiting proximity to children as described in subsection A of § 18.2-370.2, the sentencing court is authorized to impose the punishment set forth in subsection B of that section in addition to any other penalty provided by law.

TITLE 18.2. CRIMES AND OFFENSES GENERALLY CHAPTER 4. CRIMES AGAINST THE PERSON ARTICLE 1. HOMICIDE

§ 18.2-31. CAPITAL MURDER DEFINED; PUNISHMENT.

A. The following offenses shall constitute capital murder, punishable as a Class 1 felony:
1. The willful, deliberate, and premeditated killing of any person in the commission of abduction, as defined in § 18.2-48, when such abduction was committed with the intent to extort money or a pecuniary benefit or with the intent to defile the victim of such abduction;
2. The willful, deliberate, and premeditated killing of any person by another for hire;
3. The willful, deliberate, and premeditated killing of any person by a prisoner confined in a state or local correctional facility as defined in § 53.1-1, or while in the custody of an employee thereof;
4. The willful, deliberate, and premeditated killing of any person in the commission of robbery or attempted robbery;
5. The willful, deliberate, and premeditated killing of any person in the commission of, or subsequent to, rape or attempted rape, forcible sodomy, or attempted forcible sodomy or object sexual penetration;
6. The willful, deliberate, and premeditated killing of a law-enforcement officer as defined in § 9.1-101, a fire marshal appointed pursuant to § 27-30 or a deputy or an assistant fire marshal appointed pursuant to § 27-36, when such fire marshal or deputy or assistant fire marshal has police powers as set forth in §§ 27-34.2 and 27-34.2:1, an auxiliary police officer appointed or provided for pursuant to §§ 15.2-1731 and 15.2-1733, an auxiliary deputy sheriff appointed pursuant to §

15.2-1603, or any law-enforcement officer of another state or the United States having the power to arrest for a felony under the laws of such state or the United States, when such killing is for the purpose of interfering with the performance of his official duties;

7. The willful, deliberate, and premeditated killing of more than one person as a part of the same act or transaction;
8. The willful, deliberate, and premeditated killing of more than one person within a three-year period;
9. The willful, deliberate, and premeditated killing of any person in the commission of or attempted commission of a violation of § 18.2-248, involving a Schedule I or II controlled substance, when such killing is for the purpose of furthering the commission or attempted commission of such violation;
10. The willful, deliberate, and premeditated killing of any person by another pursuant to the direction or order of one who is engaged in a continuing criminal enterprise as defined in subsection I of § 18.2-248;
11. The willful, deliberate, and premeditated killing of a pregnant woman by one who knows that the woman is pregnant and has the intent to cause the involuntary termination of the woman's pregnancy without a live birth;
12. The willful, deliberate, and premeditated killing of a person under the age of 14 by a person age 21 or older;
13. The willful, deliberate, and premeditated killing of any person by another in the commission of or attempted commission of an act of terrorism as defined in § 18.2-46.4;
14. The willful, deliberate, and premeditated killing of a justice of the Supreme Court, a judge of the Court of Appeals, a judge of a circuit court or district court, a retired judge sitting by designation or under temporary recall, or a substitute judge

appointed under § 16.1-69.9:1 when the killing is for the purpose of interfering with his official duties as a judge; and

15. The willful, deliberate, and premeditated killing of any witness in a criminal case after a subpoena has been issued for such witness by the court, the clerk, or an attorney, when the killing is for the purpose of interfering with the person's duties in such case.

B. For a violation of subdivision A 6 where the offender was 18 years of age or older at the time of the offense, the punishment shall be no less than a mandatory minimum term of confinement for life.

C. If any one or more subsections, sentences, or parts of this section shall be judged unconstitutional or invalid, such adjudication shall not affect, impair, or invalidate the remaining provisions thereof but shall be confined in its operation to the specific provisions so held unconstitutional or invalid.

§ 18.2-32. FIRST AND SECOND DEGREE MURDER DEFINED; PUNISHMENT.

Murder, other than capital murder, by poison, lying in wait, imprisonment, starving, or by any willful, deliberate, and premeditated killing, or in the commission of, or attempt to commit, arson, rape, forcible sodomy, inanimate or animate object sexual penetration, robbery, burglary or abduction, except as provided in § 18.2-31, is murder of the first degree, punishable as a Class 2 felony.

All murder other than capital murder and murder in the first degree is murder of the second degree and is punishable by confinement in a state correctional facility for not less than five nor more than forty years.

TITLE 18.2. CRIMES AND OFFENSES GENERALLY CHAPTER 4. CRIMES AGAINST THE PERSON ARTICLE 3. KIDNAPPING AND RELATED OFFENSES

§ 18.2-47. ABDUCTION AND KIDNAPPING DEFINED; PUNISHMENT.

A. Any person who, by force, intimidation or deception, and without legal justification or excuse, seizes, takes, transports, detains or secretes another person with the intent to deprive such other person of his personal liberty or to withhold or conceal him from any person, authority or institution lawfully entitled to his charge, shall be deemed guilty of "abduction."

B. Any person who, by force, intimidation or deception, and without legal justification or excuse, seizes, takes, transports, detains or secretes another person with the intent to subject him to forced labor or services shall be deemed guilty of "abduction." For purposes of this subsection, the term "intimidation" shall include destroying, concealing, confiscating, withholding, or threatening to withhold a passport, immigration document, or other governmental identification or threatening to report another as being illegally present in the United States.

C. The provisions of this section shall not apply to any law-enforcement officer in the performance of his duty. The terms "abduction" and "kidnapping" shall be synonymous in this Code.

Abduction for which no punishment is otherwise prescribed shall be punished as a Class 5 felony.

D. If an offense under subsection A is committed by the parent of the person abducted and punishable as contempt of court in any proceeding then pending, the offense shall be a Class 1 misdemeanor in addition to being punishable as contempt of court. However, such offense, if committed by the parent of the person abducted and punishable as contempt of court in any proceeding then pending and the person abducted is removed from the Commonwealth by the abducting parent, shall be a Class 6 felony in addition to being punishable as contempt of court.

TITLE 18.2. CRIMES AND OFFENSES GENERALLY CHAPTER 4. CRIMES AGAINST THE PERSON ARTICLE 4. ASSAULTS AND BODILY WOUNDINGS

§ 18.2-52. MALICIOUS BODILY INJURY BY MEANS OF ANY CAUSTIC SUBSTANCE OR AGENT OR USE OF ANY EXPLOSIVE OR FIRE.

If any person maliciously causes any other person bodily injury by means of any acid, lye or other caustic substance or agent or use of any explosive or fire, he shall be guilty of a felony and shall be punished by confinement in a state correctional facility for a period of not less than five years nor more than thirty years. If such act is done unlawfully but not maliciously, the offender shall be guilty of a Class 6 felony.

§ 18.2-56.2. ALLOWING ACCESS TO FIREARMS BY CHILDREN; PENALTY.

A. It shall be unlawful for any person to recklessly leave a loaded, unsecured firearm in such a manner as to endanger the life or limb of any child under the age of fourteen. Any person violating the provisions of this subsection shall be guilty of a Class 1 misdemeanor.

B. It shall be unlawful for any person knowingly to authorize a child under the age of twelve to use a firearm except when the child is under the supervision of an adult. Any person violating this subsection shall be guilty of a Class 1 misdemeanor. For purposes of this subsection, "adult" shall mean a parent, guardian, person standing in loco parentis to the child or a person twenty-one years or over who has the permission of the parent, guardian, or person standing in loco parentis to supervise the child in the use of a firearm.

§ 18.2-57.01. POINTING LASER AT LAW-ENFORCEMENT OFFICER UNLAWFUL; PENALTY.

If any person, knowing or having reason to know another person is a law-enforcement officer as defined in § 18.2-57, a probation or parole officer appointed pursuant to § 53.1-143, a correctional officer as defined in § 53.1-1, or a person employed by the Department of Corrections directly involved in the care, treatment or supervision of inmates in the custody of the Department engaged in the performance of his public duties as such, intentionally projects at such other person a beam or a point of light from a laser, a laser gun sight, or any device that simulates a laser, shall be guilty of a Class 2 misdemeanor.

TITLE 18.2. CRIMES AND OFFENSES GENERALLY CHAPTER 4. CRIMES AGAINST THE PERSON ARTICLE 5. ROBBERY

§ 18.2-58. ROBBERY; PENALTY.

If any person commit robbery by partial strangulation, or suffocation, or by striking or beating, or by other violence to the person, or by assault or otherwise putting a person in fear of serious bodily harm, or by the threat or presenting of firearms, or other deadly weapon or instrumentality whatsoever, he shall be guilty of a felony and shall be punished by confinement in a state correctional facility for life or any term not less than five years.

TITLE 18.2. CRIMES AND OFFENSES GENERALLY CHAPTER 4. CRIMES AGAINST THE PERSON ARTICLE 6. EXTORTION AND OTHER THREATS

§ 18.2-60.3. STALKING; PENALTY.

A. Any person, except a law-enforcement officer, as defined in § 9.1-101, and acting in the performance of his official duties, and a registered private investigator, as defined in § 9.1-138, who is regulated in accordance with § 9.1-139 and acting in the course of his legitimate business, who on more than one occasion engages in conduct directed at another person with the intent to place, or when he knows or reasonably should know that the conduct places that other person in reasonable fear of death, criminal sexual assault, or bodily injury to that other person or to that other person's family or household member is guilty of a Class 1 misdemeanor. If the person contacts or follows or attempts to contact or follow the person at whom the conduct is directed after being given actual notice that the person does not want to be contacted or followed, such actions shall be prima facie evidence that the person intended to place that other person, or reasonably should have known that the other person was placed, in reasonable fear of death, criminal sexual assault, or bodily injury to himself or a family or household member.

B. Any person who is convicted of a second offense of subsection A occurring within five years of a prior conviction of such an offense under this section or for a substantially similar offense under the law of any other jurisdiction is guilty of a Class 6 felony.

C. A person may be convicted under this section irrespective of the jurisdiction or jurisdictions within the Commonwealth wherein the conduct described in subsection A occurred, if the person engaged in that conduct on at least one occasion in the jurisdiction where the person is tried. Evidence of any such conduct that occurred outside the Commonwealth may be admissible, if relevant, in any prosecution under this section provided that the prosecution is based upon conduct occurring within the Commonwealth.

D. Upon finding a person guilty under this section, the court shall, in addition to the sentence imposed, issue an order prohibiting contact between the defendant and the victim or the victim's family or household member.

E. The Department of Corrections, sheriff or regional jail director shall give notice prior to the release from a state correctional facility or a local or regional jail of any person incarcerated upon conviction of a violation of this section, to any victim of the offense who, in writing, requests notice, or to any person designated in writing by the victim. The notice shall be given at least 15 days prior to release of a person sentenced to a term of incarceration of more than 30 days or, if the person was sentenced to a term of incarceration of at least 48 hours but no more than 30 days, 24 hours prior to release. If the person escapes, notice shall be given as soon as practicable following the escape. The victim shall keep the Department of Corrections, sheriff or regional jail director informed of the current mailing address and telephone number of the person named in the writing submitted to receive notice.

All information relating to any person who receives or may receive notice under this subsection shall remain confidential and shall not be made available to the person convicted of violating this section.

For purposes of this subsection, "release" includes a release of the offender from a state correctional facility or a local or regional jail (i) upon completion of his term of incarceration or (ii) on probation or parole.

No civil liability shall attach to the Department of Corrections nor to any sheriff or regional jail director or their deputies or employees for a failure to comply with the requirements of this subsection.

F. For purposes of this section:
"Family or household member" has the same meaning as provided in § 16.1-228.

TITLE 18.2. CRIMES AND OFFENSES GENERALLY CHAPTER 4. CRIMES AGAINST THE PERSON ARTICLE 7. CRIMINAL SEXUAL ASSAULT § 18.2-61. RAPE.

A. If any person has sexual intercourse with a complaining witness, whether or not his or her spouse, or causes a complaining witness, whether or not his or her spouse, to engage in sexual intercourse with any other person and such act is accomplished (i) against the complaining witness's will, by force, threat or intimidation of or against the complaining witness or another person; or (ii) through the use of the complaining witness's mental incapacity or physical helplessness; or (iii) with a child under age 13 as the victim, he or she shall be guilty of rape.

B. A violation of this section shall be punishable, in the discretion of the court or jury, by confinement in a state correctional facility for life or for any term not less than five years; and in addition:
1. For a violation of clause (iii) of subsection A where the offender is more than three years older than the victim, if done in the commission of, or as part of the same course of conduct as, or as part of a common scheme or plan as a violation of (i) subsection A of § 18.2-47 or § 18.2-48, (ii) § 18.2-89, 18.2-90, or 18.2-91, or (iii) § 18.2-51.2, the punishment shall include a mandatory minimum term of confinement of 25 years; or
2. For a violation of clause (iii) of subsection A where it is alleged in the indictment that the offender was 18 years of age or older at the time of the offense, the punishment shall include a mandatory minimum term of confinement for life.

The mandatory minimum terms of confinement prescribed for violations of this section shall be served consecutively with any other sentence. If the term of confinement imposed for any violation of clause (iii) of subsection A, where the offender is more than three years older than the victim, is for a term less than life imprisonment, the judge shall impose, in addition to any active sentence, a suspended sentence of no less than 40 years. This suspended sentence shall be suspended for the remainder of the defendant's life, subject to revocation by the court.

There shall be a rebuttable presumption that a juvenile over the age of 10 but less than 12, does not possess the physi cal capacity to commit a violation of this section. In any case deemed appropriate by the court, all or part of any sentence imposed for a violation under this section against a spouse may be suspended upon the defendant's completion of counseling or therapy, if not already provided, in the manner prescribed under § 19.2-218.1 if, after consideration of the views of the complaining witness and such other evidence as may be relevant, the court finds such action will promote maintenance of the family unit and will be in the best interest of the complaining witness.

C. Upon a finding of guilt under this section, when a spouse is the complaining witness in any case tried by the court without a jury, the court, without entering a judgment of guilt, upon motion of the defendant who has not previously had a proceeding against him for violation of this section dismissed pursuant to this subsection and with the consent of the complaining witness and the attorney for the Commonwealth, may defer further proceedings and place the defendant on probation pending completion of counseling or therapy, if not already provided, in the manner prescribed under § 19.2-218.1. If the defendant fails to so complete such counseling or therapy, the court may make final disposition of the case and proceed as otherwise provided. If such counseling is completed as prescribed under § 19.2-218.1, the court may discharge the defendant and dismiss the proceedings against him if, after consideration of the views of the complaining witness and such other evidence as may be relevant, the court finds such action will promote maintenance of the family unit and be in the best interest of the complaining witness.

TITLE 18.2. CRIMES AND OFFENSES GENERALLY CHAPTER 5. CRIMES AGAINST PROPERTY ARTICLE 5. TRESPASS TO REALTY

§ 18.2-119. TRESPASS AFTER HAVING BEEN FORBIDDEN TO DO SO; PENALTIES.

If any person without authority of law goes upon or remains upon the lands, buildings or premises of another, or any portion or area thereof, after having been forbidden to do so, either orally or in writing, by the owner, lessee, custodian, or the agent of any such person, or other person lawfully in charge thereof, or after having been forbidden to do so by a sign or signs posted by or at the direction of such persons or the agent of any such person or by the holder of any easement or other right-of-way authorized by the instrument creating such interest to post such signs on such lands, structures, premises or portion or area thereof at a place or places where it or they may be reasonably seen, or if any person, whether he is the owner, tenant or otherwise entitled to the use of such land, building or premises, goes upon, or remains upon such land, building or premises after having been prohibited from doing so by a court of competent jurisdiction by an order issued pursuant to §§ 16.1-253, 16.1-253.1, 16.1-253.4, 16.1-278.2 through 16.1-278.6, 16.1-278.8, 16.1-278.14, 16.1-278.15, 16.1-279.1, 19.2-152.8, 19.2-152.9 or § 19.2-152.10 or an ex parte order issued pursuant to § 20-103, and after having been served with such order, he shall be guilty of a Class 1 misdemeanor. This section shall not be construed to affect in any way the provisions of §§ 18.2-132 through 18.2-136.

§ 18.2-154. SHOOTING AT OR THROWING MISSILES, ETC., AT TRAIN, CAR, VESSEL, ETC.; PENALTY.

Any person who maliciously shoots at, or maliciously throws any missile at or against, any train or cars on any railroad or other transportation company or any vessel or other watercraft, or any motor vehicle or other vehicles when occupied by one or more persons, whereby the life of any person on such train, car, vessel, or other watercraft, or in such motor vehicle or other vehicle, may be put in peril, is guilty of a Class 4 felony. In the event of the death of any such person, resulting from such malicious shooting or throwing, the person so offending is guilty of murder in the second degree. However, if the homicide is willful, deliberate, and premeditated, he is guilty of murder in the first degree.

If any such act is committed unlawfully, but not maliciously, the person so offending is guilty of a Class 6 felony and, in the event of the death of any such person, resulting from such unlawful act, the person so offending is guilty of involuntary manslaughter.

If any person commits a violation of this section by maliciously or unlawfully shooting, with a firearm, at a conspicuously marked law-enforcement, fire, or emergency medical services vehicle, the sentence imposed shall include a mandatory minimum term of imprisonment of one year to be served consecutively with any other sentence.

TITLE 18.2. CRIMES AND OFFENSES GENERALLY CHAPTER 7. CRIMES INVOLVING HEALTH AND SAFETY ARTICLE 1. DRUGS

§ 18.2-250. POSSESSION OF CONTROLLED SUBSTANCES UNLAWFUL.

A. It is unlawful for any person knowingly or intentionally to possess a controlled substance unless the substance was obtained directly from, or pursuant to, a valid prescription or order of a practitioner while acting in the course of his professional practice, or except as otherwise authorized by the Drug Control Act (§ 54.1-3400 et seq.).

Upon the prosecution of a person for a violation of this section, ownership or occupancy of premises or vehicle upon or in which a controlled substance was found shall not create a presumption that such person either knowingly or intentionally possessed such controlled substance.

(a) Any person who violates this section with respect to any controlled substance classified in Schedule I or II of the Drug Control Act shall be guilty of a Class 5 felony, except that any person other than an inmate of a penal institution as defined in § 53.1-1 or in the custody of an employee thereof who violates this section with respect to a cannabimimetic agent is guilty of a Class 1 misdemeanor.

(b) Any person other than an inmate of a penal institution as defined in § 53.1-1 or in the custody of an employee thereof, who violates this section with respect to a controlled substance classified in Schedule III shall be guilty of a Class 1 misdemeanor.

(b1) Violation of this section with respect to a controlled substance classified in Schedule IV shall be punishable as a Class 2 misdemeanor.

(b2) Violation of this section with respect to a controlled substance classified in Schedule V shall be punishable as a Class 3 misdemeanor.

(c) Violation of this section with respect to a controlled substance classified in Schedule VI shall be punishable as a Class 4 misdemeanor.

B. The provisions of this section shall not apply to members of state, federal, county, city or town law-enforcement agencies, jail officers, or correctional officers, as defined in § 53.1-1, certified as handlers of dogs trained in the detection of controlled substances when possession of a controlled substance or substances is necessary in the performance of their duties.

§ 18.2-250.1. POSSESSION OF MARIJUANA UNLAWFUL.

A. It is unlawful for any person knowingly or intentionally to possess marijuana unless the substance was obtained directly from, or pursuant to, a valid prescription or order of a practitioner while acting in the course of his professional practice, or except as otherwise authorized by the Drug Control Act (§ 54.1-3400 et seq.). The attorney for the Commonwealth or the county, city, or town attorney may prosecute such a case.

Upon the prosecution of a person for violation of this section, ownership or occupancy of the premises or vehicle upon or in which marijuana was found shall not create a presumption that such person either knowingly or intentionally possessed such marijuana.

Any person who violates this section is subject to a civil penalty of no more than $25. A violation of this section is a civil offense. Any civil penalties collected pursuant to this section shall be deposited into the Drug Offender Assessment and Treatment Fund established pursuant to § 18.2-251.02.

B. Any violation of this section shall be charged by summons. A summons for a violation of this section may be executed by a law-enforcement officer when such violation is observed by such officer. The summons used by a law-enforcement officer pursuant to this section shall be in form the same as the uniform summons for motor vehicle law violations as prescribed pursuant to § 46.2-388. No court costs shall be assessed for violations of this section. A person's criminal history record information as defined in § 9.1-101 shall not include records of any charges or judgments for a violation of this section, and records of such charges or judgments shall not be reported to the Central Criminal Records Exchange. However, if a violation of this section occurs while an individual is operating a commercial motor vehicle as defined in § 46.2-341.4, such violation shall be reported to the Department of Motor Vehicles and shall be included on such individual's driving record.

C. The procedure for appeal and trial of any violation of this section shall be the same as provided by law for misdemeanors; if requested by either party on appeal to the circuit court, trial by jury shall be as provided in Article 4 (§ 19.2-260 et seq.) of Chapter 15 of Title 19.2, and the Commonwealth shall be required to prove its case beyond a reasonable doubt.

D. The provisions of this section shall not apply to members of state, federal, county, city, or town law-enforcement agencies, jail officers, or correctional officers, as defined in § 53.1-1, certified as handlers of dogs trained in the detection of controlled substances when possession of marijuana is necessary for the performance of their duties.

E. The provisions of this section involving marijuana in the form of cannabis oil as that term is defined in § 54.1-3408.3 shall not apply to any person who possesses such oil pursuant to a valid written certification issued by a practitioner in the course of his professional practice pursuant to § 54.1-3408.3 for treatment or to alleviate the symptoms of (i) the person's diagnosed condition or disease, (ii) if such person is the parent or legal guardian of a minor or of an incapacitated adult as defined in § 18.2-369, such minor's or incapacitated adult's diagnosed condition or disease, or (iii) if such person has been designated as a registered agent pursuant to § 54.1-3408.3, the diagnosed condition or disease of his principal or, if the principal is the parent or legal guardian of a minor or of an incapacitated adult as defined in § 18.2-369, such minor's or incapacitated adult's diagnosed condition or disease.

§ 18.2-251. PERSONS CHARGED WITH FIRST OFFENSE MAY BE PLACED ON PROBATION; CONDITIONS; SUBSTANCE ABUSE SCREENING, ASSESSMENT TREATMENT AND EDUCATION PROGRAMS OR SERVICES; DRUG TESTS; COSTS AND FEES; VIOLATIONS; DISCHARGE.

Whenever any person who has not previously been convicted of any offense under this article or under any statute of the United States or of any state relating to narcotic drugs, marijuana, or stimulant, depressant, or hallucinogenic drugs, or has not previously had a proceeding against him for violation of such an offense dismissed as provided in this section, pleads guilty to or enters a plea of not guilty to possession of a controlled substance under § 18.2250 or to possession of marijuana under § 18.2-250.1, the court, upon such plea if the facts found by the court would justify a finding of guilt, without entering a judgment of guilt and with the consent of the accused, may defer further proceedings and place him on probation upon terms and conditions.

As a term or condition, the court shall require the accused to undergo a substance abuse assessment pursuant to § 18.2-251.01 or 19.2-299.2, as appropriate, and enter treatment and/or education program or services, if available, such as, in the opinion of the court, may be best suited to the needs of the accused based upon consideration of the substance abuse assessment. The program or services may be located in the judicial district in which the charge is brought or in any other judicial district as the court may provide. The services shall be provided by (i) a program licensed by the Department of Behavioral Health and Developmental Services, by a similar program which is made available through the Department of Corrections, (ii) a local community-based probation services agency established pursuant to § 9.1-174, or (iii) an ASAP program certified by the Commission on VASAP.

The court shall require the person entering such program under the provisions of this section to pay all or part of the costs of the program, including the costs of the screening, assessment, testing, and treatment, based upon the accused's ability to pay unless the person is determined by the court to be indigent.

As a condition of probation, the court shall require the accused (i) to successfully complete treatment or education program or services, (ii) to remain drug and alcohol free during the period of probation and submit to such tests during that period as may be necessary and appropriate to determine if the accused is drug and alcohol free, (iii) to make reasonable efforts to secure and maintain employment, and (iv) to comply with a plan of at least 100 hours of community service for a felony and up to 24 hours of community service for a misdemeanor. Such testing shall be conducted by personnel of the supervising probation agency or personnel of any program or agency approved by the supervising probation agency.

The court shall, unless done at arrest, order the accused to report to the original arresting law-enforcement agency to submit to fingerprinting.

Upon violation of a term or condition, the court may enter an adjudication of guilt and proceed as otherwise provided. Upon fulfillment of the terms and conditions, the court shall discharge the person and dismiss the proceedings against him. Discharge and dismissal under this section shall be without adjudication of guilt and is a conviction only for the purposes of applying this section in subsequent proceedings.

Notwithstanding any other provision of this section, whenever a court places an individual on probation upon terms and conditions pursuant to this section, such action shall be treated as a conviction for purposes of §§ 18.2-259.1, 22.1-315, and 46.2-390.1, and the driver's license forfeiture provisions of those sections shall be imposed. The provisions of this paragraph shall not be applicable to any offense for which a juvenile has had his license suspended or denied pursuant to § 16.1-278.9 for the same offense.

TITLE 18.2. CRIMES AND OFFENSES GENERALLY CHAPTER 7. CRIMES INVOLVING HEALTH AND SAFETY
ARTICLE 4. DANGEROUS USE OF FIREARMS OR OTHER WEAPONS

§ 18.2-279. DISCHARGING FIREARMS OR MISSILES WITHIN OR AT BUILDING OR DWELLING HOUSE; PENALTY.

If any person maliciously discharges a firearm within any building when occupied by one or more persons in such a manner as to endanger the life or lives of such person or persons, or maliciously shoots at, or maliciously throws any missile at or against any dwelling house or other building when occupied by one or more persons, whereby the life or lives of any such person or persons may be put in peril, the person so offending is guilty of a Class 4 felony. In the event of the death of any person, resulting from such malicious shooting or throwing, the person so offending is guilty of murder in the second degree. However, if the homicide is willful, deliberate and premeditated, he is guilty of murder in the first degree.

If any such act be done unlawfully, but not maliciously, the person so offending is guilty of a Class 6 felony; and, in the event of the death of any person resulting from such unlawful shooting or throwing, the person so offending is guilty of involuntary manslaughter. If any person willfully discharges a firearm within or shoots at any school building whether occupied or not, he is guilty of a Class 4 felony.

§ 18.2-280. WILLFULLY DISCHARGING FIREARMS IN PUBLIC PLACES.

A. If any person willfully discharges or causes to be discharged any firearm in any street in a city or town, or in any place of public business or place of public gathering, and such conduct results in bodily injury to another person, he shall be guilty of a Class 6 felony. If such conduct does not result in bodily injury to another person, he shall be guilty of a Class 1 misdemeanor.

B. If any person willfully discharges or causes to be discharged any firearm upon the buildings and grounds of any public, private or religious elementary, middle or high school, he shall be guilty of a Class 4 felony, unless he is engaged in a program or curriculum sponsored by or conducted with permission of a public, private or religious school.

C. If any person willfully discharges or causes to be discharged any firearm upon any public property within 1,000 feet of the property line of any public, private or religious elementary, middle or high school property he shall be guilty of a Class 4 felony, unless he is engaged in lawful hunting.

D. This section shall not apply to any law-enforcement officer in the performance of his official duties nor to any other person whose said willful act is otherwise justifiable or excusable at law in the protection of his life or property, or is otherwise specifically authorized by law.

E. Nothing in this statute shall preclude the Commonwealth from electing to prosecute under any other applicable provision of law instead of this section.

§ 18.2-281. Setting spring gun or other deadly weapon.

It shall be unlawful for any person to set or fix in any manner any firearm or other deadly weapon so that it may be discharged or activated by a person coming in contact therewith or with any string, wire, spring, or any other contrivance attached thereto or designed to activate such weapon remotely. Any person violating this section shall be guilty of a Class 6 felony.

§ 18.2-282. POINTING, HOLDING, OR BRANDISHING FIREARM, AIR OR GAS OPERATED WEAPON OR OBJECT SIMILAR IN APPEARANCE; PENALTY.

A. It shall be unlawful for any person to point, hold or brandish any firearm or any air or gas operated weapon or any object similar in appearance, whether capable of being fired or not, in such manner as to reasonably induce fear in the mind of another or hold a firearm or any air or gas operated weapon in a public place in such a manner as to reasonably induce fear in the mind of another of being shot or injured. However, this section shall not apply to any person engaged in excusable or justifiable self-defense. Persons violating the provisions of this section shall be guilty of a Class 1 misdemeanor or, if the violation occurs upon any public, private or religious elementary, middle or high school, including buildings and grounds or upon public property within 1,000 feet of such school property, he shall be guilty of a Class 6 felony.

B. Any police officer in the performance of his duty, in making an arrest under the provisions of this section, shall not be civilly liable in damages for injuries or death resulting to the person being arrested if he had reason to believe that the person being arrested was pointing, holding, or brandishing such firearm or air or gas operated weapon, or object that was similar in appearance, with intent to induce fear in the mind of another.

C. For purposes of this section, the word "firearm" means any weapon that will or is designed to or may readily be converted to expel single or multiple projectiles by the action of an explosion of a combustible material. The word "ammunition," as used herein, shall mean a cartridge, pellet, ball, missile or projectile adapted for use in a firearm.

§ 18.2-283. CARRYING DANGEROUS WEAPON TO PLACE OF RELIGIOUS WORSHIP.

If any person carry any gun, pistol, bowie knife, dagger or other dangerous weapon, without good and sufficient reason, to a place of worship while a meeting for religious purposes is being held at such place he shall be guilty of a Class 4 misdemeanor.

§ 18.2-283.1. CARRYING WEAPON INTO COURTHOUSE.

It is unlawful for any person to possess in or transport into any courthouse in this Commonwealth any (i) gun or other weapon designed or intended to propel a missile or projectile of any kind; (ii) frame, receiver, muffler, silencer, missile, projectile, or ammunition designed for use with a dangerous weapon; or (iii) other dangerous weapon, including explosives, stun weapons as defined in § 18.2-308.1, and those weapons specified in subsection A of § 18.2-308. Any such weapon shall be subject to seizure by a law-enforcement officer. A violation of this section is punishable as a Class 1 misdemeanor.

The provisions of this section shall not apply to any police officer, sheriff, law-enforcement agent or official, conservation police officer, conservator of the peace, magistrate, court officer, judge, city or county treasurer, or commissioner or deputy commissioner of the Virginia Workers' Compensation Commission while in the conduct of such person's official duties.

§ 18.2-283.2. CARRYING A FIREARM OR EXPLOSIVE MATERIAL WITHIN CAPITOL SQUARE AND THE SURROUNDING AREA, INTO A BUILDING OWNED OR LEASED BY THE COMMONWEALTH, ETC.; PENALTY.

A. For the purposes of this section, "Capitol Square and the surrounding area" means (i) the grounds, land, real property, and improvements in the City of Richmond bounded by Bank, Governor, Broad, and Ninth Streets, and the sidewalks of Bank Street extending from 50 feet west of the Pocahontas Building entrance to 50 feet east of the entrance of the Capitol of Virginia.

B. It is unlawful for any person to carry any firearm as defined in § 18.2-308.2:2 or explosive material as defined in § 18.2-308.2 within (i) the Capitol of Virginia; (ii) Capitol Square and the surrounding area; (iii) any building owned or leased by the Commonwealth or any agency thereof; or (iv) any office where employees of the Commonwealth or any agency thereof are regularly present for the purpose of performing their official duties.

C. A violation of this section is punishable as a Class 1 misdemeanor. Any firearm or explosive material carried in violation of this section shall be subject to seizure by a law-enforcement officer and forfeited to the Commonwealth and disposed of as provided in § 19.2-386.28.

D. The provisions of this section shall not apply to the following while acting in the conduct of such person's official duties: (i) any law-enforcement officer as defined in § 9.1-101; (ii) any authorized security personnel; (iii) any active military personnel; (iv) any fire marshal appointed pursuant to § 27-30 when such fire marshal has police powers provided by § 27-34.2:1; or (v) any member of a cadet corps who is recognized by a public institution of higher education while such member is participating in an official ceremonial event for the Commonwealth.

E. The provisions of clauses (iii) and (iv) of subsection B shall not apply to (i) any retired law-enforcement officer qualified pursuant to subsection C of § 18.2-308.016 who is visiting a gun range owned or leased by the Commonwealth; (ii) any of the following employees authorized to carry a firearm while acting in the conduct of such employee's official duties: (a) a bail bondsman as defined in § 9.1-185, (b) an employee of the Department of Corrections or a state juvenile correctional facility, (c) an employee of the Department of Conservation and Recreation, or (d) an employee of the Department of Wildlife Resources; (iii) any individual carrying a weapon into a courthouse who is exempt under § 18.2-283.1; (iv) any property owned or operated by a public institution of higher education; (v) any state park; or (vi) any magistrate acting in the conduct of the magistrate's official duties.

F. Notice of the provisions of this section shall be posted conspicuously along the boundary of Capitol Square and the surrounding area and at the public entrance of each location listed in subsection B, and no person shall be convicted of an offense under subsection B if such notice is not posted at such public entrance, unless such person had actual notice of the prohibitions in subsection B.

§ 22.1-131.1. CERTAIN SCHOOL BOARD PROPERTY; ESTABLISHMENT OF GUN-FREE ZONE PERMITTED.

Notwithstanding the provisions of § 15.2-915, in addition to ensuring compliance with the federal Gun-Free School Zones Act of 1990, 18

U.S.C. § 922(q), any school board may deem any building or property that it owns or leases where employees of such school board are regularly present for the purpose of performing their official duties, outside of school zones, as that term is defined in 18 U.S.C. § 921, as a gun-free zone and may prohibit any individual from knowingly purchasing, possessing, transferring, carrying, storing, or transporting firearms, ammunition, or components or combination thereof while such individual is upon such property. Such prohibition shall not apply to (i) any law-enforcement officer; (ii) any retired law-enforcement officer qualified to carry firearms pursuant to subsection C of § 18.2-308.016; (iii) any individual who possesses an unloaded firearm that is in a closed container in or upon a motor vehicle or an unloaded shotgun or rifle in a firearms rack in or upon a motor vehicle; or (iv) any individual who has a valid concealed handgun permit and possesses a concealed handgun while in a motor vehicle in a parking lot, traffic circle, or other means of vehicular ingress to or egress from the school board property.

§ 18.2-286. SHOOTING IN OR ACROSS ROAD OR IN STREET.

If any person discharges a firearm, crossbow or bow and arrow in or across any road, or within the right-of-way thereof, or in a street of any city or town, he shall, for each offense, be guilty of a Class 4 misdemeanor.

The provisions of this section shall not apply to firing ranges or shooting matches maintained, and supervised or approved, by lawenforcement officers and military personnel in performance of their lawful duties.

§ 18.2-287.01. CARRYING WEAPON IN AIR CARRIER AIRPORT TERMINAL.

It shall be unlawful for any person to possess or transport into any air carrier airport terminal in the Commonwealth any (i) gun or other weapon designed or intended to propel a missile or projectile of any kind, (ii) frame, receiver, muffler, silencer, missile, projectile or ammunition designed for use with a dangerous weapon, and (iii) any other dangerous weapon, including explosives, stun weapons as defined in § 18.2-308.1, and those weapons specified in subsection A of § 18.2-308. Any such weapon shall be subject to seizure by a law-enforcement officer. A violation of this section is punishable as a Class 1 misdemeanor. Any weapon possessed or transported in violation of this section shall be forfeited to the Commonwealth and disposed of as provided in § 19.2-386.28.

The provisions of this section shall not apply to any police officer, sheriff, law-enforcement agent or official, conservation police officer, conservator of the peace employed by the air carrier airport, or retired law-enforcement officer qualified pursuant to subsection C of § 18.2-308.016, nor shall the provisions of this section apply to any passenger of an airline who, to the extent otherwise permitted by law, transports a lawful firearm, weapon, or ammunition into or out of an air carrier airport terminal for the sole purposes, respectively, of (i) presenting such firearm, weapon, or ammunition to U.S. Customs agents in advance of an international flight, in order to comply with federal law, (ii) checking such firearm, weapon, or ammunition with his luggage, or (iii) retrieving such firearm, weapon, or ammunition from the baggage claim area.

Any other statute, rule, regulation, or ordinance specifically addressing the possession or transportation of weapons in any airport in the Commonwealth shall be invalid, and this section shall control.

§ 18.2-287.5. REPORTING LOST OR STOLEN FIREARMS; CIVIL PENALTY.

A. If a firearm is lost or stolen from a person who lawfully possessed it, then such person shall report the loss or theft to any local law-enforcement agency or the Department of State Police within 48 hours after such person discovers the loss or theft or is informed by a person with personal knowledge of the loss or theft. The law-enforcement agency shall enter such report information into the National Crime Information Center maintained by the Federal Bureau of Investigation. The provisions of this subsection shall not apply to the loss or theft of an antique firearm as defined in § 18.2-308.2:2.

B. A violation of this section is punishable by a civil penalty of not more than $250. The attorney for the county, city, or town in which an alleged violation of this section has occurred is authorized to enforce the provisions of this section and may bring an action to recover the civil penalty, which shall be paid into the local treasury.

C. No person who, in good faith, reports a lost or stolen firearm shall be held criminally or civilly liable for any damages from acts or omissions resulting from the loss or theft. This subsection shall not apply to any person who makes a report in violation of § 18.2-461.

TITLE 18.2. CRIMES AND OFFENSES GENERALLY CHAPTER 7. CRIMES INVOLVING HEALTH AND SAFETY ARTICLE 5. UNIFORM MACHINE GUN ACT

§ 18.2-288. MACHINE GUN & CRIME OF VIOLENCE DEFINITIONS.

When used in this article:

(1) "Machine gun" applies to any weapon which shoots or is designed to shoot automatically more than one shot, without manual reloading, by a single function of the trigger.

(2) "Crime of violence" applies to and includes any of the following crimes or an attempt to commit any of the same, namely, murder, manslaughter, kidnapping, rape, mayhem, assault with intent to maim, disable, disfigure or kill, robbery, burglary, housebreaking, breaking and entering and larceny.

(3) "Person" applies to and includes firm, partnership, association or corporation.

§ 18.2-289. USE OF MACHINE GUN FOR CRIME OF VIOLENCE.

Possession or use of a machine gun in the perpetration or attempted perpetration of a crime of violence is hereby declared to be a Class 2 felony.

§ 18.2-290. USE OF MACHINE GUN FOR AGGRESSIVE PURPOSE.

Unlawful possession or use of a machine gun for an offensive or aggressive purpose is hereby declared to be a Class 4 felony.

§ 18.2-291. AGGRESSIVE PURPOSE DEFINITION.

Possession or use of a machine gun shall be presumed to be for an offensive or aggressive purpose:
(1) When the machine gun is on premises not owned or rented for bona fide permanent residence or business occupancy by the person in whose possession the machine gun may be found;
(2) When the machine gun is in the possession of, or used by, a person who has been convicted of a crime of violence in any court of record, state or federal, of the United States of America, its territories or insular possessions;
(3) When the machine gun has not been registered as required in § 18.2-295; or
(4) When empty or loaded shells which have been or are susceptible of use in the machine gun are found in the immediate vicinity thereof.

§ 18.2-292. PRESENCE IS PRIMA FACIE EVIDENCE OF MACHINE GUN USE.

The presence of a machine gun in any room, boat or vehicle shall be prima facie evidence of the possession or use of the machine gun by each person occupying the room, boat, or vehicle where the weapon is found.

§ 18.2-293.1. MACHINE GUN ACT DOES NOT PROHIBIT.

Nothing contained in this article shall prohibit or interfere with:
(1) The possession of a machine gun for scientific purposes, or the possession of a machine gun not usable as a weapon and possessed as a curiosity, ornament, or keepsake; and

(2) The possession of a machine gun for a purpose manifestly not aggressive or offensive.

Provided, however, that possession of such machine guns shall be subject to the provisions of § 18.2-295.

§ 18.2-295. REGISTRATION OF MACHINE GUNS.

Every machine gun in this Commonwealth shall be registered with the Department of State Police within twenty-four hours after its acquisition or, in the case of semi-automatic weapons which are converted, modified or otherwise altered to become machine guns, within twenty-four hours of the conversion, modification or alteration. Blanks for registration shall be prepared by the Superintendent of State Police, and furnished upon application. To comply with this section the application as filed shall be notarized and shall show the model and serial number of the gun, the name, address and occupation of the person in possession, and from whom and the purpose for which, the gun was acquired or altered. The Superintendent of State Police shall upon registration required in this section forthwith furnish the registrant with a certificate of registration, which shall be valid as long as the registrant remains the same. Certificates of registration shall be retained by the registrant and produced by him upon demand by any peace officer. Failure to keep or produce such certificate for inspection shall be a Class 3 misdemeanor, and any peace officer, may without warrant, seize the machine gun and apply for its confiscation as provided in § 18.2-296. Upon transferring a registered machine gun, the transferor shall forthwith notify the Superintendent in writing, setting forth the date of transfer and name and address of the transferee. Failure to give the required notification shall constitute a Class 3 misdemeanor. Registration data shall not be subject to inspection by the public.

TITLE 18.2. CRIMES AND OFFENSES GENERALLY CHAPTER 7. CRIMES INVOLVING HEALTH AND SAFETY
ARTICLE 6. "SAWED-OFF" SHOTGUN AND "SAWED-OFF" RIFLE ACT

§ 18.2-299. "SAWED-OFF' SHOTGUN AND "SAWED-OFF" RIFLE DEFINITIONS.

When used in this article:

"Sawed-off shotgun" means any weapon, loaded or unloaded, originally designed as a shoulder weapon, utilizing a self-contained cartridge from which a number of ball shot pellets or projectiles may be fired simultaneously from a smooth or rifled bore by a single function of the firing device and which has a barrel length of less than 18 inches for smoothbore weapons and 16 inches for rifled weapons. Weapons of less than .225 caliber shall not be included.

"Sawed-off rifle" means a rifle of any caliber, loaded or unloaded, which expels a projectile by action of an explosion of a combustible material and is designed as a shoulder weapon with a barrel or barrels length of less than 16 inches or which has been modified to an overall length of less than 26 inches.

"Crime of violence" applies to and includes any of the following crimes or an attempt to commit any of the same, namely, murder, manslaughter, kidnapping, rape, mayhem, assault with intent to maim, disable, disfigure or kill, robbery, burglary, housebreaking, breaking and entering and larceny.

"Person" applies to and includes firm, partnership, association or corporation.

§ 18.2-300. POSSESSION OR USE OF "SAWED-OFF" SHOTGUN OR RIFLE.

A. Possession or use of a "sawed-off" shotgun or "sawed-off" rifle in the perpetration or attempted perpetration of a crime of violence is a Class 2 felony.

B. Possession or use of a "sawed-off" shotgun or "sawed-off" rifle for any other purpose, except as permitted by this article and official use by those persons permitted possession by § 18.2-303, is a Class 4 felony.

§ 18.2-303. EXEMPTIONS TO THE "SAWED-OFF" SHOTGUN AND RIFLE

The provisions of this article shall not be applicable to:
(1) The manufacture for, and sale of, "sawed-off" shotguns or "sawed-off" rifles to the armed forces or law-enforcement officers of the United States or of any state or of any political subdivision thereof, or the transportation required for that purpose; and
(2) "Sawed-off" shotguns, "sawed-off" rifles and automatic arms issued to the National Guard of Virginia by the United States or such arms used by the United States Army or Navy or in the hands of troops of the national guards of other states or territories of the United States passing through Virginia, or such arms as may be provided for the officers of the State Police or officers of penal institutions.

§ 18.2-303.1. "SAWED-OFF" SHOTGUN & RIFLE ACT DOES NOT PROHIBIT.

Nothing contained in this article shall prohibit or interfere with the possession of a "sawed-off" shotgun or "sawed-off" rifle for scientific purposes, the possession of a "sawed-off" shotgun or "sawedoff" rifle possessed in compliance with federal law or the possession of a "sawed-off" shotgun or "sawed-off" rifle not usable as a firing weapon and possessed as a curiosity, ornament, or keepsake.

TITLE 18.2. CRIMES AND OFFENSES GENERALLY CHAPTER 7. CRIMES INVOLVING HEALTH AND SAFETY
ARTICLE 6.1. CONCEALED WEAPONS AND CONCEALED HANDGUN PERMITS

§ 18.2-307.1. CONCEALED WEAPON DEFINITIONS.

As used in this article, unless the context requires a different meaning:

"Ballistic knife" means any knife with a detachable blade that is propelled by a spring-operated mechanism.

"Handgun" means any pistol or revolver or other firearm, except a machine gun, originally designed, made, and intended to fire a projectile by means of an explosion of a combustible material from one or more barrels when held in one hand.

"Law-enforcement officer" means those individuals defined as a law-enforcement officer in § 9.1-101, law-enforcement agents of the armed forces of the United States and the Naval Criminal Investigative Service, and federal agents who are otherwise authorized to carry weapons by federal law. "Law-enforcement officer" also means any sworn full-time law-enforcement officer employed by a law-enforcement agency of the United States or any state or political subdivision thereof, whose duties are substantially similar to those set forth in § 9.1-101.

"Lawfully admitted for permanent residence" means the status of having been lawfully accorded the privilege of residing permanently in the United States as an immigrant in accordance with the immigration laws, such status not having changed.

"Personal knowledge" means knowledge of a fact that a person has himself gained through his own senses, or knowledge that was gained by a law-enforcement officer or prosecutor through the performance of his official duties.

"Spring stick" means a spring-loaded metal stick activated by pushing a button that rapidly and forcefully telescopes the weapon to several times its original length.

§ 18.2-308. CARRYING CONCEALED WEAPONS; EXCEPTIONS; PENALTY.

A. If any person carries about his person, hidden from common observation, (i) any pistol, revolver, or other weapon designed or intended to propel a missile of any kind by action of an explosion of any combustible material; (ii) any dirk, bowie knife, switchblade knife, ballistic knife, machete, razor, sling bow, spring stick, metal knucks, or blackjack; (iii) any flailing instrument consisting of two or more rigid parts connected in such a manner as to allow them to swing freely, which may be known as a nun chahka, nun chuck, nunchaku, shuriken, or fighting chain; (iv) any disc, of whatever configuration, having at least two points or pointed blades which is designed to be thrown or propelled and which may be known as a throwing star or oriental dart; or (v) any weapon of like kind as those enumerated in this subsection, he is guilty of a Class 1 misdemeanor. A second violation of this section or a conviction under this section subsequent to any conviction under any substantially similar ordinance of any county, city, or town shall be punishable as a Class 6 felony, and a third or subsequent such violation shall be punishable as a Class 5 felony. For the purpose of this section, a weapon shall be deemed to be hidden from common observation when it is observable but is of such deceptive appearance as to disguise the weapon's true nature. It shall be an affirmative defense to a violation of clause (i) regarding a handgun, that a person had been issued, at the time of the offense, a valid concealed handgun permit.

B. This section shall not apply to any person while in his own place of abode or the curtilage thereof.

C. Except as provided in subsection A of § 18.2-308.012, this section shall not apply to:
1. Any person while in his own place of business;
2. Any law-enforcement officer, or retired law-enforcement officer pursuant to § 18.2-308.016, wherever such law-enforcement officer may travel in the Commonwealth;
3. Any person who is at, or going to or from, an established shooting range, provided that the weapons are unloaded and securely wrapped while being transported;
4. Any regularly enrolled member of a weapons collecting organization who is at, or going to or from, a bona fide weapons exhibition, provided that the weapons are unloaded and securely wrapped while being transported;

5. Any person carrying such weapons between his place of abode and a place of purchase or repair, provided the weapons are unloaded and securely wrapped while being transported;
6. Any person actually engaged in lawful hunting, as authorized by the Board of Wildlife Resources, under inclement weather conditions necessitating temporary protection of his firearm from those conditions, provided that possession of a handgun while engaged in lawful hunting shall not be construed as hunting with a handgun if the person hunting is carrying a valid concealed handgun permit;
7. Any attorney for the Commonwealth or assistant attorney for the Commonwealth, wherever such attorney may travel in the Commonwealth;
8. Any person who may lawfully possess a firearm and is carrying a handgun while in a personal, private motor vehicle or vessel and such handgun is secured in a container or compartment in the vehicle or vessel;
9. Any enrolled participant of a firearms training course who is at, or going to or from, a training location, provided that the weapons are unloaded and securely wrapped while being transported; and
10. Any judge or justice of the Commonwealth, wherever such judge or justice may travel in the Commonwealth.

D. This section shall also not apply to any of the following individuals while in the discharge of their official duties, or while in transit to or from such duties:
1. Carriers of the United States mail;
2. Officers or guards of any state correctional institution;
3. Conservators of the peace, except that a judge or justice of the Commonwealth, an attorney for the Commonwealth, or an assistant attorney for the Commonwealth may carry a concealed

handgun pursuant to subdivisions C 7 and 10. However, the following conservators of the peace shall not be permitted to carry a concealed handgun without obtaining a permit as provided in this article: (i) notaries public; (ii) registrars; (iii) drivers, operators, or other persons in charge of any motor vehicle carrier of passengers for hire; or (iv) commissioners in chancery; and

4. Noncustodial employees of the Department of Corrections designated to carry weapons by the Director of the Department of Corrections pursuant to § 53.1-29.

§ 18.2-308.01. CARRYING A CONCEALED HANDGUN WITH A PERMIT.

A. The prohibition against carrying a concealed handgun in clause (i) of subsection A of § 18.2-308 shall not apply to a person who has a valid concealed handgun permit issued pursuant to this article. The person issued the permit shall have such permit on his person at all times during which he is carrying a concealed handgun and shall display the permit and a photo identification issued by a government agency of the Commonwealth or by the U.S. Department of Defense or U.S. State Department (passport) upon demand by a law-enforcement officer. A person to whom a non-resident permit is issued shall have such permit on his person at all times when he is carrying a concealed handgun in the Commonwealth and shall display the permit on demand by a law-enforcement officer. A person whose permit is extended due to deployment shall carry with him and display, upon request of a law-enforcement officer, a copy of the documents required by subsection B of § 18.2-308.010.

B. Failure to display the permit and a photo identification upon demand by a law-enforcement officer shall be punishable by a $25 civil penalty, which shall be paid into the state treasury. Any attorney for the Commonwealth of the county or city in which the alleged violation occurred may bring an action to recover the civil penalty. A court may waive such penalty upon presentation to the court of a valid permit and a government-issued photo identification. Any law-enforcement officer may issue a summons for the civil violation of failure to display the concealed handgun permit and photo identification upon demand.

C. The granting of a concealed handgun permit pursuant to this article shall not thereby authorize the possession of any handgun or other weapon on property or in places where such possession is otherwise prohibited by law or is prohibited by the owner of private property.

§ 18.2-308.02. APPLICATION FOR A CONCEALED HANDGUN PERMIT; VIRGINIA RESIDENT OR DOMICILIARY.

A. Any person 21 years of age or older may apply in writing to the clerk of the circuit court of the county or city in which he resides, or if he is a member of the United States Armed Forces and stationed outside the Commonwealth, the county or city in which he is domiciled, for a five-year permit to carry a concealed handgun. There shall be no requirement regarding the length of time an applicant has been a resident or domiciliary of the county or city. The application shall be on a form prescribed by the Department of State Police, in consultation with the Supreme Court, requiring only that information necessary to determine eligibility for the permit. Additionally, the application shall request but not require that the applicant provide an email or other electronic address where a notice of permit expiration can be sent pursuant to subsection C of § 18.2-308.010. The applicant shall present one valid form of photo identification issued by a governmental agency of the Commonwealth or by the U.S. Department of Defense or U.S. State Department (passport). No information or documentation other than that which is allowed on the application in accordance with this section may be requested or required by the clerk or the court.

B. The court shall require proof that the applicant has demonstrated competence with a handgun and the applicant may demonstrate such competence by one of the following, but no applicant shall be required to submit to any additional demonstration of competence, nor shall any proof of demonstrated competence expire:
1. Completing any hunter education or hunter safety course approved by the Department of Wildlife Resources or a similar agency of another state;
2. Completing any National Rifle Association firearms safety or training course;
3. Completing any firearms safety or training course or class available to the general public offered by a law-enforcement agency, institution of higher education, or private or public institution or organization or firearms training school utilizing instructors certified by the National Rifle Association or the Department of Criminal Justice Services;
4. Completing any law-enforcement firearms safety or training course or class offered for security guards, investigators, special deputies, or any division or subdivision of law enforcement or security enforcement;
5. Presenting evidence of equivalent experience with a firearm through participation in organized shooting competition or current military service or proof of an honorable discharge from any branch of the armed services;

6. Obtaining or previously having held a license to carry a firearm in the Commonwealth or a locality thereof, unless such license has been revoked for cause;
7. Completing any firearms training or safety course or class, including an electronic, video, or online course, conducted by a state-certified or National Rifle Association-certified firearms instructor;
8. Completing any governmental police agency firearms training course and qualifying to carry a firearm in the course of normal police duties; or
9. Completing any other firearms training which the court deems adequate.

A photocopy of a certificate of completion of any of the courses or classes; an affidavit from the instructor, school, club, organization, or group that conducted or taught such course or class attesting to the completion of the course or class by the applicant; or a copy of any document that shows completion of the course or class or evidences participation in firearms competition shall constitute evidence of qualification under this subsection.

C. The making of a materially false statement in an application under this article shall constitute perjury, punishable as provided in § 18.2-434.

D. The clerk of court shall withhold from public disclosure the applicant's name and any other information contained in a permit application or any order issuing a concealed handgun permit, except that such information shall not be withheld from any law-enforcement officer acting in the performance of his official duties or from the applicant with respect to his own information. The prohibition on public disclosure of information under this subsection shall not apply to any reference to the issuance of a concealed handgun permit in any order book before July 1, 2008; however, any other concealed handgun records maintained by the clerk shall be withheld from public disclosure.

E. An application is deemed complete when all information required to be furnished by the applicant, including the fee for a concealed handgun permit as set forth in § 18.2-308.03, is delivered to and received by the clerk of court before or concomitant with the conduct of a state or national criminal history records check.

F. For purposes of this section, a member of the United States Armed Forces is domiciled in the county or city where such member claims his home of record with the United States Armed Forces. 2013, cc. 659, 746; 2014, cc. 16, 401, 549; 2017, cc. 99, 237; 2019, c. 624; 2020, c. 958.

§ 18.2-308.02. (EFFECTIVE JANUARY 1, 2021) APPLICATION FOR A CONCEALED HANDGUN PERMIT; VIRGINIA RESIDENT OR DOMICILIARY.

A. Any person 21 years of age or older may apply in writing to the clerk of the circuit court of the county or city in which he resides, or if he is a member of the United States Armed Forces and stationed outside the Commonwealth, the county or city in which he is domiciled, for a five-year permit to carry a concealed handgun. There shall be no requirement regarding the length of time an applicant has been a resident or domiciliary of the county or city. The application shall be on a form prescribed by the Department of State Police, in consultation with the Supreme Court, requiring only that information necessary to determine eligibility for the permit. Additionally, the application shall request but not require that the applicant provide an email or other electronic address where a notice of permit expiration can be sent pursuant to subsection C of § 18.2-308.010. The applicant shall present one valid form of photo identification issued by a governmental agency of the Commonwealth or by the U.S. Department of Defense or U.S. State Department (passport). No information or documentation other than that which is allowed on the application in accordance with this section may be requested or required by the clerk or the court.

B. The court shall require proof that the applicant has demonstrated competence with a handgun in person and the applicant may demonstrate such competence by one of the following, but no applicant shall be required to submit to any additional demonstration of competence, nor shall any proof of demonstrated competence expire:
1. Completing any hunter education or hunter safety course approved by the Department of Wildlife Resources or a similar agency of another state;
2. Completing any National Rifle Association firearms safety or training course;
3. Completing any firearms safety or training course or class available to the general public offered by a law-enforcement agency, institution of higher education, or private or public institution or organization or firearms training school utilizing instructors certified by the National Rifle Association or the Department of Criminal Justice Services;
4. Completing any law-enforcement firearms safety or training course or class offered for security guards, investigators, special deputies, or any division or subdivision of law enforcement or security enforcement;
5. Presenting evidence of equivalent experience with a firearm through participation in organized shooting competition or

current military service or proof of an honorable discharge from any branch of the armed services;
6. Obtaining or previously having held a license to carry a firearm in the Commonwealth or a locality thereof, unless such license has been revoked for cause;
7. Completing any in-person firearms training or safety course or class conducted by a state-certified or National Rifle Association-certified firearms instructor;
8. Completing any governmental police agency firearms training course and qualifying to carry a firearm in the course of normal police duties; or
9. Completing any other firearms training that the court deems adequate.

A photocopy of a certificate of completion of any of the courses or classes; an affidavit from the instructor, school, club, organization, or group that conducted or taught such course or class attesting to the completion of the course or class by the applicant; or a copy of any document that shows completion of the course or class or evidences participation in firearms competition shall constitute evidence of qualification under this subsection.

C. The making of a materially false statement in an application under this article shall constitute perjury, punishable as provided in § 18.2-434.

D. The clerk of court shall withhold from public disclosure the applicant's name and any other information contained in a permit application or any order issuing a concealed handgun permit, except that such information shall not be withheld from any law-enforcement officer acting in the performance of his official duties or from the applicant with respect to his own information. The prohibition on public disclosure of information under this subsection shall not apply to any reference to the issuance of a concealed handgun permit in any order book before July 1, 2008; however, any other concealed handgun records maintained by the clerk shall be withheld from public disclosure.

E. An application is deemed complete when all information required to be furnished by the applicant, including the fee for a concealed handgun permit as set forth in § 18.2-308.03, is delivered to and received by the clerk of court before or concomitant with the conduct of a state or national criminal history records check.

F. For purposes of this section, a member of the United States Armed Forces is domiciled in the county or city where such member claims his home of record with the United States Armed Forces

§ 18.2-308.2:2. CRIMINAL HISTORY RECORD INFORMATION CHECK REQUIRED FOR THE TRANSFER OF CERTAIN FIREARMS.

A. Any person purchasing from a dealer a firearm as herein defined shall consent in writing, on a form to be provided by the Department of State Police, to have the dealer obtain criminal history record information. Such form shall include only the written consent; the name, birth date, gender, race, citizenship, and social security number and/or any other identification number; the number of firearms by category intended to be sold, rented, traded, or transferred; and answers by the applicant to the following questions: (i) has the applicant been convicted of a felony offense or a misdemeanor offense listed in § 18.2-308.1:8 or found guilty or adjudicated delinquent as a juvenile 14 years of age or older at the time of the offense of a delinquent act that if committed by an adult would be a felony or a misdemeanor listed in § 18.2-308.1:8; (ii) is the applicant subject to a court order restraining the applicant from harassing, stalking, or threatening the applicant's child or intimate partner, or a child of such partner, or is the applicant subject to a protective order; (iii) has the applicant ever been acquitted by reason of insanity and prohibited from purchasing, possessing, or transporting a firearm pursuant to § 18.2-308.1:1 or any substantially similar law of any other jurisdiction, been adjudicated legally incompetent, mentally incapacitated, or adjudicated an incapacitated person and prohibited from purchasing a firearm pursuant to § 18.2-308.1:2 or any substantially similar law of any other jurisdiction, been involuntarily admitted to an inpatient facility or involuntarily ordered to outpatient mental health treatment and prohibited from purchasing a firearm pursuant to § 18.2-308.1:3 or any substantially similar law of any other jurisdiction, or been the subject of a temporary detention order pursuant to § 37.2-809 and subsequently agreed to a voluntary admission pursuant to § 37.2-805; and (iv) is the applicant subject to an emergency substantial risk order or a substantial risk order entered pursuant to § 19.2-152.13 or 19.2-152.14 and prohibited from purchasing, possessing, or transporting a firearm pursuant to § 18.2-308.1:6 or any substantially similar law of any other jurisdiction.

B. 1. No dealer shall sell, rent, trade, or transfer from his inventory any such firearm to any other person who is a resident of Virginia until he has (i) obtained written consent and the other information on the consent form specified in subsection A, and provided the

Department of State Police with the name, birth date, gender, race, citizenship, and social security and/or any other identification number and the number of firearms by category intended to be sold, rented, traded, or transferred and (ii) requested criminal history record information by a telephone call to or other communication authorized by the State Police and is authorized by subdivision 2 to complete the sale or other such transfer. To establish personal identification and residence in Virginia for purposes of this section, a dealer must require any prospective purchaser to present one photo-identification form issued by a governmental agency of the Commonwealth or by the United States Department of Defense that demonstrates that the prospective purchaser resides in Virginia. For the purposes of this section and establishment of residency for firearm purchase, residency of a member of the armed forces shall include both the state in which the member's permanent duty post is located and any nearby state in which the member resides and from which he commutes to the permanent duty post. A member of the armed forces whose photo identification issued by the Department of Defense does not have a Virginia address may establish his Virginia residency with such photo identification and either permanent orders assigning the purchaser to a duty post, including the Pentagon, in Virginia or the purchaser's Leave and Earnings Statement. When the photo identification presented to a dealer by the prospective purchaser is a driver's license or other photo identification issued by the Department of Motor Vehicles, and such identification form contains a date of issue, the dealer shall not, except for a renewed driver's license or other photo identification issued by the Department of Motor Vehicles, sell or otherwise transfer a firearm to the prospective purchaser until 30 days after the date of issue of an original or duplicate driver's license unless the prospective purchaser also presents a copy of his Virginia Department of Motor Vehicles driver's record showing that the original date of issue of the driver's license was more than 30 days prior to the attempted purchase.

In addition, no dealer shall sell, rent, trade, or transfer from his inventory any assault firearm to any person who is not a citizen of the United States or who is not a person lawfully admitted for permanent residence.

Upon receipt of the request for a criminal history record information check, the State Police shall (a) review its criminal history record information to determine if the buyer or transferee is prohibited from possessing or transporting a firearm by state or federal law, (b) inform the dealer if its record indicates that the buyer or transferee is so prohibited, and (c) provide the dealer with a unique reference number for that inquiry.

2. The State Police shall provide its response to the requesting dealer during the dealer's request or by return call without delay. A dealer who fulfills the requirements of subdivision 1 and is told by the State Police that a response will not be available by the end of the dealer's fifth business day may immediately complete the sale or transfer and shall not be deemed in violation of this section with respect to such sale or transfer.

3. Except as required by subsection D of § 9.1-132, the State Police shall not maintain records longer than 30 days, except for multiple handgun transactions for which records shall be maintained for 12 months, from any dealer's request for a criminal history record information check pertaining to a buyer or transferee who is not found to be prohibited from possessing and transporting a firearm

under state or federal law. However, the log on requests made may be maintained for a period of 12 months, and such log shall consist of the name of the purchaser, the dealer identification number, the unique approval number, and the transaction date.

4. On the last day of the week following the sale or transfer of any firearm, the dealer shall mail or deliver the written consent form required by subsection A to the Department of State Police. The State Police shall immediately initiate a search of all available criminal history record information to determine if the purchaser is prohibited from possessing or transporting a firearm under state or federal law. If the search discloses information indicating that the buyer or transferee is so prohibited from possessing or transporting a firearm, the State Police shall inform the chief law-enforcement officer in the jurisdiction where the sale or transfer occurred and the dealer without delay.

5. Notwithstanding any other provisions of this section, rifles and shotguns may be purchased by persons who are citizens of the United States or persons lawfully admitted for permanent residence but residents of other states under the terms of subsections A and B upon furnishing the dealer with one photo-identification form issued by a governmental agency of the person's state of residence and one other form of identification determined to be acceptable by the Department of Criminal Justice Services.

6. For the purposes of this subsection, the phrase "dealer's fifth business day" does not include December 25.

C. No dealer shall sell, rent, trade, or transfer from his inventory any firearm, except when the transaction involves a rifle or a shotgun and can be accomplished pursuant to the provisions of subdivision B

5, to any person who is a dual resident of Virginia and another state pursuant to applicable federal law unless he has first obtained from the Department of State Police a report indicating that a search of all available criminal history record information has not disclosed that the person is prohibited from possessing or transporting a firearm under state or federal law.

To establish personal identification and dual resident eligibility for purposes of this subsection, a dealer shall require any prospective purchaser to present one photo-identification form issued by a governmental agency of the prospective purchaser's state of legal residence and other documentation of dual residence within the Commonwealth. The other documentation of dual residence in the Commonwealth may include (i) evidence of currently paid personal property tax or real estate tax or a current (a) lease, (b) utility or telephone bill, (c) voter registration card, (d) bank check, (e) passport, (f) automobile registration, or (g) hunting or fishing license; (ii) other current identification allowed as evidence of residency by 27 C.F.R. § 178.124 and ATF Ruling 2001-5; or (iii) other documentation of residence determined to be acceptable by the Department of Criminal Justice Services and that corroborates that the prospective purchaser currently resides in Virginia.

D. If any buyer or transferee is denied the right to purchase a firearm under this section, he may exercise his right of access to and review and correction of criminal history record information under § 9.1-132 or institute a civil action as provided in § 9.1-135, provided any such action is initiated within 30 days of such denial.

E. Any dealer who willfully and intentionally requests, obtains, or seeks to obtain criminal history record information under false pretenses, or who willfully and intentionally disseminates or seeks to disseminate criminal history record information except as authorized in this section, shall be guilty of a Class 2 misdemeanor.

F. For purposes of this section:
"Actual buyer" means a person who executes the consent form required in subsection B or C, or other such firearm transaction records as may be required by federal law.

"Antique firearm" means:
1. Any firearm (including any firearm with a matchlock, flintlock, percussion cap, or similar type of ignition system) manufactured in or before 1898;
2. Any replica of any firearm described in subdivision 1 of this definition if such replica (i) is not designed or redesigned for using rimfire or conventional centerfire fixed ammunition or (ii) uses rimfire or conventional centerfire fixed ammunition that is no longer manufactured in the United States and that is not readily available in the ordinary channels of commercial trade;
3. Any muzzle-loading rifle, muzzle-loading shotgun, or muzzle-loading pistol that is designed to use black powder, or a black powder substitute, and that cannot use fixed ammunition. For purposes of this subdivision, the term "antique firearm" shall not include any weapon that incorporates a firearm frame or receiver, any firearm that is converted into a muzzle-loading weapon, or any muzzle-loading weapon that can be readily converted to fire fixed ammunition by replacing the barrel, bolt, breech-block, or any combination thereof; or
4. Any curio or relic as defined in this subsection.

5. "Assault firearm" means any semi-automatic center-fire rifle or pistol which expels single or multiple projectiles by action of an explosion of a combustible material and is equipped at the time of the offense with a magazine which will hold more than 20 rounds of ammunition or designed by the manufacturer to accommodate a silencer or equipped with a folding stock.

"Curios or relics" means firearms that are of special interest to collectors by reason of some quality other than is associated with firearms intended for sporting use or as offensive or defensive weapons. To be recognized as curios or relics, firearms must fall within one of the following categories:
1. Firearms that were manufactured at least 50 years prior to the current date, which use rimfire or conventional centerfire fixed ammunition that is no longer manufactured in the United States and that is not readily available in the ordinary channels of commercial trade, but not including replicas thereof;
2. Firearms that are certified by the curator of a municipal, state, or federal museum that exhibits firearms to be curios or relics of museum interest; and
3. Any other firearms that derive a substantial part of their monetary value from the fact that they are novel, rare, bizarre, or because of their association with some historical figure, period, or event. Proof of qualification of a particular firearm under this category may be established by evidence of present value and evidence that like firearms are not available except as collectors' items, or that the value of like firearms available in ordinary commercial channels is substantially less.

"Dealer" means any person licensed as a dealer pursuant to 18 U.S.C. § 921 et seq.

"Firearm" means any handgun, shotgun, or rifle that will or is designed to or may readily be converted to expel single or multiple projectiles by action of an explosion of a combustible material.

"Handgun" means any pistol or revolver or other firearm originally designed, made and intended to fire single or multiple projectiles by means of an explosion of a combustible material from one or more barrels when held in one hand.

"Lawfully admitted for permanent residence" means the status of having been lawfully accorded the privilege of residing permanently in the United States as an immigrant in accordance with the immigration laws, such status not having changed.

G. The Department of Criminal Justice Services shall promulgate regulations to ensure the identity, confidentiality, and security of all records and data provided by the Department of State Police pursuant to this section.

H. The provisions of this section shall not apply to (i) transactions between persons who are licensed as firearms importers or collectors, manufacturers or dealers pursuant to 18 U.S.C. § 921 et seq.; (ii) purchases by or sales to any law-enforcement officer or agent of the United States, the Commonwealth or any local government, or any campus police officer appointed under Article 3 (§ 23.1-809 et seq.) of Chapter 8 of Title 23.1; or (iii) antique firearms or curios or relics.

I. The provisions of this section shall not apply to restrict purchase, trade, or transfer of firearms by a resident of Virginia when the resident of Virginia makes such purchase, trade, or transfer in another state, in which case the laws and regulations of that state and the United States governing the purchase, trade, or transfer of firearms shall apply. A National Instant Criminal Background Check System (NICS) check shall be performed prior to such purchase, trade, or transfer of firearms.

J. All licensed firearms dealers shall collect a fee of $2 for every transaction for which a criminal history record information check is required pursuant to this section, except that a fee of $5 shall be collected for every transaction involving an out-of-state resident. Such fee shall be transmitted to the Department of State Police by the last day of the month following the sale for deposit in a special fund for use by the State Police to offset the cost of conducting criminal history record information checks under the provisions of this section.

K. Any person willfully and intentionally making a materially false statement on the consent form required in subsection B or C or on such firearm transaction records as may be required by federal law shall be guilty of a Class 5 felony.

L. Except as provided in § 18.2-308.2:1, any dealer who willfully and intentionally sells, rents, trades, or transfers a firearm in violation of this section shall be guilty of a Class 6 felony.

L1. Any person who attempts to solicit, persuade, encourage, or entice any dealer to transfer or otherwise convey a firearm other than to the actual buyer, as well as any other person who willfully and intentionally aids or abets such person, shall be guilty of a Class 6 felony. This subsection shall not apply to a federal law-enforcement officer or a law-enforcement officer as defined in § 9.1-101, in the performance of his official duties, or other person under his direct supervision.

M. Any person who purchases a firearm with the intent to (i) resell or otherwise provide such firearm to any person who he knows or has reason to believe is ineligible to purchase or otherwise receive from a dealer a firearm for whatever reason or (ii) transport such firearm out of the Commonwealth to be resold or otherwise provided to another person who the transferor knows is ineligible to purchase or otherwise receive a firearm, shall be guilty of a Class 4 felony and sentenced to a mandatory minimum term of imprisonment of one year. However, if the violation of this subsection involves such a transfer of more than one firearm, the person shall be sentenced to a mandatory minimum term of imprisonment of five years. The prohibitions of this subsection shall not apply to the purchase of a firearm by a person for the lawful use, possession, or transport thereof, pursuant to § 18.2-308.7, by his child, grandchild, or individual for whom he is the legal guardian if such child, grandchild, or individual is ineligible, solely because of his age, to purchase a firearm.

N. Any person who is ineligible to purchase or otherwise receive or possess a firearm in the Commonwealth who solicits, employs, or assists any person in violating subsection M shall be guilty of a Class 4 felony and shall be sentenced to a mandatory minimum term of imprisonment of five years.

O. Any mandatory minimum sentence imposed under this section shall be served consecutively with any other sentence.

P. All driver's licenses issued on or after July 1, 1994, shall carry a letter designation indicating whether the driver's license is an original, duplicate, or renewed driver's license.

Q. Prior to selling, renting, trading, or transferring any firearm owned by the dealer but not in his inventory to any other person, a dealer may require such other person to consent to have the dealer obtain criminal history record information to determine if such other person is prohibited from possessing or transporting a firearm by state or federal law. The Department of State Police shall establish policies and procedures in accordance with 28 C.F.R. § 25.6 to permit such determinations to be made by the Department of State Police, and the processes established for making such determinations shall conform to the provisions of this section.

R. Except as provided in subdivisions 1 and 2, it shall be unlawful for any person who is not a licensed firearms dealer to purchase more than one handgun within any 30-day period. For the purposes of this subsection, "purchase" does not include the exchange or replacement of a handgun by a seller for a handgun purchased from such seller by the same person seeking the exchange or replacement within the 30-day period immediately preceding the date of exchange or replacement. A violation of this subsection is punishable as a Class 1 misdemeanor.

1. Purchases in excess of one handgun within a 30-day period may be made upon completion of an enhanced background check, as described in this subsection, by special application to the Department of State Police listing the number and type of handguns to be purchased and transferred for lawful business or personal use, in a collector series, for collections, as a bulk

purchase from estate sales, and for similar purposes. Such applications shall be signed under oath by the applicant on forms provided by the Department of State Police, shall state the purpose for the purchase above the limit, and shall require satisfactory proof of residency and identity. Such application shall be in addition to the firearms sales report required by the federal Bureau of Alcohol, Tobacco, Firearms and Explosives (ATF). The Superintendent of State Police shall promulgate regulations, pursuant to the Administrative Process Act (§ 2.2-4000 et seq.), for the implementation of an application process for purchases of handguns above the limit.

Upon being satisfied that these requirements have been met, the Department of State Police shall immediately issue to the applicant a nontransferable certificate, which shall be valid for seven days from the date of issue. The certificate shall be surrendered to the dealer by the prospective purchaser prior to the consummation of such sale and shall be kept on file at the dealer's place of business for inspection as provided in § 54.1-4201 for a period of not less than two years. Upon request of any local law-enforcement agency, and pursuant to its regulations, the Department of State Police may certify such local law-enforcement agency to serve as its agent to receive applications and, upon authorization by the Department of State Police, issue certificates immediately pursuant to this subdivision. Applications and certificates issued under this subdivision shall be maintained as records as provided in subdivision B 3. The Department of State Police shall make available to local law-enforcement agencies all records concerning certificates issued pursuant to this subdivision and all records provided for in subdivision B 3.

2. The provisions of this subsection shall not apply to:
a. A law-enforcement agency;
b. An agency duly authorized to perform law-enforcement duties;
c. A state or local correctional facility;
d. A private security company licensed to do business within the Commonwealth;
e. The purchase of antique firearms;
f. A person whose handgun is stolen or irretrievably lost who deems it essential that such handgun be replaced immediately. Such person may purchase another handgun, even if the person has previously purchased a handgun within a 30-day period, provided that (i) the person provides the firearms dealer with a copy of the official police report or a summary thereof, on forms provided by the Department of State Police, from the law-enforcement agency that took the report of the lost or stolen handgun; (ii) the official police report or summary thereof contains the name and address of the handgun owner, a description of the handgun, the location of the loss or theft, the date of the loss or theft, and the date the loss or theft was reported to the law-enforcement agency; and (iii) the date of the loss or theft as reflected on the official police report or summary thereof occurred within 30 days of the person's attempt to replace the handgun. The firearms dealer shall attach a copy of the official police report or summary thereof to the original copy of the Virginia firearms transaction report completed for the transaction and retain it for the period prescribed by the Department of State Police;
g. A person who trades in a handgun at the same time he makes a handgun purchase and as a part of the same transaction, provided that no more than one transaction of this nature is completed per day;
h. A person who holds a valid Virginia permit to carry a concealed handgun;

i. A person who purchases a handgun in a private sale. For purposes of this subdivision, "private sale" means a purchase from a person who makes occasional sales, exchanges, or purchases of firearms for the enhancement of a personal collection of curios or relics or who sells all or part of such collection of curios and relics; or

j. A law-enforcement officer. For purposes of this subdivision, "law-enforcement officer" means any employee of a police department or sheriff's office that is part of or administered by the Commonwealth or any political subdivision thereof and who is responsible for the prevention and detection of crime and the enforcement of the penal, traffic, or highway laws of the Commonwealth.

§ 18.2-308.03. FEES FOR CONCEALED HANDGUN PERMITS.

A. The clerk shall charge a fee of $10 for the processing of an application or issuing of a permit, including his costs associated with the consultation with law-enforcement agencies. The local law-enforcement agency conducting the background investigation may charge a fee not to exceed $35 to cover the cost of conducting an investigation pursuant to this article. The $35 fee shall include any amount assessed by the U.S. Federal Bureau of Investigation for providing criminal history record information, and the local law-enforcement agency shall forward the amount assessed by the U.S. Federal Bureau of Investigation to the State Police with the fingerprints taken from any non-resident applicant. The State Police may charge a fee not to exceed $5 to cover its costs associated with processing the application. The total amount assessed for processing an application for a permit shall not exceed $50, with such fees to be paid in one sum to the person who receives the application. Payment may be made by any method accepted by that court for payment of other fees or penalties. No payment shall be required until the application is received by the court as a complete application.

B. No fee shall be charged for the issuance of such permit to a person who has retired from service (i) as a magistrate in the Commonwealth; (ii) as a special agent with the Virginia Alcoholic Beverage Control Authority or as a law-enforcement officer with the Department of State Police, the Department of Wildlife Resources, or a sheriff or police department, bureau, or force of any political subdivision of the Commonwealth, after completing 15 years of service or after reaching age 55; (iii) as a law-enforcement officer with the U.S. Federal Bureau of Investigation, Bureau of Alcohol, Tobacco and Firearms, Secret Service Agency, Drug Enforcement Administration, United States Citizenship and Immigration Services, U.S. Customs and Border Protection, Department of State Diplomatic Security Service, U.S. Marshals Service, or Naval Criminal Investigative Service, after completing 15 years of service or after reaching age 55; (iv) as a law-enforcement officer with any police or sheriff's department within the United States, the District of Columbia, or any of the territories of the United States, after completing 15 years of service; (v) as a law-enforcement officer with any combination of the agencies listed in clauses (ii) through (iv), after completing 15 years of service; (vi) as a designated boarding team member or boarding officer of the United States Coast Guard, after completing 15 years of service or after reaching age 55; (vii) as a correctional officer as defined in § 53.1-1, after completing 15 years of service; or (viii) as a probation and parole officer authorized pursuant to § 53.1-143, after completing 15 years of service.

§ 18.2-308.04. PROCESSING OF THE APPLICATION AND ISSUANCE OF A CONCEALED HANDGUN PERMIT.

A. The clerk of court shall enter on the application the date on which the application and all other information required to be submitted by the applicant is received.

B. Upon receipt of the completed application, the court shall consult with either the sheriff or police department of the county or city and receive a report from the Central Criminal Records Exchange.

C. The court shall issue the permit via United States mail and notify the State Police of the issuance of the permit within 45 days of receipt of the completed application unless it is determined that the applicant is disqualified. Any order denying issuance of the permit shall be in accordance with § 18.2-308.08. If the applicant is later found by the court to be disqualified after a five-year permit has been issued, the permit shall be revoked.

D. A court may authorize the clerk to issue concealed handgun permits, without judicial review, to applicants who have submitted complete applications, for whom the criminal history records check does not indicate a disqualification and, after consulting with either the sheriff or police department of the county or city, about which application there are no outstanding questions or issues. The court clerk shall be immune from suit arising from any acts or omissions relating to the issuance of concealed handgun permits without judicial review pursuant to this section unless the clerk was grossly negligent or engaged in willful misconduct. This section shall not be construed to limit, withdraw, or overturn any defense or immunity already existing in statutory or common law, or to affect any cause of action accruing prior to July 1, 2010.

E. The permit to carry a concealed handgun shall specify only the following information: name, address, date of birth, gender, height, weight, color of hair, color of eyes, and signature of the permittee; the signature of the judge issuing the permit, of the clerk of court who has been authorized to sign such permits by the issuing judge, or of the clerk of court who has been authorized to issue such permits pursuant to subsection D; the date of issuance; and the expiration date. The permit to carry a concealed handgun shall be of a size comparable to a Virginia driver's license, may be laminated or use a similar process to protect the permit, and shall otherwise be of a uniform style prescribed by the Department of State Police.

§ 18.2-308.05. ISSUANCE OF A DE FACTO PERMIT.

If the court has not issued the permit or determined that the applicant is disqualified within 45 days of the date of receipt noted on the application, the clerk shall certify on the application that the 45-day period has expired, and mail or send via electronic mail a copy of the certified application to the applicant within five business days of the expiration of the 45-day period. The certified application shall serve as a de facto permit, which shall expire 90 days after issuance, and shall be recognized as a valid concealed handgun permit when presented with a valid government-issued photo identification pursuant to subsection A of § 18.2-308.01, until the court issues a five-year permit or finds the applicant to be disqualified. If the applicant is found to be disqualified after the de facto permit is issued, the applicant shall surrender the de facto permit to the court and the disqualification shall be deemed a denial of the permit and a revocation of the de facto permit.

§ 18.2-308.06. NONRESIDENT CONCEALED HANDGUN PERMITS.

A. Nonresidents of the Commonwealth 21 years of age or older may apply in writing to the Virginia Department of State Police for a five-year permit to carry a concealed handgun. The applicant shall submit a photocopy of one valid form of photo identification issued by a governmental agency of the applicant's state of residency or by the U.S. Department of Defense or U.S. State Department (passport). Every applicant for a nonresident concealed handgun permit shall also submit two photographs of a type and kind specified by the Department of State Police for inclusion on the permit and shall submit fingerprints on a card provided by the Department of State Police for the purpose of obtaining the applicant's state or national criminal history record. As a condition for issuance of a concealed handgun permit, the applicant shall submit to fingerprinting by his local or state law-enforcement agency and provide personal descriptive information to be forwarded with the fingerprints through the Central Criminal Records Exchange to the U.S. Federal Bureau of Investigation for the purpose of obtaining criminal history record information regarding the applicant and obtaining fingerprint identification information from federal records pursuant to criminal investigations by state and local law-enforcement agencies. The application shall be on a form provided by the Department of State Police, requiring only that information necessary to determine eligibility for the permit. If the permittee is later found by the Department of State Police to be disqualified, the permit shall be revoked and the person shall return the permit after being so notified by the Department of State Police. The permit requirement and restriction provisions of subsection C of § 18.2-308.02 and § 18.2-308.09 shall apply, mutatis mutandis, to the provisions of this subsection.

B. The applicant shall demonstrate competence with a handgun by one of the following:
1. Completing a hunter education or hunter safety course approved by the Virginia Department of Wildlife Resources or a similar agency of another state;
2. Completing any National Rifle Association firearms safety or training course;
3. Completing any firearms safety or training course or class available to the general public offered by a law-enforcement agency, institution of higher education, or private or public institution or organization or firearms training school utilizing instructors certified by the National Rifle Association or the Department of Criminal Justice Services or a similar agency of another state;
4. Completing any law-enforcement firearms safety or training course or class offered for security guards, investigators, special deputies, or any division or subdivision of law enforcement or security enforcement;
5. Presenting evidence of equivalent experience with a firearm through participation in organized shooting competition approved by the Department of State Police or current military service or proof of an honorable discharge from any branch of the armed services;
6. Obtaining or previously having held a license to carry a firearm in the Commonwealth or a locality thereof, unless such license has been revoked for cause;
7. Completing any firearms training or safety course or class, including an electronic, video, or on-line course, conducted by a state-certified or National Rifle Association-certified firearms instructor;

8. Completing any governmental police agency firearms training course and qualifying to carry a firearm in the course of normal police duties; or
9. Completing any other firearms training that the Virginia Department of State Police deems adequate.

A photocopy of a certificate of completion of any such course or class; an affidavit from the instructor, school, club, organization, or group that conducted or taught such course or class attesting to the completion of the course or class by the applicant; or a copy of any document that shows completion of the course or class or evidences participation in firearms competition shall satisfy the requirement for demonstration of competence with a handgun.

C. The Department of State Police may charge a fee not to exceed $100 to cover the cost of the background check and issuance of the permit. Any fees collected shall be deposited in a special account to be used to offset the costs of administering the nonresident concealed handgun permit program.

D. The permit to carry a concealed handgun shall contain only the following information: name, address, date of birth, gender, height, weight, color of hair, color of eyes, and photograph of the permittee; the signature of the Superintendent of the Virginia Department of State Police or his designee; the date of issuance; and the expiration date.

E. The Superintendent of the State Police shall promulgate regulations, pursuant to the Administrative Process Act (§ 2.2-4000 et seq.), for the implementation of an application process for obtaining a nonresident concealed handgun permit. 2013, c. 746; 2017, c. 237; 2020, c. 958.

§ 18.2-308.06. (EFFECTIVE JANUARY 1, 2021) NONRESIDENT CONCEALED HANDGUN PERMITS.

A. Nonresidents of the Commonwealth 21 years of age or older may apply in writing to the Virginia Department of State Police for a five-year permit to carry a concealed handgun. The applicant shall submit a photocopy of one valid form of photo identification issued by a governmental agency of the applicant's state of residency or by the U.S. Department of Defense or U.S. State Department (passport). Every applicant for a nonresident concealed handgun permit shall also submit two photographs of a type and kind specified by the Department of State Police for inclusion on the permit and shall submit fingerprints on a card provided by the Department of State Police for the purpose of obtaining the applicant's state or national criminal history record. As a condition for issuance of a concealed handgun permit, the applicant shall submit to fingerprinting by his local or state law-enforcement agency and provide personal descriptive information to be forwarded with the fingerprints through the Central Criminal Records Exchange to the U.S. Federal Bureau of Investigation for the purpose of obtaining criminal history record information regarding the applicant and obtaining fingerprint identification information from federal records pursuant to criminal investigations by state and local law-enforcement agencies. The application shall be on a form provided by the Department of State Police, requiring only that information necessary to determine eligibility for the permit. If the permittee is later found by the Department of State Police to be disqualified, the permit shall be revoked and the person shall return the permit after being so notified by the Department of State Police. The permit requirement and restriction provisions of subsection C of § 18.2-308.02 and § 18.2-308.09 shall apply, mutatis mutandis, to the provisions of this subsection.

B. The applicant shall demonstrate competence with a handgun in person by one of the following:

1. Completing a hunter education or hunter safety course approved by the Virginia Department of Wildlife Resources or a similar agency of another state;
2. Completing any National Rifle Association firearms safety or training course;
3. Completing any firearms safety or training course or class available to the general public offered by a law-enforcement agency, institution of higher education, or private or public institution or organization or firearms training school utilizing instructors certified by the National Rifle Association or the Department of Criminal Justice Services or a similar agency of another state;
4. Completing any law-enforcement firearms safety or training course or class offered for security guards, investigators, special deputies, or any division or subdivision of law enforcement or security enforcement;
5. Presenting evidence of equivalent experience with a firearm through participation in organized shooting competition approved by the Department of State Police or current military service or proof of an honorable discharge from any branch of the armed services;
6. Obtaining or previously having held a license to carry a firearm in the Commonwealth or a locality thereof, unless such license has been revoked for cause;
7. Completing any in-person firearms training or safety course or class conducted by a state-certified or National Rifle Association-certified firearms instructor;
8. Completing any governmental police agency firearms training course and qualifying to carry a firearm in the course of normal police duties; or
9. Completing any other firearms training that the Virginia Department of State Police deems adequate.

A photocopy of a certificate of completion of any such course or class; an affidavit from the instructor, school, club, organization, or group that conducted or taught such course or class attesting to the completion of the course or class by the applicant; or a copy of any document that shows completion of the course or class or evidences participation in firearms competition shall satisfy the requirement for demonstration of competence with a handgun.

C. The Department of State Police may charge a fee not to exceed $100 to cover the cost of the background check and issuance of the permit. Any fees collected shall be deposited in a special account to be used to offset the costs of administering the nonresident concealed handgun permit program.

D. The permit to carry a concealed handgun shall contain only the following information: name, address, date of birth, gender, height, weight, color of hair, color of eyes, and photograph of the permittee; the signature of the Superintendent of the Virginia Department of State Police or his designee; the date of issuance; and the expiration date.

E. The Superintendent of the State Police shall promulgate regulations, pursuant to the Administrative Process Act (§ 2.2-4000 et seq.), for the implementation of an application process for obtaining a nonresident concealed handgun permit.

§ 18.2-308.08. DENIAL OF A CONCEALED HANDGUN PERMIT; APPEAL.

A. Only a circuit court judge may deny issuance of a concealed handgun permit to a Virginia resident or domiciliary who has applied for a permit pursuant to § 18.2-308.04. Any order denying issuance of a concealed handgun permit shall state the basis for the denial of the permit, including, if applicable, any reason under § 18.2-308.09 that is the basis of the denial, and the clerk shall provide notice, in writing, upon denial of the application, of the applicant's right to an ore tenus hearing and the requirements for perfecting an appeal of such order.

B. Upon request of the applicant made within 21 days, the court shall place the matter on the docket for an ore tenus hearing. The applicant may be represented by counsel, but counsel shall not be appointed, and the rules of evidence shall apply. The final order of the court shall include the court's findings of fact and conclusions of law.

C. Any person denied a permit to carry a concealed handgun by the circuit court may present a petition for review to the Court of Appeals. The petition for review shall be filed within 60 days of the expiration of the time for requesting an ore tenus hearing, or if an ore tenus hearing is requested, within 60 days of the entry of the final order of the circuit court following the hearing. The petition shall be accompanied by a copy of the original papers filed in the circuit court, including a copy of the order of the circuit court denying the permit. Subject to the provisions of subsection B of § 17.1410, the decision of the Court of Appeals or judge shall be final. Notwithstanding any other provision of law, if the decision to deny the permit is reversed upon appeal, taxable costs incurred by the person shall be paid by the Commonwealth.

§ 18.2-308.09. DISQUALIFICATIONS FOR A CONCEALED HANDGUN PERMIT.

The following persons shall be deemed disqualified from obtaining a permit:

1. (Effective July 1, 2021) An individual who is ineligible to possess a firearm pursuant to § 18.2-308.1:1, 18.2-308.1:2, 18.2-308.1:3, 18.2-308.1:6, or 18.2-308.1:7 or the substantially similar law of any other state or of the United States.
2. An individual who was ineligible to possess a firearm pursuant to § 18.2-308.1:1 and who was discharged from the custody of the Commissioner pursuant to § 19.2-182.7 less than five years before the date of his application for a concealed handgun permit.
3. An individual who was ineligible to possess a firearm pursuant to § 18.2-308.1:2 and whose competency or capacity was restored pursuant to § 64.2-2012 less than five years before the date of his application for a concealed handgun permit.
4. An individual who was ineligible to possess a firearm under § 18.2-308.1:3 and who was released from commitment less than five years before the date of this application for a concealed handgun permit.
5. An individual who is subject to a restraining order, or to a protective order and prohibited by § 18.2-308.1:4 from purchasing, possessing, or transporting a firearm.
6. (Effective until January 1, 2021) An individual who is prohibited by § 18.2-308.2 from possessing or transporting a firearm, except that a permit may be obtained in accordance with subsection C of that section.
6. (Effective January 1, 2021) An individual who is prohibited by § 18.2-308.2 from possessing or transporting a firearm, except

that a restoration order may be obtained in accordance with subsection C of that section.
7. An individual who has been convicted of two or more misdemeanors within the five-year period immediately preceding the application, if one of the misdemeanors was a Class 1 misdemeanor, but the judge shall have the discretion to deny a permit for two or more misdemeanors that are not Class 1. Traffic infractions and misdemeanors set forth in Title 46.2 shall not be considered for purposes of this disqualification.
8. An individual who is addicted to, or is an unlawful user or distributor of, marijuana, synthetic cannabinoids, or any controlled substance.
9. An individual who has been convicted of a violation of § 18.2-266 or a substantially similar local ordinance, or of public drunkenness, or of a substantially similar offense under the laws of any other state, the District of Columbia, the United States, or its territories within the three-year period immediately preceding the application.
10. An alien other than an alien lawfully admitted for permanent residence in the United States.
11. An individual who has been discharged from the armed forces of the United States under dishonorable conditions.
12. An individual who is a fugitive from justice.
13. An individual who the court finds, by a preponderance of the evidence, based on specific acts by the applicant, is likely to use a weapon unlawfully or negligently to endanger others. The sheriff, chief of police, or attorney for the Commonwealth may submit to the court a sworn, written statement indicating that, in the opinion of such sheriff, chief of police, or attorney for the Commonwealth, based upon a disqualifying conviction or upon the specific acts set forth in the statement, the

applicant is likely to use a weapon unlawfully or negligently to endanger others. The statement of the sheriff, chief of police, or the attorney for the Commonwealth shall be based upon personal knowledge of such individual or of a deputy sheriff, police officer, or assistant attorney for the Commonwealth of the specific acts, or upon a written statement made under oath before a notary public of a competent person having personal knowledge of the specific acts.

14. An individual who has been convicted of any assault, assault and battery, sexual battery, discharging of a firearm in violation of § 18.2-280 or 18.2-286.1 or brandishing of a firearm in violation of § 18.2-282 within the three-year period immediately preceding the application.
15. An individual who has been convicted of stalking.
16. An individual whose previous convictions or adjudications of delinquency were based on an offense that would have been at the time of conviction a felony if committed by an adult under the laws of any state, the District of Columbia, the United States or its territories. For purposes of this disqualifier, only convictions occurring within 16 years following the later of the date of (i) the conviction or adjudication or (ii) release from any incarceration imposed upon such conviction or adjudication shall be deemed to be "previous convictions." Disqualification under this subdivision shall not apply to an individual with previous adjudications of delinquency who has completed a term of service of no less than two years in the Armed Forces of the United States and, if such person has been discharged from the Armed Forces of the United States, received an honorable discharge.
17. An individual who has a felony charge pending or a charge pending for an offense listed in subdivision 14 or 15.

18. An individual who has received mental health treatment or substance abuse treatment in a residential setting within five years prior to the date of his application for a concealed handgun permit.
19. An individual not otherwise ineligible pursuant to this article, who, within the three-year period immediately preceding the application for the permit, was found guilty of any criminal offense set forth in Article 1 (§ 18.2-247 et seq.) or former § 18.2-248.1:1 or of a criminal offense of illegal possession or distribution of marijuana, synthetic cannabinoids, or any controlled substance, under the laws of any state, the District of Columbia, or the United States or its territories.
20. An individual, not otherwise ineligible pursuant to this article, with respect to whom, within the three-year period immediately preceding the application, upon a charge of any criminal offense set forth in Article 1 (§ 18.2-247 et seq.) or former § 18.2-248.1:1 or upon a charge of illegal possession or distribution of marijuana, synthetic cannabinoids, or any controlled substance under the laws of any state, the District of Columbia, or the United States or its territories, the trial court found that the facts of the case were sufficient for a finding of guilt and disposed of the case pursuant to § 18.2-251 or the substantially similar law of any other state, the District of Columbia, or the United States or its territories.

§ 18.2-308.010. RENEWAL OF CONCEALED HANDGUN PERMIT.

A. 1. Persons who previously have held a concealed handgun permit shall be issued, upon application as provided in § 18.2-308.02, a new five-year permit unless it is found that the applicant is subject to any of the disqualifications set forth in § 18.2-308.09. Persons who previously have been issued a concealed handgun permit pursuant to this article shall not be required to appear in person to apply for a new five-year permit pursuant to this section, and the application for the new permit, including a photocopy of the applicant's valid photo identification, may be submitted via the United States mail. The circuit court that receives the application shall promptly notify an applicant if the application is incomplete or if the fee submitted for the permit pursuant to § 18.2-308.03 is incorrect.

2. If a new five-year permit is issued while an existing permit remains valid, the new five-year permit shall become effective upon the expiration date of the existing permit, provided that the application is received by the court at least 90 days but no more than 180 days prior to the expiration of the existing permit.
3. Any order denying issuance of the new permit shall be in accordance with subsection A of § 18.2-308.08.

B. If a permit holder is a member of the Virginia National Guard, Armed Forces of the United States, or the Armed Forces Reserves of the United States, and his five-year permit expires during an active-duty military deployment outside of the permittee's county or city of residence, such permit shall remain valid for 90 days after the end date of the deployment. In order to establish proof of continued validity of the permit, such a permittee shall carry with him and display, upon request of a law-enforcement officer, a copy of the permittee's deployment orders or other documentation from the permittee's commanding officer that order the permittee to travel outside of his county or city of residence and that indicate the start and end date of such deployment.

C. If the clerk has an electronic system for, and issuance of, concealed handgun permits and such system has the capability of sending electronic notices to permit holders and if a permit holder requests such notice on the concealed handgun application form, the clerk that issued the permit shall notify the permit holder by electronic mail at least 90 days prior to the permit expiration date that the permit will expire. The failure of a clerk to send the notice required by this subsection or the failure of the permit holder to receive such notice shall not extend the validity of the existing permit beyond its expiration date.

§ 18.2-308.011. REPLACEMENT PERMITS.

A. The clerk of a circuit court that issued a valid concealed handgun permit shall, upon presentation of the valid permit and proof of a new address of residence by the permit holder, issue a replacement permit specifying the permit holder's new address. The clerk of court shall forward the permit holder's new address of residence to the State Police. The State Police may charge a fee not to exceed $5, and the clerk of court issuing the replacement permit may charge a fee not to exceed $5. The total amount assessed for processing a replacement permit pursuant to this subsection shall not exceed $10, with such fees to be paid in one sum to the person who receives the information for the replacement permit.

B. The clerk of a circuit court that issued a valid concealed handgun permit shall, upon submission of a notarized statement by the permit holder that the permit was lost or destroyed or that the permit holder has undergone a legal name change, issue a replacement permit. The replacement permit shall have the same expiration date as the permit that was lost, destroyed, or issued to the permit holder under a previous name. The clerk shall issue the replacement permit within 10 business days of receiving the notarized statement and may charge a fee not to exceed $5.

---

§ 18.2-308.012. PROHIBITED CONDUCT.

A. Any person permitted to carry a concealed handgun who is under the influence of alcohol or illegal drugs while carrying such handgun in a public place is guilty of a Class 1 misdemeanor. Conviction of any of the following offenses shall be prima facie evidence, subject to rebuttal, that the person is "under the influence" for purposes of this section: manslaughter in violation of § 18.236.1, maiming in violation of § 18.2-51.4, driving while intoxicated in violation of § 18.2-266, public intoxication in violation of § 18.2388, or driving while intoxicated in violation of § 46.2-341.24. Upon such conviction that court shall revoke the person's permit for a concealed handgun and promptly notify the issuing circuit court. A person convicted of a violation of this subsection shall be ineligible to apply for a concealed handgun permit for a period of five years.

B. (Effective July 1, 2018) No person who carries a concealed handgun onto the premises of any restaurant or club as defined in § 4.1-100 for which a license to sell and serve alcoholic beverages for on-premises consumption has been granted by the Virginia Alcoholic Beverage Control Authority under Title 4.1 may consume an alcoholic beverage while on the premises. A person who carries a concealed handgun onto the premises of such a restaurant or club and consumes alcoholic beverages is guilty of a Class 2 misdemeanor. However, nothing in this subsection shall apply to a federal, state, or local law-enforcement officer.

§ 18.2-308.013. SUSPENSION OR REVOCATION OF PERMIT.

A. Any person convicted of an offense that would disqualify that person from obtaining a permit under § 18.2-308.09 or who violates subsection C of § 18.2-308.02 shall forfeit his permit for a concealed handgun and surrender it to the court. Upon receipt by the Central Criminal Records Exchange of a record of the arrest, conviction, or occurrence of any other event that would disqualify a person from obtaining a concealed handgun permit under § 18.2-308.09, the Central Criminal Records Exchange shall notify the court having issued the permit of such disqualifying arrest, conviction, or other event. Upon receipt of such notice of a conviction, the court shall revoke the permit of a person disqualified pursuant to this subsection, and shall promptly notify the State Police and the person whose permit was revoked of the revocation.

B. An individual who has a felony charge pending or a charge pending for an offense listed in subdivision 14 or 15 of § 18.2-308.09, holding a permit for a concealed handgun, may have the permit suspended by the court before which such charge is pending or by the court that issued the permit.

C. The court shall revoke the permit of any individual for whom it would be unlawful to purchase, possess, or transport a firearm under § 18.2-308.1:2 or 18.2-308.1:3, and shall promptly notify the State Police and the person whose permit was revoked of the revocation.

§ 18.2-308.014. RECIPROCITY.

A. A valid concealed handgun or concealed weapon permit or license issued by another state shall authorize the holder of such permit or license who is at least 21 years of age to carry a concealed handgun in the Commonwealth, provided (i) the issuing authority provides the means for instantaneous verification of the validity of all such permits or licenses issued within that state, accessible 24 hours a day if available; (ii) the permit or license holder carries a photo identification issued by a government agency of any state or by the U.S. Department of Defense or U.S. Department of State and displays the permit or license and such identification upon demand by a law-enforcement officer; and (iii) the permit or license holder has not previously had a Virginia concealed handgun permit revoked.

The Superintendent of State Police shall enter into agreements for reciprocal recognition with such other states that require an agreement to be in place before such state will recognize a Virginia concealed handgun permit as valid in such state. The Attorney General shall provide the Superintendent with any legal assistance or advice necessary for the Superintendent to perform his duties set forth in this subsection. If the Superintendent determines that another state requires that an agreement for reciprocal recognition be executed by the Attorney General or otherwise formally approved by the Attorney General as a condition of such other state's entering into an agreement for reciprocal recognition, the Attorney General shall (a) execute such agreement or otherwise formally approve such agreement and (b) return to the Superintendent the executed agreement or, in a form deemed acceptable by such other state, documentation of his formal approval of such agreement within 30 days after the Superintendent notifies the Attorney General, in writing, that he is required to execute or otherwise formally approve such agreement.

B. For the purposes of participation in concealed handgun reciprocity agreements with other jurisdictions, the official government-issued law-enforcement identification card issued to an active-duty law-enforcement officer in the Commonwealth who is exempt from obtaining a concealed handgun permit under this article shall be deemed a concealed handgun permit.

§ 18.2-308.016. (EFFECTIVE OCTOBER 1, 2016, UNTIL JULY 1, 2018) RETIRED LAW-ENFORCEMENT OFFICERS; CARRYING A CONCEALED HANDGUN.

A. Except as provided in subsection A of § 18.2-308.012, § 18.2-308 shall not apply to:

1. Any State Police officer retired from the Department of State Police, any officer retired from the Division of Capitol Police, any local law-enforcement officer, auxiliary police officer or animal control officer retired from a police department or sheriff's office within the Commonwealth, any special agent retired from the State Corporation Commission or the Virginia Alcoholic Beverage Control Board, any employee with internal investigations authority designated by the Department of Corrections pursuant to subdivision 11 of § 53.1-10 retired from the Department of Corrections, any conservation police officer retired from the Department of Game and Inland Fisheries, any Virginia Marine Police officer retired from the Law Enforcement Division of the Virginia Marine Resources Commission, any campus police officer appointed under Article 3 (§ 23.1-809 et seq.) of Chapter 8 of Title 23.1 retired from a campus police department, any retired member of the enforcement division of the Department of Motor Vehicles appointed pursuant to § 46.2217, and any retired investigator of the security division of the Virginia Lottery, other than an officer or agent terminated for cause, (i) with a service-related

disability; (ii) following at least 10 years of service with any such law-enforcement agency, commission, board, or any combination thereof; (iii) who has reached 55 years of age; or (iv) who is on long-term leave from such law-enforcement agency or board due to a service-related injury, provided such officer carries with him written proof of consultation with and favorable review of the need to carry a concealed handgun issued by the chief law-enforcement officer of the last such agency from which the officer retired or the agency that employs the officer or, in the case of special agents, issued by the State Corporation Commission or the Virginia Alcoholic Beverage Control Board. A copy of the proof of consultation and favorable review shall be forwarded by the chief, Commission, or Board to the Department of State Police for entry into the Virginia Criminal Information Network. The chief law-enforcement officer shall not without cause withhold such written proof if the retired law-enforcement officer otherwise meets the requirements of this section. An officer set forth in clause (iv) who receives written proof of consultation to carry a concealed handgun shall surrender such proof of consultation upon return to work or upon termination of employment with the law-enforcement agency. Notice of the surrender shall be forwarded to the Department of State Police for entry into the Virginia Criminal Information Network. However, if such officer retires on disability because of the service-related injury, and would be eligible under clause (i) for written proof of consultation to carry a concealed handgun, he may retain the previously issued written proof of consultation.

2. Any person who is eligible for retirement with at least 20 years of service with a law-enforcement agency, commission,

or board mentioned in subdivision 1 who has resigned in good standing from such law-enforcement agency, commission, or board to accept a position covered by a retirement system that is authorized under Title 51.1, provided such person carries with him written proof of consultation with and favorable review of the need to carry a concealed handgun issued by the chief law-enforcement officer of the agency from which he resigned or, in the case of special agents, issued by the State Corporation Commission or the Virginia Alcoholic Beverage Control Board. A copy of the proof of consultation and favorable review shall be forwarded by the chief, Commission, or Board to the Department of State Police for entry into the Virginia Criminal Information Network. The chief law-enforcement officer shall not without cause withhold such written proof if the law-enforcement officer otherwise meets the requirements of this section.

3. Any State Police officer who is a member of the organized reserve forces of any of the Armed Services of the United States or National Guard, while such officer is called to active military duty, provided such officer carries with him written proof of consultation with and favorable review of the need to carry a concealed handgun issued by the Superintendent of State Police. The proof of consultation and favorable review shall be valid as long as the officer is on active military duty and shall expire when the officer returns to active law-enforcement duty. The issuance of the proof of consultation and favorable review shall be entered into the Virginia Criminal Information Network. The Superintendent of State Police shall not without cause withhold such written proof if the officer is in good standing and is qualified to carry a weapon while on active law-enforcement duty.

B. For purposes of complying with the federal Law Enforcement Officers Safety Act of 2004, a retired or resigned law-enforcement officer who receives proof of consultation and review pursuant to this section shall have the opportunity to annually participate, at the retired or resigned law-enforcement officer's expense, in the same training and testing to carry firearms as is required of active law-enforcement officers in the Commonwealth. If such retired or resigned law-enforcement officer meets the training and qualification standards, the chief law-enforcement officer shall issue the retired or resigned officer certification, valid one year from the date of issuance, indicating that the retired or resigned officer has met the standards of the agency to carry a firearm.

C. A retired or resigned law-enforcement officer who receives proof of consultation and review pursuant to this section may annual ly participate and meet the training and qualification standards to carry firearms as is required of active law-enforcement officers in the Commonwealth. If such retired or resigned law-enforcement officer meets the training and qualification standards, the chief law-enforcement officer shall issue the retired or resigned officer certification, valid one year from the date of issuance, indicating that the retired or resigned officer has met the standards of the Commonwealth to carry a firearm. A copy of the certification indicating that the retired or resigned officer has met the standards of the Commonwealth to carry a firearm shall be forwarded by the chief, Commission, or Board to the Department of State Police for entry into the Virginia Criminal Information Network.

D. For all purposes, including for the purpose of applying the reciprocity provisions of § 18.2-308.014, any person granted the privilege to carry a concealed handgun pursuant to this section, while carrying the proof of consultation and favorable review required, shall be deemed to have been issued a concealed handgun permit.

TITLE 18.2. CRIMES AND OFFENSES GENERALLY CHAPTER 7. CRIMES INVOLVING HEALTH AND SAFETY ARTICLE 7. OTHER ILLEGAL WEAPONS

§ 18.2-308.1. POSSESSION OF FIREARM, STUN WEAPON, OR OTHER WEAPON ON SCHOOL PROPERTY PROHIBITED; PENALTY.

A. If any person knowingly possesses any (i) stun weapon as defined in this section; (ii) knife, except a pocket knife having a folding metal blade of less than three inches; or (iii) weapon, including a weapon of like kind, designated in subsection A of § 18.2-308, other than a firearm; upon (a) the property of any child day center or public, private, or religious preschool, elementary, middle, or high school, including buildings and grounds; (b) that portion of any property open to the public and then exclusively used for school-sponsored functions or extracurricular activities while such functions or activities are taking place; or (c) any school bus owned or operated by any such school, he is guilty of a Class 1 misdemeanor.

B. If any person knowingly possesses any firearm designed or intended to expel a projectile by action of an explosion of a combustible material while such person is upon (i) the property of any child day center or public, private, or religious preschool, elementary, middle, or high school, including buildings and grounds; (ii) that portion of any property open to the public and then exclusively used for school-sponsored functions or extracurricular activities while such functions or activities are taking place; or (iii) any school bus owned or operated by any such school, he is guilty of a Class 6 felony.

C. If any person knowingly possesses any firearm designed or intended to expel a projectile by action of an explosion of a combustible material within the building of a child day center or public, private, or religious preschool, elementary, middle, or high school and intends to use, or attempts to use, such firearm, or displays such weapon in a threatening manner, such person is guilty of a Class 6 felony and sentenced to a mandatory minimum term of imprisonment of five years to be served consecutively with any other sentence.

D. The child day center and private or religious preschool provisions of this section (i) shall apply only during the operating hours of such child day center or private or religious preschool and (ii) shall not apply to any person (a) whose residence is on the property of a child day center or a private or religious preschool and (b) who possesses a firearm or other weapon prohibited under this section while in his residence.

E. The exemptions set out in §§ 18.2-308 and 18.2-308.016 shall apply, mutatis mutandis, to the provisions of this section. The provisions of this section shall not apply to (i) persons who possess such weapon or weapons as a part of the school's curriculum or activities; (ii) a person possessing a knife customarily used for food preparation or service and using it for such purpose; (iii) persons who possess such weapon or weapons as a part of any program sponsored or facilitated by either the school or any organization authorized by the school to conduct its programs either on or off the school premises; (iv) any law-enforcement officer, or retired law-enforcement officer qualified pursuant to subsection C of § 18.2-308.016; (v) any person who possesses a knife or blade which he uses customarily in his trade; (vi) a person who possesses an unloaded firearm or a stun weapon that is in a closed container, or a knife having a metal blade, in or upon a motor vehicle, or an unloaded shotgun or rifle in a firearms rack in or upon a motor vehicle; (vii) a person who has a valid concealed handgun permit and possesses a concealed handgun or a stun weapon while in a motor vehicle in a parking lot, traffic circle, or other means of vehicular ingress or egress to the school; (viii) a school security officer authorized to carry a firearm pursuant to § 22.1-280.2:1; or (ix) an armed security officer, licensed pursuant to Article 4 (§ 9.1-138 et seq.) of Chapter 1 of Title 9.1, hired by a child day center or a private or religious school for the protection of students and employees as authorized by such school. For the purposes of this subsection, "weapon" includes a knife having a metal blade of three inches or longer and "closed container" includes a locked vehicle trunk.

F. Nothing in subsection E or any other provision of law shall be construed as providing an exemption to the provisions of this section for a special conservator of the peace appointed pursuant to § 19.2-13, other than the specifically enumerated exemptions that apply to the general population as provided in subsection E.

G. As used in this section:
"Child day center" means a child day center, as defined in § 22.1-289.02, that is licensed in accordance with the provisions of Chapter 14.1 (§ 22.1-289.02 et seq.) of Title 22.1 and is not operated at the residence of the provider or of any of the children.

"Stun weapon" means any device that emits a momentary or pulsed output, which is electrical, audible, optical or electromagnetic in nature and which is designed to temporarily incapacitate a person.

§ 18.2-308.1:1. PURCHASE, POSSESSION OR TRANSPORTATION OF FIREARMS BY PERSONS ACQUITTED BY REASON OF INSANITY; PENALTY.

A. It shall be unlawful for any person acquitted by reason of insanity and committed to the custody of the Commissioner of Behavioral Health and Developmental Services, pursuant to Chapter 11.1 (§ 19.2-182.2 et seq.) of Title 19.2, on a charge of treason, any felony or any offense punishable as a misdemeanor under Title 54.1 or a Class 1 or Class 2 misdemeanor under this title, except those misdemeanor violations of (i) Article 2 (§ 18.2-266 et seq.) of Chapter 7 of this title, (ii) Article 2 (§ 18.2-415 et seq.) of Chapter 9 of this title, or (iii) § 18.2-119, or (iv) an ordinance of any county, city, or town similar to the offenses specified in (i), (ii), or (iii), to knowingly and intentionally purchase, possess, or transport any firearm. A violation of this subsection shall be punishable as a Class 1 misdemeanor.

B. Any person so acquitted may, upon discharge from the custody of the Commissioner, petition the general district court in the city or county in which he resides to restore his right to purchase, possess or transport a firearm. A copy of the petition shall be mailed or delivered to the attorney for the Commonwealth for the jurisdiction where the petition was filed who shall be entitled to respond and represent the interests of the Commonwealth. The court shall conduct a hearing if requested by either party. If the court determines, after receiving and considering evidence concerning the circumstances regarding the disability referred to in subsection A and the person's criminal history, treatment record, and reputation as developed through character witness statements, testimony, or other character evidence, that the person will not be likely to act in a manner dangerous to public safety and that the granting of the relief would not be contrary to the public interest, the court shall grant the petition. Any person denied relief by the general district court may petition the circuit court for a de novo review of the denial. Upon a grant of relief in any court, the court shall enter a written order granting the petition, in which event the provisions of subsection A do not apply. The clerk of court shall certify and forward forthwith to the Central Criminal Records Exchange, on a form provided by the Exchange, a copy of any such order.

C. As used in this section, "treatment record" shall include copies of health records detailing the petitioner's psychiatric history, which shall include the records pertaining to the commitment or adjudication that is the subject of the request for relief pursuant to this section.

§ 18.2-308.1:2. PURCHASE, POSSESSION OR TRANSPORTATION OF FIREARM BY PERSONS ADJUDICATED LEGALLY INCOMPETENT OR MENTALLY INCAPACITATED; PENALTY.

A. It shall be unlawful for any person who has been adjudicated (i) legally incompetent pursuant to former § 37.1-128.02 or former § 37.1-134, (ii) mentally incapacitated pursuant to former § 37.1-128.1 or former § 37.1-132 or (iii) incapacitated pursuant to Chapter 20 (§ 64.2-2000 et seq.) of Title 64.2 to purchase, possess, or transport any firearm. A violation of this subsection shall be punishable as a Class 1 misdemeanor.

B. Any person whose competency or capacity has been restored pursuant to former § 37.1-134.1, former § 37.2-1012, or § 64.22012 may petition the general district court in the city or county in which he resides to restore his right to purchase, possess or transport a firearm. A copy of the petition shall be mailed or delivered to the attorney for the Commonwealth for the jurisdiction where the petition was filed who shall be entitled to respond and represent the interests of the Commonwealth. The court shall conduct a hearing if requested by either party. If the court determines, after receiving and considering evidence concerning the circumstances regarding the disability referred to in subsection A and the person's criminal history, treatment record, and reputation as developed through character witness statements, testimony, or other character evidence, that the person will not be likely to act in a manner dangerous to public safety and that the granting of the relief would not be contrary to the public interest, the court shall grant the petition. Any person denied relief by the general district court may petition the circuit court for a de novo review of the denial. Upon a grant of relief in any court, the court shall enter a writte+9+n order granting the petition, in which event the provisions of subsection A do not apply. The clerk of court shall certify and forward forthwith to the Central Criminal Records Exchange, on a form provided by the Exchange, a copy of any such order.

C. As used in this section, "treatment record" shall include copies of health records detailing the petitioner's psychiatric history, which shall include the records pertaining to the commitment or adjudication that is the subject of the request for relief pursuant to this section.

§ 18.2-308.1:3. PURCHASE, POSSESSION OR TRANSPORTATION OF FIREARM BY PERSONS INVOLUNTARILY ADMITTED OR ORDERED TO OUTPATIENT TREATMENT; PENALTY.

A. It shall be unlawful for any person (i) involuntarily admitted to a facility or ordered to mandatory outpatient treatment pursuant to § 19.2-169.2; (ii) involuntarily admitted to a facility or ordered to mandatory outpatient treatment as the result of a commitment hearing pursuant to Article 5 (§ 37.2-814 et seq.) of Chapter 8 of Title 37.2, notwithstanding the outcome of any appeal taken pursuant to § 37.2-821; (iii) involuntarily admitted to a facility or ordered to mandatory outpatient treatment as a minor 14 years of age or older as the result of a commitment hearing pursuant to Article 16 (§ 16.1-335 et seq.) of Chapter 11 of Title 16.1, notwithstanding the outcome of any appeal taken pursuant to § 16.1-345.6; (iv) who was the subject of a temporary detention order pursuant to § 37.2-809 and subsequently agreed to voluntary admission pursuant to § 37.2-805; (v) who, as a minor 14 years of age or older, was the subject of a temporary detention order pursuant to § 16.1-340.1 and subsequently agreed to voluntary admission pursuant to § 16.1-338; or (vi) who was found incompetent to stand trial and likely to remain so for the foreseeable future and whose case was disposed of in accordance with § 19.2-169.3, to purchase, possess, or transport a firearm. A violation of this subsection shall be punishable as a Class 1 misdemeanor.

B. Any person prohibited from purchasing, possessing or transporting firearms under this section may, at any time following his release from involuntary admission to a facility, his release from an order of mandatory outpatient treatment, his release from voluntary admission pursuant to § 37.2-805 following the issuance of a temporary detention order, his release from a training center, or his release as provided by § 19.2-169.3, petition the general district court in the city or county in which he resides or, if the person is not a resident of the Commonwealth, the general district court of the city or county in which the most recent of the proceedings described in subsection A occurred to restore his right to purchase, possess, or transport a firearm. A copy of the petition shall be mailed or delivered to the attorney for the Commonwealth for the jurisdiction where the petition was filed who shall be entitled to respond and represent the interests of the Commonwealth. The court shall conduct a hearing if requested by either party. If the court determines, after receiving and considering evidence concerning the circumstances regarding the disabilities referred to in subsection A and the person's criminal history, treatment record, and reputation as developed through character witness statements, testimony, or other character evidence, that the person will not likely act in a manner dangerous to public safety and that granting the relief would not be contrary to the public interest, the court shall grant the petition. Any person denied relief by the general district court may petition the circuit court for a de novo review of the denial. Upon a grant of relief in any court, the court shall enter a written order granting the petition, in which event the provisions of subsection A do not apply. The clerk of court shall certify and forward forthwith to the Central Criminal Records Exchange, on a form provided by the Exchange, a copy of any such order.

C. As used in this section, "treatment record" shall include copies of health records detailing the petitioner's psychiatric history, which shall include the records pertaining to the commitment or adjudication that is the subject of the request for relief pursuant to this section.

§ 18.2-308.1:4. PURCHASE OR TRANSPORTATION OF FIREARM BY PERSONS SUBJECT TO PROTECTIVE ORDERS; PENALTIES.

A. It is unlawful for any person who is subject to (i) a protective order entered pursuant to § 16.1-253.1, 16.1-253.4, 16.1-278.2, 16.1-279.1, 19.2-152.8, 19.2-152.9, or 19.2-152.10; (ii) an order issued pursuant to subsection B of § 20-103; (iii) an order entered pursuant to subsection D of § 18.2-60.3; (iv) a preliminary protective order entered pursuant to subsection F of § 16.1-253 where a petition alleging abuse or neglect has been filed; or (v) an order issued by a tribunal of another state, the United States or any of its territories, possessions, or commonwealths, or the District of Columbia pursuant to a statute that is substantially similar to those cited in clauses (i), (ii), (iii), or (iv) to purchase or transport any firearm while the order is in effect. Any person with a concealed handgun permit shall be prohibited from carrying any concealed firearm, and shall surrender his permit to the court entering the order, for the duration of any protective order referred to herein. A violation of this subsection is a Class 1 misdemeanor.

B. In addition to the prohibition set forth in subsection A, it is unlawful for any person who is subject to a protective order entered pursuant to § 16.1-279.1 or 19.2-152.10 or an order issued by a tribunal of another state, the United States or any of its territories, possessions, or commonwealths, or the District of Columbia pursuant to a statute that is substantially similar to § 16.1-279.1 or 19.2-152.10 to knowingly possess any firearm while the order is in effect, provided that for a period of 24 hours after being served with a protective order in accordance with subsection C of § 16.1-279.1 or subsection D of § 19.2-152.10 such person may continue to possess and, notwithstanding the provisions of subsection A, transport any firearm possessed by such person at the time of service for the purposes of surrendering any such firearm to a law-enforcement agency in accordance with subsection C or selling or transferring any such firearm to a dealer as defined in § 18.2-308.2:2 or to any person who is not otherwise prohibited by law from possessing such firearm in accordance with subsection C. A violation of this subsection is a Class 6 felony.

C. Upon issuance of a protective order pursuant to § 16.1-279.1 or 19.2-152.10, the court shall order the person who is subject to the protective order to (i) within 24 hours after being served with a protective order in accordance with subsection C of § 16.1-279.1 or subsection D of § 19.2-152.10 (a) surrender any firearm possessed by such person to a designated local law-enforcement agency, (b) sell or transfer any firearm possessed by such person to a dealer as defined in § 18.2-308.2:2, or (c) sell or transfer any firearm possessed by such person to any person who is not otherwise prohibited by law from possessing such firearm and (ii) within 48 hours after being served with a protective order in accordance with subsection C of § 16.1-279.1 or subsection D of § 19.2-152.10, certify in writing, on a form provided by the Office of the Executive Secretary of the Supreme Court, that such person does not possess any firearms or that all firearms possessed by such person have been surrendered, sold, or transferred and file such certification with the clerk of the court that entered the protective order. The willful failure of any person to certify in writing in accordance with this section that all firearms possessed by such person have been surrendered, sold, or transferred or that such person does not possess any firearms shall constitute contempt of court.

D. The person who is subject to a protective order pursuant to § 16.1-279.1 or 19.2-152.10 shall be provided with the address and hours of operation of a designated local law-enforcement agency and the certification forms when such person is served with a protective order in accordance with subsection C of § 16.1-279.1 or subsection D of § 19.2-152.10.

E. A law-enforcement agency that takes into custody a firearm surrendered to such agency pursuant to subsection C by a person who is subject to a protective order pursuant to § 16.1-279.1 or 19.2-152.10 shall prepare a written receipt containing the name of the person who surrendered the firearm and the manufacturer, model, and serial number of the firearm and provide a copy to such person. Any firearm surrendered to and held by a law-enforcement agency pursuant to subsection C shall be returned by such agency to the person who surrendered the firearm upon the expiration or dissolution of the protective order entered pursuant to § 16.1-279.1 or 19.2-152.10. Such agency shall return the firearm within five days of receiving a written request for the return of the firearm by the person who surrendered the firearm and a copy of the receipt provided to such person by the agency. Prior to returning the firearm to such person, the law-enforcement agency holding the firearm shall confirm that such person is no longer subject to a protective order issued pursuant to § 16.1-279.1 or 19.2-152.10 and is not otherwise prohibited by law from possessing a firearm. A firearm surrendered to a law-enforcement agency pursuant to subsection C may be disposed of in accordance with the provisions of § 15.2-1721 if (i) the person from whom the firearm was seized provides written authorization for such disposal to the agency or (ii) the firearm remains in the possession of the agency more than 120 days after such person is no longer subject to a protective order issued pursuant to § 16.1-279.1 or 19.2-152.10 and such person has not submitted a request in writing for the return of the firearm.

F. Any law-enforcement agency or law-enforcement officer that takes into custody, stores, possesses, or transports a firearm pursuant to this section shall be immune from civil or criminal liability for any damage to or deterioration, loss, or theft of such firearm.

G. The law-enforcement agencies of the counties, cities, and towns within each judicial circuit shall designate, in coordination with each other, and provide to the chief judges of all circuit and district courts within the judicial circuit, one or more local law-enforcement agencies to receive and store firearms pursuant to this section. The law-enforcement agencies shall provide the chief judges with a list that includes the addresses and hours of operation for any law-enforcement agencies so designated that such addresses and hours of operation may be provided to a person served with a protective order in accordance with subsection C of § 16.1-279.1 or subsection D of § 19.2-152.10.

§ 18.2-308.1:5. PURCHASE OR TRANSPORTATION OF FIREARM BY PERSONS CONVICTED OF CERTAIN DRUG OFFENSES PROHIBITED.

Any person who, within a 36-consecutive-month period, has been convicted of two misdemeanor offenses under subsection B of former § 18.2-248.1:1, § 18.2-250 or 18.2-250.1 shall be ineligible to purchase or transport a handgun. However, upon expiration of a period of five years from the date of the second conviction and provided the person has not been convicted of any such offense within that period, the ineligibility shall be removed.

§ 18.2-308.1:6. PURCHASE, POSSESSION, OR TRANSPORTATION OF FIREARM BY PERSONS ENROLLED INTO THE VOLUNTARY DO NOT SELL FIREARMS LIST; PENALTY.

It is unlawful for any person enrolled into the Voluntary Do Not Sell Firearms List pursuant to Chapter 12 (§ 52-50 et seq.) of Title 52 to purchase, possess, or transport a firearm. A violation of this section is punishable as a Class 3 misdemeanor.

§ 18.2-308.1:8. PURCHASE, POSSESSION, OR TRANSPORTATION OF FIREARM FOLLOWING AN ASSAULT AND BATTERY OF A FAMILY OR HOUSEHOLD MEMBER; PENALTY.

A. Any person who knowingly and intentionally purchases, possesses, or transports any firearm following a misdemeanor conviction for an offense that occurred on or after July 1, 2021, for (i) the offense of assault and battery of a family or household member or (ii) an offense substantially similar to clause (i) under the laws of any other state or of the United States is guilty of a Class 1 misdemeanor.

B. For the purposes of this section, "family or household member" means (i) the person's spouse, whether or not he resides in the same home with the person; (ii) the person's former spouse, whether or not he resides in the same home with the person; or (iii) any individual who has a child in common with the person, whether or not the person and that individual have been married or have resided together at any time.

C. Any person prohibited from purchasing, possessing, or transporting a firearm pursuant to subsection A shall be prohibited from purchasing, possessing, or transporting a firearm for three years following the date of the conviction at which point the person convicted of such offense shall no longer be prohibited from purchasing, possessing, or transporting a firearm pursuant to subsection A. Such person shall have his firearms rights restored, unless such person receives another disqualifying conviction, is subject to a protective order that would restrict his rights to carry a firearm, or is otherwise prohibited by law from purchasing, possessing, or transporting a firearm.

---

§ 18.2-308.2.

A. It shall be unlawful for (i) any person who has been convicted of a felony; (ii) any person adjudicated delinquent as a juvenile 14 years of age or older at the time of the offense of murder in violation of § 18.2-31 or 18.2-32, kidnapping in violation of § 18.2-47, robbery by the threat or presentation of firearms in violation of § 18.2-58, or rape in violation of § 18.2-61; or (iii) any person under the age of 29 who was adjudicated delinquent as a juvenile 14 years of age or older at the time of the offense of a delinquent act which would be a felony if committed by an adult, other than those felonies set forth in clause (ii), whether such conviction or adjudication occurred under the laws of the Commonwealth, or any other state, the District of Columbia, the United States or any territory thereof, to knowingly and intentionally possess or transport any firearm or ammunition for a firearm, any stun weapon as defined by § 18.2-308.1, or any explosive material, or to knowingly and intentionally carry about his person, hidden from common observation, any weapon described in subsection A of § 18.2-308. However, such person may possess in his residence or the curtilage thereof a stun weapon as defined by § 18.2-308.1. Any person who violates this section shall be guilty of a Class 6 felony. However, any person who violates this section by knowingly and intentionally possessing or transporting any firearm and who was previously convicted of a violent felony as defined in § 17.1-805 shall be sentenced to a mandatory minimum term of imprisonment of five years. Any person who violates this section by knowingly and intentionally possessing or transporting any firearm and who was previously convicted of any other felony within the prior 10 years shall be sentenced to a mandatory minimum term of imprisonment of two years. The mandatory minimum terms of imprisonment prescribed for violations of this section shall be served consecutively with any other sentence.

B. The prohibitions of subsection A shall not apply to (i) any person who possesses a firearm, ammunition for a firearm, explosive material or other weapon while carrying out his duties as a member of the Armed Forces of the United States or of the National Guard of Virginia or of any other state, (ii) any law-enforcement officer in the performance of his duties, (iii) any person who has been pardoned or whose political disabilities have been removed pursuant to Article V, Section 12 of the Constitution of Virginia provided the Governor, in the document granting the pardon or removing the person's political disabilities, may expressly place conditions upon the reinstatement of the person's right to ship, transport, possess or receive firearms, (iv) any person whose right to possess firearms or ammunition has been restored under the law of another state subject to conditions placed upon the reinstatement of the person's right to ship, transport, possess, or receive firearms by such state, or (v) any person adjudicated delinquent as a juvenile who has completed a term of service of no less than two years in the Armed Forces of the United States and, if such person has been discharged from the Armed Forces of the United States, received an honorable discharge and who is not otherwise prohibited under clause (i) or (ii) of subsection A.

C. Any person prohibited from possessing, transporting, or carrying a firearm, ammunition for a firearm, or a stun weapon under subsection A may petition the circuit court of the jurisdiction in which he resides or, if the person is not a resident of the Commonwealth, the circuit court of any county or city where such person was last convicted of a felony or adjudicated delinquent of a disqualifying offense pursuant to subsection A, for a permit to possess or carry a firearm, ammunition for a firearm, or a stun weapon; however, no person who has been convicted of a felony shall be qualified to petition for such a permit unless his civil rights have been restored by the Governor or other appropriate authority. A copy of the petition shall be mailed or delivered to the attorney for the Commonwealth for the jurisdiction where the petition was filed who shall be entitled to respond and represent the interests of the Commonwealth. The court shall conduct a hearing if requested by either party. The court may, in its discretion and for good cause shown, grant such petition and issue a permit. The provisions of this section relating to firearms, ammunition for a firearm, and stun weapons shall not apply to any person who has been granted a permit pursuant to this subsection.

C1. Any person who was prohibited from possessing, transporting or carrying explosive material under subsection A may possess, transport or carry such explosive material if his right to possess, transport or carry explosive material has been restored pursuant to federal law.

C2. The prohibitions of subsection A shall not prohibit any person other than a person convicted of an act of violence as defined in § 19.2-297.1 or a violent felony as defined in subsection C of § 17.1-805 from possessing, transporting, or carrying (i) antique firearms or (ii) black powder in a quantity not exceeding five pounds if it is intended to be used solely for sporting, recreational, or cultural purposes in antique firearms. For the purposes of this subsection, "antique firearms" means any firearm described in subdivision 3 of the definition of "antique firearm" in subsection F of § 18.2-308.2:2.

D. For the purpose of this section:
"Ammunition for a firearm" means the combination of a cartridge, projectile, primer, or propellant designed for use in a firearm other than an antique firearm as defined in § 18.2-308.2:2.

"Explosive material" means any chemical compound mixture, or device, the primary or common purpose of which is to function by explosion; the term includes, but is not limited to, dynamite and other high explosives, black powder, pellet powder, smokeless gun powder, detonators, blasting caps and detonating cord but shall not include fireworks or permissible fireworks as defined in § 27-95.

§ 24.2-604. POLLING PLACES; PROHIBITED ACTIVITIES; PROHIBITED AREA; PENALTIES.

A. During the times the polls are open and ballots are being counted, or within one hour of opening or after closing, it is unlawful for any person (i) to loiter or congregate within 40 feet of any entrance of any polling place; (ii) within such distance to give, tender, or exhibit any ballot, ticket, or other campaign material to any person or to solicit or in any manner attempt to influence any person in casting his vote; (iii) to hinder or delay a qualified voter in entering or leaving a polling place; or (iv) to knowingly possess any firearm as defined in § 18.2-308.2:2 within 40 feet of any building, or part thereof, used as a polling place.

B. Prior to opening the polls, the officers of election shall post, in the area within 40 feet of any entrance to the polling place, sufficient notices that state "Prohibited Area" in two-inch type. The notices shall also state the provisions of this section in not less than 24-point type. The officers of election shall post the notices within the prohibited area to be visible to voters and the public.

C. It is unlawful for any authorized representative permitted in the polling place pursuant to § 24.2-604.4, any voter, or any other person in the room to (i) hinder or delay a qualified voter; (ii) give, tender, or exhibit any ballot, ticket, or other campaign material to any person; (iii) solicit or in any manner attempt to influence any person in casting his vote; (iv) hinder or delay any officer of election; (v) be in a position to see the marked ballot of any other voter; or (vi) otherwise impede the orderly conduct of the election.

D. The provisions of subsections A and C shall not be construed to prohibit a person who approaches or enters the polling place for the purpose of voting from wearing a shirt, hat, or other apparel on which a candidate's name or a political slogan appears or from having a sticker or button attached to his apparel on which a candidate's name or a political slogan appears. This exemption shall not apply to candidates, representatives of candidates, or any other person who approaches or enters the polling place for any purpose other than voting.

E. This section shall not be construed to prohibit a candidate from entering any polling place on the day of the election to vote, or to visit a polling place for no longer than 10 minutes per polling place per election day, provided that he complies with the restrictions stated in subsections A, C, and D.

F. The provisions of clause (iv) of subsection A shall not apply to (i) any law-enforcement officer or any retired law-enforcement officer qualified pursuant to subsection C of § 18.2-308.016; (ii) any person occupying his own private property that falls within 40 feet of a polling place; or (iii) an armed security officer, licensed pursuant to Article 4 (§ 9.1-138 et seq.) of Chapter 1 of Title 9.1, whose employment or performance of his duties occurs within 40 feet of any building, or part thereof, used as a polling place.

G. The officers of election may require any person who is found by a majority of the officers present to be in violation of this section to remain outside of the prohibited area. Any person violating subsection A or C is guilty of a Class 1 misdemeanor.

§ 18.2-308.2. (EFFECTIVE JANUARY 1, 2021) POSSESSION OR TRANSPORTATION OF FIREARMS, FIREARMS AMMUNITION, STUN WEAPONS, EXPLOSIVES OR CONCEALED WEAPONS BY CONVICTED FELONS; PENALTIES; PETITION FOR RESTORATION ORDER; WHEN ISSUED.

A. It shall be unlawful for (i) any person who has been convicted of a felony; (ii) any person adjudicated delinquent as a juvenile 14 years of age or older at the time of the offense of murder in violation of § 18.2-31 or 18.2-32, kidnapping in violation of § 18.2-47, robbery by the threat or presentation of firearms in violation of § 18.2-58, or rape in violation of § 18.2-61; or (iii) any person under the age of 29 who was adjudicated delinquent as a juvenile 14 years of age or older at the time of the offense of a delinquent act which would be a felony if committed by an adult, other than those felonies set forth in clause (ii), whether such conviction or adjudication occurred under the laws of the Commonwealth, or any other state, the District of Columbia, the United States or any territory thereof, to knowingly and intentionally possess or transport any firearm or ammunition for a firearm, any stun weapon as defined by § 18.2-308.1, or any explosive material, or to knowingly and intentionally carry about his person, hidden from common observation, any weapon described in subsection A of § 18.2-308. However, such person may possess in his residence or the curtilage thereof a stun weapon as defined by § 18.2-308.1. Any person who violates this section shall be guilty of a Class 6 felony. However, any person who violates this section by knowingly and intentionally possessing or transporting any firearm and who was previously convicted of a violent felony as defined in § 17.1-805 shall be sentenced to a mandatory minimum term of imprisonment of five years. Any person who violates this section by knowingly and intentionally possessing or transporting any firearm and who was previously convicted of any other felony within the prior 10 years shall be sentenced to a mandatory minimum term of imprisonment of two years. The mandatory minimum terms of imprisonment prescribed for violations of this section shall be served consecutively with any other sentence.

B. The prohibitions of subsection A shall not apply to (i) any person who possesses a firearm, ammunition for a firearm, explosive material or other weapon while carrying out his duties as a member of the Armed Forces of the United States or of the National

Guard of Virginia or of any other state, (ii) any law-enforcement officer in the performance of his duties, (iii) any person who has been pardoned or whose political disabilities have been removed pursuant to Article V, Section 12 of the Constitution of Virginia provided the Governor, in the document granting the pardon or removing the person's political disabilities, may expressly place conditions upon the reinstatement of the person's right to ship, transport, possess or receive firearms, (iv) any person whose right to possess firearms or ammunition has been restored under the law of another state subject to conditions placed upon the reinstatement of the person's right to ship, transport, possess, or receive firearms by such state, or (v) any person adjudicated delinquent as a juvenile who has completed a term of service of no less than two years in the Armed Forces of the United States and, if such person has been discharged from the Armed Forces of the United States, received an honorable discharge and who is not otherwise prohibited under clause (i) or (ii) of subsection A.

C. Any person prohibited from possessing, transporting, or carrying a firearm, ammunition for a firearm, or a stun weapon under subsection A may petition the circuit court of the jurisdiction in which he resides or, if the person is not a resident of the Commonwealth, the circuit court of any county or city where such person was last convicted of a felony or adjudicated delinquent of a disqualifying offense pursuant to subsection A, for a restoration order that unconditionally authorizes possessing, transporting, or carrying a firearm, ammunition for a firearm, or a stun weapon; however, no person who has been convicted of a felony shall be qualified to petition for such an order unless his civil rights have been restored by the Governor or other appropriate authority. A copy of the petition shall be mailed or delivered to the attorney for the Commonwealth for the jurisdiction where the petition was filed who shall be entitled to respond and represent the interests of the Commonwealth. The court shall conduct a hearing if requested by either party. The court may, in its discretion and for good cause shown, grant such petition and issue a restoration order. Such order shall contain the petitioner's name and date of birth. The clerk shall certify and forward forthwith to the Central Criminal Records Exchange (CCRE), on a form provided by the CCRE, a copy of the order to be accompanied by a complete set of the petitioner's fingerprints. The Department of State Police shall forthwith enter the petitioner's name and description in the CCRE so that the order's existence will be made known to law-enforcement personnel accessing the computerized criminal history records for investigative purposes. The provisions of this section relating to firearms, ammunition for a firearm, and stun weapons shall not apply to any person who has been issued a restoration order pursuant to this subsection.

C1. Any person who was prohibited from possessing, transporting or carrying explosive material under subsection A may possess, transport or carry such explosive material if his right to possess, transport or carry explosive material has been restored pursuant to federal law.

C2. The prohibitions of subsection A shall not prohibit any person other than a person convicted of an act of violence as defined in § 19.2-297.1 or a violent felony as defined in subsection C of § 17.1-805 from possessing, transporting, or carrying (i) antique firearms or (ii) black powder in a quantity not exceeding five pounds if it is intended to be used solely for sporting, recreational, or cultural purposes in antique firearms. For the purposes of this subsection, "antique firearms" means any firearm described in subdivision 3 of the definition of "antique firearm" in subsection F of § 18.2-308.2:2.

D. For the purpose of this section:
"Ammunition for a firearm" means the combination of a cartridge, projectile, primer, or propellant designed for use in a firearm other than an antique firearm as defined in § 18.2-308.2:2.

"Explosive material" means any chemical compound mixture, or device, the primary or common purpose of which is to function by explosion; the term includes, but is not limited to, dynamite and other high explosives, black powder, pellet powder, smokeless gun powder, detonators, blasting caps and detonating cord but shall not include fireworks or permissible fireworks as defined in § 27-95.

§ 18.2-308.2:01. POSSESSION OR TRANSPORTATION OF CERTAIN FIREARMS BY CERTAIN PERSONS.

A. It shall be unlawful for any person who is not a citizen of the United States or who is not a person lawfully admitted for permanent residence to knowingly and intentionally possess or transport any assault firearm or to knowingly and intentionally carry about his person, hidden from common observation, an assault firearm.

B. It shall be unlawful for any person who is not a citizen of the United States and who is not lawfully present in the United States to knowingly and intentionally possess or transport any firearm or to knowingly and intentionally carry about his person, hidden from common observation, any firearm. A violation of this section shall be punishable as a Class 6 felony.

C. For purposes of this section, "assault firearm" means any semi-automatic center-fire rifle or pistol that expels single or multiple projectiles by action of an explosion of a combustible material and is equipped at the time of the offense with a magazine which will hold more than 20 rounds of ammunition or designed by the manufacturer to accommodate a silencer or equipped with a folding stock.

§ 18.2-308.2:1. PROHIBITING THE SELLING, ETC., OF FIREARMS TO CERTAIN PERSONS.

Any person who sells, barters, gives or furnishes, or has in his possession or under his control with the intent of selling, bartering, giving or furnishing, any firearm to any person he knows is prohibited from possessing or transporting a firearm pursuant to § 18.2-308.1:1, 18.2-308.1:2, or 18.2-308.1:3, subsection B of § 18.2-308.1:4, § 18.2-308.1:6 or 18.2-308.2, subsection B of § 18.2-308.2:01, or § 18.2-308.7 is guilty of a Class 4 felony. However, this prohibition shall not be applicable when the person convicted of the felony, adjudicated delinquent, or acquitted by reason of insanity has (i) been issued a permit pursuant to subsection C of § 18.2-308.2 or been granted relief pursuant to subsection B of § 18.2-308.1:1, or § 18.2-308.1:2 or 18.2-308.1:3; (ii) been pardoned or had his political disabilities removed in accordance with subsection B of § 18.2-308.2; or (iii) obtained a permit to ship, transport, possess or receive firearms pursuant to the laws of the United States. 1988, c. 327; 1990, c. 692; 1993, cc. 467, 494, 882, 926; 2004, c. 995; 2008, c. 408; 2011, c. 775; 2013, c. 797; 2020, cc. 887, 888, 1221, 1260.

§ 18.2-308.2:1. (EFFECTIVE JULY 1, 2021) PROHIBITING THE SELLING, ETC., OF FIREARMS TO CERTAIN PERSONS; PENALTIES.

A. Any person who sells, barters, gives, or furnishes, or has in his possession or under his control with the intent of selling, bartering, giving, or furnishing, any firearm to any person he knows is prohibited from possessing or transporting a firearm pursuant to § 18.2-308.1:1, 18.2-308.1:2, or 18.2-308.1:3, subsection B of § 18.2-308.1:4, § 18.2-308.1:6 or 18.2-308.2, subsection B of § 18.2-308.2:01, or § 18.2-308.7 is guilty of a Class 4 felony. However, this prohibition shall not be applicable when the person convicted of the felony, adjudicated delinquent, or acquitted by reason of insanity has (i) been issued a permit pursuant to subsection C of § 18.2-308.2 or been granted relief pursuant to subsection B of § 18.2-308.1:1 or § 18.2-308.1:2 or 18.2-308.1:3; (ii) been pardoned or had his political disabilities removed in accordance with subsection B of § 18.2-308.2; or (iii) obtained a permit to ship, transport, possess, or receive firearms pursuant to the laws of the United States.

B. Any person who sells, barters, gives, or furnishes, or has in his possession or under his control with the intent of selling, bartering, giving, or furnishing, any firearm to any person he knows is prohibited from purchasing, possessing or transporting a firearm pursuant to § 18.2-308.1:7 is guilty of a Class 1 misdemeanor.

§ 18.2-308.2:2. CRIMINAL HISTORY RECORD INFORMATION CHECK REQUIRED FOR THE TRANSFER OF CERTAIN FIREARMS.

A. Any person purchasing from a dealer a firearm as herein defined shall consent in writing, on a form to be provided by the Department of State Police, to have the dealer obtain criminal history record information. Such form shall include only the written consent; the name, birth date, gender, race, citizenship, and social security number and/or any other identification number; the number of firearms by category intended to be sold, rented, traded, or transferred; and answers by the applicant to the following questions: (i) has the applicant been convicted of a felony offense or found guilty or adjudicated delinquent as a juvenile 14 years of age or older at the time of the offense of a delinquent act that would be a felony if committed by an adult; (ii) is the applicant subject to a court order restraining the applicant from harassing, stalking, or threatening the applicant's child or intimate partner, or a child of such partner, or is the applicant subject to a protective order; and (iii) has the applicant ever been acquitted by reason of insanity and prohibited from purchasing, possessing or transporting a firearm pursuant to § 18.2-308.1:1 or any substantially similar law of any other jurisdiction, been adjudicated legally incompetent, mentally incapacitated or adjudicated an incapacitated person and prohibited from purchasing a firearm pursuant to § 18.2-308.1:2 or any substantially similar law of any other jurisdiction, or been involuntarily admitted to an inpatient facility or involuntarily ordered to outpatient mental health treatment and prohibited from purchasing a firearm pursuant to § 18.2-308.1:3 or any substantially similar law of any other jurisdiction.

B. 1. No dealer shall sell, rent, trade or transfer from his inventory any such firearm to any other person who is a resident of Virginia until he has (i) obtained written consent and the other information on the consent form specified in subsection A, and provided the Department of State Police with the name, birth date, gender, race, citizenship, and social security and/or any other identification number and the number of firearms by category intended to be sold, rented, traded or transferred and (ii) requested criminal history record information by a telephone call to or other communication authorized by the State Police and is authorized by subdivision 2 to complete the sale or other such transfer. To establish personal identification and residence in Virginia for purposes of this section, a dealer must require any prospective purchaser to present one photo-identification form issued by a governmental agency of the Commonwealth or by the United States Department of Defense that demonstrates that the prospective purchaser resides in Virginia. For the purposes of this section and establishment of residency for firearm purchase, residency of a member of the armed forc es shall include both the state in which the member's permanent duty post is located and any nearby state in which the member resides and from which he commutes to the permanent duty post. A member of the armed forces whose photo identification issued by the Department of Defense does not have a Virginia address may establish his Virginia residency with such photo identification and either permanent orders assigning the purchaser to a duty post, including the Pentagon, in Virginia or the purchaser's Leave and Earnings Statement. When the photo identification presented to a dealer by the prospective purchaser is a driver's license or other photo identification issued by the Department of Motor Vehicles, and such identification form contains a date of issue, the dealer shall not, except for a renewed driver's license or other photo identification issued by the Department of Motor Vehicles, sell or otherwise transfer a firearm to the prospective purchaser until 30 days after the date of issue of an original or duplicate driver's license unless the prospective purchaser also presents a copy of his Virginia Department of Motor Vehicles driver's record showing that the original date of issue of the driver's license was more than 30 days prior to the attempted purchase.

In addition, no dealer shall sell, rent, trade, or transfer from his inventory any assault firearm to any person who is not a citizen of the United States or who is not a person lawfully admitted for permanent residence.

Upon receipt of the request for a criminal history record information check, the State Police shall (a) review its criminal history record information to determine if the buyer or transferee is prohibited from possessing or transporting a firearm by state or federal law, (b) inform the dealer if its record indicates that the buyer or transferee is so prohibited, and (c) provide the dealer with a unique reference number for that inquiry.

2. The State Police shall provide its response to the requesting dealer during the dealer's request, or by return call without delay. If the criminal history record information check indicates the prospective purchaser or transferee has a disqualifying criminal record or has been acquitted by reason of insanity and committed to the custody of the Commissioner of Behavioral Health and Developmental Services, the State Police shall have until the end of the dealer's next business day to advise the dealer if its records indicate the buyer or transferee is prohibited from possessing or transporting a firearm by state or federal law. If not so advised by the end of the dealer's next business day, a dealer who has fulfilled the requirements of subdivision 1 may immediately complete the sale or transfer and shall not be deemed in violation of this section with respect to such sale or transfer. In case of electronic failure or other circumstances beyond the control of the State Police, the dealer shall be advised immediately of the reason for such delay and be given an estimate of the length of such delay. After such notification, the State Police

shall, as soon as possible but in no event later than the end of the dealer's next business day, inform the requesting dealer if its records indicate the buyer or transferee is prohibited from possessing or transporting a firearm by state or federal law. A dealer who fulfills the requirements of subdivision 1 and is told by the State Police that a response will not be available by the end of the dealer's next business day may immediately complete the sale or transfer and shall not be deemed in violation of this section with respect to such sale or transfer.
3. Except as required by subsection D of § 9.1-132, the State Police shall not maintain records longer than 30 days, except for multiple handgun transactions for which records shall be maintained for 12 months, from any dealer's request for a criminal history record information check pertaining to a buyer or transferee who is not found to be prohibited from possessing and transporting a firearm under state or federal law. However, the log on requests made may be maintained for a period of 12 months, and such log shall consist of the name of the purchaser, the dealer identification number, the unique approval number and the transaction date.
4. On the last day of the week following the sale or transfer of any firearm, the dealer shall mail or deliver the written consent form required by subsection A to the Department of State Police. The State Police shall immediately initiate a search of all available criminal history record information to determine if the purchaser is prohibited from possessing or transporting a firearm under state or federal law. If the search discloses information indicating that the buyer or transferee is so prohibited from possessing or transporting a firearm, the State Police shall inform the chief law-enforcement officer in

the jurisdiction where the sale or transfer occurred and the dealer without delay.

5. Notwithstanding any other provisions of this section, rifles and shotguns may be purchased by persons who are citizens of the United States or persons lawfully admitted for permanent residence but residents of other states under the terms of subsections A and B upon furnishing the dealer with one photo-identification form issued by a governmental agency of the person's state of residence and one other form of identification determined to be acceptable by the Department of Criminal Justice Services.

6. For the purposes of this subsection, the phrase "dealer's next business day" shall not include December 25.

C. No dealer shall sell, rent, trade or transfer from his inventory any firearm, except when the transaction involves a rifle or a shotgun and can be accomplished pursuant to the provisions of subdivision B 5 to any person who is not a resident of Virginia unless he has first obtained from the Department of State Police a report indicating that a search of all available criminal history record information has not disclosed that the person is prohibited from possessing or transporting a firearm under state or federal law. The dealer shall obtain the required report by mailing or delivering the written consent form required under subsection A to the State Police within 24 hours of its execution. If the dealer has complied with the provisions of this subsection and has not received the required report from the State Police within 10 days from the date the written consent form was mailed to the Department of State Police, he shall not be deemed in violation of this section for thereafter completing the sale or transfer.

D. Nothing herein shall prevent a resident of the Commonwealth, at his option, from buying, renting or receiving a firearm from a dealer in Virginia by obtaining a criminal history record information check through the dealer as provided in subsection C.

E. If any buyer or transferee is denied the right to purchase a firearm under this section, he may exercise his right of access to and review and correction of criminal history record information under § 9.1-132 or institute a civil action as provided in § 9.1-135, provided any such action is initiated within 30 days of such denial.

F. Any dealer who willfully and intentionally requests, obtains, or seeks to obtain criminal history record information under false pretenses, or who willfully and intentionally disseminates or seeks to disseminate criminal history record information except as authorized in this section shall be guilty of a Class 2 misdemeanor.

G. For purposes of this section:
"Actual buyer" means a person who executes the consent form required in subsection B or C, or other such firearm transaction records as may be required by federal law.

"Antique firearm" means:
1. Any firearm (including any firearm with a matchlock, flintlock, percussion cap, or similar type of ignition system) manufactured in or before 1898;
2. Any replica of any firearm described in subdivision 1 of this definition if such replica (i) is not designed or redesigned for using rimfire or conventional centerfire fixed ammunition or (ii) uses rimfire or conventional centerfire fixed ammunition that is no longer manufactured in the United States and that is

not readily available in the ordinary channels of commercial trade;

3. Any muzzle-loading rifle, muzzle-loading shotgun, or muzzle-loading pistol that is designed to use black powder, or a black powder substitute, and that cannot use fixed ammunition. For purposes of this subdivision, the term "antique firearm" shall not include any weapon that incorporates a firearm frame or receiver, any firearm that is converted into a muzzle-loading weapon, or any muzzle-loading weapon that can be readily converted to fire fixed ammunition by replacing the barrel, bolt, breech-block, or any combination thereof; or

4. Any curio or relic as defined in this subsection.

"Assault firearm" means any semi-automatic center-fire rifle or pistol which expels single or multiple projectiles by action of an explosion of a combustible material and is equipped at the time of the offense with a magazine which will hold more than 20 rounds of ammunition or designed by the manufacturer to accommodate a silencer or equipped with a folding stock.

"Curios or relics" means firearms that are of special interest to collectors by reason of some quality other than is associated with firearms intended for sporting use or as offensive or defensive weapons. To be recognized as curios or relics, firearms must fall within one of the following categories:

1. Firearms that were manufactured at least 50 years prior to the current date, which use rimfire or conventional centerfire fixed ammunition that is no longer manufactured in the United States and that is not readily available in the ordinary channels of commercial trade, but not including replicas thereof;

2. Firearms that are certified by the curator of a municipal, state, or federal museum that exhibits firearms to be curios or relics of museum interest; and
3. Any other firearms that derive a substantial part of their monetary value from the fact that they are novel, rare, bizarre, or because of their association with some historical figure, period, or event. Proof of qualification of a particular firearm under this category may be established by evidence of present value and evidence that like firearms are not available except as collectors' items, or that the value of like firearms available in ordinary commercial channels is substantially less.

"Dealer" means any person licensed as a dealer pursuant to 18 U.S.C. § 921 et seq.

"Firearm" means any handgun, shotgun, or rifle that will or is designed to or may readily be converted to expel single or multiple projectiles by action of an explosion of a combustible material.

"Handgun" means any pistol or revolver or other firearm originally designed, made and intended to fire single or multiple projectiles by means of an explosion of a combustible material from one or more barrels when held in one hand.

"Lawfully admitted for permanent residence" means the status of having been lawfully accorded the privilege of residing permanently in the United States as an immigrant in accordance with the immigration laws, such status not having changed.

H. The Department of Criminal Justice Services shall promulgate regulations to ensure the identity, confidentiality and security of all records and data provided by the Department of State Police pursuant to this section.

I. (Effective October 1, 2016) The provisions of this section shall not apply to (i) transactions between persons who are licensed as firearms importers or collectors, manufacturers or dealers pursuant to 18 U.S.C. § 921 et seq.; (ii) purchases by or sales to any law-enforcement officer or agent of the United States, the Commonwealth or any local government, or any campus police officer appointed under Article 3 (§ 23.1-809 et seq.) of Chapter 8 of Title 23.1; or (iii) antique firearms, curios or relics.

J. The provisions of this section shall not apply to restrict purchase, trade or transfer of firearms by a resident of Virginia when the resident of Virginia makes such purchase, trade or transfer in another state, in which case the laws and regulations of that state and the United States governing the purchase, trade or transfer of firearms shall apply. A National Instant Criminal Background Check System (NICS) check shall be performed prior to such purchase, trade or transfer of firearms.

J1. All licensed firearms dealers shall collect a fee of $2 for every transaction for which a criminal history record information check is required pursuant to this section, except that a fee of $5 shall be collected for every transaction involving an out-of-state resident. Such fee shall be transmitted to the Department of State Police by the last day of the month following the sale for deposit in a special fund for use by the State Police to offset the cost of conducting criminal history record information checks under the provisions of this section.

K. Any person willfully and intentionally making a materially false statement on the consent form required in subsection B or C or on such firearm transaction records as may be required by federal law, shall be guilty of a Class 5 felony.

L. Except as provided in § 18.2-308.2:1, any dealer who willfully and intentionally sells, rents, trades or transfers a firearm in violation of this section shall be guilty of a Class 6 felony.

L1. Any person who attempts to solicit, persuade, encourage, or entice any dealer to transfer or otherwise convey a firearm other than to the actual buyer, as well as any other person who willfully and intentionally aids or abets such person, shall be guilty of a Class 6 felony. This subsection shall not apply to a federal law-enforcement officer or a law-enforcement officer as defined in § 9.1-101, in the performance of his official duties, or other person under his direct supervision.

M. Any person who purchases a firearm with the intent to (i) resell or otherwise provide such firearm to any person who he knows or has reason to believe is ineligible to purchase or otherwise receive from a dealer a firearm for whatever reason or (ii) transport such firearm out of the Commonwealth to be resold or otherwise provided to another person who the transferor knows is ineligible to purchase or otherwise receive a firearm, shall be guilty of a Class 4 felony and sentenced to a mandatory minimum term of imprisonment of one year. However, if the violation of this subsection involves such a transfer of more than one firearm, the person shall be sentenced to a mandatory minimum term of imprisonment of five years. The prohibitions of this subsection shall not apply to the purchase of a firearm by a person for the lawful use, possession, or transport thereof, pursuant to § 18.2-308.7, by his child, grandchild, or individual for whom he is the legal guardian if such child, grandchild, or individual is ineligible, solely because of his age, to purchase a firearm.

N. Any person who is ineligible to purchase or otherwise receive or possess a firearm in the Commonwealth who solicits, employs or assists any person in violating subsection M shall be guilty of a Class 4 felony and shall be sentenced to a mandatory minimum term of imprisonment of five years.

O. Any mandatory minimum sentence imposed under this section shall be served consecutively with any other sentence.

P. All driver's licenses issued on or after July 1, 1994, shall carry a letter designation indicating whether the driver's license is an original, duplicate or renewed driver's license.

Q. Prior to selling, renting, trading, or transferring any firearm owned by the dealer but not in his inventory to any other person, a dealer may require such other person to consent to have the dealer obtain criminal history record information to determine if such other person is prohibited from possessing or transporting a firearm by state or federal law. The Department of State Police shall establish policies and procedures in accordance with 28 C.F.R. § 25.6 to permit such determinations to be made by the Department of State Police, and the processes established for making such determinations shall conform to the provisions of this section.

§ **18.2-308.2:5.**

A. No person shall sell a firearm for money, goods, services or anything else of value unless he has obtained verification from a licensed dealer in firearms that information on the prospective purchaser has been submitted for a criminal history record information check as set out in § 18.2-308.2:2 and that a determination has been received from the Department of State Police that the prospective purchaser is not prohibited under state or federal law from possessing a firearm or such sale is specifically exempted by state or federal law. The Department of State Police shall provide a means by which sellers may obtain from designated licensed dealers the approval or denial of firearm transfer requests, based on criminal history record information checks. The processes established shall conform to the provisions of § 18.2-308.2:2, and the definitions and provisions of § 18.2-308.2:2 regarding criminal history record information checks shall apply to this section mutatis mutandis. The designated dealer shall collect and disseminate the fees prescribed in § 18.2-308.2:2 as required by that section. The dealer may charge and retain an additional fee not to exceed $15 for obtaining a criminal history record information check on behalf of a seller.

B. Notwithstanding the provisions of subsection A and unless otherwise prohibited by state or federal law, a person may sell a firearm to another person if:
1. The sale of a firearm is to an authorized representative of the Commonwealth or any subdivision thereof as part of an authorized voluntary gun buy-back or give-back program; or
2. The sale occurs at a firearms show, as defined in § 54.1-4200, and the seller has received a determination from the Department of State Police that the purchaser is not prohibited under state or federal law from possessing a firearm in accordance with § 54.1-4201.2.

C. Any person who willfully and intentionally sells a firearm to another person without obtaining verification in accordance with this section is guilty of a Class 1 misdemeanor.

D. Any person who willfully and intentionally purchases a firearm from another person without obtaining verification in accordance with this section is guilty of a Class 1 misdemeanor.

§ 18.2-308.3. USE OR ATTEMPTED USE OF RESTRICTED AMMUNITION IN COMMISSION OR ATTEMPTED COMMISSION OF CRIMES PROHIBITED; PENALTY.

A. When used in this section:
"Restricted firearm ammunition" applies to bullets, projectiles or other types of ammunition that are: (i) coated with or contain, in whole or in part, polytetrafluorethylene or a similar product, (ii) commonly known as "KTW" bullets or "French Arcanes," or (iii) any cartridges containing bullets coated with a plastic substance with other than lead or lead alloy cores, jacketed bullets with other than lead or lead alloy cores, or cartridges of which the bullet itself is wholly comprised of a metal or metal alloy other than lead. This definition shall not be construed to include shotgun shells or solid plastic bullets.

B. It shall be unlawful for any person to knowingly use or attempt to use restricted firearm ammunition while committing or attempting to commit a crime. Violation of this section shall constitute a separate and distinct felony and any person found guilty thereof shall be guilty of a Class 5 felony.

§ 18.2-308.5. MANUFACTURE, IMPORT, SALE, TRANSFER OR POSSESSION OF PLASTIC FIREARM PROHIBITED.

It shall be unlawful for any person to manufacture, import, sell, transfer or possess any plastic firearm. As used in this section, "plastic firearm" means any firearm, including machine guns and sawed-off shotguns as defined in this chapter, containing less than 3.7 ounces of electromagnetically detectable metal in the barrel, slide, cylinder, frame or receiver of which, when subjected to inspection by X-ray machines commonly used at airports, does not generate an image that accurately depicts its shape. A violation of this section shall be punishable as a Class 5 felony.

§ 18.2-308.5:1. MANUFACTURE, IMPORTATION, SALE, POSSESSION, TRANSFER, OR TRANSPORTATION OF TRIGGER ACTIVATORS PROHIBITED; PENALTY.

A. As used in this section, "trigger activator" means a device designed to allow a semi-automatic firearm to shoot more than one shot with a single pull of the trigger by harnessing the recoil energy of any semi-automatic firearm to which it is affixed so that the trigger resets and continues firing without additional physical manipulation of the trigger by the shooter.

B. It is unlawful for any person to manufacture, import, sell, offer for sale, possess, transfer, or transport a trigger activator in the Commonwealth.

C. A violation of this section is punishable as a Class 6 felony.

D. Nothing in this section shall be construed to prohibit a person from manufacturing, importing, selling, offering for sale, possessing, receiving, transferring, or transporting any item for which such person is in compliance with the National Firearms Act (26 U.S.C. § 5801 et seq.).

§ 18.2-308.7. POSSESSION OR TRANSPORTATION OF CERTAIN FIREARMS BY PERSONS UNDER THE AGE OF 18; PENALTY.

It shall be unlawful for any person under 18 years of age to knowingly and intentionally possess or transport a handgun or assault firearm anywhere in the Commonwealth. For the purposes of this section, "handgun" means any pistol or revolver or other firearm originally designed, made and intended to fire single or multiple projectiles by means of an explosion of a combustible material from one or more barrels when held in one hand and "assault firearm" means any (i) semi-automatic centerfire rifle or pistol which expels single or multiple projectiles by action of an explosion of a combustible material and is equipped at the time of the offense with a magazine which will hold more than 20 rounds of ammunition or designed by the manufacturer to accommodate a silencer or equipped with a folding stock or (ii) shotgun with a magazine which will hold more than seven rounds of the longest ammunition for which it is chambered. A violation of this section shall be a Class 1 misdemeanor.

This section shall not apply to:
1. Any person (i) while in his home or on his property; (ii) while in the home or on the property of his parent, grandparent, or legal guardian; or (iii) while on the property of another who has provided prior permission, and with the prior permission of

his parent or legal guardian if the person has the landowner's written permission on his person while on such property;
2. Any person who, while accompanied by an adult, is at, or going to and from, a lawful shooting range or firearms educational class, provided that the weapons are unloaded while being transported;
3. Any person actually engaged in lawful hunting or going to and from a hunting area or preserve, provided that the weapons are unloaded while being transported; and
4. Any person while carrying out his duties in the Armed Forces of the United States or the National Guard of this Commonwealth or any other state.

§ 18.2-308.8. IMPORTATION, SALE, POSSESSION OR TRANSFER OF STRIKER 12'S PROHIBITED; PENALTY.

It shall be unlawful for any person to import, sell, possess or transfer the following firearms: the Striker 12, commonly called a "streetsweeper," or any semi-automatic folding stock shotgun of like kind with a spring tension drum magazine capable of holding twelve shotgun shells. A violation of this section shall be punishable as a Class 6 felony.

§ 18.2-309. FURNISHING CERTAIN WEAPONS TO MINORS; PENALTY.

A. If any person sells, barters, gives or furnishes, or causes to be sold, bartered, given or furnished, to any minor a dirk, switchblade knife or bowie knife, having good cause to believe him to be a minor, such person shall be guilty of a Class 1 misdemeanor.

B. If any person sells, barters, gives or furnishes, or causes to be sold, bartered, given or furnished, to any minor a handgun, having good cause to believe him to be a minor, such person shall be guilty of a Class 6 felony. This subsection shall not apply to any transfer made between family members or for the purpose of engaging in a sporting event or activity.

§ 18.2-311. PROHIBITING THE SELLING OR HAVING IN POSSESSION BLACKJACKS, ETC.

If any person sells or barters, or exhibits for sale or for barter, or gives or furnishes, or causes to be sold, bartered, given or furnished, or has in his possession, or under his control, with the intent of selling, bartering, giving or furnishing, any blackjack, brass or metal knucks, any disc of whatever configuration having at least two points or pointed blades which is designed to be thrown or propelled and which may be known as a throwing star or oriental dart, switchblade knife, ballistic knife as defined in § 18.2-307.1, or like weapons, such person is guilty of a Class 4 misdemeanor. The having in one's possession of any such weapon shall be prima facie evidence, except in the case of a conservator of the peace, of his intent to sell, barter, give or furnish the same.

TITLE 18.2. CRIMES AND OFFENSES GENERALLY CHAPTER 7. CRIMES INVOLVING HEALTH AND SAFETY ARTICLE 8. MISCELLANEOUS DANGEROUS CONDUCT

§ 18.2-312. ILLEGAL USE OF TEAR GAS, PHOSGENE AND OTHER GASES.

If any person maliciously release or cause or procure to be released in any private home, place of business or place of public gathering any tear gas, mustard gas, phosgene gas or other noxious or nauseating gases or mixtures of chemicals designed to, and capable of, producing vile or injurious or nauseating odors or gases, and bodily injury results to any person from such gas or odor, the offending person shall be guilty of a Class 3 felony.

If such act be done unlawfully, but not maliciously, the offending person shall be guilty of a Class 6 felony.

Nothing herein contained shall prevent the use of tear gas or other gases by police officers or other peace officers in the proper performance of their duties, or by any person or persons in the protection of person, life or property.

§ 18.2-324. THROWING OR DEPOSITING CERTAIN SUBSTANCES UPON HIGHWAY; REMOVAL OF SUCH SUBSTANCES.

No person shall throw or deposit or cause to be deposited upon any highway any glass bottle, glass, nail, tack, wire, can, or any other substance likely to injure any person or animal, or damage any vehicle upon such highway, nor shall any person throw or deposit or cause to be deposited upon any highway any soil, sand, mud, gravel or other substances so as to create a hazard to the traveling public. Any person who drops, or permits to be dropped or thrown, upon any highway any destructive, hazardous or injurious material shall immediately remove the same or cause it to be removed. Any person removing a wrecked or damaged vehicle from a highway shall remove any glass or other injurious substance dropped upon the highway from such vehicle. Any persons violating the provisions of this section shall be guilty of a Class 1 misdemeanor.

This section shall not apply to the use, by a law-enforcement officer while in the discharge of official duties, of any device designed to deflate tires. The Division of Purchase and Supply shall, pursuant to § 2.2-1112, set minimum standards for such devices and shall give notice of such standards to law-enforcement offices in the Commonwealth. No such device shall be used which does not meet or exceed the standards

TITLE 18.2. CRIMES AND OFFENSES GENERALLY CHAPTER 8. CRIMES INVOLVING MORALS AND DECENCY ARTICLE 5. OBSCENITY AND RELATED OFFENSES

§ 18.2-388. PROFANE SWEARING AND INTOXICATION IN PUBLIC; PENALTY; TRANSPORTATION OF PUBLIC INEBRIATES TO DETOXIFICATION CENTER.

If any person is intoxicated in public, whether such intoxication results from alcohol, narcotic drug, or other intoxicant or drug of whatever nature, he is guilty of a Class 4 misdemeanor. In any area in which there is located a court-approved detoxification center, a law-enforcement officer may authorize the transportation, by police or otherwise, of public inebriates to such detoxification center in lieu of arrest; however, no person shall be involuntarily detained in such center.

TITLE 18.2. CRIMES AND OFFENSES GENERALLY CHAPTER 9. CRIMES AGAINST PEACE AND ORDER ARTICLE 8. UNLAWFUL PARAMILITARY ACTIVITY

§ 18.2-433.1. DEFINITIONS.

As used in this article:

"Civil disorder" means any public disturbance within the United

States or any territorial possessions thereof involving acts of violence by assemblages of three or more persons, which causes an immediate danger of or results in damage or injury to the property or person of any other individual.

"Explosive or incendiary device" means (i) dynamite and all other forms of high explosives, (ii) any explosive bomb, grenade, missile, or similar device, or (iii) any incendiary bomb or grenade, fire bomb, or similar device, including any device which consists of or includes a breakable container including a flammable liquid or compound, and a wick composed of any material which, when ignited, is capable of igniting such flammable liquid or compound, and can be carried or thrown by one individual acting alone.

"Firearm" means any weapon that will or is designed to or may readily be converted to expel single or multiple projectiles by the action of an explosion of a combustible material; or the frame or receiver of any such weapon.

"Law-enforcement officer" means any officer as defined in § 9.1101 or any such officer or member of the armed forces of the United States, any state, any political subdivision of a state, or the District of Columbia, and such term shall specifically include, but shall not be limited to, members of the National Guard, as defined in § 101(c) of Title 10, United States Code, members of the organized militia of any state or territory of the United States, the Commonwealth of Puerto Rico, or the District of Columbia, not included within the definition of National Guard as defined by such § 101(c), and members of the Armed Forces of the United States.

TITLE 19.2. CRIMINAL PROCEDURE CHAPTER 9.1. PROTECTIVE ORDERS

§ 19.2-56. TO WHOM SEARCH WARRANT DIRECTED; WHAT IT SHALL COMMAND; WARRANT TO SHOW DATE AND TIME OF ISSUANCE; COPY OF AFFIDAVIT TO BE PART OF WARRANT AND SERVED THEREWITH; WARRANTS NOT EXECUTED WITHIN 15 DAYS.

A. The judge, magistrate, or other official authorized to issue criminal warrants, shall issue a search warrant only if he finds from the facts or circumstances recited in the affidavit that there is probable cause for the issuance thereof.

Every search warrant shall be directed (i) to the sheriff, sergeant, or any policeman of the county, city, or town in which the place to be searched is located; (ii) to any law-enforcement officer or agent employed by the Commonwealth and vested with the powers of sheriffs and police; or (iii) jointly to any such sheriff, sergeant, policeman, or law-enforcement officer or agent and an agent, special agent, or officer of the Federal Bureau of Investigation, the Bureau of Alcohol, Tobacco and Firearms of the United States Treasury, the United States Naval Criminal Investigative Service, the United States Department of Homeland Security, any inspector, law-enforcement official, or police personnel of the United States Postal Service, or the Drug Enforcement Administration. The warrant shall (a) name the affiant, (b) recite the offense or the identity of the person to be arrested for whom a warrant or process for arrest has been issued in relation to which the search is to be made, (c) name or describe the place to be searched, (d) describe the property or person to be searched for, and (e) recite that the magistrate has found probable cause to believe that the property or person constitutes evidence of a crime (identified in the warrant) or tends to show that a person (named or described therein) has committed or is committing a crime or that the person to be arrested for whom a warrant or process for arrest has been issued is located at the place to be searched.

The warrant shall command that the place be forthwith searched and that the objects or persons described in the warrant, if found there, be seized. An inventory shall be produced before a court having jurisdiction of the offense or over the person to be arrested for whom a warrant or process for arrest has been issued in relation to which the warrant was issued as provided in § 19.2-57.

Any such warrant as provided in this section shall be executed by the policeman or other law-enforcement officer or agent into whose hands it shall come or be delivered. If the warrant is directed jointly to a sheriff, sergeant, policeman, or law-enforcement officer or agent of the Commonwealth and a federal agent or officer as otherwise provided in this section, the warrant may be executed jointly or by the policeman, law-enforcement officer, or agent into whose hands it is delivered. No other person may be permitted to be present during or participate in the execution of a warrant to search a place except (1) the owners and occupants of the place to be searched when permitted to be present by the officer in charge of the conduct of the search and (2) persons designated by the officer in charge of the conduct of the search to assist or provide expertise in the conduct of the search.

Any search warrant for records or other information pertaining to a subscriber to, or customer of, an electronic communication service or remote computing service, whether a domestic corporation or foreign corporation, that is transacting or has transacted any business in the Commonwealth, to be executed upon such service provider may be executed within or outside the Commonwealth by hand, United States mail, commercial delivery service, facsimile, or other electronic means upon the service provider. Notwithstanding the provisions of § 19.2-57, the officer executing a warrant pursuant to this paragraph shall endorse the date of execution thereon and shall file the warrant, with the inventory attached (or a notation that no property was seized) and the accompanying affidavit, unless such affidavit was made by voice or videotape recording, within three days after the materials ordered to be produced are received by the officer from the service provider. The return shall be made in the circuit court clerk's office for the jurisdiction wherein the warrant was (A) executed, if executed within the Commonwealth, and a copy of the return shall also be delivered to the clerk of the circuit court of the county or city where the warrant was issued or (B) issued, if executed outside the Commonwealth. Saturdays, Sundays, or any federal or state legal holiday shall not be used in computing the three-day filing period.

Electronic communication service or remote computing service providers, whether a foreign or domestic corporation, shall also provide the contents of electronic communications pursuant to a search warrant issued under this section and § 19.2-70.3 using the same process described in the preceding paragraph.

Notwithstanding the provisions of § 19.2-57, any search warrant for records or other information pertaining to a customer of a financial institution as defined in § 6.2-604, money transmitter as defined in § 6.2-1900, commercial business providing credit history or credit reports, or issuer as defined in § 6.2-424 may be executed within the Commonwealth by hand, United States mail, commercial delivery service, facsimile, or other electronic means upon the financial institution, money transmitter, commercial business providing credit history or credit reports, or issuer. The officer executing such warrant shall endorse the date of execution thereon and shall file the warrant, with the inventory attached (or a notation that no property was seized) and the accompanying affidavit, unless such affidavit was made by voice or videotape recording, within three days after the materials ordered to be produced are received by the officer from the financial institution, money transmitter, commercial business providing credit history or credit reports, or issuer. The return shall be made in the circuit court clerk's office for the jurisdiction wherein the warrant was executed. Saturdays, Sundays, or any federal or state legal holiday shall not be used in computing the three-day filing period. For the purposes of this section, the warrant will be considered executed in the jurisdiction where the entity on which the warrant is served is located.

Every search warrant shall contain the date and time it was issued. However, the failure of any such search warrant to contain the date and time it was issued shall not render the warrant void, provided that the date and time of issuing of said warrant is established by competent evidence.

The judge, magistrate, or other official authorized to issue criminal warrants shall attach a copy of the affidavit required by § 19.2-54, which shall become a part of the search warrant and served therewith. However, this provision shall not be applicable in any case in which the affidavit is made by means of a voice or videotape recording or where the affidavit has been sealed pursuant to § 19.2-54.

Any search warrant not executed within 15 days after issuance thereof shall be returned to, and voided by, the officer who issued such search warrant.

B. No law-enforcement officer shall seek, execute, or participate in the execution of a no-knock search warrant. A search warrant for any place of abode authorized under this section shall require that a law-enforcement officer be recognizable and identifiable as a uniformed law-enforcement officer and provide audible notice of his authority and purpose reasonably designed to be heard by the occupants of such place to be searched prior to the execution of such search warrant.

After entering and securing the place to be searched and prior to undertaking any search or seizure pursuant to the search warrant, the executing law-enforcement officer shall give a copy of the search warrant and affidavit to the person to be searched or the owner of the place to be searched or, if the owner is not present, to any occupant of the place to be searched. If the place to be searched is unoccupied, the executing law-enforcement officer shall leave a copy of the search warrant and affidavit in a conspicuous place within or affixed to the place to be searched.

Search warrants authorized under this section for the search of any place of abode shall be executed by initial entry of the abode only in the daytime hours between 8:00 a.m. and 5:00 p.m. unless (i) a judge or a magistrate, if a judge is not available, authorizes the execution of such search warrant at another time for good cause shown by particularized facts in an affidavit or (ii) prior to the issuance of the search warrant, law-enforcement officers lawfully entered and secured the place to be searched and remained at such place continuously.

A law-enforcement officer shall make reasonable efforts to locate a judge before seeking authorization to execute the warrant at another time, unless circumstances require the issuance of the warrant after 5 p.m., pursuant to the provisions of this subsection, in which case the law-enforcement officer may seek such authorization from a magistrate without first making reasonable efforts to locate a judge. Such reasonable efforts shall be documented in an affidavit and submitted to a magistrate when seeking such authorization.

Any evidence obtained from a search warrant executed in violation of this subsection shall not be admitted into evidence for the Commonwealth in any prosecution.

C. For the purposes of this section:
"Foreign corporation" means any corporation or other entity, whose primary place of business is located outside of the boundaries of the Commonwealth, that makes a contract or engages in a terms of service agreement with a resident of the Commonwealth to be performed in whole or in part by either party in the Commonwealth, or a corporation that has been issued a certificate of authority pursuant to § 13.1-759 to transact business in the Commonwealth. The making of the contract or terms of service agreement or the issuance of a certificate of authority shall be considered to be the agreement of the foreign corporation or entity that a search warrant or subpoena, which has been properly served on it, has the same legal force and effect as if served personally within the Commonwealth.

"Properly served" means delivery of a search warrant or subpoena by hand, by United States mail, by commercial delivery service, by facsimile or by any other manner to any officer of a corporation or its general manager in the Commonwealth, to any natural person designated by it as agent for the service of process, or if such corporation has designated a corporate agent, to any person named in the latest annual report filed pursuant to § 13.1-775.

§ 19.2-152.8. EMERGENCY PROTECTIVE ORDERS AUTHORIZED.

A. Any judge of a circuit court, general district court, juvenile and domestic relations district court or magistrate may issue a written or oral ex parte emergency protective order pursuant to this section in order to protect the health or safety of any person.

B. When a law-enforcement officer or an alleged victim asserts under oath to a judge or magistrate that such person is being or has been subjected to an act of violence, force, or threat and on that assertion or other evidence the judge or magistrate finds that (i) there is probable danger of a further such act being committed by the respondent against the alleged victim or (ii) a petition or warrant for the arrest of the respondent has been issued for any criminal offense resulting from the commission of an act of violence, force, or threat, the judge or magistrate shall issue an ex parte emergency protective order imposing one or more of the following conditions on the respondent:

1. Prohibiting acts of violence, force, or threat or criminal offenses resulting in injury to person or property;
2. Prohibiting such contacts by the respondent with the alleged victim or the alleged victim's family or household members, including prohibiting the respondent from being in the physical presence of the alleged victim or the alleged victim's family or household members, as the judge or magistrate deems necessary to protect the safety of such persons;
3. Such other conditions as the judge or magistrate deems necessary to prevent (i) acts of violence, force, or threat, (ii) criminal offenses resulting in injury to person or property, or (iii) communication or other contact of any kind by the respondent; and
4. Granting the petitioner the possession of any companion animal as defined in § 3.2-6500 if such petitioner meets the definition of owner in § 3.2-6500.

C. An emergency protective order issued pursuant to this section shall expire at 11:59 p.m. on the third day following issuance. If the expiration occurs on a day that the court is not in session, the emergency protective order shall be extended until 11:59 p.m. on the next day that the court which issued the order is in session. The respondent may at any time file a motion with the court requesting a hearing to dissolve or modify the order. The hearing on the motion shall be given precedence on the docket of the court.

D. A law-enforcement officer may request an emergency protective order pursuant to this section and, if the person in need of protection is physically or mentally incapable of filing a petition pursuant to § 19.2-152.9 or 19.2-152.10, may request the extension of an emergency protective order for an additional period of time not to exceed three days after expiration of the original order. The request for an emergency protective order or extension of an order may be made orally, in person or by electronic means, and the judge of a circuit court, general district court, or juvenile and domestic relations district court or a magistrate may issue an oral emergency protective order. An oral emergency protective order issued pursuant to this section shall be reduced to writing, by the law-enforcement officer requesting the order or the magistrate, on a preprinted form approved and provided by the Supreme Court of Virginia. The completed form shall include a statement of the grounds for the order asserted by the officer or the alleged victim of such crime.

E. The court or magistrate shall forthwith, but in all cases no later than the end of the business day on which the order was issued, enter and transfer electronically to the Virginia Criminal Information Network the respondent's identifying information and the name, date of birth, sex, and race of each protected person provided to the court or magistrate. A copy of an emergency protective order issued pursuant to this section containing any such identifying information shall be forwarded forthwith to the primary law-enforcement agency responsible for service and entry of protective orders. Upon receipt of the order by the primary law-enforcement agency, the agency shall forthwith verify and enter any modification as necessary to the identifying information and other appropriate information required by the Department of State Police into the Virginia Criminal Information Network established and maintained by the Department pursuant to Chapter 2 (§ 52-12 et seq.) of Title 52 and the order shall be served forthwith upon the respondent and due return made to the court. However, if the order is issued by the circuit court, the clerk of the circuit court shall forthwith forward an attested copy of the order containing the respondent's identifying information and the name, date of birth, sex, and race of each protected person provided to the court to the primary law-enforcement agency providing service and entry of protective orders and upon receipt of the order, the primary law-enforcement agency shall enter the name of the person subject to the order and other appropriate information required by the Department of State Police into the Virginia Criminal Information Network established and maintained by the Department pursuant to Chapter 2 (§ 52-12 et seq.) of Title 52 and the order shall be served forthwith upon the respondent. Upon service, the agency making service shall enter the date and time of service and other appropriate information required into the Virginia Criminal Information Network and make due return to the court. One copy of the order shall be given to the alleged victim of such crime. The judge or magistrate who issues an oral order pursuant to an electronic request by a law-enforcement officer shall verify the written order to determine whether the officer who reduced it to writing accurately transcribed the contents of the oral order. The original copy shall be filed with the clerk of the appropriate district court within five business days of the issuance of the order. If the order is later dissolved or modified, a copy of the dissolution or modification order shall also be attested, forwarded forthwith to the primary law-enforcement agency responsible for service and entry of protective orders, and upon receipt of the order by the primary law-enforcement agency, the agency shall forthwith verify and enter any modification as necessary to the identifying information and other appropriate information required by the Department of State Police into the Virginia Criminal Information Network as described above and the order shall be served forthwith and due return made to the court. Upon request, the clerk shall provide the alleged victim of such crime with information regarding the date and time of service.

F. The issuance of an emergency protective order shall not be considered evidence of any wrongdoing by the respondent.

G. As used in this section, a "law-enforcement officer" means any (i) person who is a full-time or part-time employee of a police department or sheriff's office which is part of or administered by the Commonwealth or any political subdivision thereof and who is responsible for the prevention and detection of crime and the enforcement of the penal, traffic or highway laws of the Commonwealth and (ii) member of an auxiliary police force established pursuant to § 15.2-1731. Part-time employees are compensated officers who are not full-time employees as defined by the employing police department or sheriff's office.

H. Neither a law-enforcement agency, the attorney for the Commonwealth, a court nor the clerk's office, nor any employee of them, may disclose, except among themselves, the residential address, telephone number, or place of employment of the person protected by the order or that of the family of such person, except to the extent that disclosure is (i) required by law or the Rules of the Supreme Court, (ii) necessary for law-enforcement purposes, or (iii) permitted by the court for good cause.

I. As used in this section:

"Copy" includes a facsimile copy.

"Physical presence" includes (i) intentionally maintaining direct visual contact with the petitioner or (ii) unreasonably being within 100 feet from the petitioner's residence or place of employment.

J. No fee shall be charged for filing or serving any petition pursuant to this section.

K. No emergency protective order shall be issued pursuant to this section against a law-enforcement officer for any action arising out of the lawful performance of his duties.

L. Upon issuance of an emergency protective order, the clerk of the court shall make available to the petitioner information that is published by the Department of Criminal Justice Services for victims of domestic violence or for petitioners in protective order cases.

§ 19.2-152.9. PRELIMINARY PROTECTIVE ORDERS.

A. Upon the filing of a petition alleging that (i) the petitioner is or has been, within a reasonable period of time, subjected to an act of violence, force, or threat, or (ii) a petition or warrant has been issued for the arrest of the alleged perpetrator for any criminal offense resulting from the commission of an act of violence, force, or threat, the court may issue a preliminary protective order against the alleged perpetrator in order to protect the health and safety of the petitioner or any family or household member of the petitioner. The order may be issued in an ex parte proceeding upon good cause shown when the petition is supported by an affidavit or sworn testimony before the judge or intake officer. If an ex parte order is issued without an affidavit or a completed form as prescribed by subsection D of § 19.2-152.8 being presented, the court, in its order, shall state the basis upon which the order was entered, including a summary of the allegations made and the court's findings. Immediate and present danger of any act of violence, force, or threat or evidence sufficient to establish probable cause that an act of violence, force, or threat has recently occurred shall constitute good cause.

A preliminary protective order may include any one or more of the following conditions to be imposed on the respondent:
1. Prohibiting acts of violence, force, or threat or criminal offenses that may result in injury to person or property;
2. Prohibiting such other contacts by the respondent with the petitioner or the petitioner's family or household members as the court deems necessary for the health and safety of such persons;
3. Such other conditions as the court deems necessary to prevent (i) acts of violence, force, or threat, (ii) criminal offenses that may result in injury to person or property, or (iii) communication or other contact of any kind by the respondent; and
4. Granting the petitioner the possession of any companion animal as defined in § 3.2-6500 if such petitioner meets the definition of owner in § 3.2-6500.

B. The court shall forthwith, but in all cases no later than the end of the business day on which the order was issued, enter and transfer electronically to the Virginia Criminal Information Network the respondent's identifying information and the name, date of birth, sex, and race of each protected person provided to the court. A copy of a preliminary protective order containing any such identifying information shall be forwarded forthwith to the primary law-enforcement agency responsible for service and entry of protective orders. Upon receipt of the order by the primary law-enforcement agency, the agency shall forthwith verify and enter any modification as necessary to the identifying information and other appropriate information required by the Department of State Police into the Virginia Criminal Information Network established and maintained by the Department pursuant to Chapter 2 (§ 52-12 et seq.) of Title 52 and the order shall be served forthwith on the alleged perpetrator in person as provided in § 16.1-264, and due return made to the court. However, if the order is issued by the circuit court, the clerk of the circuit court shall forthwith forward an attested copy of the order containing the respondent's identifying information and the name, date of birth, sex, and race of each protected person provided to the court to the primary law-enforcement agency providing service and entry of protective orders and upon receipt of the order, the primary law-enforcement agency shall enter the name of the person subject to the order and other appropriate information required by the Department of State Police into the Virginia Criminal Information Network established and maintained by the Department pursuant to Chapter 2 (§ 52-12 et seq.) of Title 52 and the order shall be served forthwith on the alleged perpetrator in person as provided in § 16.1-264. Upon service, the agency making service shall enter the date and time of service and other appropriate information required by the Department of State Police into the Virginia

Criminal Information Network and make due return to the court. The preliminary order shall specify a date for the full hearing. The hearing shall be held within 15 days of the issuance of the preliminary order, unless the court is closed pursuant to § 16.1-69.35 or 17.1-207 and such closure prevents the hearing from being held within such time period, in which case the hearing shall be held on the next day not a Saturday, Sunday, legal holiday, or day on which the court is lawfully closed. If such court is closed pursuant to § 16.1-69.35 or 17.1-207, the preliminary protective order shall remain in full force and effect until it is dissolved by such court, until another preliminary protective order is entered, or until a protective order is entered. If the respondent fails to appear at this hearing because the respondent was not personally served, the court may extend the protective order for a period not to exceed six months. The extended protective order shall be served as soon as possible on the respondent. However, upon motion of the respondent and for good cause shown, the court may continue the hearing. The preliminary order shall remain in effect until the hearing. Upon request after the order is issued, the clerk shall provide the petitioner with a copy of the order and information regarding the date and time of service. The order shall further specify that either party may at any time file a motion with the court requesting a hearing to dissolve or modify the order. The hearing on the motion shall be given precedence on the docket of the court. Upon petitioner's motion to dissolve the preliminary protective order, a dissolution order may be issued ex parte by the court with or without a hearing. If an ex parte hearing is held, it shall be heard by the court as soon as practicable. If a dissolution order is issued ex parte, the court shall serve a copy of such dissolution order on respondent in conformity with §§ 8.01-286.1 and 8.01-296.

Upon receipt of the return of service or other proof of service pursuant to subsection C of § 16.1-264, the clerk shall forthwith forward an attested copy of the preliminary protective order to primary law-enforcement agency and the agency shall forthwith verify and enter any modification as necessary into the Virginia Criminal Information Network as described above. If the order is later dissolved or modified, a copy of the dissolution or modification order shall also be attested, forwarded forthwith to the primary law-enforcement agency responsible for service and entry of protective orders, and upon receipt of the order by the primary law-enforcement agency, the agency shall forthwith verify and enter any modification as necessary to the identifying information and other appropriate information required by the Department of State Police into the Virginia Criminal Information Network as described above and the order shall be served forthwith and due return made to the court.

C. The preliminary order is effective upon personal service on the alleged perpetrator. Except as otherwise provided, a violation of the order shall constitute contempt of court.

D. At a full hearing on the petition, the court may issue a protective order pursuant to § 19.2-152.10 if the court finds that the petitioner has proven the allegation that the petitioner is or has been, within a reasonable period of time, subjected to an act of violence, force, or threat by a preponderance of the evidence.

E. No fees shall be charged for filing or serving petitions pursuant to this section.

F. Neither a law-enforcement agency, the attorney for the Commonwealth, a court nor the clerk's office, nor any employee of them, may disclose, except among themselves, the residential address, telephone number, or place of employment of the person protected by the order or that of the family of such person, except to the extent that disclosure is (i) required by law or the Rules of the Supreme Court, (ii) necessary for law-enforcement purposes, or (iii) permitted by the court for good cause.

G. As used in this section, "copy" includes a facsimile copy.

H. Upon issuance of a preliminary protective order, the clerk of the court shall make available to the petitioner information that is published by the Department of Criminal Justice Services for victims of domestic violence or for petitioners in protective order cases.

§ 19.2-152.10. PROTECTIVE ORDER.

A. The court may issue a protective order pursuant to this chapter to protect the health and safety of the petitioner and family or household members of a petitioner upon (i) the issuance of a petition or warrant for, or a conviction of, any criminal offense resulting from the commission of an act of violence, force, or threat or (ii) a hearing held pursuant to subsection D of § 19.2-152.9. A protective order issued under this section may include any one or more of the following conditions to be imposed on the respondent:
1. Prohibiting acts of violence, force, or threat or criminal offenses that may result in injury to person or property;
2. Prohibiting such contacts by the respondent with the petitioner or family or household members of the petitioner as the court deems necessary for the health or safety of such persons;
3. Any other relief necessary to prevent (i) acts of violence,

force, or threat, (ii) criminal offenses that may result in injury to person or property, or (iii) communication or other contact of any kind by the respondent; and

4. Granting the petitioner the possession of any companion animal as defined in § 3.2-6500 if such petitioner meets the definition of owner in § 3.2-6500.

B. Except as provided in subsection C, the protective order may be issued for a specified period of time up to a maximum of two years. The protective order shall expire at 11:59 p.m. on the last day specified or at 11:59 p.m. on the last day of the two-year period if no date is specified. Prior to the expiration of the protective order, a petitioner may file a written motion requesting a hearing to extend the order. Proceedings to extend a protective order shall be given precedence on the docket of the court. The court may extend the protective order for a period not longer than two years to protect the health and safety of the petitioner or persons who are family or household members of the petitioner at the time the request for an extension is made. The extension of the protective order shall expire at 11:59 p.m. on the last day specified or at 11:59 p.m. on the last day of the two-year period if no date is specified. Nothing herein shall limit the number of extensions that may be requested or issued.

C. Upon conviction for an act of violence as defined in § 19.2-297.1 and upon the request of the victim or of the attorney for the Commonwealth on behalf of the victim, the court may issue a protective order to the victim pursuant to this chapter to protect the health and safety of the victim. The protective order may be issued for any reasonable period of time, including up to the lifetime of the defendant, that the court deems necessary to protect the health and safety of the victim. The protective order shall expire at 11:59 p.m. on the last day specified in the protective order, if any. Upon a conviction for violation of a protective order issued pursuant to this subsection, the court that issued the original protective order may extend the protective order as the court deems necessary to protect the health and safety of the victim. The extension of the protective order shall expire at 11:59 p.m. on the last day specified, if any. Nothing herein shall limit the number of extensions that may be issued.

D. A copy of the protective order shall be served on the respondent and provided to the petitioner as soon as possible. The court, including a circuit court if the circuit court issued the order, shall forthwith, but in all cases no later than the end of the business day on which the order was issued, enter and transfer electronically to the Virginia Criminal Information Network the respondent's identifying information and the name, date of birth, sex, and race of each protected person provided to the court and shall forthwith forward the attested copy of the protective order and containing any such identifying information to the primary law-enforcement agency responsible for service and entry of protective orders. Upon receipt of the order by the primary law-enforcement agency, the agency shall forthwith verify and enter any modification as necessary to the identifying information and other appropriate information required by the Department of State Police into the Virginia Criminal Information Network established and maintained by the Department pursuant to Chapter 2 (§ 52-12 et seq.) of Title 52 and the order shall be served forthwith upon the respondent and due return made to the court. Upon service, the agency making service shall enter the date and time of service and other appropriate information required into the Virginia Criminal Information

Network and make due return to the court. If the order is later dissolved or modified, a copy of the dissolution or modification order shall also be attested, forwarded forthwith to the primary law-enforcement agency responsible for service and entry of protective orders, and upon receipt of the order by the primary law-enforcement agency, the agency shall forthwith verify and enter any modification as necessary to the identifying information and other appropriate information required by the Department of State Police into the Virginia Criminal Information Network as described above and the order shall be served forthwith and due return made to the court.

E. Except as otherwise provided, a violation of a protective order issued under this section shall constitute contempt of court.

F. The court may assess costs and attorneys' fees against either party regardless of whether an order of protection has been issued as a result of a full hearing.

G. Any judgment, order or decree, whether permanent or temporary, issued by a court of appropriate jurisdiction in another state, the United States or any of its territories, possessions or Commonwealths, the District of Columbia or by any tribal court of appropriate jurisdiction for the purpose of preventing violent or threatening acts or harassment against or contact or communication with or physical proximity to another person, including any of the conditions specified in subsection A, shall be accorded full faith and credit and enforced in the Commonwealth as if it were an order of the Commonwealth, provided reasonable notice and opportunity to be heard were given by the issuing jurisdiction to the person against whom the order is sought to be enforced sufficient to protect such person's due process rights and consistent with federal law. A person entitled to protection under such a foreign order may file the order in any appropriate district court by filing with the court, an attested or exemplified copy of the order. Upon such a filing, the clerk shall forthwith forward an attested copy of the order to the primary law-enforcement agency responsible for service and entry of protective orders which shall, upon receipt, enter the name of the person subject to the order and other appropriate information required by the Department of State Police into the Virginia Criminal Information Network established and maintained by the Department pursuant to Chapter 2 (§ 52-12 et seq.) of Title 52. Where practical, the court may transfer information electronically to the Virginia Criminal Information Network.

Upon inquiry by any law-enforcement agency of the Commonwealth, the clerk shall make a copy available of any foreign order filed with that court. A law-enforcement officer may, in the performance of his duties, rely upon a copy of a foreign protective order or other suitable evidence which has been provided to him by any source and may also rely upon the statement of any person protected by the order that the order remains in effect.

H. Either party may at any time file a written motion with the court requesting a hearing to dissolve or modify the order. Proceedings to modify or dissolve a protective order shall be given precedence on the docket of the court. Upon petitioner's motion to dissolve the protective order, a dissolution order may be issued ex parte by the court with or without a hearing. If an ex parte hearing is held, it shall be heard by the court as soon as practicable. If a dissolution order is issued ex parte, the court shall serve a copy of such dissolution order on respondent in conformity with §§ 8.01-286.1 and 8.01-296.

I. Neither a law-enforcement agency, the attorney for the Commonwealth, a court nor the clerk's office, nor any employee of them, may disclose, except among themselves, the residential address, telephone number, or place of employment of the person protected by the order or that of the family of such person, except to the extent that disclosure is (i) required by law or the Rules of the Supreme Court, (ii) necessary for law-enforcement purposes, or (iii) permitted by the court for good cause.

J. No fees shall be charged for filing or serving petitions pursuant to this section.

K. As used in this section:
"Copy" includes a facsimile copy; and "Protective order" includes an initial, modified or extended protective order.

L. Upon issuance of a protective order, the clerk of the court shall make available to the petitioner information that is published by the Department of Criminal Justice Services for victims of domestic violence or for petitioners in protective order cases.

§ 19.2-152.13. EMERGENCY SUBSTANTIAL RISK ORDER.

A. Upon the petition of an attorney for the Commonwealth or a law-enforcement officer, a judge of a circuit court, general district court, or juvenile and domestic relations district court or a magistrate, upon a finding that there is probable cause to believe that a person poses a substantial risk of personal injury to himself or others in the near future by such person's possession or acquisition of a firearm, shall issue an ex parte emergency substantial risk order. Such order shall prohibit the person who is subject to the order from purchasing, possessing, or transporting a firearm for the duration of the order. In determining whether probable cause for the issuance of an order exists, the judge or magistrate shall consider any relevant evidence, including any recent act of violence, force, or threat as defined in § 19.2-152.7:1 by such person directed toward another person or toward himself. No petition shall be filed unless an independent investigation has been conducted by law enforcement that determines that grounds for the petition exist. The order shall contain a statement (i) informing the person who is subject to the order of the requirements and penalties under § 18.2-308.1:6, including that it is unlawful for such person to purchase, possess, or transport a firearm for the duration of the order and that such person is required to surrender his concealed handgun permit if he possesses such permit, and (ii) advising such person to voluntarily relinquish any firearm within his custody to the law-enforcement agency that serves the order.

B. The petition for an emergency substantial risk order shall be made under oath and shall be supported by an affidavit.

C. Upon service of an emergency substantial risk order, the person who is subject to the order shall be given the opportunity to voluntarily relinquish any firearm in his possession. The law-enforcement agency that executed the emergency substantial risk order shall take custody of all firearms that are voluntarily relinquished by such person. The law-enforcement agency that takes into custody a firearm pursuant to the order shall prepare a written receipt containing the name of the person who is subject to the order and the manufacturer, model, condition, and serial number of the firearm and shall provide a copy thereof to such person. Nothing in this subsection precludes a law-enforcement officer from later obtaining a search warrant for any firearms if the law-enforcement officer has reason to believe that the person who is subject to an emergency substantial risk order has not relinquished all firearms in his possession.

D. An emergency substantial risk order issued pursuant to this section shall expire at 11:59 p.m. on the fourteenth day following issuance of the order. If the expiration occurs on a day that the circuit court for the jurisdiction where the order was issued is not in session, the order shall be extended until 11:59 p.m. on the next day that the circuit court is in session. The person who is subject to the order may at any time file with the circuit court a motion to dissolve the order.

E. An emergency substantial risk order issued pursuant to this section is effective upon personal service on the person who is subject to the order. The order shall be served forthwith after issuance. A copy of the order, petition, and supporting affidavit shall be given to the person who is subject to the order together with a notice informing the person that he has a right to a hearing under § 19.2-152.14 and may be represented by counsel at the hearing.

F. The court or magistrate shall forthwith, but in all cases no later than the end of the business day on which the emergency substantial risk order was issued, enter and transfer electronically to the Virginia Criminal Information Network (VCIN) established and maintained by the Department of State Police (Department) pursuant to Chapter 2 (§ 52-12 et seq.) of Title 52 the identifying information of the person who is subject to the order provided to the court or magistrate. A copy of an order issued pursuant to this section containing any such identifying information shall be forwarded forthwith to the primary law-enforcement agency responsible for service and entry of the order. Upon receipt of the order by the primary law-enforcement agency, the agency shall forthwith verify and enter any modification as necessary to the identifying information and other appropriate information required by the Department into the VCIN, and the order shall be served forthwith upon the person who is subject to the order. However, if the order is issued by the circuit court, the clerk of the circuit court shall forthwith forward an attested copy of the order containing the identifying information of the person who is subject to the order provided to the court to the primary law-enforcement agency providing service and entry of the order. Upon receipt of the order by the primary law-enforcement agency, the agency shall enter the name of the person subject to the order and other appropriate information required by the Department into the VCIN and the order shall be served forthwith upon the person who is subject to the order. Upon service, the agency making service shall enter the date and time of service and other appropriate information required into the VCIN and make due return to the court. If the order is later dissolved or modified, a copy of the dissolution or modification order shall also be attested and forwarded forthwith to the primary law-enforcement agency responsible for service and entry of the order. Upon receipt of the dissolution or modification order by the primary law-enforcement agency, the agency shall forthwith verify and enter any modification as necessary to the identifying information and other appropriate information required by the Department into the VCIN and the order shall be served forthwith.

G. The law-enforcement agency that serves the emergency substantial risk order shall make due return to the circuit court, which shall be accompanied by a written inventory of all firearms relinquished.

H. Proceedings in which an emergency substantial risk order is sought pursuant to this section shall be commenced where the person who is subject to the order (i) has his principal residence or (ii) has engaged in any conduct upon which the petition for the emergency substantial risk order is based.

I. A proceeding for a substantial risk order shall be a separate civil legal proceeding subject to the same rules as civil proceedings.

§ 19.2-152.14. SUBSTANTIAL RISK ORDER.

A. Not later than 14 days after the issuance of an emergency substantial risk order pursuant to § 19.2-152.13, the circuit court for the jurisdiction where the order was issued shall hold a hearing to determine whether a substantial risk order should be entered. The attorney for the Commonwealth for the jurisdiction that issued the emergency substantial risk order shall represent the interests of the Commonwealth. Notice of the hearing shall be given to the person subject to the emergency substantial risk order and the attorney for the Commonwealth. Upon motion of the respondent and for good cause shown, the court may continue the hearing, provided that the order shall remain in effect until the hearing. The Commonwealth shall have the burden of proving all material facts by clear and convincing evidence. If the court finds by clear and convincing evidence that the person poses a substantial risk of personal injury to himself or to other individuals in the near future by such person's possession or acquisition of a firearm, the court shall issue a substantial risk order. Such order shall prohibit the person who is subject to the order from purchasing, possessing, or transporting a firearm for the duration of the order. In determining whether clear and convincing evidence for the issuance of an order exists, the judge shall consider any relevant evidence including any recent act of violence, force, or threat as defined in § 19.2-152.7:1 by such person directed toward another person or toward himself. The order shall contain a statement (i) informing the person who is subject to the order of the requirements and penalties under § 18.2-308.1:6, including that it is unlawful for such person to purchase, possess, or transport a firearm for the duration of the order and that such person is required to surrender his concealed handgun permit if he possesses such permit, and (ii) advising such person to voluntarily relinquish any firearm that has not been taken into custody to the law-enforcement agency that served the emergency substantial risk order.

B. If the court issues a substantial risk order pursuant to subsection A, the court shall (i) order that any firearm that was previously relinquished pursuant to § 19.2-152.13 from the person who is subject to the substantial risk order continue to be held by the agency that has custody of the firearm for the duration of the order and (ii) advise such person that a law-enforcement officer may obtain a search warrant to search for any firearms from such person if such law-enforcement officer has reason to believe that such person has not relinquished all firearms in his possession.

If the court finds that the person does not pose a substantial risk of personal injury to himself or to other individuals in the near future, the court shall order that any firearm that was previously relinquished be returned to such person in accordance with the provisions of § 19.2-152.15.

C. The substantial risk order may be issued for a specified period of time up to a maximum of 180 days. The order shall expire at 11:59 p.m. on the last day specified or at 11:59 p.m. on the last day of the 180-day period if no date is specified. Prior to the expiration of the order, an attorney for the Commonwealth or a law-enforcement officer may file a written motion requesting a hearing to extend the order. Proceedings to extend an order shall be given precedence on the docket of the court. The court may extend the order for a period not longer than 180 days if the court finds by clear and convincing evidence that the person continues to pose a substantial risk of personal injury to himself or to other individuals in the near future by such person's possession or acquisition of a firearm at the time the request for an extension is made. The extension of the order shall expire at 11:59 p.m. on the last day specified or at 11:59 p.m. on the last day of the 180-day period if no date is specified. Nothing herein shall limit the number of extensions that may be requested or issued. The person who is subject to the order may file a motion to dissolve the order one time during the duration of the order; however, such motion may not be filed earlier than 30 days from the date the order was issued.

D. Any person whose firearm has been voluntarily relinquished pursuant to § 19.2-152.13 or this section, or such person's legal representative, may transfer the firearm to another individual 21 years of age or older who is not otherwise prohibited by law from possessing such firearm, provided that:
1. The person subject to the order and the transferee appear at the hearing;
2. At the hearing, the attorney for the Commonwealth advises the court that a law-enforcement agency has determined that the transferee is not prohibited from possessing or transporting a firearm;

3. The transferee does not reside with the person subject to the order;
4. The court informs the transferee of the requirements and penalties under § 18.2-308.2:1; and
5. The court, after considering all relevant factors and any evidence or testimony from the person subject to the order, approves the transfer of the firearm subject to such restrictions as the court deems necessary.

The law-enforcement agency holding the firearm shall deliver the firearm to the transferee within five days of receiving a copy of the court's approval of the transfer.

E. The court shall forthwith, but in all cases no later than the end of the business day on which the substantial risk order was issued, enter and transfer electronically to the Virginia Criminal Information Network (VCIN) established and maintained by the Department of State Police (Department) pursuant to Chapter 2 (§ 52-12 et seq.) of Title 52 the identifying information of the person who is subject to the order provided to the court and shall forthwith forward the attested copy of the order containing any such identifying information to the primary law-enforcement agency responsible for service and entry of the order. Upon receipt of the order by the primary law-enforcement agency, the agency shall forthwith verify and enter any modification as necessary to the identifying information and other appropriate information required by the Department into the VCIN and the order shall be served forthwith upon the person who is subject to the order and due return made to the court. Upon service, the agency making service shall enter the date and time of service and other appropriate information required by the Department into the VCIN and make due return to the court. If the person who is subject to an emergency substantial risk order fails to appear at the hearing conducted pursuant to this section because such person was not personally served with notice of the hearing pursuant to subsection A, or if personally served was incarcerated and not transported to the hearing, the court may extend the emergency substantial risk order for a period not to exceed 14 days. The extended emergency substantial risk order shall specify a date for a hearing to be conducted pursuant to this section and shall be served forthwith on such person and due return made to the court. If the order is later dissolved or modified, a copy of the dissolution or modification order shall also be attested and forwarded forthwith to the primary law-enforcement agency responsible for service and entry of the order. Upon receipt of the dissolution or modification order by the primary law-enforcement agency, the agency shall forthwith verify and enter any modification as necessary to the identifying information and other appropriate information required by the Department of State Police into the Virginia Criminal Information Network, and the order shall be served forthwith and due return made to the court.

§ 19.2-152.15. RETURN OR DISPOSAL OF FIREARMS.

A. Any firearm taken into custody pursuant to § 19.2-152.13 or 19.2-152.14 and held by a law-enforcement agency shall be returned by such agency to the person from whom the firearm was taken upon a court order for the return of the firearm issued pursuant to § 19.2-152.14 or the expiration or dissolution of an order issued pursuant to § 19.2-152.13 or 19.2-152.14. Such agency shall return the firearm within five days of receiving a written request for the return of the firearm by the person from whom the firearm was taken and a copy of the receipt provided to such person pursuant to § 19.2-152.13. Prior to returning the firearm to such person, the law-enforcement agency holding the firearm shall confirm that such person is no longer subject to an order issued pursuant to § 19.2-152.13 or 19.2-152.14 and is not otherwise prohibited by law from possessing a firearm.

B. A firearm taken into custody pursuant to pursuant to § 19.2-152.13 or 19.2-152.14 and held by a law-enforcement agency may be disposed of in accordance with the provisions of § 15.2-1721 if (i) the person from whom the firearm was taken provides written authorization for such disposal to the agency or (ii) the firearm remains in the possession of the agency more than 120 days after such person is no longer subject to an order issued pursuant to § 19.2-152.13 or 19.2-152.14 and such person has not submitted a request in writing for the return of the firearm.

PROCEDURE
CHAPTER 11. PROCEEDINGS ON QUESTION OF INSANITY

§ 19.2-169.2. DISPOSITION WHEN DEFENDANT FOUND INCOMPETENT.

A. Upon finding pursuant to subsection E of § 19.2-169.1 that the defendant, including a juvenile transferred pursuant to § 16.1-269.1, is incompetent, the court shall order that the defendant receive treatment to restore his competency on an outpatient basis or, if the court specifically finds that the defendant requires inpatient hospital treatment, at a hospital designated by the Commissioner of Behavioral Health and Developmental Services as appropriate for treatment of persons under criminal charge. Outpatient treatment may occur in a local correctional facility or at a location determined by the appropriate community services board or behavioral health authority. Notwithstanding the provisions of § 19.2-178, if the court orders inpatient hospital treatment, the defendant shall be transferred to and accepted by the hospital designated by the Commissioner as soon as practicable, but no later than 10 days, from the receipt of the court order requiring treatment to restore the defendant's competency. If the 10-day period expires on a Saturday, Sunday, or other legal holiday, the 10 days shall be extended to the next day that is not a Saturday, Sunday, or legal holiday. Any psychiatric records and other information that have been deemed relevant and submitted by the attorney for the defendant pursuant to subsection C of § 19.2-169.1 and any reports submitted pursuant to subsection D of § 19.2-169.1 shall be made available to the director of the community services board or behavioral health authority or his designee or to the director of the treating inpatient facility or his designee within 96 hours of the issuance of the court order requiring treatment to restore the defendant's competency. If the 96-hour period expires on a Saturday, Sunday, or other legal holiday, the 96 hours shall be extended to the next day that is not a Saturday, Sunday, or legal holiday.

B. If, at any time after the defendant is ordered to undergo treatment under subsection A of this section, the director of the community services board or behavioral health authority or his designee or the director of the treating inpatient facility or his designee believes the defendant's competency is restored, the director or his designee shall immediately send a report to the court as prescribed in subsection D of § 19.2-169.1. The court shall make a ruling on the defendant's competency according to the procedures specified in subsection E of § 19.2-169.1.

C. The clerk of court shall certify and forward forthwith to the Central Criminal Records Exchange, on a form provided by the Exchange, a copy of an order for treatment issued pursuant to subsection A.

§ 19.2-387.3. SUBSTANTIAL RISK ORDER REGISTRY; MAINTENANCE; ACCESS.

A. The Department of State Police shall keep and maintain a computerized Substantial Risk Order Registry (the Registry) for the entry of orders issued pursuant to § 19.2-152.13 or 19.2-152.14. The purpose of the Registry shall be to assist the efforts of law-enforcement agencies to protect their communities and their citizens. The Department of State Police shall make the Registry information available, upon request, to criminal justice agencies, including local law-enforcement agencies, through the Virginia Criminal Information Network. Registry information provided under this section shall be used only for the purposes of the administration of criminal justice as defined in § 9.1-101.

B. No liability shall be imposed upon any law-enforcement official who disseminates information or fails to disseminate information in good-faith compliance with the requirements of this section, but this provision shall not be construed to grant immunity for gross negligence or willful misconduct.

TITLE 19.2. CRIMINAL PROCEDURE
CHAPTER 23.1. EXPUNGEMENT OF CRIMINAL RECORDS

§ 19.2-392.2. EXPUNGEMENT OF POLICE AND COURT RECORDS.
A. If a person is charged with the commission of a crime, a civil offense, or any offense defined in Title 18.2, and
1. Is acquitted, or
2. A nolle prosequi is taken or the charge is otherwise dismissed, including dismissal by accord and satisfaction pursuant to § 19.2-151, he may file a petition setting forth the relevant facts and requesting expungement of the police records and the court records relating to the charge.

B. If any person whose name or other identification has been used without his consent or authorization by another person who has been charged or arrested using such name or identification, he may file a petition with the court disposing of the charge for relief pursuant to this section. Such person shall not be required to pay any fees for the filing of a petition under this subsection. A petition filed under this subsection shall include one complete set of the petitioner's fingerprints obtained from a law-enforcement agency.

C. The petition with a copy of the warrant, summons, or indictment if reasonably available shall be filed in the circuit court of the county or city in which the case was disposed of by acquittal or being otherwise dismissed and shall contain, except where not reasonably available, the date of arrest and the name of the arresting agency. Where this information is not reasonably available, the petition shall state the reason for such unavailability. The petition shall further state the specific criminal charge or civil offense to be expunged, the date of final disposition of the charge as set forth in the petition, the petitioner's date of birth, and the full name used by the petitioner at the time of arrest.

D. A copy of the petition shall be served on the attorney for the Commonwealth of the city or county in which the petition is filed. The attorney for the Commonwealth may file an objection or answer to the petition or may give written notice to the court that he does not object to the petition within 21 days after it is served on him.

E. The petitioner shall obtain from a law-enforcement agency one complete set of the petitioner's fingerprints and shall provide that agency with a copy of the petition for expungement. The law-enforcement agency shall submit the set of fingerprints to the Central Criminal Records Exchange (CCRE) with a copy of the petition for expungement attached. The CCRE shall forward under seal to the court a copy of the petitioner's criminal history, a copy of the source documents that resulted in the CCRE entry that the petitioner wishes to expunge, if applicable, and the set of fingerprints. Upon completion of the hearing, the court shall return the fingerprint card to the petitioner. If no hearing was conducted, upon the entry of an order of expungement or an order denying the petition for expungement, the court shall cause the fingerprint card to be destroyed unless, within 30 days of the date of the entry of the order, the petitioner requests the return of the fingerprint card in person from the clerk of the court or provides the clerk of the court a self-addressed, stamped envelope for the return of the fingerprint card.

F. After receiving the criminal history record information from the CCRE, the court shall conduct a hearing on the petition. If the court finds that the continued existence and possible dissemination of information relating to the arrest of the petitioner causes or may cause circumstances which constitute a manifest injustice to the petitioner, it shall enter an order requiring the expungement of the police and court records, including electronic records, relating to the charge. Otherwise, it shall deny the petition. However, if the petitioner has no prior criminal record and the arrest was for a misdemeanor violation or the charge was for a civil offense, the petitioner shall be entitled, in the absence of good cause shown to the contrary by the Commonwealth, to expungement of the police and court records relating to the charge, and the court shall enter an order of expungement. If the attorney for the Commonwealth of the county or city in which the petition is filed (i) gives written notice to the court pursuant to subsection D that he does not object to the petition and (ii) when the charge to be expunged is a felony, stipulates in such written notice that the continued existence and possible dissemination of information relating to the arrest of the petitioner causes or may cause circumstances which constitute a manifest injustice to the petitioner, the court may enter an order of expungement without conducting a hearing.

G. The Commonwealth shall be made party defendant to the proceeding. Any party aggrieved by the decision of the court may appeal, as provided by law in civil cases.

H. Notwithstanding any other provision of this section, when the charge is dismissed because the court finds that the person arrested or charged is not the person named in the summons, warrant, indictment or presentment, the court dismissing the charge shall, upon motion of the person improperly arrested or charged, enter an order requiring expungement of the police and court records relating to the charge. Such order shall contain a statement that the dismissal and expungement are ordered pursuant to this subsection and shall be accompanied by the complete set of the petitioner's fingerprints filed with his petition. Upon the entry of such order, it shall be treated as provided in subsection K.

I. Notwithstanding any other provision of this section, upon receiving a copy pursuant to § 2.2-402 of an absolute pardon for the commission of a crime that a person did not commit, the court shall enter an order requiring expungement of the police and court records relating to the charge and conviction. Such order shall contain a statement that the expungement is ordered pursuant to this subsection. Upon the entry of such order, it shall be treated as provided in subsection K.

J. Upon receiving a copy of a writ vacating a conviction pursuant to § 19.2-327.5 or 19.2-327.13, the court shall enter an order requiring expungement of the police and court records relating to the charge and conviction. Such order shall contain a statement that the expungement is ordered pursuant to this subsection. Upon the entry of the order, it shall be treated as provided in subsection

K. Upon the entry of an order of expungement, the clerk of the court shall cause a copy of such order to be forwarded to the Department of State Police, which shall, pursuant to rules and regulations adopted pursuant to § 9.1-134, direct the manner by which the appropriate expungement or removal of such records shall be effected.

L. Costs shall be as provided by § 17.1-275, but shall not be recoverable against the Commonwealth. If the court enters an order of expungement, the clerk of the court shall refund to the petitioner such costs paid by the petitioner.

M. Any order entered where (i) the court or parties failed to strictly comply with the procedures set forth in this section or (ii) the court enters an order of expungement contrary to law, shall be voidable upon motion and notice made within three years of the entry of such order.

TITLE 20. DOMESTIC RELATIONS
CHAPTER 6. DIVORCE, AFFIRMATION AND ANNULMENT

§ 20-103. COURT MAY MAKE ORDERS PENDING SUIT FOR DIVORCE, CUSTODY OR VISITATION, ETC.

A. In suits for divorce, annulment and separate maintenance, and in proceedings arising under subdivision A 3 or subsection L of § 16.1-241, the court having jurisdiction of the matter may, at any time pending a suit pursuant to this chapter, in the discretion of such court, make any order that may be proper (i) to compel a spouse to pay any sums necessary for the maintenance and support of the petitioning spouse, including (a) an order that the other spouse provide health care coverage for the petitioning spouse, unless it is shown that such coverage cannot be obtained, or (b) an order that a party pay secured or unsecured debts incurred jointly or by either party, (ii) to enable such spouse to carry on the suit, (iii) to prevent either spouse from imposing any restraint on the personal liberty of the other spouse, (iv) to provide for the custody and maintenance of the minor children of the parties, including an order that either party or both parties provide health care coverage or cash medical support, or both, for the children, (v) to provide support, calculated in accordance with § 20-108.2, for any child of the parties to whom a duty of support is owed and to pay or continue to pay support for any child over the age of 18 who meets the requirements set forth in subsection C of § 20-124.2, (vi) for the exclusive use and possession of the family residence during the pendency of the suit, (vii) to preserve the estate of either spouse, so that it be forthcoming to meet any decree which may be made in the suit, (viii) to compel either spouse to give security to abide such decree, or (ix)(a) to compel a party to maintain any existing policy owned by that party insuring the life of either party or to require a party to name as a beneficiary of the policy the other party or an appropriate person for the exclusive use and benefit of the minor children of the parties and (b) to allocate the premium cost of such life insurance between the parties, provided that all premiums are billed to the policyholder. Nothing in clause (ix) shall be construed to create an independent cause of action on the part of any beneficiary against the insurer or to require an insurer to provide information relating to such policy to any person other than the policyholder without the written consent of the policyholder. The parties to any petition where a child whose custody, visitation, or support is contested shall show proof that they have attended within the 12 months prior to their court appearance or that they shall attend within 45 days thereafter an educational seminar or other like program conducted by a qualified person or organization approved by the court except that the court may require the parties to attend such seminar or program in uncontested cases only if the court finds good cause. The seminar or other program shall be a minimum of four hours in length and shall address the effects of separation or divorce on children, parenting responsibilities, options for conflict resolution and financial responsibilities. Once a party has completed one educational seminar or other like program, the required completion of additional programs shall be at the court's discretion. Parties under this section shall include natural or adoptive parents of the child, or any person with a legitimate interest as defined in § 20-124.1. The fee charged a party for participation in such program shall be based on the party's ability to pay; however, no fee in excess of $50 may be charged. Whenever possible, before participating in mediation or alternative dispute resolution to address custody, visitation or support, each party shall have attended the educational seminar or other like program.

The court may grant an exemption from attendance of such program for good cause shown or if there is no program reasonably available. Other than statements or admissions by a party admitting criminal activity or child abuse, no statement or admission by a party in such seminar or program shall be admissible into evidence in any subsequent proceeding.

A1. Any award or order made by the court pursuant to subsection A shall be paid from the post-separation income of the obligor unless the court, for good cause shown, orders otherwise. Upon the request of either party, the court may identify and state in such order or award the specific source from which the financial obligation imposed is to be paid.

B. In addition to the terms provided in subsection A, upon a showing by a party of reasonable apprehension of physical harm to that party by such party's family or household member as that term is defined in § 16.1-228, and consistent with rules of the Supreme Court of Virginia, the court may enter an order excluding that party's family or household member from the jointly owned or jointly rented family dwelling. In any case where an order is entered under this paragraph, pursuant to an ex parte hearing, the order shall not exclude a family or household member from the family dwelling for a period in excess of 15 days from the date the order is served, in person, upon the person so excluded. The order may provide for an extension of time beyond the 15 days, to become effective automatically. The person served may at any time file a written motion in the clerk's office requesting a hearing to dissolve or modify the order. Nothing in this section shall be construed to prohibit the court from extending an order entered under this subsection for such longer period of time as is deemed appropriate, after a hearing on notice to the parties. If the party subject to the order fails to appear at this hearing, the court may extend the order for a period not to exceed six months.

C. In cases other than those for divorce in which a custody or visitation arrangement for a minor child is sought, the court may enter an order providing for custody, visitation or maintenance pending the suit as provided in subsection A. The order shall be directed to either parent or any person with a legitimate interest who is a party to the suit.

D. Orders entered pursuant to this section which provide for custody or visitation arrangements pending the suit shall be made in accordance with the standards set out in Chapter 6.1 (§ 20-124.1 et seq.). Orders entered pursuant to subsection B shall be certified by the clerk and forwarded as soon as possible to the local police department or sheriff's office which shall, on the date of receipt, enter the name of the person subject to the order and other appropriate information required by the Department of State Police into the Virginia crime information network system established and maintained by the Department of State Police pursuant to Chapter 2 (§ 52-12 et seq.) of Title 52. If the order is later dissolved or modified, a copy of the dissolution or modification shall also be certified, forwarded and entered in the system as described above.

E. There shall be a presumption in any judicial proceeding for pendente lite spousal support and maintenance under this section that the amount of the award that would result from the application of the formula set forth in this section is the correct amount of spousal support to be awarded. The court may deviate from the presumptive amount as provided in subsection H.

F. If the court is determining both an award of pendente lite spousal support and maintenance and an award of child support, the court shall first make a determination of the amount of the award of pendente lite spousal support, if any, owed by one party to the other under this section.

G. If the parties have minor children in common, the presumptive amount of an award of pendente lite spousal support and maintenance shall be the difference between 26 percent of the payor spouse's monthly gross income and 58 percent of the payee spouse's monthly gross income. If the parties have no minor children in common, the presumptive amount of the award shall be the difference between 27 percent of the payor spouse's monthly gross income and 50 percent of the payee spouse's monthly gross income. For the purposes of this section, monthly gross income shall have the same meaning as it does in section § 20-108.2.

H. The court may deviate from the presumptive amount for good cause shown, including any relevant evidence relating to the parties' current financial circumstances or the impact of any tax exemption and any credits resulting from such exemptions that indicates the presumptive amount is inappropriate.

I. The presumptive formula set forth in this section shall only apply to cases where the parties' combined monthly gross income does not exceed $10,000.

J. An order entered pursuant to this section shall have no presumptive effect and shall not be determinative when adjudicating the underlying cause.

TITLE 29.1. WILDLIFE, INLAND FISHERIES AND BOATING
CHAPTER 1. ADMINISTRATION OF GAME AND INLAND FISHERIES
ARTICLE 1. GENERAL PROVISIONS

§ 29.1-100. DEFINITIONS.

As used in and for the purposes of this title only, or in any of the regulations of the Board, unless the context clearly requires a different meaning:

"Bag or creel limit" means the quantity of game, fish or fur-bearing animals that may be taken, caught, or possessed during a period fixed by the Board.

"Board" means the Board of Wildlife Resources.

"Closed season" means that period of time fixed by the Board during which wild animals, birds or fish may not be taken, captured, killed, pursued, hunted, trapped or possessed.

"Conservation police officers" means supervising officers, and regular and special conservation police officers.

"Department" means the Department of Wildlife Resources.

"Director" means the Director of the Department of Wildlife Resources.

"Firearm" means any weapon that will or is designed to or may readily be converted to expel single or multiple projectiles by the action of an explosion of a combustible material.

"Fishing" means taking, capturing, killing, or attempting to take, capture or kill any fish in and upon the inland waters of this Commonwealth.

"Fur-bearing animals" includes beaver, bobcat, fisher, fox, mink, muskrat, opossum, otter, raccoon, skunk, and weasel.

"Game" means wild animals and wild birds that are commonly hunted for sport or food.

"Game animals" means deer (including all Cervidae), bear, rabbit, fox, squirrel, bobcat and raccoon.

"Game fish" means trout (including all Salmonidae), all of the sunfish family (including largemouth bass, smallmouth bass and spotted bass, rock bass, bream, bluegill and crappie), walleye or pike perch, white bass, chain pickerel or jackfish, muskellunge, and northern pike, wherever such fish are found in the waters of this Commonwealth and rockfish or striped bass where found above tidewaters or in streams which are blocked from access from tidewaters by dams.

"Hunting and trapping" includes the act of or the attempted act of taking, hunting, trapping, pursuing, chasing, shooting, snaring or netting birds or animals, and assisting any person who is hunting, trapping or attempting to do so regardless of whether birds or animals are actually taken; however, when hunting and trapping are allowed, reference is made to such acts as being conducted by lawful means and in a lawful manner. The Board of Wildlife Resources may authorize by regulation the pursuing or chasing of wild birds or wild animals during any closed hunting season where persons have no intent to take such birds or animals.

"Lawful," "by law," or "law" means the statutes of this Commonwealth or regulations adopted by the Board which the Director is empowered to enforce.

"Migratory game birds" means doves, ducks, brant, geese, swan, coot, gallinules, sora and other rails, snipe, woodcock and other species of birds on which open hunting seasons are set by federal regulations.

"Muzzleloader" means any firearm described in subdivision 3 of the definition of antique firearm in § 18.2-308.2:2.

"Muzzleloading pistol" means a muzzleloader originally designed, made or intended to fire a projectile (bullet) from one or more barrels when held in one hand and that is loaded from the muzzle or forward end of the cylinder.

"Muzzleloading rifle" means a muzzleloader firing a single projectile that is loaded along with the propellant from the muzzle of the gun.

"Muzzleloading shotgun" means a muzzleloader with a smooth bore firing multiple projectiles that are loaded along with the propellant from the muzzle of the gun.

"Nonmigratory game birds" means grouse, bobwhite quail, turkey and all species of birds introduced into the Commonwealth by the Board.

"Nuisance species" means blackbirds, coyotes, crows, cowbirds, feral swine, grackles, English sparrows, starlings, or those species designated as such by regulations of the Board, and those species found committing or about to commit depredation upon ornamental or shade trees, agricultural crops, wildlife, livestock or other property or when concentrated in numbers and manners as to constitute a health hazard or other nuisance. However, the term nuisance does not include (i) animals designated as endangered or threatened pursuant to §§ 29.1-563, 29.1-564, and 29.1-566, (ii) animals classified as game or fur-bearing animals, and (iii) those species protected by state or federal law.

"Open season" means that period of time fixed by the Board during which wild animals, wild birds and fish may be taken, captured, killed, pursued, trapped or possessed.

"Pistol" means a weapon originally designed, made, and intended to fire a projectile (bullet) from one or more barrels when held in one hand, and having one or more chambers as an integral part of or permanently aligned with the bore and a short stock at an angle to and extending below the line of the bore that is designed to be gripped by one hand.

"Possession" means the exercise of control of any wild animal, wild bird, fish or fur-bearing animal, or any part of the carcass thereof.

"Properly licensed person" means a person who, while engaged in hunting, fishing or trapping, or in any other activity permitted under this title, in and upon the lands and inland waters of this Commonwealth, has upon his person all the licenses, permits and stamps required by law.

"Regulation" means a regulation duly adopted by the Board pursuant to the authority vested by the provisions of this title.

"Revolver" means a projectile weapon of the pistol type, having a breechloading chambered cylinder arranged so that the cocking of the hammer or movement of the trigger rotates it and brings the next cartridge in line with the barrel for firing.

"Rifle" means a weapon designed or redesigned, made or remade, and intended to be fired from the shoulder, and designed or redesigned and made or remade to use the energy of the explosive in a fixed metallic cartridge to fire only a single projectile through a rifled bore for each single pull of the trigger.

"Shotgun" means a weapon designed or redesigned, made or remade, and intended to be fired from the shoulder, and designed or redesigned and made or remade to use the energy of the explosive in a fixed shotgun shell to fire through a smooth bore or rifled shotgun barrel either a number of ball shot or a single projectile for each single pull of the trigger.

"Transportation" means the transportation, either upon the person or by any other means, of any wild animal or wild bird or fish.

"Wildlife" means all species of wild animals, wild birds and freshwater fish in the public waters of this Commonwealth.

TITLE 29.1. WILDLIFE, INLAND FISHERIES AND BOATING CHAPTER 5. WILDLIFE AND FISH LAWS

ARTICLE 2. HUNTING AND TRAPPING
§ 29.1-512. CLOSED SEASON ON OTHER SPECIES.

There shall be a continuous closed hunting season on all birds and wild animals which are not nuisance species as defined in § 29.1100, except as provided by law.

§ 29.1-529. KILLING OF DEER, ELK OR BEAR DAMAGING FRUIT TREES, CROPS, LIVESTOCK, OR PERSONAL PROPERTY; WILDLIFE CREATING A HAZARD TO AIRCRAFT OR MOTOR VEHICLES.

A. Whenever deer, elk or bear are damaging fruit trees, crops, livestock or personal property utilized for commercial agricultural production in the Commonwealth, the owner or lessee of the lands on which such damage is done shall immediately report the damage to the Director or his designee for investigation. If after investigation the Director or his designee finds that deer or bear are responsible for the damage, he shall authorize in writing the owner, lessee or any other person designated by the Director or his designee to kill such deer or bear when they are found upon the land upon which the damages occurred. However, the Director or his designee shall have the option of authorizing nonlethal control measures rather than authorizing the killing of elk or bear, provided that such measures occur within a reasonable period of time; and whenever deer cause damage on parcels of land of five acres or less, except when such acreage is used for commercial agricultural production, the Director or his designee shall have discretion as to whether to issue a written authorization to kill the deer. The Director or his designee may limit such authorization by specifying in writing the number of animals to be killed and duration for which the authorization is effective and may in proximity to residential areas and under other appropriate circumstances limit or prohibit the authorization between 11:00 p.m. and one-half hour before sunrise of the following day. The Director or his designees issuing these authorizations shall specify in writing that only antlerless deer shall be killed, unless the Director or his designee determines that there is clear and convincing evidence that the damage was done by deer with antlers. Any owner or lessee of land who has been issued a written authorization shall not be issued an authorization in subsequent years unless he can demonstrate to the satisfaction of the Director or his designee that during the period following the prior authorization, the owner or his designee has hunted bear or deer on the land for which he received a previous authorization.

B. Subject to the provisions of subsection A, the Director or his designee may issue a written authorization to kill deer causing damage to residential plants, whether ornamental, noncommercial agricultural, or other types of residential plants. The Director may charge a fee not to exceed actual costs. The holder of this written authorization shall be subject to local ordinances, including those regulating the discharge of firearms.

C. Whenever wildlife is creating a hazard to the operation of any aircraft or to the facilities connected with the operation of aircraft, the person or persons responsible for the safe operation of the aircraft or facilities shall report such fact to the Director or his designee for investigation. If after investigation the Director or his designee finds that wildlife is creating a hazard, he shall authorize such person or persons or their representatives to kill wildlife when the wildlife is found to be creating such a hazard. As used in this subsection, the term "wildlife" shall not include any federally protected species.

D. Whenever deer are creating a hazard to the operation of motor vehicle traffic within the corporate limits of any city or town, the operator of a motor vehicle or chief law-enforcement officer of the city or town may report such fact to the Director or his designee for investigation. If after investigation the Director or his designee finds that deer are creating a hazard within such city or town, he may authorize responsible persons, or their representatives, to kill the deer when they are found to be creating such a hazard.

E. Whenever deer are damaging property in a locality in which deer herd population reduction has been recommended in the current Deer Management Plan adopted by the Board, the owner or lessee of the lands on which such damage is being done may report such damage to the Director or his designee for investigation. If after investigation the Director or his designee finds that deer are responsible for the damage, he may authorize in writing the owner, lessee or any other person designated by the Director or his designee to kill such deer when they are found upon the land upon which the damages occurred. The Director or his designee also may limit such authorization by specifying in writing the number of animals to be killed and the period of time for which the authorization is effective. The requirement in subsection A of this section, that an owner or lessee of land demonstrate that during the period following the prior authorization deer or bear have been hunted on his land, shall not apply to any locality that conducts a deer population control program authorized by the Department.

F. The Director or his designee may revoke or refuse to reissue any authorization granted under this section when it has been shown by a preponderance of the evidence that an abuse of the authorization has occurred. Such evidence may include a complaint filed by any person with the Department alleging that an abuse of the written authorization has occurred. Any person aggrieved by the issuance, denial or revocation of a written authorization can appeal the decision to the Department of Game and Inland Fisheries. Any person convicted of violating any provision of the hunting and trapping laws and regulations shall be entitled to receive written authorization to kill deer or bear. However, such person shall not (i) be designated as a shooter nor (ii) carry out the authorized activity for a person who has received such written authorization for a period of at least two years and up to five years following his most recent conviction for violating any provision of the hunting and trapping laws and regulations. In determining the appropriate length of this restriction, the Director shall take into account the nature and severity of the most recent violation and of any past violations of the hunting and trapping laws and regulations by the applicant. No person shall be designated as a shooter under this section during a period when such person's hunting license or privileges to hunt have been suspended or revoked.

G. The Director or his designee may authorize, subject to the provisions of this section, the killing of deer over bait within the political boundaries of any city or town, or any county with a special late antlerless season, in the Commonwealth when requested by a certified letter from the governing body of such locality.

H. The parts of any deer or bear killed pursuant to this section or wildlife killed pursuant to subsection C shall not be used for the purposes of taxidermy, mounts, or any public display unless authorized by the Director or his designee. However, the meat of any such animal may be used for human consumption. The carcass and any unused meat of any such animal shall be disposed of within 24 hours of being killed.

Any person who violates any provision of this subsection is guilty of a Class 3 misdemeanor.

I. It is unlawful to willfully and intentionally impede any person who is engaged in the lawful killing of a bear or deer pursuant to written authorization issued under this section. Any person convicted of a violation of this subsection is guilty of a Class 3 misdemeanor.

TITLE 29.1. WILDLIFE, INLAND FISHERIES AND BOATING
CHAPTER 7. BOATING LAWS

ARTICLE 1. BOAT REGISTRATION AND IDENTIFICATION

§ 29.1-700. DEFINITIONS.
As used in this chapter, unless the context clearly requires a different meaning:

"Motorboat" means any vessel propelled by machinery whether or not the machinery is the principal source of propulsion.

"No wake" means operation of a motorboat at the slowest possible speed required to maintain steerage and headway.

"Operate" means to navigate or otherwise control the movement of a motorboat or a vessel.

"Owner" means a person, other than a lien holder, having the property in or title to a motorboat. The term includes a person entitled to the use or possession of a motorboat subject to an interest in another person, reserved or created by agreement and securing payment of performance of an obligation, but the term excludes a lessee under a lease not intended as security.

"Personal watercraft" means a motorboat less than sixteen feet in length which uses an inboard motor powering a jet pump, as its primary motive power and which is designed to be operated by a person sitting, standing, or kneeling on, rather than in the conventional manner of sitting or standing inside, the vessel.

"Vessel" means every description of watercraft, other than a seaplane on the water, used or capable of being used as a means of transportation on water.

"Waters of the Commonwealth" means any public waters within the territorial limits of the Commonwealth, the adjacent marginal sea and the high seas when navigated as a part of a journey or ride to or from the Virginia shore.

TITLE 29.1. WILDLIFE, INLAND FISHERIES AND BOATING
CHAPTER 7. BOATING LAWS

ARTICLE 2.1. VIRGINIA UNIFORM CERTIFICATE OF TITLE FOR WATERCRAFT ACT

§ 29.1-733.2. DEFINITIONS.

The definitions in this section do not apply to any Virginia or federal law governing licensing, numbering, or registration if the same term is used in that law. As used in this article, unless the context requires a different meaning:

"Abandoned watercraft" means a watercraft that is left unattended on private property for more than 10 days without the consent of the property's owner, regardless of whether it was brought onto the private property with the consent of the owner or person in control of the private property.

"Agreement" means the same as that term is defined in subdivision (b)(3) of § 8.1A-201.

"Barge" means a watercraft that is not self-propelled or fitted for propulsion by sail, paddle, oar, or similar device.

"Builder's certificate" means a certificate of the facts of the build of a vessel described in 46 C.F.R. § 67.99, as amended.

"Buyer" means a person that buys or contracts to buy a watercraft.

"Buyer in ordinary course of business" means the same as that term is defined in subdivision (b)(9) of § 8.1A-201.

"Cancel," with respect to a certificate of title, means to make the certificate ineffective.

"Certificate of origin" means a record created by a manufacturer or importer as the manufacturer's or importer's proof of identity of a watercraft. The term includes a manufacturer's certificate or statement of origin and an importer's certificate or statement of origin. The term does not include a builder's certificate.

"Certificate of title" means a record, created by the Department under this article or by a governmental agency of another jurisdiction under the law of that jurisdiction that is designated as a certificate of title by the Department or agency and is evidence of ownership of a watercraft.

"Conspicuous" means the same as that term is defined in subdivision (b)(10) of § 8.1A-201.

"Consumer goods" means the same as that term is defined in subdivision (a)(23) of § 8.9A-102.

"Dealer" means any watercraft dealer as defined in § 29.1-801.

"Debtor" means the same as that term is defined in subdivision (a)(28) of § 8.9A-102.

"Documented vessel" means a watercraft covered by a certificate of documentation issued pursuant to 46 U.S.C. § 12105, as amended. The term does not include a foreign-documented vessel.

"Electronic" means relating to technology having electrical, digital, magnetic, wireless, optical, electromagnetic, or similar capabilities.

"Electronic certificate of title" means a certificate of title consisting of information that is stored solely in an electronic medium and is retrievable in perceivable form.

"Foreign-documented vessel" means a watercraft whose ownership is recorded in a registry maintained by a country other than the

United States that identifies each person that has an ownership interest in a watercraft and includes a unique alphanumeric designation for the watercraft.

"Good faith" means honesty in fact and the observance of reasonable commercial standards of fair dealing.

"Hull damaged" means compromised with respect to the integrity of a watercraft's hull by a collision, allision, lightning strike, fire, explosion, running aground, or similar occurrence, or the sinking of a watercraft in a manner that creates a significant risk to the integrity of the watercraft's hull.

"Hull identification number" means the alphanumeric designation assigned to a watercraft pursuant to 33 C.F.R. Part 181, as amended. "Knowledge" means the same as that term is defined in § 8.1A-202.

"Lease" means the same as that term is defined in subdivision (1) (j) of § 8.2A-103.

"Lessor" means the same as that term is defined in subdivision (1) (p) of § 8.2A-103.

"Lien creditor," with respect to a watercraft, means:
1. A creditor that has acquired a lien on the watercraft by attachment, levy, or the like;
2. An assignee for benefit of creditors from the time of assignment;
3. A trustee in bankruptcy from the date of the filing of the petition; or
4. A receiver in equity from the time of appointment.

"Notice" means the same as that term is defined in § 8.1A-202.

"Owner" means a person that has legal title to a watercraft.

"Owner of record" means the owner indicated in the files of the Department or, if the files indicate more than one owner, the one first indicated.

"Person" means an individual, corporation, business trust, estate, trust, statutory trust, partnership, limited liability company, association, joint venture, public corporation, government or governmental subdivision, agency or instrumentality, or any other legal or commercial entity.

"Purchase" means to take by sale, lease, mortgage, pledge, consensual lien, security interest, gift, or any other voluntary transaction that creates an interest in a watercraft.

"Purchaser" means a person that takes by purchase.

"Record" means information that is inscribed on a tangible medium or that is stored in an electronic or other medium and is retrievable in perceivable form.

"Registration number" means the alphanumeric designation for a vessel issued pursuant to 46 U.S.C. § 12301, as amended.

"Representative" means the same as that term is defined in subdivision (b)(33) of § 8.1A-201.

"Sale" means the same as that term is defined in § 8.2-106.

"Secured party," with respect to a watercraft, means a person:
1. In whose favor a security interest is created or provided for under a security agreement, whether or not any obligation to be secured is outstanding;
2. That is a consignor under Title 8.9A; or
3. That holds a security interest arising under § 8.2-401 or 8.2505, subsection (3) of § 8.2-711, or subsection (5) of § 8.2A508.

"Secured party of record" means the secured party whose name is indicated as the name of the secured party in the files of the Department or, if the files indicate more than one secured party, the one first indicated.

"Security agreement" means the same as that term is defined in subdivision (a)(74) of § 8.9A-102.

"Security interest" means an interest in a watercraft that secures payment or performance of an obligation if the interest is created by contract or arises under § 8.2-401 or 8.2-505, subsection (3) of § 8.2-711, or subsection (5) of § 8.2A-508. The term includes any interest of a consignor in a watercraft in a transaction that is subject to Title 8.9A. The term does not include the special property interest of a buyer of a watercraft on identification of that watercraft to a contract for sale under § 8.2-401, but a buyer also may acquire a security interest by complying with Title 8.9A. Except as otherwise provided in § 8.2-505, the right of a seller or lessor of a watercraft under Title 8.2 or Title 8.2A to retain or acquire possession of the watercraft is not a security interest, but a seller or lessor also may acquire a security interest by complying with Title 8.9A. The retention or reservation of title by a seller of a watercraft notwithstanding shipment or delivery to the buyer under

§ 8.2-401 is limited in effect to a reservation of a security interest. Whether a transaction in the form of a lease creates a security interest is determined by § 8.1A-304.

"Seller" means the same as that term is defined in subdivision (1) (o) of § 8.2A-103.

"Send" means the same as that term is defined in subdivision (b) (36) of § 8.1A-201.

"Sign" means, with present intent to authenticate or adopt a record, to:
1. Make or adopt a tangible symbol; or
2. Attach to or logically associate with the record an electronic symbol, sound, or process.

"State" means a state of the United States, the District of Columbia, Puerto Rico, the United States Virgin Islands, or any territory or insular possession subject to the jurisdiction of the United States.

"State of principal use" means the state on whose waters a watercraft is or will be used, operated, navigated, or employed more than on the waters of any other state during a calendar year.

"Title brand" means a designation of previous damage, use, or condition that shall be indicated on a certificate of title.

"Transfer of ownership" means a voluntary or involuntary conveyance of an interest in a watercraft.

"Value" means the same as that term is defined in § 8.1A-204.

"Watercraft" means any vessel that is used or capable of being used as a means of transportation on water and is propelled by machinery, whether or not the machinery is the principal source of propulsion, except:
1. A seaplane;
2. An amphibious vehicle for which a certificate of title is issued pursuant to Chapter 6 (§ 46.2-600 et seq.) of Title 46.2 or a similar statute of another state;
3. A vessel that measures 18 feet or less in length along the centerline and is propelled by sail;
4. A vessel that operates only on a permanently fixed, manufactured course and whose movement is restricted to or guided by means of a mechanical device to which the vessel is attached or by which the vessel is controlled;
5. A stationary floating structure that:
    a. Does not have and is not designed to have a mode of propulsion of its own;
    b. Is dependent for utilities upon a continuous utility hookup to a source originating on shore; and
    c. Has a permanent, continuous hookup to a shoreside sewage system;
6. A vessel owned by the United States, a state, or a foreign government or a political subdivision of any of them;
7. A vessel used solely as a lifeboat on another vessel; or
8. A vessel that has a valid marine document issued by the United States Coast Guard.

"Written certificate of title" means a certificate of title consisting of information inscribed on a tangible medium.

TITLE 37.2. BEHAVIORAL HEALTH AND DEVELOPMENTAL SERVICES
CHAPTER 8. EMERGENCY CUSTODY AND VOLUNTARY AND INVOLUNTARY CIVIL ADMISSIONS
ARTICLE 2. VOLUNTARY ADMISSION

§ 37.2-805. VOLUNTARY ADMISSION.

Any state facility shall admit any person requesting admission who has been (i) screened by the community services board or behavioral health authority that serves the county or city where the person resides or, if impractical, where the person is located, (ii) examined by a physician on the staff of the state facility, and (iii) deemed by the board or authority and the state facility physician to be in need of treatment, training, or habilitation in a state facility. Upon motion of the treating physician, a family member or personal representative of the person, or the community services board serving the county or city where the facility is located, the county or city where the person resides, or the county or city where the person receives treatment, a hearing shall be held prior to the release date of any person who has been the subject of a temporary detention order and voluntarily admitted himself in accordance with subsection B of § 37.2-814 to determine whether such person should be ordered to mandatory outpatient treatment pursuant to subsection D of § 37.2-817 upon his release if such person, on at least two previous occasions within 36 months preceding the date of the hearing, has been (a) the subject of a temporary detention order and voluntarily admitted himself in accordance with subsection B of § 37.2-814 or (b) involuntarily admitted pursuant to § 37.2-817. A district court judge or special justice shall hold the hearing within 72 hours after receiving the motion for a mandatory outpatient treatment order; however, if the 72-hour period expires on a Saturday, Sunday, or legal holiday, the hearing shall be held by the close of business on the next day that is not a Saturday, Sunday, or legal holiday.

TITLE 37.2. BEHAVIORAL HEALTH AND DEVELOPMENTAL SERVICES
CHAPTER 8. EMERGENCY CUSTODY AND VOLUNTARY AND INVOLUNTARY CIVIL ADMISSIONS

ARTICLE 4. EMERGENCY CUSTODY AND INVOLUNTARY TEMPORARY DETENTION

§ 37.2-809. INVOLUNTARY TEMPORARY DETENTION; ISSUANCE AND EXECUTION OF ORDER.

A. For the purposes of this section:

"Designee of the local community services board" means an examiner designated by the local community services board who (i) is skilled in the assessment and treatment of mental illness, (ii) has completed a certification program approved by the Department, (iii) is able to provide an independent examination of the person, (iv) is not related by blood or marriage to the person being evaluated, (v) has no financial interest in the admission or treatment of the person being evaluated, (vi) has no investment interest in the facility detaining or admitting the person under this article, and (vii) except for employees of state hospitals and of the U.S. Department of Veterans Affairs, is not employed by the facility.

"Employee" means an employee of the local community services board who is skilled in the assessment and treatment of mental illness and has completed a certification program approved by the Department.

"Investment interest" means the ownership or holding of an equity or debt security, including shares of stock in a corporation, interests or units of a partnership, bonds, debentures, notes, or other equity or debt instruments.

B. A magistrate shall issue, upon the sworn petition of any responsible person, treating physician, or upon his own motion and only after an evaluation conducted in-person or by means of a two-way electronic video and audio communication system as authorized in § 37.2-804.1 by an employee or a designee of the local community services board to determine whether the person meets the criteria for temporary detention, a temporary detention order if it appears from all evidence readily available, including any recommendation from a physician, clinical psychologist, or clinical social worker treating the person, that the person (i) has a mental illness and that there exists a substantial likelihood that, as a result of mental illness, the person will, in the near future, (a) cause serious physical harm to himself or others as evidenced by recent behavior causing, attempting, or threatening harm and other relevant information, if any, or (b) suffer serious harm due to his lack of capacity to protect himself from harm or to provide for his basic human needs; (ii) is in need of hospitalization or treatment; and (iii) is unwilling to volunteer or incapable of volunteering for hospitalization or treatment. The magistrate shall also consider, if available, (a) information provided by the person who initiated emergency custody and (b) the recommendations of any treating or examining physician licensed in Virginia either verbally or in writing prior to rendering a decision. Any temporary detention order entered pursuant to this section shall provide for the disclosure of medical records pursuant to § 37.2-804.2. This subsection shall not preclude any other disclosures as required or permitted by law.

C. When considering whether there is probable cause to issue a temporary detention order, the magistrate may, in addition to the petition, consider (i) the recommendations of any treating or examining physician, psychologist, or clinical social worker licensed in Virginia, if available, (ii) any past actions of the person, (iii) any past mental health treatment of the person, (iv) any relevant hearsay evidence, (v) any medical records available, (vi) any affidavits submitted, if the witness is unavailable and it so states in the affidavit, and (vii) any other information available that the magistrate considers relevant to the determination of whether probable cause exists to issue a temporary detention order.

D. A magistrate may issue a temporary detention order without an emergency custody order proceeding. A magistrate may issue a temporary detention order without a prior evaluation pursuant to subsection B if (i) the person has been personally examined within the previous 72 hours by an employee or a designee of the local community services board or (ii) there is a significant physical, psychological, or medical risk to the person or to others associated with conducting such evaluation.

E. An employee or a designee of the local community services board shall determine the facility of temporary detention in accordance with the provisions of § 37.2-809.1 for all individuals detained pursuant to this section. An employee or designee of the local community services board may change the facility of temporary detention and may designate an alternative facility for temporary detention at any point during the period of temporary detention if it is determined that the alternative facility is a more appropriate facility for temporary detention of the individual given the specific security, medical, or behavioral health needs of the person. In cases in which the facility of temporary detention is changed following transfer of custody to an initial facility of temporary custody, transportation of the individual to the alternative facility of temporary detention shall be provided in accordance with the provisions of § 37.2-810. The initial facility of temporary detention shall be identified on the preadmission screening report and indicated on the temporary detention order; however, if an employee or designee of the local community services board designates an alternative facility, that employee or designee shall provide written notice forthwith, on a form developed by the Executive Secretary of the Supreme Court of Virginia, to the clerk of the issuing court of the name and address of the alternative facility. Subject to the provisions of § 37.2-809.1, if a facility of temporary detention cannot be identified by the time of the expiration of the period of emergency custody pursuant to § 37.2-808, the individual shall be detained in a state facility for the treatment of individuals with mental illness and such facility shall be indicated on the temporary detention order. Except as provided in § 37.2-811 for inmates requiring hospitalization in accordance with subdivision A 2 of § 19.2-169.6, the person shall not be detained in a jail or other place of confinement for persons charged with criminal offenses and shall remain in the custody of law enforcement until the person is either detained within a secure facility or custody has been accepted by the appropriate personnel designated by either the initial facility of temporary detention identified in the temporary detention order or by the alternative facility of temporary detention designated by the employee or designee of the local community services board pursuant to this subsection. The person detained or in custody pursuant to this section shall be given a written summary of the temporary detention procedures and the statutory protections associated with those procedures.

F. Any facility caring for a person placed with it pursuant to a temporary detention order is authorized to provide emergency medical and psychiatric services within its capabilities when the facility determines that the services are in the best interests of the person within its care. The costs incurred as a result of the hearings and by the facility in providing services during the period of temporary detention shall be paid and recovered pursuant to § 37.2-804. The maximum costs reimbursable by the Commonwealth pursuant to this section shall be established by the State Board of Medical Assistance Services based on reasonable criteria. The State Board of Medical Assistance Services shall, by regulation, establish a reasonable rate per day of inpatient care for temporary detention.

G. The employee or the designee of the local community services board who is conducting the evaluation pursuant to this section shall determine, prior to the issuance of the temporary detention order, the insurance status of the person. Where coverage by a third party payor exists, the facility seeking reimbursement under this section shall first seek reimbursement from the third party payor. The Commonwealth shall reimburse the facility only for the balance of costs remaining after the allowances covered by the third party payor have been received.

H. The duration of temporary detention shall be sufficient to allow for completion of the examination required by § 37.2-815, preparation of the preadmission screening report required by § 37.2-816, and initiation of mental health treatment to stabilize the person's psychiatric condition to avoid involuntary commitment where possible, but shall not exceed 72 hours prior to a hearing. If the 72-hour period herein specified terminates on a Saturday, Sunday, legal holiday, or day on which the court is lawfully closed, the person may be detained, as herein provided, until the close of business on the next day that is not a Saturday, Sunday, legal holiday, or day on which the court is lawfully closed. The person may be released, pursuant to § 37.2-813, before the 72-hour period herein specified has run.

I. If a temporary detention order is not executed within 24 hours of its issuance, or within a shorter period as is specified in the order, the order shall be void and shall be returned unexecuted to the office of the clerk of the issuing court or, if the office is not open, to any magistrate serving the jurisdiction of the issuing court. Subsequent orders may be issued upon the original petition within 96 hours after the petition is filed. However, a magistrate must again obtain the advice of an employee or a designee of the local community services board prior to issuing a subsequent order upon the original petition. Any petition for which no temporary detention order or other process in connection therewith is served on the subject of the petition within 96 hours after the petition is filed shall be void and shall be returned to the office of the clerk of the issuing court.

J. The Executive Secretary of the Supreme Court of Virginia shall establish and require that a magistrate, as provided by this section, be available seven days a week, 24 hours a day, for the purpose of performing the duties established by this section. Each community services board shall provide to each general district court and magistrate's office within its service area a list of its employees and designees who are available to perform the evaluations required herein.

K. For purposes of this section, a health care provider or designee of a local community services board or behavioral health authority shall not be required to encrypt any email containing information or medical records provided to a magistrate unless there is reason to believe that a third party will attempt to intercept the email.

L. If the employee or designee of the community services board who is conducting the evaluation pursuant to this section recommends that the person should not be subject to a temporary detention order, such employee or designee shall (i) inform the petitioner, the person who initiated emergency custody if such person is present, and an onsite treating physician of his recommendation; (ii) promptly inform such person who initiated emergency custody that the community services board will facilitate communication between the person and the magistrate if the person disagrees with recommendations of the employee or designee of the community services board who conducted the evaluation and the person who initiated emergency custody so requests; and (iii) upon prompt request made by the person who initiated emergency custody, arrange for such person who initiated emergency custody to communicate with the magistrate as soon as is practicable and prior to the expiration of the period of emergency custody. The magistrate shall consider any information provided by the person who initiated emergency custody and any recommendations of the treating or examining physician and the employee or designee of the community services board who conducted the evaluation and consider such information and recommendations in accordance with subsection B in making his determination to issue a temporary detention order. The individual who is the subject of emergency custody shall remain in the custody of law enforcement or a designee of law enforcement and shall not be released from emergency custody until communication with the magistrate pursuant to this subsection has concluded and the magistrate has made a determination regarding issuance of a temporary detention order.

M. For purposes of this section, "person who initiated emergency custody" means any person who initiated the issuance of an emergency custody order pursuant to § 37.2-808 or a law-enforcement officer who takes a person into custody pursuant to subsection G of § 37.2-808.

TITLE 37.2. BEHAVIORAL HEALTH AND DEVELOPMENTAL SERVICES CHAPTER 8. EMERGENCY CUSTODY AND VOLUNTARY AND INVOLUNTARY CIVIL ADMISSIONS

ARTICLE 5. INVOLUNTARY ADMISSIONS

§ 37.2-814. COMMITMENT HEARING FOR INVOLUNTARY ADMISSION; WRITTEN EXPLANATION; RIGHT TO COUNSEL; RIGHTS OF PETITIONER.

A. The commitment hearing for involuntary admission shall be held after a sufficient period of time has passed to allow for completion of the examination required by § 37.2-815, preparation of the preadmission screening report required by § 37.2-816, and initiation of mental health treatment to stabilize the person's psychiatric condition to avoid involuntary commitment where possible, but shall be held within 72 hours of the execution of the temporary detention order as provided for in § 37.2-809; however, if the 72-hour period herein specified terminates on a Saturday, Sunday, legal holiday, or day on which the court is lawfully closed, the person may be detained, as herein provided, until the close of business on the next day that is not a Saturday, Sunday, legal holiday, or day on which the court is lawfully closed.

B. At the commencement of the commitment hearing, the district court judge or special justice shall inform the person whose involuntary admission is being sought of his right to apply for voluntary admission for inpatient treatment as provided for in § 37.2-805 and shall afford the person an opportunity for voluntary admission. The district court judge or special justice shall advise the person whose involuntary admission is being sought that if the person chooses to be voluntarily admitted pursuant to § 37.2-805, such person will be prohibited from possessing, purchasing, or transporting a firearm pursuant to § 18.2-308.1:3. The judge or special justice shall ascertain if the person is then willing and capable of seeking voluntary admission for inpatient treatment. In determining whether a person is capable of consenting to voluntary admission, the judge or special justice may consider evidence regarding the person's past compliance or noncompliance with treatment. If the judge or special justice finds that the person is capable and willingly accepts voluntary admission for inpatient treatment, the judge or special justice shall require him to accept voluntary admission for a minimum period of treatment not to exceed 72 hours. After such minimum period of treatment, the person shall give the facility 48 hours' notice prior to leaving the facility. During this notice period, the person shall not be discharged except as provided in § 37.2-837, 37.2-838, or 37.2840. The person shall be subject to the transportation provisions as provided in § 37.2-829 and the requirement for preadmission screening by a community services board as provided in § 37.2-805.

C. If a person is incapable of accepting or unwilling to accept voluntary admission and treatment, the judge or special justice shall inform the person of his right to a commitment hearing and right to counsel. The judge or special justice shall ascertain if the person whose admission is sought is represented by counsel, and, if he is not represented by counsel, the judge or special justice shall appoint an attorney to represent him. However, if the person requests an opportunity to employ counsel, the judge or special justice shall give him a reasonable opportunity to employ counsel at his own expense.

D. A written explanation of the involuntary admission process and the statutory protections associated with the process shall be given to the person, and its contents shall be explained by an attorney prior to the commitment hearing. The written explanation shall describe, at a minimum, the person's rights to (i) retain private counsel or be represented by a court-appointed attorney, (ii) present any defenses including independent evaluation and expert testimony or the testimony of other witnesses, (iii) be present during the hearing and testify, (iv) appeal any order for involuntary admission to the circuit court, and (v) have a jury trial on appeal. The judge or special justice shall ascertain whether the person whose involuntary admission is sought has been given the written explanation required herein.

E. To the extent possible, during or before the commitment hearing, the attorney for the person whose involuntary admission is sought shall interview his client, the petitioner, the examiner described in § 37.2-815, the community services board staff, and any other material witnesses. He also shall examine all relevant diagnostic and other reports, present evidence and witnesses, if any, on his client's behalf, and otherwise actively represent his client in the proceedings. A health care provider shall disclose or make available all such reports, treatment information, and records concerning his client to the attorney, upon request. The role of the attorney shall be to represent the wishes of his client, to the extent possible.

F. The petitioner shall be given adequate notice of the place, date, and time of the commitment hearing. The petitioner shall be entitled to retain counsel at his own expense, to be present during the hearing, and to testify and present evidence. The petitioner shall be encouraged but shall not be required to testify at the hearing, and the person whose involuntary admission is sought shall not be released solely on the basis of the petitioner's failure to attend or testify during the hearing.

TITLE 54.1. PROFESSIONS AND OCCUPATIONS CHAPTER 42. DEALERS IN FIREARMS

§ 54.1-4201.2. FIREARM TRANSACTIONS BY PERSONS OTHER THAN DEALERS; VOLUNTARY BACKGROUND CHECKS.

A. The Department of State Police shall be available at every firearms show held in the Commonwealth and shall make determinations in accordance with the procedures set out in § 18.2-308.2:2 of whether a prospective purchaser or transferee is prohibited under state or federal law from possessing a firearm prior to the completion of any firearm transaction at a firearms show held in the Commonwealth. The Department of State Police shall establish policies and procedures in accordance with 28 C.F.R. § 25.6 to permit such determinations to be made by the Department of State Police.

The Department of State Police may charge a reasonable fee for the determination.

B. The promoter, as defined in § 54.1-4201.1, shall give the Department of State Police notice of the time and location of a firearms show at least 30 days prior to the show. The promoter shall provide the Department of State Police with adequate space, at no charge, to conduct such prohibition determinations. The promoter shall ensure that a notice that such determinations are available is prominently displayed at the show.

C. No person who sells or transfers a firearm at a firearms show after receiving a determination from the Department of State Police that the purchaser or transferee is not prohibited by state or federal law from possessing a firearm shall be liable for selling or transferring a firearm to such person.

D. The provisions of § 18.2-308.2:2, including definitions, procedures, and prohibitions, shall apply, mutatis mutandis, to the provisions of this section.

TITLE 63.2 WELFARE
CHAPTER 17: LICENSURE AND REGISTRATION PROCEDURES

§ 63.2-1701.01. STORAGE OF FIREARMS IN CERTAIN FAMILY DAY HOMES.

During hours of operation, all firearms in a licensed family day home, registered family day home, or family day home approved by a family day system shall be stored unloaded in a locked container, compartment, or cabinet, and all ammunition shall be stored in a separate locked container, compartment, or cabinet. The key or combination to such locked containers, compartments, or cabinets shall be inaccessible to all children in the home.

> APPENDICES <

APPENDIX B
Selected Federal Forms

ATF Form 1 Page 1

U.S. Department of Justice
Bureau of Alcohol, Tobacco, Firearms and Explosives

OMB No. 1140-0011 (08/31/2022)

Application to Make and Register a Firearm

ATF Control Number

To: National Firearms Act Division, Bureau of Alcohol, Tobacco, Firearms and Explosives, P.O. Box 5015, Portland, OR 97208-5015
(Submit in duplicate. Please do not staple documents. See instructions attached.)

As required by Sections 5821 (b), 5822, and 5841 of the National Firearms Act, Title 26 U.S.C., Chapter 53, the undersigned hereby submits application to make and register the firearm described below.

1. Type of Application *(check one)*

   a. Tax Paid. Submit your tax payment of $200 with the application. The tax may be paid by credit or debit card, check, or money order. Please complete item 17. Upon approval of the application, we will affix and cancel the required National Firearms Act Stamp. *(See instruction 2c and 3)*

   b. Tax Exempt because firearm is being made on behalf of the United States, or any department, independent establishment, or agency thereof.

   c. Tax Exempt because firearm is being made by or on behalf of any State or possession of the United States, or any political subdivision thereof, or any official police organization of such a government entity engaged in criminal investigations.

2. Application is made by: ☐ Corporation ☐ Individual ☐ Other Legal Entity ☐ Trust ☐ Government Entity

3a. Trade name *(If any)*

3b. Applicant's Full Legal Name and Mailing Address *(Type or print below) (See instruction 2d)*

3d. County/Parish

3e. Telephone Number

3f. E-mail address

3c. If P.O. Box is shown above, street address must be given here

4. Description of Firearm *(complete items a through k) (See instruction 2j)*

   a. Name and Address of Original Manufacturer and/or Importer of Firearm *(If any)*
   b. Type of Firearm to be made *(See definition 2k) If a destructive device, complete item 4j*
   c. Caliber or Gauge *(Specify one)*
   d. Model *(As marked on firearm)*
   e. Barrel length:
   f. Overall length:
   g. Serial Number
   h. Additional Description *(Indicate required maker's markings to include maker's name (as registered), city and state as each will appear on firearm)*
   i. Specify Why You Intend To Make Firearm *(Use additional sheet if necessary)*
   j. Type of destructive device *(check one box):* ☐ Firearm ☐ Explosives *(If the Explosives box is checked, complete item 5 and see instruction 2m)*
   If an explosive type destructive device, identify the type of explosive(s): _____
   k. Is this firearm being reactivated? ☐ Yes ☐ No *(See definition 1k)*

5. Applicant's Federal Firearms License *(If any)* or Explosives License or Permit Number
   (Give complete 15-digit Number)

6. Special *(Occupational)* Tax Status *(if applicable) (See definitions)*
   a. Employer Identification Number
   b. Class

Under Penalties of Perjury, I Declare that I have examined this application, including accompanying documents, and to the best of my knowledge and belief it is true, accurate and complete and the making and possession of the firearm described above would not constitute a violation of Title 18, U.S.C., Chapter 44, Title 26, U.S.C., Chapter 53; or any provisions of State or local law.

7. Signature of Applicant
8. Name and Title of Authorized Official
9. Date

The space below is for the use of the Bureau of Alcohol, Tobacco, Firearms and Explosives

By authority of the Director, Bureau of Alcohol, Tobacco, Firearms and Explosives, this application has been examined and the applicant's making and registration of the firearm described above is:

☐ Approved *(With the following conditions, if any)*
☐ Disapproved *(For the following reasons)*

Authorized ATF Official

Date

Previous Editions Are Obsolete

ATF Copy

ATF Form 1 (5320.1)
Revised September 2019

ATF Form 1 Page 2

MAKER'S CERTIFICATION *(not completed by a GOVERNMENT ENTITY)*

10. Law Enforcement Notification *(See instruction 2I)*
Each applicant is to provide notification of the proposed making and possession of the firearm described on this Form 1 by providing a copy of the completed form to the chief law enforcement officer in the agency identified below.

Agency or Department Name _____ Name and Title of Official _____

Address (Street address or P.O. Box, City, State and Zip Code) to which sent (mailed or delivered) _____

Information for the Chief Law Enforcement Officer

This form provides notification of the applicant's intent to make and register a National Firearms Act (NFA) firearm. No action on your part is required. However, should you have information that may disqualify this person from making or possessing a firearm, please contact the NFA Division at (304) 616-4500 or NFA@atf.gov. A "Yes" answer to items 11 a. through 11 h. or 15 d. or 15 e. could disqualify a person from acquiring or possessing a firearm. Also, ATF will not approve an application if the making or possession of the firearm is in violation of State or local law.

12. Photograph

Affix a 2" x 2" Photograph Here
No Stapling. Please Tape Sides of Photo to the Application.

1. Photo must have been taken within the last year.
2. Photo must have been taken in full face view without a hat or head covering that obscures the hair or hairline.
3. On back of photograph print full name, last 4 of SSN.

Maker's Questions *(complete only when the maker is an individual)*

A maker who is an individual must complete this Section.

11. Answer questions 11 a. through 11 h. Answer questions 13, 15, 16 and 17 if applicable. For any "Yes" answer the applicant shall provide details on a separate sheet. *(See instruction 7c and definitions)*

	Yes	No
a. Are you under indictment or information in any court for a felony, or any other crime, for which the judge could imprison you for more than one year? *(See definition 1n)*		
b. Have you ever been convicted in any court for a felony, or any other crime, for which the judge could have imprisoned you for more than one year, even if you received a shorter sentence including probation? *(See definition 1n)*		
c. Are you a fugitive from justice? *(See definition 1t)*		
d. Are you an unlawful user of, or addicted to, marijuana or any depressant, stimulant, narcotic drug, or any other controlled substance? **Warning: The use or possession of marijuana remains unlawful under Federal law regardless of whether it has been legalized or decriminalized for medicinal or recreational purposes in the state where you reside.**		
e. Have you ever been adjudicated as a mental defective OR have you ever been committed to a mental institution? *(See definition 1o and 1p)*		
f. Have you been discharged from the Armed Forces under **dishonorable** conditions?		
g. Are you subject to a court order restraining you from harassing, stalking, or threatening your child or an intimate partner or child of such partner? *(See definition 1q)*		
h. Have you ever been convicted in any court of a misdemeanor crime of domestic violence? *(See definition 1r)*		

13. Social Security Number: *(See instruction 2f)* _____ Date of Birth: _____

14a. Ethnicity	☐ Hispanic or Latino	14b. Race	☐ American Indian or Alaska Native	☐ Black or African American	☐ White
	☐ Not Hispanic or Latino		☐ Asian	☐ Native Hawaiian or Other Pacific Islander	

15a. Country of Citizenship: *(Check/List more than one, if applicable. Nationals of the United States may check U.S.A.) (See definition 1s)*
☐ United States of America   ☐ Other Country/Countries *(specify)*: _____

15b. State of Birth _____ 15c. Country of Birth _____

	Yes	No
d. Have you ever renounced your United States citizenship?		
e. Are you an alien illegally or unlawfully in the United States?		
f.1. Are you an alien who has been admitted to the United States under a nonimmigrant visa?		
f.2. If "yes", do you fall within any of the exceptions stated in the instructions? Attach the documentation to the application ☐ N/A		

16. If you are an alien, record your U.S.-Issued Alien or Admission number (AR#, USCIS#, or I94#): _____

17. Have you been issued a Unique Personal Identification Number (UPIN)? *(See instruction 2f)* ☐ Yes ☐ No If yes please list _____

CERTIFICATION: Under penalties imposed by 18 U.S.C. § 924 and 26 U.S.C. § 5861, I certify that, upon submission of this form to ATF, a completed copy of this form will be directed to the chief law enforcement officer (CLEO) shown in item 10, that the statements, as applicable, contained in this certification, and any attached documents in support thereof, are true and correct to the best of my knowledge and belief. NOTE: See instructions 2.d(2) and 2.d(3) for the items to be completed depending on the type of applicant.

Signature of Maker _____ Date _____

ATF Copy

ATF Form 1 Page 3

18. Number of Responsible Persons *(see definitions)* associated with the applicant trust or legal entity _____

19. Provide the full name (printed or typed) below for each Responsible Person associated with the applicant trust or legal entity *(if there are more Responsible Persons than can be listed on the form, attach a separate sheet listing the additional Responsible Person(s))*. Please note that a completed Form 5320.23, National Firearms Act (NFA) Responsible Person Questionnaire, must be submitted with the Form 1 application for each Responsible Person.

Full Name _____ Full Name _____

20. **Method of Payment** *(Check one) (See instruction 21) (if paying by credit/debit card, complete the sections below)*

☐ Check *(Enclosed)*   ☐ Cashier's Check or Money Order *(Enclosed)*   ☐ Visa   ☐ Mastercard   ☐ American Express   ☐ Discover   ☐ Diners Club

Credit/Debit Card Number *(No dashes)* _____ Name as Printed on the Credit/Debit Card _____ Expiration Date *(Month & year)* _____

Credit/Debit Card Billing Address:
Address: _____
City: _____ State: _____ Zip Code: _____

Tax Amount: $ _____

I Authorize ATF to Charge my Credit/Debit Card the Above Amount.

Signature of Cardholder _____   Date _____

Your credit/debit card will be charged the above stated amount upon receipt of your application. The charge will be reflected on your credit/debit card statement. In the event your application is NOT approved, the above amount will be credited to the credit/debit card noted above.

Important Information for Currently Registered Firearms

If you are the current registrant of the firearm described on this form, please note the following information.

Estate Procedures: For procedures regarding the transfer of firearms in an estate resulting from the death of the registrant identified in item 3b, the executor should contact the NFA Division, Bureau of ATF, 244 Needy Road, Martinsburg, WV 25405.

Interstate Movement: If the firearm identified in item 4 is a machinegun, short-barreled rifle, short-barreled shotgun, or destructive device, the registrant may be required by 18 U.S.C. § 922(a)(4) to obtain permission from ATF prior to any transportation in interstate or foreign commerce. ATF Form 5320.20 can be used to request this permission.

Change of Description or Address: The registrant shall notify the NFA Division, Bureau of Alcohol, Tobacco, Firearms and Explosives, 244 Needy Road, Martinsburg, WV 25405, in writing, of any change to the description of the firearm in item 4, or any change to the address of the registrant.

Restrictions on Possession: Any restriction *(see approval block on face of form)* on the possession of the firearm identified in item 4 continues with the further transfer of the firearm.

Persons Prohibited from Possessing Firearms: If the registrant becomes prohibited from possessing a firearm, please contact the NFA Division for procedures on how to dispose of the firearm.

Proof of Registration: A person possessing a firearm registered as required by the NFA shall retain proof of registration which shall be made available to any ATF officer upon request.

Paperwork Reduction Act Notice

This form is in accordance with the Paperwork Reduction Act of 1995. The information you provide is used to establish that the applicant's making and possession of the firearm would be in conformance with Federal, State, and local law. The data is used as proof of lawful registration of a firearm to the manufacturer. The furnishing of this information is mandatory *(26 U.S.C. § 5822)*.

The estimated average burden associated with this collection of information is 4.0 hours per respondent or recordkeeper, depending on individual circumstances. Comments concerning the accuracy of this burden estimate and suggestion for reducing this burden should be addressed to Reports Management Officer, Information Technology Coordination Staff, Bureau of Alcohol, Tobacco, Firearms and Explosives, Washington, DC 20226.

An agency may not conduct or sponsor, and a person is not required to respond to, a collection of information unless it displays a currently valid OMB control number.

ATF Copy

ATF Form 1 (5320.1)
Revised September 2019

ATF Form 4 Page 1

U.S. Department of Justice
Bureau of Alcohol, Tobacco, Firearms and Explosives

OMB No. 1140-0014 (08/31/2022)

Application for Tax Paid Transfer and Registration of Firearm

ATF Control Number

SUBMIT in DUPLICATE to: National Firearms Act Division
Bureau of Alcohol, Tobacco, Firearms and Explosives, P.O. Box 5015, Portland, OR 97208-5015

1. Type of Transfer *(Check one)*
   - [ ] $5
   - [ ] $200

Submit the appropriate tax payment with the application. The tax may be paid by credit or debit card, check, or money order. Please complete item 20. Upon approval of the application, we will affix and cancel the required National Firearms Act stamp. (See instructions 2b, 2j and 3)

2a. Transferee's Full Legal Name and Address *(Include trade name, if any) (See instruction 2d)*

- [ ] Corporation
- [ ] Individual
- [ ] Other Legal Entity
- [ ] Trust

2b. County/Parish

3a. Transferor's Full Legal Name and Address *(Include trade name, if any)* *(Executors: see instruction 2l)*

3b. E-mail address

3c. Transferor's Telephone *(Area Code and Number)*

3d. If Applicable: Decedent's Name, Address, and Date of Death

3e. Number, Street, City, State and Zip Code of Residence *(or Firearms Business Premises)* If Different from Item 3a.

The above-named and undersigned transferor hereby makes application as required by Section 5812 of the National Firearms Act to transfer and register the firearm described below to the transferee.

4. Description of Firearm *(Complete items a through h) (See instruction 2n)*

a. Name and Address of Maker Manufacturer and/or Importer of Firearm	b. Type of Firearm *(see definitions 1c)*	c. Caliber or Gauge	d. Model
			e. Barrel Length: f. Overall Length:
			g. Serial Number

h. Additional Description or Data Appearing on Firearm *(Attach additional sheet if necessary)*

5. Transferee's Federal Firearms License *(if any)* or Explosives License or Permit Number *(Give complete 15-digit number) (See instruction 2c)*

First 6 digits	2 digits	2 digits	5 digits

6. Transferee's Special (Occupational) Tax Status *(If any)*

a. Employer Identification Number	b. Class

7. Transferor's Federal Firearms License *(If any)*

First 6 digits	2 digits	2 digits	5 digits

8. Transferor's Special (Occupational) Tax Status *(If any)*

a. Employer Identification Number	b. Class

Under Penalties of Perjury, I Declare that I have examined this application, and to the best of my knowledge and belief it is true, correct and complete, and that the transfer of the described firearm to the transferee and receipt and possession of it by the transferee are not prohibited by the provisions of Title 18, United States Code; Chap 44; Title 26, United States Code; Chap 53; or any provisions of State or local law.

9. Signature of Transferor *(Or authorized official)*

10. Name and Title of Authorized Official *(Print or type)*

11. Date

The Space Below is for the use of the Bureau of Alcohol, Tobacco, Firearms and Explosives

By Authority of The Director, This Application Has Been Examined, and the Transfer and Registration of the Firearm Described Herein and the Interstate Movement of that Firearm, When Applicable, to the Transferee are:

Stamp Denomination

- [ ] Approved *(With the following conditions, if any)*
- [ ] Disapproved *(For the following reasons)*

Signature of Authorized ATF Official

Date

Previous Editions Are Obsolete

ATF Copy

ATF Form 4 (5320.4)
Revised September 2019

APPENDIX B | 603

ATF Form 4 Page 2

Transferee Certification

12. Law Enforcement Notification *(See instruction 2f)*

The transferee is to provide notification of the proposed acquisition and possession of the firearm described on this Form 4 by providing a copy of the completed form to the chief law enforcement officer in the agency identified below:

Agency or Department Name	Name and Title of Official

Address *(Street address or P.O. Box, City, State and Zip Code)* to which sent *(mailed or delivered)*

Information for the Chief Law Enforcement Officer

This form provides notification of the transferee's intent to acquire and possess a National Firearms Act (NFA) firearm. No action on your part is required. However, should you have information that may disqualify this person from acquiring or possessing a firearm, please contact the NFA Division at (304) 616-4500 or NFA@atf.gov. A "Yes" answer to items 14.a. through 14.h. or 18.d. or 18.e. could disqualify a person from acquiring or possessing a firearm. Also, ATF will not approve an application if the transfer or possession of the firearm is in violation of State or local law.

13. Transferee Necessity Statement *(See instruction 2e)*

I, _____, have a reasonable necessity to possess the machinegun, short-barreled rifle,
(Name and Title of Transferee)

short-barreled shotgun, or destructive device described on this application for the following reason(s) _____

and my possession of the device or weapon would be consistent with public safety (18 U.S.C. § 922(b) (4) and 27 CFR § 478.98).

Transferee Questions *(Complete Only When Transferee is An Individual)*

14. Answer questions 14.a. through 14.h. Answer questions 16, 17, 18, 19 and 20, if applicable. For any "Yes" answer the transferee shall provide details on a separate sheet. *(See instruction 7b and definitions)*

		Yes	No
a.	Are you under indictment or information in any court for a felony, or any other crime, for which the judge could imprison you for more than one year? *(See definition 1m)*		
b.	Have you ever been convicted in any court for a felony, or any other crime, for which the judge could have imprisoned you for more than one year, even if you received a shorter sentence including probation? *(See definition 1m)*		
c.	Are you a fugitive from justice? *(See definition 1s)*		
d.	Are you an unlawful user of, or addicted to, marijuana or any depressant, stimulant, narcotic drug, or any other controlled substance? **Warning: The use or possession of marijuana remains unlawful under Federal law regardless of whether it has been legalized or decriminalized for medicinal or recreational purposes in the state where you reside.**		
e.	Have you ever been adjudicated as a mental defective **OR** have you ever been committed to a mental institution? *(See definitions 1n and 1o)*		
f.	Have you ever been discharged from the Armed Forces under **dishonorable** conditions?		
g.	Are you subject to a court order restraining you from harassing, stalking, or threatening your child or an intimate partner or child of such partner? *(See definition 1p)*		
h.	Have you ever been convicted in any court of a misdemeanor crime of domestic violence? *(See definition 1q)*		

15. Photograph

Affix a 2" x 2" Photograph here. No Stapling. Tape Sides of Photo to the Application.

1. Photo must have been taken within the last year.
2. Photo must have been taken in full face view without a hat or head covering that obscures the hair or hairline.
3. On back of photograph print full name, last 4 of SSN.

16. Social Security Number: *(See instruction 2h)*	Date of Birth:

17a. Ethnicity	☐ Hispanic or Latino ☐ Not Hispanic or Latino	17b. Race	☐ American Indian or Alaska Native ☐ Asian	☐ Black or African American ☐ Native Hawaiian or Other Pacific Islander	☐ White

18a. Country of Citizenship: *(Check/List more than one, if applicable. Nationals of the United States may check U.S.A.) (See definition 1r)*
☐ United States of America   ☐ Other Country/Countries *(specify)*:

18b. State of Birth	18c. Country of Birth

		Yes	No
d.	Have you ever renounced your United States citizenship?		
e.	Are you an alien illegally or unlawfully in the United States?		
f.1.	Are you an alien who has been admitted to the United States under a nonimmigrant visa?		
f.2.	If "yes", do you fall within any of the exceptions stated in the instructions? Attach the documentation to the application	☐ N/A	

19. If you are an alien, record your U.S.-Issued Alien or Admission number (AR#, USCIS#, or 194#): _____

20. Have you been issued a Unique Personal Identification Number *(UPIN)*? *(See instruction 2h)* ☐ Yes ☐ No If yes please list _____

ATF Copy

ATF Form 4 (5320.4)
Revised September 2019

ATF Form 4 Page 3

CERTIFICATION: Under penalties imposed by 18 U.S.C. § 924 and 26 U.S.C. § 5861, I certify that, upon submission of this form to ATF, a completed copy of this form will be directed to the chief law enforcement officer *(CLEO)* shown in item 12, that the statements, as applicable, contained in this certification, and any attached documents in support thereof, are true and correct to the best of my knowledge and belief. NOTE: See instructions 2.d(2) and 2.d(3) for the items to be completed depending on the type of transferee.

_____ _____
Signature of Transferee   Date

21. Number of Responsible Persons *(see definitions)* associated with the transferee trust or legal entity _____

22. Provide the full name (printed or typed) below for each Responsible Person associated with the applicant trust or legal entity (if there are more Responsible Persons than can be listed on the form, attach a separate sheet listing the additional Responsible Person(s)). Please note that a completed Form 5320.23, National Firearms Act (NFA) Responsible Person Questionnaire, must be submitted with the Form 4 application for each Responsible Person.

Full Name   Full Name

23. **Method of Payment** *(Check one) (See instruction 2j)* (if paying by credit/debit card, complete the section below)

☐ Check *(Enclosed)* ☐ Cashier's Check or Money Order *(Enclosed)* ☐ Visa ☐ Mastercard ☐ American Express ☐ Discover ☐ Diners Club

Credit/Debit Card Number *(No dashes)* | Name as Printed on the Credit/Debit Card | Expiration Date *(Month & year)*

Credit/Debit Card Billing Address:
Address:
City: State: Zip Code:

Tax Amount: $

I Authorize ATF to Charge my Credit/Debit Card the Tax Amount.

_____ _____
Signature of Cardholder   Date

Your credit/debit card will be charged the above stated amount upon receipt of the application. The charge will be reflected on your credit/debit card statement. In the event your application is NOT approved, the above amount will be credited to the credit/debit card noted above.

Important Information for Currently Registered Firearms

If you are the current registrant of the firearm described on this form, please note the following information.

Estate Procedures: For procedures regarding the transfer of firearms in an estate resulting from the death of the registrant identified in item 2a, the executor should contact the NFA Division, Bureau of Alcohol, Tobacco, Firearms and Explosives, 244 Needy Road, Martinsburg, WV 25405.

Change of Address: Unless currently licensed under the Gun Control Act, the registrant shall notify the NFA Division, Bureau of Alcohol, Tobacco, Firearms and Explosives, 244 Needy Road, Martinsburg, WV 25405, in writing, of any change to the address in item 2a.

Change of Description: The registrant shall notify the NFA Division, Bureau of Alcohol, Tobacco, Firearms and Explosives, 244 Needy Road, Martinsburg, WV 25405, in writing, of any change to the description of the firearm(s) in item 4.

Interstate Movement: If the firearm identified in item 4 is a **machinegun, short-barreled rifle, short-barreled shotgun,** or **destructive device**, the registrant may be required by 18 U.S.C. § 922(a)(4) to obtain permission from ATF prior to any transportation in interstate or foreign commerce. ATF Form 5320. 20 can be used to request this permission.

Restrictions on Possession: Any restriction *(see approval block on face of form)* on the possession of the firearm identified in item 4 continues with the further transfer of the firearm.

Persons Prohibited from Possessing Firearms: If the registrant becomes prohibited from possessing a firearm, please contact the NFA Division for procedures on how to dispose of the firearm.

Proof of Registration: A person possessing a firearm registered as required by the NFA shall retain proof of registration which shall be made available to any ATF officer upon request.

Paperwork Reduction Act Notice

This form meets the clearance requirements of the Paperwork Reduction Act of 1995. The information you provide is used in applying to transfer serviceable firearms taxpaid. Data is used to identify transferor, transferee, and firearm, and to ensure legality for transfer under Federal, State and local laws. The furnishing of this information is mandatory (26 U.S.C. § 5812).

The estimated average burden associated with this collection of information is 3.78 hours per respondent or recordkeeper, depending on individual circumstances. Comments concerning the accuracy of this burden estimate and suggestion for reducing this burden should be addressed to Reports Management Officer, Information Technology Coordination Staff, Bureau of Alcohol, Tobacco, Firearms and Explosives, Washington, DC 20226.

An agency may not conduct or sponsor, and a person is not required to respond to, a collection of information unless it displays a currently valid OMB control number.

ATF Form 4 (5320.4)
Revised September 2019

ATF Copy

ATF Form 4473 Page 1

U.S. Department of Justice
Bureau of Alcohol, Tobacco, Firearms and Explosives

OMB No. 1140-0020

Firearms Transaction Record

WARNING: The information you provide will be used to determine whether you are prohibited by Federal or State law from receiving a firearm. Certain violations of the Gun Control Act, 18 U.S.C. 921 et. seq., are punishable by up to 10 years imprisonment and/or up to a $250,000 fine. Any person who exports a firearm without a proper authorization from either the Department of Commerce or the Department of State, as applicable, is subject to a fine of not more than $1,000,000 and up to 20 years imprisonment.

Transferor's/Seller's Transaction Serial Number (if any)

Read the Notices, Instructions, and Definitions on this form. Prepare in original only at the licensed premises (including business temporarily conducted from a qualifying gun show or event in the same State in which the premises is located) unless the transaction qualifies under 18 U.S.C. 922(c). **All entries must be handwritten in ink unless completed under ATF Rul. 2016-2. PLEASE PRINT.**

Section A - Must Be Completed By Transferor/Seller Before Transferee/Buyer Completes Section B

	1. Manufacturer and Importer (if any) (If the manufacturer and importer are different, include both.)	2. Model (if designated)	3. Serial Number	4. Type	5. Caliber or Gauge
1.					
2.					
3.					

6. Total Number of Firearms to be Transferred (Please spell total number e.g., one, two, etc. Do not use numerals.)

7. Check if any part of this transaction is a pawn redemption. ☐
Record Line Number(s) From Question 1:

8. Check if this transaction is to facilitate a private party transfer. ☐

Section B - Must Be Completed Personally By Transferee/Buyer

9. Transferee's/Buyer's Full Name (If legal name contains an initial only, record the initial followed by "IO" in quotes. If no middle initial or name, record "NMN".)

Last Name (including suffix, e.g., Jr, Sr, II, III) | First Name | Middle Name

10. Current State of Residence and Address (U.S. postal abbreviations are acceptable. Cannot be a post office box.)
Number and Street Address | City | State | ZIP Code | County/Parish/Borough

11. Place of Birth
U.S. City **and** State -OR- Foreign Country

12. Height Ft. ___ In. ___
13. Weight (lbs.)
14. Sex ☐ Male ☐ Female ☐ Non-Binary
15. Birth Date Month | Day | Year

16. Social Security Number (optional, but will help prevent misidentification)

17. Unique Personal Identification Number (UPIN) or Appeals Management Database Identification (AMD ID) (if applicable)

18.a. Ethnicity
☐ Hispanic or Latino
☐ Not Hispanic or Latino

18.b. Race (Select one or more race in 18.b. Both 18.a. and 18.b. must be answered.)
☐ American Indian or Alaska Native
☐ Asian
☐ Black or African American
☐ Native Hawaiian or Other Pacific Islander
☐ White

19. Country of Citizenship: (Check/List more than one, if applicable. Nationals of the United States may check U.S.A.)
☐ United States of America (U.S.A.) ☐ Other Country/Countries (Specify):

20. If you are an alien, record your U.S.-issued alien or admission number (AR#, USCIS#, or I94#):

21. Answer the following questions by checking or marking either the "yes" or "no" box to the right of the questions:	Yes	No
a. Are you the actual transferee/buyer of the firearm(s) listed on this form and any continuation sheet(s) (ATF Form 5300.9A)? **Warning: You are not the actual transferee/buyer if you are acquiring the firearm(s) on behalf of another person. If you are not the actual transferee/buyer, the licensee cannot transfer the firearm(s) to you.** Exception: If you are only picking up a repaired firearm(s) for another person, you are not required to answer 21.a. and may proceed to question 21.b.	☐	☐
b. Are you under indictment or information in any court for a **felony**, or any other crime for which the judge could imprison you for more than one year, or are you a current member of the military who has been charged with violation(s) of the Uniform Code of Military Justice and whose charge(s) have been referred to a general court-martial?	☐	☐
c. Have you ever been convicted in any court, including a military court, of a **felony**, or any other crime for which the judge could have imprisoned you for more than one year, even if you received a shorter sentence including probation?	☐	☐
d. Are you a fugitive from justice?	☐	☐
e. Are you an unlawful user of, or addicted to, marijuana or any depressant, stimulant, narcotic drug, or any other controlled substance? **Warning:** The use or possession of marijuana remains unlawful under Federal law regardless of whether it has been legalized or decriminalized for medicinal or recreational purposes in the state where you reside.	☐	☐

Previous Editions Are Obsolete
STAPLE IF PAGES BECOME SEPARATED
ATF Form 4473 (5300.9)
Revised May 2020

ATF Form 4473 Page 2

		Yes	No
f.	Have you ever been adjudicated as a mental defective **OR** have you ever been committed to a mental institution?	☐	☐
g.	Have you ever been discharged from the Armed Forces under dishonorable conditions?	☐	☐
h.	Are you subject to a court order, including a Military Protection Order issued by a military judge or magistrate, restraining you from harassing, stalking, or threatening your child or an intimate partner or child of such partner?	☐	☐
i.	Have you ever been convicted in any court of a misdemeanor crime of domestic violence, or are you or have you ever been a member of the military and been convicted of a crime that included, as an element, the use of force against a person as identified in the instructions?	☐	☐
j.	Have you ever renounced your United States citizenship?	☐	☐
k.	Are you an alien **illegally** or **unlawfully** in the United States?	☐	☐
21.l.1.	Are you an alien who has been admitted to the United States under a nonimmigrant visa?	☐	☐
21.l.2.	If you are such an alien do you fall within any of the exceptions stated in the instructions? (U.S. citizens/nationals leave 21.l.2. blank)	☐	☐

I certify that my answers in Section B are true, correct, and complete. I have read and understand the Notices, Instructions, and Definitions on ATF Form 4473. I understand that answering "yes" to question 21.a. if I am not the actual transferee/buyer is a crime punishable as a felony under Federal law, and may also violate State and/or local law. I understand that a person who answers "yes" to any of the questions 21.b. through 21.k. is prohibited from receiving or possessing a firearm. I understand that a person who answers "yes" to question 21.l.1. is prohibited from receiving or possessing a firearm, unless the person answers "yes" to question 21.l.2. and provides the documentation required in 26.d. I also understand that making any false oral or written statement, or exhibiting any false or misrepresented identification with respect to this transaction, is a crime punishable as a felony under Federal law, and may also violate State and/or local law. I further understand that the repetitive purchase of firearms for the purpose of resale for livelihood and profit without a Federal firearms license is a violation of Federal law.

22. Transferee's/Buyer's Signature	23. Certification Date
	Month / Day / Year

Section C - Must Be Completed By Transferor/Seller Prior To The Transfer Of The Firearm(s)

24. Category of firearm(s) to be transferred (check or mark all that apply):
☐ Handgun ☐ Long Gun (rifle or shotgun) ☐ Other Firearm (frame, receiver, etc.)

25. If sale or transfer is at a qualifying gun show or event:
Name of Function: _____
City, State: _____

26.a. Identification (e.g., Virginia driver's license (VA DL) or other valid government-issued photo identification including military ID.)

Issuing Authority and Type of Identification	Number on Identification	Expiration Date of Identification (if any) Month / Day / Year

26.b. Supplemental Government Issued Documentation (if identification document does not show current residence address or full legal name)

26.c. Official Military Orders Establishing Permanent Change of Station (PCS):

PCS Base/City and State:	PCS Effective Date:	PCS Order Number (if any):

26.d. Exception to the Nonimmigrant Alien Prohibition: If the transferee/buyer answered "yes" to 21.1.2. record the type of documentation showing the exception to the prohibition and attach a copy to this ATF Form 4473:

27.a. Date the transferee's/buyer's identifying information in Section B was transmitted to NICS or the appropriate State agency:
Month / Day / Year

27.b. The NICS or State transaction number (if provided) was:

27.c. The response initially provided by NICS or the appropriate State agency was:
☐ Proceed
☐ Delayed _____ [The firearm(s) may be transferred on _____ if State law permits (optional)]
☐ Denied
☐ Cancelled

27.d. Prior to transfer the following response(s) was/were later provided by NICS or the appropriate State agency:
☐ Proceed _____ (date)   ☐ Overturned
☐ Denied _____ (date)
☐ Cancelled _____ (date)
☐ No response was provided within 3 business days.

27.e. After the firearm was transferred, the following response was provided by NICS or the appropriate State agency (if applicable) on:
_____ (date).   ☐ Proceed   ☐ Denied   ☐ Cancelled

27.f. Name and Brady identification number of the NICS examiner. (optional)
_____ (name)   _____ (number)

27.g. Name of FFL Employee Completing NICS check. (optional)

☐ No NICS check is required because a background check was completed during the NFA approval process on the individual who will receive the NFA firearm(s), as reflected on the approved NFA application.

ATF Form 4473 (5300.9)

ATF Form 4473 Page 3

29. ☐ No NICS check is required because the transferee/buyer has a valid permit from the State where the transfer is to take place, which qualifies as an exemption to NICS.

Issuing State and Permit Type	Date of Issuance (if any)	Expiration Date (if any)	Permit Number (if any)

Section D - Must Be Completed Personally By Transferee/Buyer

If the transfer of the firearm(s) takes place on a different day from the date that the transferee/buyer signed Section B, the transferee/buyer must complete Section D immediately prior to the transfer of the firearm(s).

I certify that all of my responses in Section B of this form are still true, correct, and complete.

30. Transferee's/Buyer's Signature	31. Recertification Date Month	Day	Year

Section E - Must Be Completed By Transferor/Seller

32. For Use by Licensee	33. Trade/corporate name and address of transferor/seller and Federal Firearm License Number (must contain at least first three and last five digits X-XX-XXXXX; hand stamp may be used)

The Individual Transferring The Firearm(s) Must Complete Questions 34-36.
For Denied/Cancelled Transactions, The Individual Who Completed Section C Must Complete Questions 34-35.

I certify that: (1) I have read and understand the Notices, Instructions, and Definitions on this ATF Form 4473; (2) the information recorded in Sections A, C and E is true, correct, and complete; and (3) this entire transaction record has been completed at the licensed business premises ("licensed premises" includes business temporarily conducted from a qualifying gun show or event in the same State in which the licensed premises is located) unless this transaction has met the requirements of 18 U.S.C. 922(c). Unless this transaction has been denied or cancelled by NICS or State agency, I further certify on the basis of — (1) the transferee's/buyer's responses in Section B (and Section D, if applicable); (2) the verification of the identification recorded in question 26 (and the re-verification at the time of transfer, if Section D was completed); and (3) State or local law applicable to the firearms business — it is my belief that it is not unlawful for me to sell, deliver, transport, or otherwise dispose of the firearm(s) listed on this form to the person identified in Section B.

34. Transferor's/Seller's Name (please print)	35. Transferor's/Seller's Signature	36. Date Transferred Month	Day	Year

REMINDER - By the Close of Business Complete ATF Form 3310.4 for Multiple Sales of Handguns Within 5 Consecutive Business Days

NOTICES, INSTRUCTIONS, AND DEFINITIONS

Purpose of the Form: The information and certification on this form are designed so that a person licensed under 18 U.S.C. 923 may determine if he/she may lawfully sell or deliver a firearm to the person identified in Section B, and to alert the transferee/buyer of certain restrictions on the receipt and possession of firearms. The transferor/seller of a firearm must determine the lawfulness of the transaction and maintain proper records of the transaction. Consequently, the transferor/seller must be familiar with the provisions of 18 U.S.C. 921-931 and the regulations in 27 CFR Parts 478 and 479. In determining the lawfulness of the sale or delivery of a rifle or shotgun to a resident of another State, the transferor/seller is presumed to know the applicable State laws and published ordinances in both the transferor's/seller's State and the transferee's/buyer's State. (See State Laws and Published Ordinances -Firearms (ATF Electronic Publication 5300.5) on https://www.atf.gov/.)

Generally, ATF Form 4473 must be completed at the licensed business premises when a firearm is transferred over-the-counter. Federal law, 18 U.S.C. 922(c), allows a licensed importer, manufacturer, or dealer to sell a firearm to a nonlicensee who does not appear in person at the licensee's business premises only if the transferee/buyer meets certain requirements. These requirements are set forth in section 922(c), 27 CFR 478.96(b), and ATF Procedure 2013-2 (or subsequent update).

After the transferor/seller has completed the firearms transaction, he/she must make the completed, original ATF Form 4473 (which includes the Notices, General Instructions, and Definitions), and any supporting documents, part of his/her permanent records. Such Forms 4473 must be retained for at least 20 years and after that period may be submitted to ATF. Filing may be chronological (by date of disposition), alphabetical (by name of purchaser), or numerical (by transaction serial number), as long as all of the transferor's/seller's completed Forms 4473 are filed in the same manner.

FORMS 4473 FOR DENIED/CANCELLED TRANSFERS MUST BE RETAINED: If the transfer of a firearm is denied/cancelled by NICS, or if for any other reason the transfer is not completed after a NICS check is initiated, the licensee must retain the ATF Form 4473 in his/her records for at least 5 years. Forms 4473 with respect to which a sale, delivery, or transfer did not take place shall be separately retained in alphabetical (by name of transferee) or chronological (by date of transferee's certification) order.

If the transferor/seller or the transferee/buyer discovers that an ATF Form 4473 is incomplete or improperly completed after the firearm has been transferred, and the transferor/seller or the transferee/buyer wishes to correct the omission(s) or error(s), photocopy the inaccurate form and make any necessary additions or revisions to the photocopy. The transferor/seller should only make changes to Sections A, C, and E. The transferee/buyer should only make changes to Sections B and D. Whoever made the changes should initial and date the changes. The corrected photocopy should be attached to the original Form 4473 and retained as part of the transferor's/seller's permanent records.

Section A

Questions 1-6. Firearm(s) Description: These blocks must be completed with the firearm(s) information. All firearms manufactured after 1968 by Federal firearms licensees should be marked with a serial number. Should you acquire a firearm that is legally not marked with a serial number (i.e. pre-1968); you may answer question 3 with "NSN" (No Serial Number), "N/A" or "None".

If more than three firearms are involved in a transaction, please provide the information required by Section A, Questions 1-5, on ATF Form 5300.9A, Firearms Transaction Record Continuation Sheet. The completed Form 5300.9A must be attached to this ATF Form 4473.

ATF Form 5320.23 Page 1

U.S. Department of Justice
Bureau of Alcohol, Tobacco, Firearms and Explosives

OMB No. 1140-0107 (08/31/2022)

National Firearms Act *(NFA)* Responsible Person Questionnaire

Complete the form in duplicate. The ATF copy of the form, with fingerprints on Form FD-258 and photograph, will be submitted with the ATF Form 1, 4, or 5 *(to the address shown on the specific form)* and the other copy will be directed to the responsible person's chief law enforcement officer. *(See Instructions)*

1. Please check the appropriate box to indicate with which ATF form this questionnaire will be submitted.

   ☐ ATF Form 1   ☐ ATF Form 4   ☐ ATF Form 5

2. Full Legal Name and Address of Applicant or Transferee *(as shown on the ATF Form 1, 4 or 5) (see instruction 2)*

3a. Full Legal Name and Home Address of Responsible Person	3b. Telephone *(Area code and Number)*	3e. Photograph
	3c. E-mail address	Affix recent Photograph Here
	3d. Other names used *(including alias and maiden name)*	*(Approximately 2" x 2")* *(See instruction 3b)*

4a. Type of Firearm *(see definition 5)*	
4b. Name and Address of Maker, Manufacturer and/or Importer of Firearm	

4c. Firearm Model	4d. Caliber or Gauge	4e. Firearm Serial Number

5. Social Security Number: *(See instructions 3C)*	Date of Birth:

6a. Ethnicity   ☐ Hispanic or Latino   6b. Race   ☐ American Indian or Alaska Native   ☐ Black or African American   ☐ White
                ☐ Not Hispanic or Latino   ☐ Asian   ☐ Native Hawaiian or Other Pacific Islander

7. Law Enforcement Notification *(See instruction 5)*

As a responsible person *(see definition 4)* of the trust or legal entity identified in Item 2 of this form, I am required to provide notification of the proposed making or acquisition and possession of the firearm described in item 4 of this form by providing a copy of the completed form to the chief law enforcement officer (CLEO) in the agency identified below:

Agency or Department Name	Name and Title of Official

Address (Street address or P.O. Box, City, State and Zip Code) to which sent (mailed or delivered)

Information for the Chief Law Enforcement Officer

This form provides notification of the maker or transferee's intent to make or acquire and possess a National Firearms Act (NFA) firearm. No action on your part is required. However, should you have information that may disqualify this person from making or possessing a firearm, please contact the NFA Branch at *(304)* 616-4500 or NFA@atf.gov. A "Yes" answer to items 8.a. through 8.h. or item 9.d. or 9.e. could disqualify a person from acquiring or possessing a firearm. Also, ATF may not approve an application if the transfer or possession of the firearm would be in violation of State or local law.

ATF Form 5320. 23

ATF Form 5320.23 Page 2

8. Answer questions 8.a. through 8.h. Answer questions 9 and 10, if applicable. For any "Yes" answer the transferee shall provide details on a separate sheet. *(See definitions 8-14)*

		Yes	No
a.	Are you under indictment or information in any court for a felony, or any other crime, for which the judge could imprison you for more than one year? *(See definition 8)*		
b.	Have you ever been convicted in any court for a felony, or any other crime, for which the judge could have imprisoned you for more than one year, even if you received a shorter sentence including probation? *(See definition 8)*		
c.	Are you a fugitive from justice? *(See definition 13)*		
d.	Are you an unlawful user of, or addicted to, marijuana or any depressant, stimulant, narcotic drug, or any other controlled substance? **Warning: The use or possession of marijuana remains unlawful under Federal law regardless of whether it has been legalized or decriminalized for medicinal or recreational purposes in the state where you reside.**		
e.	Have you ever been adjudicated as a mental defective **OR** have you ever been committed to a mental institution? *(See definitions 9 and 10)*		
f.	Have you been discharged from the Armed Forces under **dishonorable** conditions?		
g.	Are you subject to a court order restraining you from harassing, stalking, or threatening your child or an intimate partner or child of such partner? *(See definition 11)*		
h.	Have you ever been convicted in any court of a misdemeanor crime of domestic violence? *(See definition 14)*		

9a. Country of Citizenship: *(Check/List more than one, if applicable. Nationals of the United States may check U.S.A.) (See definition 12)*

☐ United States of America   ☐ Other Country/Countries *(specify)*: _____

9b. State of Birth	9c. Country of Birth

		Yes	No
d.	Have you ever renounced your United States citizenship?		
e.	Are you an alien illegally or unlawfully in the United States?		
f.1.	Are you an alien who has been admitted to the United States under a nonimmigrant visa?		
f.2.	If "yes", do you fall within any of the exceptions stated in the instructions? Attach the documentation to the questionnaire ☐ N/A		

10. If you are an alien, record your U.S.-Issued Alien or Admission number (AR#, USCIS#, or I94#): _____

11. Have you been issued a Unique Personal Identification Number *(UPIN)*? *(See instructions 3C)* ☐ Yes ☐ No If yes please list _____

CERTIFICATION: Under penalties imposed by 18 U.S.C. § 924 and 26 U.S.C. § 5861, I certify that, upon submission of this form to ATF, a completed copy of this form will be directed to the chief law enforcement officer (CLEO) shown in item 5, that the statements contained in this certification, and any attached documents in support thereof, are true and correct to the best of my knowledge and belief.

_____   _____
Signature of Responsible Person   Date

Instructions

1. Completion: Each responsible person (see definition 4) of a trust or legal entity seeking to make or acquire a National Firearms Act *(NFA)* firearm shall complete this form in duplicate. (see instruction 9)
    a. Each responsible person must submit his/her fingerprints and photograph with this form *(see below)*.
    b. Please note that this form is not required when the applicant on Form 1, 4 or 5 is an individual.
2. Item 2- Enter the name, trade name *(if any)* and address of the trust or legal entity identified on the Form 1 *(items 3a and b)*; Form 4 *(item 2a)*; or Form 5 *(item 2a)*
3. Item 3- Responsible Person information
    a. Provide the information for the responsible person in items 3a through 3e.
    b. Item 3e - Photograph: The responsible person shall attach, in item 3e on the ATF copy of the form only, a 2-inch by 2-inch frontal view photograph taken within one year prior to the date of the filing of the form. Item 3c is obscured on the CLEO copy.
    c. Social Security Number and UPIN. The Social Security number and UPIN are not required. However, this information assists with the efficient completion of the NICS background check. Please be aware that refusal to provide this information may result in a delay in the NICS background check process.
4. Firearm information
    a. Type of NFA firearm: see definition 5 and as identified in item 4b of Form 1, 4, or 5
    b. Name of maker, manufacturer and/or importer: as identified in item 4a of Form 1, 4 or 5
    c. Firearm Model: identified in item 4d of Form 1, 4 or 5
    d. Caliber or Gauge: identified in item 4c of Form 1, 4 or 5
    e. Firearm Serial Number: identified in item 4g of Form 1, 4 or 5. Item 4e is obscured on the CLEO copy.
5. Item 6- Law Enforcement Notification: Each responsible person must provide a notification on this form of the proposed making or acquisition of an NFA firearm to his/her chief law enforcement officer having jurisdiction where the responsible person is located. The chief law enforcement officer is considered to be the Chief of Police; the Sheriff; the Head of the State Police; or a State or local district attorney or prosecutor.
6. Complete items 7 through 10
7. Fingerprints: The responsible person shall submit, in duplicate with the ATF copy of this form, his or her fingerprints on FBI Form FD-258 and the fingerprints must be clear for accurate classification and taken by someone properly equipped to take them. No fingerprints are required with the copy of the form sent to the chief law enforcement officer.
8. State or Local Permit: If the State in which the responsible person resides requires the responsible person to have a State or Local permit or licensee, a copy of the permit or license must be submitted with this form.
9. Disposition: The ATF copy of the form, with the fingerprints and photograph, shall be submitted with the ATF Form 1, 4 or 5. The other copy shall be directed to the responsible person's chief law enforcement officer identified in item 5 of this form.
10. Sign and date the form. The signature must be original. **Exceptions:** In the case of eforms or where a variance has been granted a Digital/Electronic signature may be used.

ATF Copy

ATF Form 5320.23 Page 3

U.S. Department of Justice
Bureau of Alcohol, Tobacco, Firearms and Explosives

OMB No. 1140-0107 (08/31/2022)

National Firearms Act *(NFA)*
Responsible Person Questionnaire

Complete the form in duplicate. The ATF copy of the form, with fingerprints on Form FD-258 and photograph, will be submitted with the ATF Form 1, 4, or 5 *(to the address shown on the specific form)* and the other copy will be directed to the responsible person's chief law enforcement officer. *(See Instructions)*

Please check the appropriate box to indicate with which ATF form this questionnaire will be submitted.

[ ] ATF Form 1   [ ] ATF Form 4   [ ] ATF Form 5

1. Full Legal Name and Address of Applicant or Transferee *(as shown on the ATF Form 1, 4 or 5) (see instruction 2)*

3a. Full Legal Name and Home Address of Responsible Person

3b. Telephone *(Area code and Number)*

3c. E-mail address

3d. Other names used *(including alias and maiden name)*

4a. Type of Firearm *(see definition 5)*

4b. Name and Address of Maker, Manufacturer and/or Importer of Firearm

4c. Firearm Model   4d. Caliber or Gauge

5. Date of Birth:

6a. Ethnicity
[ ] Hispanic or Latino
[ ] Not Hispanic or Latino

6b. Race
[ ] American Indian or Alaska Native
[ ] Asian
[ ] Black or African American
[ ] Native Hawaiian or Other Pacific Islander
[ ] White

Law Enforcement Notification *(See instruction 5)*

As a responsible person *(see definition 4)* of the trust or legal entity identified in Item 2 of this form, I am required to provide notification of the proposed making or acquisition and possession of the firearm described in item 4 of this form by providing a copy of the completed form to the chief law enforcement officer (CLEO) in the agency identified below:

Agency or Department Name   Name and Title of Official

Address (Street address or P.O. Box, City, State and Zip Code) to which sent (mailed or delivered)

Information for the Chief Law Enforcement Officer

This form provides notification of the maker or transferee's intent to make or acquire and possess a National Firearms Act (NFA) firearm. No action on your part is required. However, should you have information that may disqualify this person from making or possessing a firearm, please contact the NFA Branch at *(304)* 616-4500 or NFA@atf.gov. A "Yes" answer to items 8.a. through 8.h. or item 9.d. or 9.e. could disqualify a person from acquiring or possessing a firearm. Also, ATF may not approve an application if the transfer or possession of the firearm would be in violation of State or local law.

CLEO Copy

ATF Form 5320.23
Revised September 2019

APPENDIX B | 611

ATF Form 5320.23 Page 4

8. Answer questions 8.a. through 8.h. Answer questions 9 and 10, if applicable. For any "Yes" answer the transferee shall provide details on a separate sheet. *(See definitions 8-14)*

		Yes	No
a.	Are you under indictment or information in any court for a felony, or any other crime, for which the judge could imprison you for more than one year? *(See definition 8)*		
b.	Have you ever been convicted in any court for a felony, or any other crime, for which the judge could have imprisoned you for more than one year, even if you received a shorter sentence including probation? *(See definition 8)*		
c.	Are you a fugitive from justice? *(See definition 13)*		
d.	Are you an unlawful user of, or addicted to, marijuana or any depressant, stimulant, narcotic drug, or any other controlled substance? **Warning: The use or possession of marijuana remains unlawful under Federal law regardless of whether it has been legalized or decriminalized for medicinal or recreational purposes in the state where you reside.**		
e.	Have you ever been adjudicated as a mental defective **OR** have you ever been committed to a mental institution? *(See definitions 9 and 10)*		
f.	Have you been discharged from the Armed Forces under **dishonorable** conditions?		
g.	Are you subject to a court order restraining you from harassing, stalking, or threatening your child or an intimate partner or child of such partner? *(See definition 11)*		
h.	Have you ever been convicted in any court of a misdemeanor crime of domestic violence? *(See definition 14)*		

9a. Country of Citizenship: *(Check/List more than one, if applicable. Nationals of the United States may check U.S.A.) (See definition 12)*

☐ United States of America   ☐ Other Country/Countries *(specify)*: _____

9b. State of Birth _____   9c. Country of Birth _____

		Yes	No
d.	Have you ever renounced your United States citizenship?		
e.	Are you an alien illegally or unlawfully in the United States?		
f.1.	Are you an alien who has been admitted to the United States under a nonimmigrant visa?		
f.2.	If "yes", do you fall within any of the exceptions stated in the instructions? Attach the documentation to the questionnaire ☐ N/A		

10. If you are an alien, record your U.S.-Issued Alien or Admission number (AR#, USCIS#, or I94#): _____

11. Have you been issued a Unique Personal Identification Number *(UPIN)*? *(See instructions 3C)* ☐ Yes ☐ No If yes please list _____

CERTIFICATION: Under penalties imposed by 18 U.S.C. § 924 and 26 U.S.C. § 5861, I certify that, upon submission of this form to ATF, a completed copy of this form will be directed to the chief law enforcement officer (CLEO) shown in item 5, that the statements contained in this certification, and any attached documents in support thereof, are true and correct to the best of my knowledge and belief.

Signature of Responsible Person _____   Date _____

Instructions

1. Completion: Each responsible person (see definition 4) of a trust or legal entity seeking to make or acquire a National Firearms Act *(NFA)* firearm shall complete this form in duplicate. (see instruction 9)
    a. Each responsible person must submit his/her fingerprints and photograph with this form *(see below)*.
    b. Please note that this form is not required when the applicant on Form 1, 4 or 5 is an individual.
2. Item 2- Enter the name, trade name *(if any)* and address of the trust or legal entity identified on the Form 1 *(items 3a and b)*; Form 4 *(item 2a)*; or Form 5 *(item 2a)*
3. Item 3- Responsible Person information
    a. Provide the information for the responsible person in items 3a through 3e.
    b. Item 3e - Photograph: The responsible person shall attach, in item 3e on the ATF copy of the form only, a 2-inch by 2-inch frontal view photograph taken within one year prior to the date of the filing of the form. Item 3c is obscured on the CLEO copy.
    c. Social Security Number and UPIN. The Social Security number and UPIN are not required. However, this information assists with the efficient completion of the NICS background check. Please be aware that refusal to provide this information may result in a delay in the NICS background check process.
4. Firearm information
    a. Type of NFA firearm: see definition 5 and as identified in item 4b of Form 1, 4, or 5
    b. Name of maker, manufacturer and/or importer: as identified in item 4a of Form 1, 4 or 5
    c. Firearm Model: identified in item 4d of Form 1, 4 or 5
    d. Caliber or Gauge: identified in item 4c of Form 1, 4 or 5
    e. Firearm Serial Number: identified in item 4g of Form 1, 4 or 5. Item 4e is obscured on the CLEO copy.
5. Item 6- Law Enforcement Notification: Each responsible person must provide a notification on this form of the proposed making or acquisition of an NFA firearm to his/her chief law enforcement officer having jurisdiction where the responsible person is located. The chief law enforcement officer is considered to be the Chief of Police; the Sheriff; the Head of the State Police; or a State or local district attorney or prosecutor.
6. Complete items 7 through 10
7. Fingerprints: The responsible person shall submit, in duplicate with the ATF copy of this form, his or her fingerprints on FBI Form FD-258 and the fingerprints must be clear for accurate classification and taken by someone properly equipped to take them. No fingerprints are required with the copy of the form sent to the chief law enforcement officer.
8. State or Local Permit: If the State in which the responsible person resides requires the responsible person to have a State or Local permit or licensee, a copy of the permit or license must be submitted with this form.
9. Disposition: The ATF copy of the form, with the fingerprints and photograph, shall be submitted with the ATF Form 1, 4 or 5. The other copy shall be directed to the responsible person's chief law enforcement officer identified in item 5 of this form.
10. Sign and date the form. The signature must be original. **Exceptions:** In the case of eforms or where a variance has been granted a Digital/Electronic signature may be used.

ATF Form 5320. 23
Revised September 201

CLEO Copy

ABOUT THE ATTORNEY AUTHOR

GILBERT AMBLER
AUTHOR

Attorney Gilbert Ambler focuses on constitutional issues and criminal defense throughout Virginia and in central and western Pennsylvania, with many of his cases involving weapons or self-defense related issues. He has experience representing both individuals and Federal Firearm Licensees (FFLs) in compliance with the ATF. Gilbert also has represented various firearms organizations such as Gun Owners of America, Gun Owners Foundation, and Virginia Citizens Defense league. Gilbert is a contributor to multiple firearms blogs, has taught CLE (continuing legal education) to other attorneys on the subject of firearms law, and has been a featured guest on radio programming to discuss important constitutional concepts. Gilbert is one of the founding members of the American Council of 2nd Amendment Lawyers (*see* 2alawyers.org). He is also the co-author of "The Ultimate FFL Resource Guide," a comprehensive guidebook for Federal Firearm Licensees. In his free time, Gilbert enjoys watching baseball, shooting, and spending time with his wife, Sylvia.

The U.S. LawShield® Legal Defense for Self Defense® Program is dedicated to preserving its members' fundamental and Constitutional right to self-defense through zealous legal representation by Independent Program Attorneys experienced in self-defense and gun laws. A cornerstone of the U.S. LawShield program is legal education.

U.S. LawShield boasts hundreds of thousands of members, including civilians, law enforcement and security officers, and military personnel. U.S. LawShield is honored to be affiliated with thousands of gun ranges, gun stores, FFL dealers, instructors, educators, and other firearms experts and professionals. U.S. LawShield is one of the largest civilian repositories of state-specific self-defense and gun law legal information available anywhere.

For more information about the U.S. LawShield Legal Defense for Self Defense Program, visit www.uslawshield.com.

Gilbert Ambler is an Independent Program Attorney for U.S. LawShield with the law firm of Ambler Law Offices, LLC. This publication is not an endorsement or solicitation for any product or service. The content in Virginia Gun Law: Armed And Educated was produced for educational purposes only as a general legal overview of the law in Virginia. No legal advice is being provided and no attorney-client relationship is being created. This publication is not a substitute for legal advice. You should contact an attorney regarding your specific legal circumstances.